# THE LONE HERETIC

*A Biography of*
*Miguel de Unamuno y Jugo*

*To My Parents*
*Who Gave Me the Key*

# the Lone Heretic

### A Biography of
## MIGUEL de UNAMUNO y JUGO
*by* MARGARET THOMAS RUDD

*Introduction by* FEDERICO de ONÍS

**GORDIAN PRESS**
**NEW YORK**
**1976**

**Library of Congress Cataloging in Publication Data**

Rudd, Margaret Thomas.
   The lone heretic.

   Reprint of the 1963 ed. published by University
of Texas Press, Austin; with new pref.
   Bibliography: p.
   Includes index.
   1. Unamuno y Jugo, Miguel de, 1864-1936--Biog-
raphy. I. Title.
PQ6639.N3Z835   1975     868'.6'209 [B]    75-31688
ISBN 0-87752-181-6

# PREFACE     *2*

The quantity and quality of bibliography on Unamuno is the most eloquent proof of his value and significance. Federico de Onís made this statement in his introduction to the University of Puerto Rico's July - December, 1961 issue of *La Torre* honoring Don Miguel de Unamuno. Accordingly, the last thirty-five of that volume's 636 pages list the vast bibliography compiled by Don Federico himself who claimed Don Miguel as his "Spanish master." Now, thirty-eight years since the death of the Salamancan poet — he was essentially a poet — and twelve since Federico de Onís wrote the introduction to *The Lone Heretic,* I rejoice to write a second preface to this biography while I grieve for the tragic death of Don Federico who I claim as *my* Spanish master.

Before considering Unamuno's bibliography since this book's publication in 1963, I feel impelled to write a word about my involvement with two great exponents of Hispanism: Federico de Onís and Miguel de Unamuno. Their personalities are so inextricably mingled in me that I cannot write or even think the name of one without the other. The former I knew in person; the latter, in spirit only, which is, after all, the truest form of knowing. But such knowing alone does not qualify one to be linked with them. During the past eleven years I have watched the tenuous existence of *The Lone Heretic* "with my soul hanging by a thread," as the Spanish saying goes, feeling increasingly humble that my name should be associated with theirs in the same theme, expressed by Don Federico as "the inception of the process of defining and transmitting a human value to posterity." The errors in my work — the majority of them technical rather than of the spirit or of fact — are wholly mine. If my telling of Don Miguel's "novel" transmits some slight particle of human value I shall not hesitate to ask the reader's indulgence of its faults.

Now, to bibliography. Since 1962 the Library of Congress in Washington, D. C. has catalogued some eighty books under "Unamuno y Jugo, Miguel de." Among them are books including studies on other writers; most, however, focus entirely on Don Miguel. Some comprise collected studies by numerous Unamuno scholars. A few are new editions of former studies, while others are translations of works published in Spanish before 1963. Bear in mind, however, that I have referred to books only; neither time nor space allow for considering articles or unpublished dissertations.

During the period in question, the year 1964 leads with the largest number of books published, possibly because it marked the first centennial of the maestro's birth. Celebrations of the occasion were widespread in Europe and America where outstanding scholars gathered on university campuses testifying to the continued depth and expansion of Unamuno's influence. Five volumes of the collected papers presented on such occasions in Spain (Bilbao and Salamanca), Brazil, Chile and the United States (the University of California in Los Angeles) appear in the catalogue. During the week of September 3 - 7 I was privileged to be among seventy-nine participants in an International Symposium on the Vanderbilt campus. Eight of the participants came from Spain, some of them scheduled to attend similar celebrations on other U. S. campuses. Notable among these were Carlos Clavería, Manuel García Blanco, (the noted Unamuno scholar from Salamanca), Julián Marías and Fernando de Unamuno (Don Miguel's eldest son).

Of the translated studies I should mention Julián Marías' *Miguel de Unamuno*. Its original Spanish edition, published in 1943 and many times re-edited in that language, was the first philosophical review of Unamuno's thought, which Dr. Marías defines as essentially a problem of philosophy. Its English version by Frances M. López-Morillas (Harvard University Press, 1966) brings to English readers the penetrating insight into Spain's most influential modern thinker by one who is perhaps her most widely known philosopher-essayist in this country today.

M. T. R.<br>
Richmond, Virginia

# PREFACE

WHAT IS THE USE OF HEALTH OR OF LIFE, IF NOT TO DO SOME WORK therewith? And what work nobler than transplanting foreign thought into the barren domestic soil, except, indeed, planting thought of your own, which the fewest are privileged to do?"[1] Thus wrote Carlyle in *Sartor Resartus*. And in the same chapter, which is appropriately titled "Prospective," Professor Teufelsdrockh, quoting Goethe, says "'. . . man is properly the *only* object that interests man'." And, he adds, "thus I too have noted that in Weissnichtwo our whole conversation is little or nothing else but biography or autobiography; ever human—anecdotal. Biography is by nature the most universally profitable, universally pleasant of all this; especially biography of distinguished individuals."[2]

That Don Miguel de Unamuno y Jugo was a distinguished individual is incontrovertible. He was professor of Greek and rector of the University of Salamanca in Spain; as essayist, dramatist, novelist, poet, and philosophical thinker, he is Spain's most outstanding literary figure of the twentieth century; and as a disturbing, contradictory, controversial man whose influence has spread beyond the boundaries of the Iberian Peninsula into the infinite realm of the human spirit, he is one of the most fascinating individuals of modern times.

[1] Thomas Carlyle, *Sartor Resartus*, p. 61.
[2] *Ibid.*, pp. 57–58.

Unamuno's bibliography has continued to grow since before his death in 1936. From the first serious study of his works, which was the doctor's dissertation by his distinguished countryman, Romera-Navarro, in 1928, to the detailed analysis of one of his key works in *Unamuno en su "Nivola"* by the Peruvian scholar, Dr. Armando Zubizarreta, in 1960, and the monumental July–December, 1961, number of the University of Puerto Rico's publication, *La Torre,* dedicated to Unamuno, the list of Unamuno studies and translations has grown to impressive proportions. Of Unamuno's own works, available in English translation are *Essays and Soliloquies, The Agony of Christianity, Mist* (a novel), *Life of Don Quijote and Sancho, The Christ of Velázquez* (a long poem), *Poems* (a selected anthology with Spanish originals included), and his masterpiece of religious-metaphysical thinking, *The Tragic Sense of Life in Men and in Peoples.* The essence of *el pensamiento unamuniano* (Unamunian thinking) is contained in a comprehensive, critical essay by Arturo Barea entitled simply *Unamuno* and published in English translation by the Yale University Press in 1952.

Unamuno's definitive biography has yet to be written. *The Lone Heretic* is the first critical biography of this distinguished Spaniard to date. It is the result of many years of study and a six-months' sabbatical from university teaching, most of which was spent in Salamanca. A letter of introduction from Professor Federico de Onís to Don Manuel García Blanco, who is currently editing Unamuno's *Obras completas* from the University of Salamanca, opened many doors—the University Library, the Casa Museo Unamuno—to say nothing of the hearts of Unamuno's family and friends in Salamanca and in Bilbao.

The aim of this biography is to pass on to the English reading public the essence of this man, a "distinguished individual," as he existed in "circumstantial time" and as he continues to exist in the *"intra-historia"* of his people, in Spain's *"tradición eterna."*

Unamuno is not altogether unknown in the United States, though outside of the Hispanic field the number of those acquainted with him is all too small. He is studied along with Gide, Sartre, Kapec, and Maurois in courses on European literature, selections from his works appear in the best anthologies of modern writers, and he is occasionally quoted by ministers and lecturers. Unamuno's thinking permeates portions of the one-time best seller, *Witness,* by Whittaker Chambers, who quoted Unamuno almost verbatim both in his book and during the Hiss trial.[3]

[3] Whittaker Chambers, *Witness,* pp. 505–507.

As a man who fought for spiritual qualities in a world of physical values, Don Miguel has been called "The Don Quijote of twentieth century Spanish literature." [4] If this characterization is apt, surely Unamuno is the Don Quijote of all modern literature, for who but a Spaniard could answer to that name? He promised to extend quixotism to all of Europe and he accomplished this during a lifetime of seventy-two years (1864–1936) fraught with agony of soul (*agonía*, in the Greek sense of *struggle*) which was the conflict between his head and his heart. Never has a man so completely revealed the intimate contradiction of his paradoxical self as man, the paradox. Unamuno called it "the struggle of the soul, the soul-fight that has in it something of the bullfight." [5] He revealed it in his life and in his writings, the struggle that results from the divine contradiction in man and in society, the jealousies, hatreds and envies between Cain and Abel—both within and without, for, as Kierkegaard said before Unamuno, each man carries his adversary within himself. And from this struggle springs life, existence, spiritual progress which, as Unamuno said before Le Compte de Nouys, is man's future realm—an existence ennobled by love and faith; faith in man's future life, faith in immortality. Only thus shall man become divine, though here and now he can merely play at being God.

To struggle, to exist, and so create his own soul—this is man's task. Existentialism? Perhaps! Whether directly from the Danish Kierkegaard, through the Spanish Unamuno to the Germans, Heidegger and Jaspers (the chronological sequence allows such a possibility), or whether by coincidence, this course of European existentialist thought has not yet been established. However, Antonio Machado, the Spanish poet, was right when he wrote that "Any critical study . . . should point out that coincident with Unamuno's last years, there flourished in Europe a complete system of existentialist metaphysics, profoundly human, which has in Unamuno not simply one of its ablest exponents, but—let us say it frankly—one of its precursors." [6] And it may even be as Machado added: "Theology always results when fantasy is used to serve life. To live, to live! Unamuno, the great existentialist, the father of this great philosophical, poetic movement." [7]

---

[4] Syllabus for a telecourse taught by Joseph Remenye, Western Reserve University, 1951.

[5] Unamuno, *La ciudad de Henoc: comentario 1933*, p. 70.

[6] Manuel Altolaguirre, "Don Miguel de Unamuno," in *Revista hispánica moderna* (New York), (January 1940), pp. 17–24.

[7] *Ibid.*

Unamuno was certainly not the precursor of the Godless existentialism of Sartre, or of his distinguished contemporary and countryman,
the philosopher, José Ortega y Gasset. Though Unamuno and Ortega
were basically different in personality and approach, they coincided
in much of their thinking and especially in their emphasis on life.
While both were called existentialists, they came to the opposite ends
of the pole of ultimate values: one, Unamuno, came to God; the other,
Ortega, came to the individual, to man as his own ultimate. A scholarly
study of the thinking of Unamuno and Ortega has been made by the
Mexican, Dr. Agustín Basave, Jr., entitled *Miguel de Unamuno y José
Ortega y Gasset; un bosquejo valorativo.* An incurable Germanophile,
Ortega turned his back on the intrinsic value in Spain's spiritual tradition and held human life as its own ultimate. This change in direction
from the divine object to the human, points more directly to the thinking of Sartre than does the philosophy of Unamuno who came to faith
in God and in immortality—faith through doubt and by dint of constant struggle.

He carried this quixotic struggle far beyond the confines of his
nation. Although Unamuno spent almost his entire life in Spain, except
for six years of exile in France, he heard, from his study desk in the
medieval university town of Salamanca, the heartbeat of all nations.
"He seems alert to the cry of all people," wrote Dr. Alfonso Reyes, the
Mexican humanist. "At times, like a physician, he seems to apply his
ear to our hearts." [8]

Like Miguel de Cervantes, the creator of Don Quijote, Miguel de
Unamuno was conscious of his role, for he wrote: "I shall soon come
to be the writer of most authority if not of the largest public, among
Spanish-speaking peoples, and I don't despair of reaching people of
other tongues. As I feel it, I say it!" [9] So it has come to pass for besides
the English translations, some of his works have appeared in French,
German, Italian, Czech, Dutch, and other languages.

That Don Miguel was sure of himself was obvious. On what did he
base this confidence; what is his claim to fame? Unamuno has made
a unique contribution in the realm of knowledge concerning the basic
nature of man. He proclaimed his own paradoxical nature and affirmed
his faith in an existence based on struggle as opposed to speculation.

[8] Alfonso Reyes, "Unamuno dibujante," in *Simpatías y diferencias* from *Colección de escritores mexicanos,* II, 223–225.
[9] Hernán Benítez (ed.), "Cartas inéditas de Miguel de Unamuno y de Pedro
Jiménez Ilundain," in *Revista de la universidad de Buenos Aires,* Vol. III, No. 9
(January–March 1949), p. 111.

He demonstrated the ability of man to "swim in deep, unknown waters" or, to use another of Kierkegaard's metaphors, "to go out on a limb" in order to push forward the frontier into the spiritual realm of the future. Today, somewhat belatedly, writers are pointing out and nations are realizing at last that, engulfed in a multitude of *things*—inventions, gadgets, to say nothing of atom bombs—all products of science which make for horizontal progress, twentieth-century man feels the need for something more profound. Dr. Alexis Carrel makes this confession in *Man the Unknown*. Max Scheler, in his *Philosophical Anthology*, says that we do not possess a unified idea of man. Francisco Ichaso, a Cuban, says in essence: We are acquainted with several "styles" of man such as "pagan man," "Christian man," "primitive man," but "the *man* man is left out. Man in his haste to advance horizontally, forgot about himself . . . What matters is not what one has, but what one is." [10] He writes that modern man goes into politics with the same devotion that medieval man went into religion. And he adds, that "the primary politics of man is to save his soul." [11] Many would agree with his conclusion that, "this fall into absolutism is the great tragedy of modern man." [12]

Unamuno's contribution to the deep stream of human progress was himself and his ability so clearly to reveal himself in his life and in his writings that he had drawn a distinct picture of universal man, his spiritual and physical aspects, his Cain and his Abel:

. . . a man is human, is alive according to what he has in common with other men. The somber man without his joys would not be a man, as neither would the joyful man without his somber moods. The weaknesses of the strong, the decisions of the indecisive, the brave sallies of the cowards, the cowardly moments of the valiant, the commonplaces of the geniuses and the aspirations of the simple, all of this, the intimate contradictions of men, is what makes them brothers. Never do our hearts beat with such love for Christ as when we read the story of his despair on the cross. Without this, he would not be a man.[13]

I wish to express gratitude to all of those who have made this work possible: to Professor Federico de Onís and his brother Don Carlos; to Professor Manuel García Blanco and Dr. Armando Zubizarreta; to Felisa Unamuno and her life-long friend, Doña Pilar Cuadrado with her children, Paquita and Federico; to Don Pablo Beltrán de Heredia

---

[10] Francisco Ichaso, *Defensa del hombre*, pp. 22, 23, 28.
[11] *Ibid.*, p. 32.
[12] *Ibid.*, p. 33.
[13] Unamuno, *Contra esto y aquello*, p. 110.

and to Antonio Lizárraga in Bilbao; to Conchita Vicéntiz who was a faithful Lazarillo in that town; and to His Excellency, Dr. José María de Areílza, Ambassador of Spain to the U.S.A., who corrected certain parts of this manuscript pertaining to Bilbao, which is his own, as well as Unamuno's, birthplace. I am especially indebted to members of my family for their aid in typing the manuscript, as well as in encouraging me in my endeavor, *i.e.*, Mrs. Harry T. Harris and Mrs. A. B. Rudd, Jr.

Finally, I wish to express appreciation to the University of Richmond and to the Research Council of the Richmond Area University Center for several grants without which this work could not have been completed.

M. T. R.
Richmond, Virginia

# Table of Contents

# List of Illustrations

# INTRODUCTION

IT IS A SOURCE OF SATISFACTION TO ME TO WRITE THESE WORDS OF introduction to the book about my Spanish master, Miguel de Unamuno, by my North American student, Margaret Thomas Rudd—three separate persons linked by the same theme, in the inception of the process of defining and transmitting a human value to posterity. They represent three generations: grandfather, son, and granddaughter, whose association carries within itself the series of actions and reactions which determine the continuity and the variety of history.

To the generation which preceded his, Unamuno was a man of innovation and dissent, what was known at the end of the nineteenth century as a "modernista," the most outstanding of the various subjective, individualistic writers who appeared at that time and who have been grouped, against all their wills, under the denomination of "the generation of '98." I have always felt that this name, which was invented by one of them, Azorín, when the members of this group had achieved individual triumph, thanks to the emergence of a new generation, was erroneous and misleading, although it has become the term generally employed. It is a mistake to associate this literary revolution which was already clearly defined in Spain in 1892, and ten years earlier in Spanish America, with the historic event of the war with the United States which signified the failure of the Spanish government and the end of the Spanish empire in the world. The men of that generation had been characterized from the beginning by their reaction against the nineteenth century and had undertaken a revision of values with regard to Spain, as well as to everything, which was in keeping with the new trends throughout Europe at the end of the century. The national debacle of ninety-eight was only one of the events foreseen in this new interpretation of Spain, as well as all the others which followed.

The new generation which appeared around 1910 with Ortega y Gasset at its head, and to which I belong, was the offspring and heir of Unamuno, and received from him its first cultural stimuli. But as good children do, we soon began to react against our father, working to give his subjective ideas and attitudes an objectivity which led us to the fields of science and the building of a new Spain. I recall that when in 1912, as professor of the University of Oviedo, I gave the commencement address, I paid homage to Unamuno as the teacher to whom my generation and I were most indebted, but I added: "The intervening years have led me to a way of thinking diametrically opposed to his, and to a completely different evaluation of his ideas." And I summed up my opinion of him in these words:

All this was what Unamuno stood for in the University of Salamanca, and we, who had the good fortune to encounter him when we were young, owe him all this. In short, almost everything in the way of culture came to us through his words. The nation owes him a similar debt; he has performed the task of arousing its sleeping or paralyzed spirits and breaking the monotony and vulgarity of our spiritual ambience. And if today, to pass a more mature judgement on Unamuno, I would have to take many other things into consideration, I prefer not to do so at this moment, but to leave you with the optimistic and ingenuous impression of those days which are already coming to form a store of imperishable memories for me: that gay and noble city which the Spanish Renaissance filled with carved stone; those fields, created anew by the poets; that University where the only men I can consider the forebears of my tradition one day struggled; all that, gentlemen, which is my native land. And looming large on its horizon and giving it new life, this extraordinary man, refined and rustic, modern and medieval, mystic and scientist, with the fervor of an apostle and the shrewdness of a rogue, in whom all the defects and all the virtues of our race would seem to achieve their fullest expression.

This attitude of the rising generation toward Unamuno can be clearly seen in the relationship between him and José Ortega y Gasset, which I analyzed in my study *Ortega, joven* (published in *Cursos y Conferencias*, Buenos Aires, 1957, Vol. L, no. 277.)

The third generation, that of the grandchildren, to which Margaret
Rudd belongs, was contemporary with the last years of Unamuno's
life, which, like Spain itself, was being dissolved in the national
tragedy. Some of them were fortunate enough to still see and hear
him on his return from exile during the time of the Republic; others
knew him only by hearsay, through the echo of his participation in
the national events which led to the civil war, that coincided with his
timely death. Free from prejudice, this generation is the one which is
devoting itself to studying and understanding Unamuno, who, in their
eyes, has taken on the stature of a classic of Spanish literature, the
most outstanding figure of the epoch which has just come to an end,
and, at the same time, one of the forerunners and creators of the new
epoch in world literature.

This awakened interest in Unamuno is characterized by the fact that
it is markedly international and is not limited to writers and thinkers.
The bibliography I prepared for the *Homenaje a Unamuno*, which has
just been published by the University of Puerto Rico, bears this out;
it lists forty-two theses, of which twenty-six were presented from 1944
to the present date in universities of the United States. Unamuno's
renown is growing in all the world and his values are being established by the young people who, removed from him in time and space,
approach him to study the manifold aspects of his work and personality.
This is not in the nature of a discovery, for Unamuno's work had been
translated by the preceding generation from 1913 in Italy, from 1917
in France, from 1921 in England and the United States, and from 1925
in Germany. In the United States around 1920 or a little later Unamuno was the object of attention on the part of critics like Ernest
Boyd, Mark Van Doren, John Dos Passos, Warner Fite, and Samuel
Putnam, to name only a few.

Margaret Rudd, who has devoted herself to Hispanic studies, has
fallen heir to all this; but her interest in Unamuno and the work which
this book of hers represents has a different purpose than that of her
predecessors, who discovered him, or that of her contemporaries, who
analyze and study aspects of his work. Rather she has tried to recon-
struct the intimate life of this widely admired and discussed writer.
For that she went to Spain, where she lived for five months in the
places where Unamuno had lived: Salamanca and Bilbao. There she
came to know his family and friends, and had access to the museum
founded by the University of Salamanca, where his things are preserved as when he was living in the rectoral house. In the light of all

this she has examined the dramatic process of development of the man of flesh and bone who was Unamuno (as he said referring to himself); she has evoked his share in the history and the life of his Spain, and has endeavored to discover and define the originality and unity of his literary creation which, for all its diversity, is always the expression of the deepest and most intimate wellsprings of his personality. As with every human being, at Unamuno's roots lie his religious sense, his need for self-affirmation, his longing for immortality, which inform all his acts and his writing. The author of this book has contributed greatly to the interpretation of the human entity who was Unamuno, and who will continue to be, with his outstanding significance, at one and the same time individual, Spanish, and universal.

Federico de Onís

# THE LONE HERETIC

*A Biography of*
*Miguel de Unamuno y Jugo*

# For After My Death

. . .

Listen you who read this
after I have left the earth, when
I that have written it
can no longer see myself in the mirror;
listen and meditate!
Meditate, that is, dream!
"He, that nucleus
of ideas, sentiments and emotions,
feelings, desires, disgusts,
voices and gestures,
inspirations and reasonings,
memories, hopes,
joys and sorrows,
he who called himself I, shadow of life,
flung his plaint into time
and today is not;
it is mine now, not his!"
Yes, my solitary reader, you that
hear the voice of the dead
these my words will be yours.

. . .

I am not, but my song lives after me
and carries round the world
the shadow of my shadow,
sad non-existence!

. . .

From POEMS by Miguel de Unamuno
translated by Eleanor Turnbull
Johns Hopkins Press, 1952

# The Waning Star

CHAPTER *1*

DEEP IN THE HEART OF THE ancient Spanish kingdom of León, now a part of old Castile, on the banks of the River Tormes, lies the town of Salamanca. Rising from the distant blue mountains are the peaks of Gredos and Peña de Francia, brooding over the town. Across them blow the fitful winds from Portugal, and beneath them came, all the way from Lisbon, the mighty earth tremor that shivered up the tallest tower of the Salamancan cathedrals to leave it leaning just off the 90 degree angle. But that was nearly two centuries ago. Today this land of old Castile lies hard and high and deep.

When God fashioned the bit of earth and water that forms the southern tip of Europe He must have said,

You are different, you are separate. In you I will hide a heart-land, a rocky core where only strong men can endure. And my sun shall beat upon you in summer, and my cold breath shall blow upon you in winter, for you shall be close to my heavens. But you shall be hidden from most men, for I will encircle you with waters and a pleasant, lush land where man can till the soil and it will bear fruit. But you, Castile, I shall hold so fast that you shall be split by deep gorges and lofty rocks to mold strong men, austere men, men who shall suffer and love, but endure. And your men will struggle to seek me, for they will thirst after my divinity.

From this rocky heart-land of Spain have come a Saint Teresa, a Fray Luis de León, and a Don Miguel de Unamuno.

It was here in Salamanca that the first university of Catholic Spain was established in 1218. Cervantes, Ruiz de Alarcón, and Góngora paced its rectangular courtyards, and Fray Luis de León, teacher and poet, still stands carved in bronze, in the little square outside the University's main entrance. Facing the heavy wooden doors, his statue seems to brood as watchfully over the University as the distant mountains over the town whose "golden stones" hold "recollections of glorious yesterdays."

> In silence, alone, Fray Luis de León
> meditates on the misfortunes of Job,
> or in his orisons savors the sweet
> names of our Lord.
> Names of peace and of love that in the strife
> he sought for his comfort, and bravely then
> he returned to the struggle singing love
> peace and repose.[1]

Passing centuries heap high their recollections and golden stones may not forget, but the truths of the twentieth century must be writ clear while there are still those who remember, lest the secrets die locked within them. The course of two bright stars traversed the Spanish heavens to meet, to struggle briefly, and to part in Salamanca— one was waxing, newly born in the year of 1936, the other, already old, was waning in its natural span.

It was Tuesday, October 6, 1936. The headlines on page one of *La Gaceta Regional* read:

## SALAMANCA PRESENTS BRILLIANT SPECTACLE TO HONOR THE SPANISH CHIEF OF STATE, HIS EXCELLENCY GENERAL DON FRANCISCO FRANCO

### THE DECREE OF HIS PROCLAMATION WAS READ TO MORE THAN 15,000 PEOPLE ON SUNDAY IN THE PLAZA MAYOR

All Military and Patriotic Organizations of the City and the Surrounding Province in Imposing Parade

Outstanding Feature of the Celebration was the Parade of the Civil Guard Flying over Seventy Different Banners

[1] From "Salamanca" by Miguel de Unamuno, translated by Eleanor Turnbull in *Poems*, p. 16. Unless otherwise indicated all translations have been rendered by the author.

A long article goes on to describe the details. At dawn autos and special trams, all loaded with people, began to arrive. By ten A.M., one hour before the scheduled time, the crowds started moving toward Salamanca's huge Main Square. The national colors of red and yellow were proudly displayed along the streets, the flags were hanging from the three stories of balconies that topped the arcade around the public square, reviving the splendor of the bullfights that were held in the middle ages when Salamanca was more Roman than Arabic. Soon the Square was filled to capacity and agile spectators began to appear on the roofs where the voices of the crowds below sounded like the shrill chatter of blackbirds at nesting time. The place was packed and still the eager spectators came; soon the little squares outside the Main Square were filled—the Plaza del Corrillo leading from the east corner, then the Plaza of the Poeta Iglesias in front of the Gran Hotel to the northeast, even the streets around the old marketplace on the north just outside the archway of the bull [2] and all the way to the church of San Julián. Within the Square on the west side is the city hall, its imposing facade topped with the symbolical figures of Justice, Agriculture, and the Arts. Large double-doored windows opened onto the balconies where the dignitaries were seen by the crowd below and heard with the aid of loudspeakers. Somehow the assembled parade made its way along the narrow town streets into the enclosure to draw up in full array beneath these balconies, while the "authorities" and local "official entities" were assembling by invitation in the auditorium of the city hall.

The lead-off name was "His Excellency the Bishop of the Diocese Dr. Plá y Deniel." Franco was making Salamanca his headquarters during the war and he was careful to become identified with the Catholic Church. Following were the names of the military and civil authorities, in that order: next was an item reading, "representing the University, the rector, Don Miguel de Unamuno, and the vice-rector, Don Esteban Madruga," followed by two columns of names. Thus, the star that wanes upon the local scene. But Franco, the rising star, did not appear on this occasion. A shorter article in the same paper reports that "Passing through Salamanca from Valladolid, his excellency Francisco Franco arrived yesterday at 6:25 P.M. Upon his arrival he was greeted by local authorities and hailed by the public as he rode through the streets"—modest, unassuming, a busy soldier fighting a war. That

[2] So called for the bull's head above the entrance, commemorating the spot where a man is said to have been gored during a bullfight.

was on Monday; but back again to the preceding Sunday's celebration:
at eleven A.M. the "authorities" appeared on the balcony of the city
hall to receive the applause and the reverent silence of the crowd.
". . . Colonel Don José María Baigorri, his excellency the Military
Governor of the Square, read the Decree in which his excellency General Don Francisco Franco Bahamonde, was named head of the
Government of the Spanish State, and *Generalísimo* of the armed
forces on land, on the sea, and in the air." The applause was long and
loud, and the answering speech of the governor of the Square was
topped off with the thrice roared, "VIVA ESPAÑA, VIVA ESPAÑA, VIVA
ESPAÑA!"

Other speeches followed for the people must be told why they were
fighting and against whom. In the absence of the civil governor, his
secretary read a statement identifying the enemy as traitors and as
"that hoard of wicked highwaymen in the service of Moscow that came
with their savage intentions of assassinating and destroying the most
cherished values of our Spain."

Only music and a parade would keep the crowd any longer. It was
past the two o'clock dinner hour and so they dispersed, their senses
stirred by the brilliance of the new star, with never a thought for the
other, their Don Miguel, for whom the time was fast running out as
October 12, his day of destiny, drew near.

Yes, Don Miguel was "among those present" on that Sunday, October 4, 1936. A strange role for him to play, especially in Salamanca
where for the past forty-five years, excepting the six years of exile in
France, he had dominated most public events and the private lives of
many of the townspeople. Even the humblest among them, the children, the beggars, the blind, claimed him, Don Miguel, professor of
Greek and rector of the University. Indeed, the blind vendor of lottery
tickets waited for his greeting as anxiously as did the Bishop of Salamanca, but for different reasons.

He was a stalwart old gentleman—seventy-two years old then—and
he wore always what he called his "civil uniform," an immaculate dark
blue suit, a solid-fronted black vest that fitted closely up around his
white collar, thus eliminating the need of a tie. His much worn black
felt hat was usually in evidence, if not on his head, then stuffed hastily
into a pocket. He never wore an overcoat, not even when it snowed—
and it snows in Salamanca! Take for instance that February day of
his triumphal return from exile back in 1930. The crowds were here

for *him* that day—but that's another story. Now he was "among those present." What was he thinking as his deep-set, penetrating eyes peered owlishly from under his shaggy eyebrows through his old gold-rimmed spectacles? His white mustache and pointed goatee seemed to quiver with emotion. Was he thinking of his friend and former student who had been shot in cold blood by Franco's men? Young Salvador Vila Hernández, brilliant, promising professor of Arabic and Hebrew at the University of Granada, had been appointed acting rector there to handle certain political difficulties. Unfortunately, his wife's Jewish blood, and especially her German origin, had made him the object of persecution in Granada. Salvador had spent the past summer vacation in Salamanca where, protected by Unamuno, he had remained until the first of October. Then, without warning and without trial, he was carried off to Granada and summarily shot. Had Don Miguel heard of this? Or was he thinking perhaps of the treatment his old friend and associate, Don Filiberto Villalobos was receiving? Prior to February of 1936 Don Filiberto had been Minister of Public Education, and a long-time resident of Salamanca. He was almost as well-known and beloved in the town as the Rector himself. Like practically everyone in Spain before the outbreak of the war, he had been a "republican," just as everyone—that is, everyone who enjoys any position of status today—vociferously supports the *Movimiento*, i.e., Franco. Well, since September Don Filiberto had been languishing in the Salamancan jail. That too rankled the soul of Don Miguel. It was only a question of time before he should have to speak out. Knowing him, his friends and family kept a close watch to see that his customarily outspoken tongue should not get him in trouble. It had cost him his freedom once before but he seemed not to have profited by the experience. Freedom and justice were two of his ruling passions, and as though to prove that his beloved Spain really was a free country, Don Miguel often spoke harsh and brutal truths when silence would have implied no subterfuge. "This is a free country," he wrote once to a friend in Paris, a friend who for his own good had enjoined that he refrain from uttering unpleasantries. The year 1936 had brought crucial times to Spain and it was definitely not the time to "shoot off his mouth," as the vice-rector, Don Esteban, had cautioned him. By tacit agreement his friends tried now to anticipate events and so prevent Don Miguel from involving himself and them in any unnecessary tangle with the authorities.

Nor did the authorities seem anxious to tangle with Unamuno. Twice rector of Spain's oldest university, retired in 1934 with the honorary title of Lifetime Rector, Spain's candidate for the Nobel prize for literature, a figure of unquestioned international prestige, it would ill behoove Franco to alienate such a literary light just when he himself was aspiring to an equal, if not higher, position in the political world. No, the part of wisdom was to befriend him, keep him *with* the *Movimiento*, and so claim him for Falange. Was Unamuno on Franco's side? Did he die a Falangist? The answer is no! As he said to a reporter after he was named Lifetime Rector, "Never shall I be on the conqueror's side." And talking to the Dutch Hispanist, Dr. J. Brouwer, in September 1936, Unamuno made the following statements, "There is no culture that can come to life and flourish under a military regime . . . It's impossible, impossible! Under militarism nothing can prosper; they're just blustering fools." [3] And two months later, a prisoner in his own home, a prisoner of that same military regime, Unamuno exclaimed to a Greek novelist who had come to seek him out, "Don't pay any attention to what they tell you about me! I have not turned rightist; I have not betrayed freedom! But for the time being order must be preserved. You shall see within the near future, very soon now, I shall be the first to resume the fight for freedom. I am not a Fascist nor a Bolshevik. I stand alone!" [4]

However, twenty-three years later, with Franco's *Movimiento* still riding the crest of the wave, Spaniards insist that the answer is yes. Even his former associates, still in Spain, those who live and work under the regime, say "yes." Franco still wants the world to believe that the great Salamancan rector, the man who said, "I am my people," whose voice is today the voice of Spain, was one with El Caudillo.

Perhaps the only reason Don Miguel did not speak out in a loud voice on this occasion—besides the fact that he was given no opportunity, and that no one would have listened if he had—was that he carried in his pocket a written protest signed by him as rector of the University and dated September 26, 1936. It was printed four days later on October 8, a two-columned neatly boxed statement on page one of the local paper:

[3] J. Brouwer, "Entrevista del hispanista holandés Dr. J. Brouwer con don Miguel de Unamuno, en el mes de setiembre de 1936," in *Repertorio americano* (San José, Costa Rica), Vol. XXXIII, No. 14 (April 10, 1937), pp. 217–218.
[4] Luis Araquistain, "Una entrevista con Unamuno," a typewritten article.

### Message from the University of Salamanca to the universities and academies of the world concerning the SPANISH CIVIL WAR

The University of Salamanca that has known how to maintain its spiritual horizon calmly and austerely apart from all political activity, knows likewise that her secular tradition obliges her at times to raise her voice above men's struggles to fulfill her duty to justice. Faced with the tremendous struggle to defend our western Christian civilization, the civilization that has built Europe, against a destructive Oriental ideology, the University of Salamanca notes with heartfelt grief that in addition to the cruel violence of the Civil War, certain bitter acts have been perpetrated that force her to fulfill this duty of registering her strong protest to the civilized world. Unnecessary acts of cruelty—assassinations of lay and ecclesiastical personnel—and of useless destruction—bombardments of national sanctuaries (such as "El Pilar" and "La Rabida"), of hospitals and schools, to say nothing of the bombardment of open cities—crimes of lesser intelligence, in fine, committed by forces directly controlled, or at least they should be, by the government today recognized *de jure*, by world governments.

The university is purposely referring exclusively to such acts, passing over in silence, through a sense of decorum and national honor, the innumerable crimes and engrossing devastation by the wave of collective dementia that has broken over a part of our land—for such acts revealed that unnecessary and useless cruelty and destruction are either ordered or cannot be controlled by that organization which moreover has not uttered a single word of condemnation or excuse that might reflect the least sentiment of humility or intention of rectification.

We make known the foregoing painful relation of facts to our companions in the world of the sciences, and request an expression of solidarity, referring strictly to the field of cultural values, in keeping with the spirit of this document.

Salamanca, 26 September 1936

THE RECTOR, MIGUEL DE UNAMUNO

Perhaps this document was stuffed in his pocket with his old felt hat that Sunday. The record does not say. Perhaps, too, he made his way slowly back to his home at No. 4 Bordadores Street (the Street of the Weavers).

His old friend and landlady, Doña Pilar, sighed now as she heard the slow footsteps ascending the stairs. Those footsteps, once so eager

and firm, had changed gradually since the death of his wife in 1934.
She recalled fondly her best friend, Concha, as he coughed and
fumbled for his key upon reaching the head of the stairs. She hoped
he'd not forgotten it again. He was a patient man; he never rang twice.
Several times on her way out she had found him standing there waiting for her to come and let him in. "Heavens, man, why didn't you
ring my bell?" she had so often asked. "I did," he would answer, "and
I was just waiting." Poor man, he just seemed to be thinking; she
wondered what.

He was thinking now as he coughed again, and fingered the protesting document in his pocket. Tomorrow he would take it down to
the paper himself. His blood stirred with something of the old eagerness at the thought. He opened the door and turned from the hall to
enter his study, a large room across the front of the house. In the
center of the tiled floor stood a long heavy work table piled high with
papers and books—everywhere there were books, books, books. They
filled the shelves that lined the walls. Two tall windows gave onto the
iron-railinged balconies that overhung the street below. From one he
could see directly down the Street of the Ursulas leading to his beloved
San Francisco Park, and to the left he could see the tower of the
Monterrey Palace, its lacy stones etched clear against the sky. Now
as he entered this familiar room he glanced hurriedly around for his
mail, realized his mistake, and went back to his work table that stood
by the window in the back room overlooking the little balcony and
the garden below. Mail was scarce in these troubled times, not like it
used to be when each day brought as many as a dozen or more com-
munications—requests for articles, fan letters, letters from publishers
in Argentina and France and Madrid, letters he answered himself, all
by hand. Now there was only one locally stamped envelope on his
table. No doubt Felisa had put it there. He tore it open and read
hastily. It was from the Municipal Government, another edict he supposed. Yes—October 12 was Día de la Raza in Spain, the anniversary
of Columbus' landing in America and celebrated as the Day of the
Race in all Spanish-speaking countries. ". . . The Municipal Government in cooperation with the University of Salamanca would celebrate
. . . in the Paraninfo—the university auditorium . . ." Well, he was
still the rector even if in name only, so he'd have to do something
about it. But now he was tired, dead tired, and he felt a cold coming
on. He took to his bed, a custom not uncommon with Don Miguel,
drank something hot the maid brought in, and was soon sound asleep.

The record of events which followed is tangled and confused. Newspaper accounts are clear enough as far as they go, but what they leave unrecorded is far more vital to the understanding of the remaining months of life and the death of Don Miguel de Unamuno y Jugo, one of the most influential men of modern Spain, a great teacher, writer, and existentialist thinker of the twentieth century.

# The Living Rock

CHAPTER $2$

ENCIRCLING THE HIGH TABLE-
land of Castile whose deep river gorges and arid peaks suggest "the
pocked and cratered surface of the moon,"[1] lie mountain ranges which
drop suddenly to fertile lands, as in Andalucía, or to the pleasant
beaches along the Mediterranean coast of Cataluña or the Atlantic
coastline of Portugal and, to the north, the Bay of Biscay. The mountains of this northern region are fresh and green. Their lofty peaks
overlook the ocean and their forests of silver-barked beeches hide
sweet streams, running between fern-covered banks. This is the home
of the Basques, a proud and hardy people.

Both the Unamuno and Jugo families were rooted for generations
in the Basque race. Legend has it that the first man, the father of the
human race, was a Basque. History also points to the possibility of
this race having been the primitive Iberians of the peninsula. Though
Spanish is spoken in the cities where there is contact with the outside
world, the peasants and even a number of the educated class still
speak Basque, said to be the most difficult of all languages. Among
the many separate regions that comprise Spain, the three Basque
provinces, Guipúzcoa, Alava, and Vizcaya, form one of the most closely-
knit units in the country. They are held together not only by geography,
but by language, perhaps the strongest common denominator of all.
Bilbao, the port of contact with the outside world, at the mouth of the

[1] V. S. Pritchett, *The Spanish Temper.*

Nervión River, and the capital of Vizcaya, is the most important city, having been for centuries an industrial center.

Ships and cargo boats coming from other parts of Spain, Europe, and even America, enter the river's mouth and go up, the smaller ones, all the way to the very heart of the town, for the Nervión flows from high in the Pyrenees straight through the center of Bilbao, by the imposing city hall on the left and on the right along the Arenal, Bilbao's central park with its tall old trees, its graveled paths, its monuments, and its bandstand. Spanning the river and overlooking the busy wharves below are a series of drawbridges that open to let the ships pass by. The wharves are glutted with cargo, iron pipes cast in Bilbao's smoke-belching factories of iron mined from the surrounding mountains, cattle and sheep that graze on the lush green hillsides, rubber from the Orient, cork from southern Spain, and machinery from America.

The life of the town that nestles around the mouth of the river and extends up the hillsides depends on this shipping and the old part of Bilbao, as though conscious of this fact, huddles here below. On the northern end of the Arenal is the old church of San Nicolás; to the south across the street is Bilbao's theater, the Teatro Arriaga. A short block away from the Arenal to the east is the Plaza Nueva—the new park which is no longer new. Much like the Main Square of Salamanca and countless other parks of olden Spain, it consists of a large square surrounded by an arcaded walkway that forms the facade of shops and cafés. The windows and balconies of the dwellings above command an excellent view of the cultural, social and other events that are often held here.

Around the corner from San Nicolás are the old narrow streets of Bilbao, the well known *siete calles* (seven streets), probably the original ones of the town. They lead to the Basílica de Santiago with its massive stone pillars and the old Door of the Angel which leads to the cool patio within just off the main sanctuary. The sounds of the street names carry somehow the impression of the tall dark buildings that look down from their many stories of protruding glassed-in windows: La Ronda, Artecalle, Tendería, Somera, Belosticalle, Carnicería Vieja, and Barrencalle. Other streets with other names wind aimlessly among these seven: the Calle de la Cruz, with its quaint old church of Los Santos Juanes on the corner, and the Calle Bidebarrieta, the final resting place of El Sitio, once Bilbao's club of young intellectuals. These streets are narrow but not very straight; Calle de la Ronda, as its name implies, follows a winding pathway, while Calle de la Cruz leads into a flight of wide stone steps up the hillside. The climb is long and steep, up past the Mallona graveyard, long since overgrown in weeds, all the way to the top where the shrine of Our Lady of Begoña, patron saint of Vizcaya, overlooks the whole town, the river's mouth, and the surrounding blue mountains topped by Arnótegui and Pagasarri. A graceful avenue of trees leads to the entrance of the shrine, and within the spirit of the gentle virgin above the altar pervades the place. Outside again one looks at the town below. The river's mouth, its spanning bridges, the *Ayuntamiento*, the smokestacks of the factories—they can scarcely be distinguished through the heavy cold mist, the *sirimiri*, that envelops Bilbao much of the time. One comprehends the pervading feeling of sadness, of depression, that overshadowed Unamuno's boyhood, and the lines of his poem "En La Basílica del Señor Santiago de Bilbao" come to mind:

> *Como tu cielo es el de mi alma triste*
> *y él llueve tristeza a fino orvallo*
> *y como tú entre férreas montañas*
> *sueño agitándome.*[2]

> The fine mist of sadness rains in my
> soul like that of your sky, and like you,
> I dream my dream of restlessness among
> the iron-cored mountains.

On the way down a sign catches the eye; directly in front of a turn in the road an abandoned little vendor's sign bears the words "*Churrería Zabalbide.*" It recalls Pachico Zabalbide who depicts the author himself in Unamuno's novel *Paz en la guerra.* Down below on one of those seven streets, there is a house; another of those tall dark buildings on Ronda Street. The plaque to the right of the door is its only distinguishing mark: "Don Miguel de Unamuno y Jugo was born in this house on September 29, 1864." It happened at 7:15 A.M., according to the baptismal record:

In the town of Bilbao, Señorío of Vizcaya, diócesis of Vitoria, on the 29th of September of Eighteen Hundred and Sixty-Four, I, D. Pascual de Zuazo, presbyter, chaplain and priest of the parochial church of the Saints John, did solemnly baptize a boy born today at seven and a quarter of the morning, legitimate son of D. Félix Unamuno, a native of Vergara, a merchant, and Da. Salomé de Jugo, a native and a resident of this town. *Paternal*

[2] Joaquín Zuazagoitia, *Algunos escritores vascongados desde 1874*, pp. 13–14.

*grandparents* D. Melchor de Unamuno and Da. Josefa Ignacia de Larraza, natives of Vergara. *Maternal* D. José Antonio de Jugo and Da. Benita de Unamuno, natives, he of Ceberio, and she of Vergara: I named him Miguel and the Godparents were D. Félix de Aranzadi, a merchant, and Da. Valentina de Unamuno, natives, he of Arechabaleta, and she of Vergara, who will act as spiritual parents: *Witnesses,* Ramón de Arrugaeta and Lucas de Ayesta, the sacristans, and I, Pascual de Zuazo, sign it.[3]

Of his grandparents Unamuno himself was to write that the only information he had of his father's father was that he ran a candy store in Vergara, but he possessed the record of his mother's parentage all the way back to the eighth Juan de Jugo whose son, Pedro de Jugo Sáez Abendaño, was born in Galdácano in 1608.[4]

No one knows in which room, or exactly on which floor Unamuno was born in that house on Ronda Street. It all reeks of "dampness and gloom," and there is not a room in it but what "the light enters only filteringly," as Don Miguel himself described it. He also wrote that Juan Crisóstomo was born in this same house fifty-eight years earlier. However, according to Don Antonio Lizárraga, a nephew of Unamuno's wife, who as the nearest relative in Bilbao officiated at the unveiling of the dedicatory plaque on December 31, 1941, it has been found that the musician, Juan Crisóstomo de Arriaga, was born in a nearby house on Somera Street, hence the sign bearing his name, which for years had been on this house, was moved when Unamuno's plaque was put up. The townspeople, and especially the occupants of the house, still argue the question.

The family moved from this house when Miguel was still a nursing infant to another gloomy house just around the corner from the church of the Saints John, No. 7 on the Calle de la Cruz. This was to be his home for the next twenty-six years until he left to take up his life work at the University of Salamanca in 1891. The stairway leads from story to story, turning along a short hallway on each floor around to the right where a small built-in seat faces the next flight up. Just before the turn to the alcove and the second flight up a heavy door leads into a narrow hallway. Off of this hallway across the front of the building are the rooms that were home for Don Félix Unamuno, his wife who was also his niece, Doña Salomé de Jugo, and their four children: the old-fashioned traditionally Basque parlor, used only on

[3] This is a copy of the original, signed, sealed, and given to the author by the parish priest in Bilbao, June 16, 1959.

[4] Unamuno, *Rosario de sonetos líricos,* Notes, p. 159.

special occasions, the anteroom that was the family's living room, and the dark bedroom beyond it. Here around the glassed-in balcony window (mirador) and the encircling raised floor space within, the family, relatives, and friends, accustomed to gather for the seven o'clock evening *tertulia,* while the children would play in the open space in front of the church of the Saints John. They could be seen from the aptly named mirador and called at will. This area of the house—the bed, the mirador—was to hold many memories for the boy and the man as he grew to maturity. It was from this window that, on February 21, 1874, he witnessed the Carlist bomb exploding on the house next door during the second Carlist war. To this bed he brought his Concha as a bride in 1891, and standing here in the same mirador his mother was taken fatally ill in the summer of 1908.

The Basque lineage of Unamuno is a dominant factor in his whole life history. He was proudly, sometimes even belligerently, a Basque, as far back as memory and records go. Referring to himself and his country, *i.e.,* the Basque provinces, Unamuno once wrote: ". . . he who was born of parents from that very country (and of grandparents and of great grandparents and . . . forefathers as far back as my information goes) and where he was born and reared." [5] His father's mother was a Larraza, which in Basque means "pasture," and in Spanish, "the race." This name was to offer Don Miguel opportunities for word play of which he always availed himself. "I do not wish to devour other people;" he once wrote, "rather let them devour me! How beautiful to be a victim! To give oneself in spiritual pasture! To be consumed . . . to become diluted in the souls of others! Thus we shall arise on that day when all are united, and when God shall be all in all, as St. Paul says . . ." [6]

Although Don Félix died before Miguel was six years old, the influence of his teachings and especially of his personality left a permanent and indelible mark upon his son. The *"carácter* Unamuno" is a term frequently used among the family, especially with reference to a quality of outspoken frankness, a certain bent they seem to have toward contention. Of his maternal grandmother, Doña Benita de Unamuno from Vergara, Don Miguel once wrote that she was "fault-finding and terrible tempered." To her fulminations against the Carlists Miguel would only retort, "grandmother's exaggerations." [7]

[5] *Obras completas,* VI, 34.
[6] Unamuno, *El espejo de la muerte,* p. 130.
[7] *La Gaceta Regional* (Salamanca), December 31, 1948.

On one occasion Félix, Miguel's older brother who was at odds with the entire family on some financial questions, went for consolation and support to visit his elder sister, the nun Susana. The interview took place in one of those quiet peaceful little rooms in the convent. Félix, thinking to startle his prayerful sister into agreement, pounded the table and exclaimed, "Damn it, I'm tired of it!" "And I am even more so," answered Susana with an equally resounding pound of her fist.

Whenever a relative was particularly hard to get along with it was immediately ascribed to the "*carácter* Unamuno." Juan Cruz de Unamuno, the bachelor brother of Don Félix, once chided his nephew Miguel: "You must be an Unamuno." "No," retorted Miguel, "you are the Unamuno, I am a Jugo!" Indeed this feeling of kinship with his Jugo ancestry was what stirred him to write those virile lines of majestic rhythm which he composed on a visit to the old homestead in Galdácano entitled "Near the Jugo Homestead." It reads:

> Aquí, en la austeridad de la montaña,
> con el viento del cielo que entre robles
> se cierne, redondearon pechos nobles
> mis abuelos . . .[8]

> Here, in the austerity of these mountains,
> with the wind of heaven that purifies itself
> among the oaks, my forefathers held high
> their noble breasts . . .

In later life Don Miguel often referred to "that rich uncle with the sullen temperament and intolerable temper who left all of his fortune to his servant because no relative was willing to put up with his violent character." Then he would add, "but he did exactly right."[9]

As a young man Miguel's father, Don Félix, had gone to America with Juan Cruz and two of his other brothers. After several years on the Pacific coast of Mexico he had returned to Spain richer by a library of some five hundred "useful" books which he brought with him; Juan Cruz returned rich in the more literal sense of the word and accompanied by a manservant who attended to his wants the rest of his life and inherited his money when he died. As Don Miguel often remarked, the servant had won it honestly for putting up with his uncle for so long; even his money didn't compensate for his terrible disposition ("*ni con el dinero era aguantable*").

[8] *Rosario de sonetos líricos*, No. 20.
[9] *La Gaceta Regional* (Salamanca), December 31, 1948.

Miguel's father, however, was a merchant occupying a position of trust in Bilbao and of admiration and love in his son's memories. A comparatively widely read man of culture, he was for years the official auditor (*contador*) of the town government.

The religion of both the Unamuno and Jugo families was Catholic. "Catholic heart—the Unamunos and the Jugos. Catholic to the Bone," is the title of a part of a study which Dr. Hernán Benítez, a Catholic priest and professor at the University of Buenos Aires wrote on *La crisis religiosa de Unamuno*. He writes of the prayers offered before pictures of saints and the receptacles for holy water that hung beside almost every door of the home on the Calle de la Cruz. Antonio Lizárraga relates with pride that as a boy Unamuno was secretary of the Congregación de las Koscas (a church organization for boys from ten to twelve) whose chief occupation seems to have been playing in the inner churchyard of the Basílica de Santiago.

In such a town and to such a home was born Miguel, a serious, sad-looking boy, the youngest of four children. Don Miguel, the man, pondered often and deeply on the influences of his childhood, turning with increasing frequency and intensity to it as he neared the end of his life. An awareness of self, of his *yo*, took him back constantly to his beginnings. "I am I, my uncle and my nephew," he would say. And so he was. That father who by marrying his own niece had made him so, was hard to remember. Once reminiscing in Salamanca, he imagined himself back in the old house on Calle de la Cruz in Bilbao, hearing again a voice—the voice of his father. The face escaped him but the voice was clear—it was speaking French. Miguel, the object of his father's special devotion, was listening outside the parlor door. He could hear clearly his father's voice but he could not distinguish the words. Overcome by curiosity, on an impulse, he pulled open the heavy door and went in. On one wall hung a picture of Moses, striking the rock; on another was one of those large bevelled mirrors that distort the image, making one appear first tall and angular, then short and round. Thus he remembered the parlor of the old house on Calle de la Cruz.

Just around the corner was the old slaughterhouse which occupied one entire block. In *Mi bochito* he draws later a vivid picture of it. He writes that it was bounded by the Calle de la Cruz, the Calle de la Sombrerería, Calle del Correo and Calle del Matadero (this latter, he writes, was changed to Calle del Banco de España, indicating that the slaughterhouse no longer existed). He goes on to say, my world, my real world, the placenta of my embryonic spirit, that forged the rock on which is based my vision of the universe, was, above all, the square where the slaughterhouse was located. What mysterious relations could there have been between the sights which were constantly before our eyes when our comprehension of the universe was taking shape, and the path our lives take later? The slaughterhouse, its tiled floor streaming with water and blood, and those women who seemed to dance with the aid of a rope a silent, ritualistic dance, beating out with their feet the blood of the slain cattle—the influence that the frequent sight of all this may have had on my conception of life, is, I believe, a wonderful mystery.[10]

Then he added, "But I don't know just why my *bochito* [hole] is symbolized for me . . . by something much more modern; the "New Park."

The surrounding mountains challenged something in the boy and he writes of Arnótegui whose top seems to crown the buildings of Bilbao. This mountain, as it appeared, framed by the old houses of Bilbao, first disclosed nature to him.

First revelation of nature framed by the dark, drafty old houses with their crude wooden porches, their doorways, half-hidden by all sorts of implements and wearing apparel: barets, suspenders, scarfs, oxen yokes! And gazing down upon the human anthill . . . the mountain, impassive, in its enduring mantle of green. When would I be able to scale its peak up there, where at times the clouds would rest to bathe themselves in God's air and sunshine?[11]

No wonder the boy Miguel wanted to scale the mountain peak, to escape from the confines of gloomy homes and narrow streets! This early longing was sensed by his father who led the boy into the open air and taught him the wonder of life and nature. From him, too, Miguel learned his first history lesson. He was four years old when his father took him to see the wax works, the little figures of Maximilian with his two Mexican generals, Miramón and Mejía. They were lined up, standing stiffly, before a firing squad. That, his father explained, was history. Only later did he realize that the shooting of those men, what actually happened to them, was an incident in history which had passed, but what he felt about that incident, as it entered into and helped mold his spirit, remained. This latter element of history, the part which remained, he later termed *la intra-historia*.

Unamuno sometimes thought he carried all of his childhood within

[10] Unamuno, *Obras selectas*, pp. 836–837.
[11] *Ibid.*, p. 836.

the very core of his being. In times of crisis, in that *intra-historia* of his spiritual struggle, some instinct invariably took him back to his childhood where faith and strength were renewed. He often sought an explanation of these returns to the simple feelings of his boyhood. Writing of this in *Cómo se hace una novela* he quotes a writer as saying, ". . . it is always and every time the child in us who believes . . . believing is a function of the sense of childhood. There is in us as much ability to believe as there is infancy." [12] In the same work, Don Miguel has his hero (himself) go back to his homeland and childhood, "and he would find his true childhood, his eternal childhood, that age when he could not yet read, when he was not yet a man of books. And in that childhood he would discover his inner man, the 'oso anthropos'." [13] Another great teacher said that in order to enter the Kingdom of Heaven, we must become as little children.

All of his childhood and early youth, until the age of sixteen when he left to study in Madrid, Miguel spent in Bilbao. It was a good thing to spend one's childhood in one country, in one town even, ". . . one should not be a child in two different countries, and to be a poet one must have been a child in one country, and, in a certain sense, continue being one; for it is the poet who cherishes his childhood in his soul." [14]

The house, the town, the lesson in history, and, most of all, the eternal wonder of nature which he learned from his father formed what he later called his "intimate culture" (*cultura íntima*).[15] Before the boy was six the two would take long walks across the open fields, usually at dusk. "On these walks," he writes, "my father would talk to me about the moon, the clouds and how they were formed, and about how grain is sown and grows and is gathered; and about the insects and their lives and habits. I am sure that those lessons, even the ones I have forgotten, are the best that I have been taught, the living rock of my *cultura íntima*." [16]

[12] Unamuno, *Cómo se hace una novela*, p. 133.
[13] *Ibid.*, p. 132.
[14] Unamuno, *Contra esto y aquello*, p. 133.
[15] This recurrent return to nature in search of his "intimate culture" or the intrahistory of his people is analyzed by Carlos Blanco Aguinaga in his *El Unamuno contemplativo*. Señor Blanco Aguinaga relates it to the Spaniard's persistent dwelling on his childhood memories and the maternal instinct of his women: his wife and his fictional characters. Señor Blanco Aguinaga contrasts this contemplative, mystical Unamuno with the agonizing, struggling Unamuno, the latter identified with his idea of history.
[16] Unamuno, *La ciudad de Henoc: comentario 1933*, p. 134.

# The Rock Is Split

CHAPTER  *3*

THE LUSH, GREEN MOUNTAINS
of Vizcaya and the growing wonder of the natural world that formed
this rock of his *cultura íntima* might have produced a romantic poet.
But Unamuno was not a romantic. In his life and writings there is
struggle, contradiction, vacillation between faith and doubt and the
agony of life and death. Somewhere the rock was split, like the yellow
crags of Castile, by nature itself, by death as he discovered it in that
first history lesson and perhaps by the sudden and traumatic experience of the death of his father.

The actual details of Señor Unamuno's death are not clear. Don
Miguel tells the story in a short sketch, "El abejorro" (The Bumblebee), which is found in *El espejo de la muerte.* It happened when
Miguel was nearly six years old, on one of those long walks when
father and son would share the world around them. In the story an
old man is explaining his fear of bumblebees to a young companion:

When I was a boy my father would frequently take me for long walks
across the field, just at dusk, and the two of us alone, and about all I can
remember is that those long walks used to sadden me [1] . . . Then suddenly,
as if seized by an overwhelming longing, he would take me in his arms
and smother me with kisses, asking me repeatedly "Gabriel, will you always
be good?" . . . At times he would even weep, his tears falling on my cheeks;

[1] Unamuno, *El espejo de la muerte,* p. 133.

and I remember that I began to cry, a silent weeping like his, a weeping that welled up from the deepest recesses of my spirit as though expressing all the sadness which has molded our flesh, griefs from beyond the cradle . . . Who knows? Inherited griefs, perhaps.[2]

Then somewhere a bumblebee was buzzing and the father with his last passionate breath, asked, "Will you always be good, Gabriel?" Scarcely had the question been formed before the father died. The last gasp of death must have horrified the boy. Here the story ends abruptly, adding only that in that moment the child "discovered" death, while the bumblebee buzzed on. At the end of the collection of sketches in *El espejo de la muerte*, Unamuno states that he has been writing about himself. We have but to substitute "Miguel" for "Gabriel" and this picture comes to life. But the transfer from fiction to fact may not be justified. However, Unamuno makes reference to an incident in his own life which also points to his early awareness of death. Referring to the death of one of his schoolmates in the days when he had scarcely entered puberty, he writes in *Recuerdos de niñez y mocedad*: "It is a solemn moment when death is revealed to us for the first time, when we feel that we are to die." [3]

Beginning thus in his childhood and increasing throughout his lifetime, the idea of death was the dominant preoccupation of Unamuno. Sometimes he would try to imagine death as nothing and the effort filled him with such terror that, as he once wrote, all the torments of hell seemed preferable to *la nada* (nonexistence). As he expressed it, death transforms everything into nothing. It is the supreme contradiction of life—life's greatest paradox.

The facts of Miguel's childhood are veiled in fiction and scattered throughout his writings, although the spirit of the man breathes in almost every line he wrote. A mixture of fact and fiction reveals a few incidents, such as the foregoing experience, though for the most part those early years in Bilbao are shrouded in silence. After the death of Don Félix Unamuno economic difficulties of the family may have been relieved somewhat by Juan Cruz. Recalling his childhood Christmases in Bilbao Don Miguel once referred to ". . . that distant kinsman who lived alone in Bilbao and used to come during those days to spend them with my family, bringing a Christmas present to the children." [4]

[2] *Ibid.*, p. 134.
[3] Luis S. Granjel, *Retrato de Unamuno*, p. 70.
[4] Unamuno, *Obras completas*, VI, 11.

Of the four children, María, who was ten years older than Miguel, had the longest association with him, though the two were never close to each other. In fact, even during the long years that María lived in his large household in Salamanca, from 1908 until her death from tuberculosis in 1931, their relations were so strained that they hardly ever spoke directly to each other. Any communicating between them was always done through a third person. María must have been generously endowed with the "*carácter* Unamuno" for this situation is common knowledge in Salamanca where it is also said that she was anything but a favorite with her nieces and nephews. This left only Doña Concha who seemed to handle María very well. One can only wonder when and where this antagonism started between the oldest and the youngest of the children in the Bilbao household. There is no mention of María's name in her brother's works; not so, however, with Susana. There are frequent references to his "adored" Susana. Her letters written from the convent affected him deeply and he mentions his joy when, for reasons of health, she was a visitor in his home.

Of the four Unamuno children, Félix, the third child, was the least favored by fortune. Referred to by some as *el tonto* (the fool), he could not have been too bright, but was bright enough to feel keenly the difference between Miguel and himself. It is still related in Bilbao that when that town was preparing a welcoming celebration for Don Miguel as he was making his triumphal trek from Hendaye back to Salamanca in 1930, poor old Félix, always the object of gibes and practical jokes, paraded in front of the station arrogantly opening and closing his coat and wearing a sign on his hat that read, "*No me hablen de mi hermano*" (don't talk to me about my brother).

The theme of brotherly relationships appears frequently in Unamuno's works as that of Cain and Abel with the novel twist of blaming Abel for becoming the victim rather than Cain for being the victimizer. Undoubtedly Miguel felt no love in his heart for Félix. His brother's death in Bilbao some time in May of 1931 brought Don Miguel from Madrid to attend the funeral, accompanied by two of his daughters. Félix had the reputation for hoarding money and it was rumored then that he had a billfold full of it. However, Don Miguel refused to look for it among his brother's effects. "Let the family he lived with have it for their trouble," he said.

A rich source of information about those early years is Don Miguel's first novel *Paz en la guerra*, and it is to this book that Unamuno re-

peatedly referred friends and critics for biographical details. The
central character of this novel, Francisco Zabalbide, is undoubtedly
himself, and the circumstances of the Carlist uprising with the details
of the bombing of Bilbao he affirms to be physical and historical fact.
Further than this it is misleading to accept other facts as entirely
autobiographical for there is a wide discrepancy between the age of
Zabalbide and Unamuno's own age in the crucial year of the city's
siege. Orphaned at the age of seven, Zabalbide was raised by a rich
uncle and witnessed the bombing as an adolescent, not as a child of
ten years old as was Miguel.

The language of the Unamuno home was Spanish though the parents
may have used the Basque tongue occasionally. The latter had probably been familiar to them in childhood, particularly to Don Félix
who was reared in Vergara. Don Miguel recalls the ease with which
he and his playmates would pick up *éuscaro* from the peasants, a
pastime of his boyhood that led to the serious study of Basque which
was the theme of his major thesis when he graduated from the University of Madrid in 1884.

Miguel's first teacher after his father was Don Higinio, the schoolmaster of the local Colegio de San Nicolás—*colegio* was for boys who
could pay; *escuela* meant free tuition. At first the child was stoically
silent. *"Pero, hombre, Miguel, di algo!"* said the teacher. (Heavens,
Miguel, say something!) *"Algo,"* said Miguel.

There is another incident that happened in that Colegio de San
Nicolás which stood out in his memory years afterward. Don Higinio
was a strict disciplinarian, as were many educators of two generations
ago. He dispensed punishment of two different kinds: *juicio general*
and *juicio individual.* By means of a stout stick which he termed his
*junquillo de Indias* (little cane from the Indies) he would rain blows
indiscriminately among the pupils who took refuge under the benches.
This was his *juicio general.* Even the *juicio individual* concerned them
all for each child was expected to contribute a blow on one of his
more unfortunate schoolmates. One day the victim was Miguel's class-
mate, Ene. The children were forced to strike the boy, one by one.
Not a tear was shed but they suffered with Ene and each one in his
heart passed judgment on the teacher. The one principle which Don
Higinio taught Miguel, as he recorded in *Recuerdos de niñez y de
mocedad,* was that "theatrical punishments are, by virtue of their
theatrical nature, the least exemplary of all." [5]

[5] Unamuno, *Obras selectas,* p. 844.

Fortunately for Miguel the schoolmaster was not his only teacher. A curious incident related by Dr. José María de Areílza, Spain's Ambassador to Washington 1958–1959, in *La Estafeta Literaria* (Madrid, December 15, 1944), reveals the enlightening fact that a Spanish artist of some national renown, one Antonio Lecuona, lived in one of those upper stories in the house on Calle de la Cruz. A Basque from Guipúzcoa, Lecuona painted the portraits of Don Carlos VII, the famous king without a kingdom of the Carlist wars, and he occasionally visited the royal garrison at Durango. Among other well-known people who sat for him was one Sabino Arana, the initiator of the Basque nationalist movement whose forefathers were friends of the artist's family. But of all his subjects, the Basque poet, Antonio Trueba, was the one who most directly influenced the young Miguel. Areílza writes that Trueba often visited Lecuona in his studio, and the artist did a drawing of the poet on his deathbed. He also states that Miguel was a frequent visitor in the studio and his article is accompanied by a painting by Lecuona as evidence of the fact. In the picture Ignacio de Loyola lies wounded on the battlefield of Pamplona. He is attended by a priest and a young surgeon who is none other than Unamuno. His young face peers down at Loyola from under a beplumed dark velvet hat as he binds up the leg of the founder of the Jesuit order. Now Don Miguel has repeatedly proclaimed his admiration and boyhood devotion to the simple lines of Trueba's poetry that first taught him to love the natural charms of his Vasconia and, as Areílza points out by quoting Unamuno himself, ". . . as a young man, Unamuno was a dilettante at caricature and drawing. Lecuona gave him his first classes in copying on canvas, copying in plaster of Paris, and even in oils . . ."

Listening to the Basque artist and the Basque poet here in the studio just above his own home, the boy Miguel learned many things that were to bear fruit: a love and understanding of his native Vasconia, stories of Don Carlos and the Carlist wars, an appreciation and sensitivity to line and color, and a deep feeling for poetry and nature.

In these short years of his childhood Unamuno, who might have been another romantic poet, became acquainted with the great paradoxes of life—the beauty and cruelty of nature, the struggle between life and nonexistence in death, the kindness and justice of his first teacher, his father, and the sadistic injustice of Don Higinio. These experiences were the celt, the wedge, which was to split the living rock of his *cultura íntima* and so produce a writer whose philosophy was based on struggle, a man of contradiction and paradoxes, and an existentialist who thirsted after immortality, even as the hart of the psalmist "panteth after the water brook." They were of a personal, intimate nature and affected him deeply. As he grew older he was affected also by events of a sociological nature—events which split his home community of Bilbao and the entire nation, his beloved España, with which he grew to identify himself. These events comprise the civil wars which rent the people in twain and in 1873 split the city of Bilbao in those tragic days when it was bombed.

# The Siege of Bilbao

CHAPTER 4

UNAMUNO WAS BORN AND LIVED
in a world torn by political and ideological strife: the Carlist wars in
Spain, Spain's colonial disaster, World War I in Europe, and, at the
end of his seventy-two years, another civil war in his own country.
Small wonder, then, that he should build his philosophy on struggle,
on a tragic sense of life!

In 1864, the year of his birth, Isabel II, daughter of the Bourbon
king, Fernando VII, was queen, while her cousin, Don Carlos, con-
tested the crown. The country was split into warring factions, divided
not primarily by the question of legal succession, which served as a
mere pretext, but by ideological differences rooted deep in tradition
and in divergent ways of life.

Around the queen in Madrid rallied the liberals, suspected of har-
boring "progressive" European ideas, even protestant sympathies.
Their opponents, the "Carlists," whose strongholds lay in the mountain
regions of the north around Asturias and old Castile, fought heroically
for traditionalism and Catholicism. Repeated bloody uprisings, intensified by individual loyalties to one or another of the many guerrilla
heroes created by circumstances and the uniting loyalty to Don Carlos
whose very name was a symbol of the causes which stir the Spanish
heart, produced the bitter Carlist wars which split Spain during the
latter half of the nineteenth century.

It was perhaps in Vizcaya and certainly in Bilbao where these divergent ways of life most vitally came to grips. The last Carlist war culminated in the siege of Bilbao which lasted from November 1873 until May of the following year.

Bilbao is a seaport town, but winding up from the river's mouth its narrow streets lead back to the mountains, back to the hidden source of the river—which is well-named the Nervión, for it is the connecting nerve between the primitive life of Vizcaya and the modern life of the town. This meeting of the two in the struggle of the last Carlist war, its effect on the people of Bilbao and his own part in it, all are vividly described by Unamuno in his novel, *Paz en la guerra*.

Bilbao itself, or at least those who chose to stay on through the siege, sided with the liberals. As the merchant, Don Juan Arana, explained it ". . . Even if we of Bilbao should turn Carlist, Bilbao would keep right on being liberal or it would no longer be Bilbao. Otherwise no commerce is possible and without commerce this town has no reason for being." [1] The reason for the struggle, however, lay deeper than that. Unamuno saw it as "The ancient feud . . . the feud between the man of the country and the man of the city, between the man of the mountain and of frugality and the man of the sea and of greed." [2]

The conflict was reflected in the two town newspapers: *La Guerra*, the liberal publication, and *El Cuartel*, the Carlist mouthpiece. As rumors of the coming struggle began to reach Bilbao, they became the current topic both in print and in friendly discussion. The groups which gathered every evening in the popular eating place or in the shop of the *chocolatero* (the chocolate vendor), would speculate on the outcome of the present issues and drink in tales of bygone battles, told by some veteran of the Spanish war of independence against the forces of Napoleon. Such gatherings were made up of neighbors, who lived peacefully side by side, and whose forefathers might never have spoken Spanish, having lived and died in some hidden mountain village. But here and now, they shared their thoughts and feelings and were united as one family.

However, families frequently quarrel and brother turns upon brother, even as Cain slew his brother, Abel. As the Carlist forces drew nearer, emotions were aroused and the family feud began. The "shameless" anti-Catholic campaign of *La Guerra* added fuel to the emotional fire. "The whole thing was like a heated family fight, it was as though the

---

[1] Unamuno, *Paz en la guerra*, p. 187.
[2] *Ibid.*, p. 139.

whole town were brothers." [3] Recalling this fraternal aspect of the conflict, Unamuno often expressed the conviction that war is a confirmation of the essential brotherhood of man, the eternal struggle between Cain and Abel: "In wartime," he wrote once, "the child and the savage in man, always twin brothers, stand revealed." [4]

As the Carlists approached, Bilbao gradually became an isolated island of liberals. The time for quarreling was over and each one had to take some decisive action. The roots of tradition are strong roots for a Spaniard and most of the people of peasant stock left Bilbao. Some carried their entire families back to their native villages—to Guernica, to Tolosa or to Vitoria. The younger men went to the hills to swell the Carlist forces by joining one of the guerrilla bands whose members would fight like heroes when occasion demanded or run like rats to their holes when this seemed the better part of strategy. Those whose livelihood and interests depended upon and were allied with the world beyond the confines of the peninsula stayed behind, determined to maintain shipping, to keep the traffic moving on those wharves along the river.

Miguel was nine years old when the siege began. Many a long evening he must have listened to the voices arguing; his uncle, no doubt a liberal, arguing with the priest, perhaps, while the women sat listening, fearing, and planning. But for him and his classmates the war was a game, a holiday from Don Higinio's dreaded cane. Some of those children can still be identified either because of kinship ties or long friendships nourished by common experiences and associations. One of them was Miguel's first cousin, Claudio Aranzadi y Unamuno. The son of Valentina, Don Félix's sister, Claudio and his brother Telesforo, lived with their parents on the third floor of the same building with their cousins. Just four years younger than Miguel, Claudio was a spectator of, if not a participant in, those childish war games.

Another lifelong friend who belonged to that early group was Mario Sagárduy. The two of them "saw the bombing of Bilbao together and were schoolmates through their high school studies [bachillerato] at the Instituto Vizcaíno." When Mario was sixteen he started his long business career with an insurance company in Bilbao. Miguel, who visited Bilbao regularly throughout his lifetime, was a frequent visitor in Mario's home, sometimes accompanied by his son Fernando, and

---

[3] *Ibid.*, p. 189.
[4] *Ibid.*, p. 190.

it was due to Don Miguel's influence and connection with the University of Salamanca that Mario took up the study of law in 1897. He even passed the required examinations in Salamanca and completed the course, on a bet, in nineteen months, just under the two year time limit set by himself. During that period Mario was in Salamanca three times for examinations on which occasions he stayed in Don Miguel's home. On one of these visits Don Miguel presented his old schoolmate to the board of examiners and added, "Watch out for this fellow; he won the prize in psychology and in logic right out from under my nose in the instituto." Correspondence between these two is further evidence of their close friendship, for Don Miguel wrote of his personal, intimate problems to Mario during that most crucial period in his life, the years of 1896 and 1897.

Among those children who in the midst of war were starting lifelong friendships, there may have been one who has left evidence of that friendship in the assembly room of Bilbao's town fathers, in the *Ayuntamiento*. Prominently displayed in the center aisle at the rear of the hall is a sculptured head of Unamuno. It was executed by Moisés de Huerta, a life-long friend (*amigo de vida*).

Then of course there was Pedro Eguillor who lived and died in Bilbao. To him Unamuno was to dedicate a part of his *Rosario de sonetos líricos*, written in the years 1910 to 1911. That rosary of songs entwined his childhood memories of his Vizcaya—"Dulce recuerdo," "Junto al caserío Jugo," "Mi vieja cama"—with his "Castilla enjuta," where the image of Vizcaya's sweet green forests comforted him in his life's struggle. The dedication begins, "To my dear friend, Pedro Eguillor . . . *Guárdemelas*," he writes " *en tu abrigada cilla por si algún día en mí la fe desmaye.*" (Keep them for me in your sheltered storehouse in case some day my faith should falter.)

War to them there in Bilbao in 1874 was a holiday from school. The roll call came later to each in his own time: Claudio Aranzadi, Telesforo Aranzadi, Mario Sagárduy, Moisés de Huerta, Pedro Eguillor, and Miguel de Unamuno. Like all children they poetized the war seeing neither its causes nor its consequences, only "its pure form, a game pregnant with new emotions." [5] Indeed, before the strenuous days of the siege, the grownups also felt the holiday spirit, and a strong community feeling united children and adults alike. Religious

[5] *Ibid.*, p. 216.

fiestas and *romerías* [6] seemed never so fervent and gay. Miguel remembered especially the observance of his saint's day, the *día de San Miguel,* that September of 1873. All the men and boys who bore this popular name gathered in the Arenal instead of at the *romería de Basauri* over the mountain on the road to Ceberio where the *romerías* were usually held. It was a gay company. The boys were wearing "red berets and coarse white pants." Some, dressed for hunting, wore leggings. All carried lunches, even if they consisted only of "bread and dried fish," and the street vendors mixed freely among the crowd crying their wares: ". . . cigars, sweet water, and hot fritters for sale." The path to the picnic grounds led past the cemetery. Unamuno later recalled that the words of the sign over the entrance, "Do not enter," impressed him deeply, although for the rest of the company fun and frolic was the order of the day. Every able-bodied person joined enthusiastically in the energetic folk dances of Vizcaya.

However, this holiday spirit could not last. Eventually the adults had to face the realities of war. In December the bombing began and the Carlists closed the mouth of the river, cutting off the supply of ammunition and food. Rumors that the liberals were sending an army from Madrid to engage the Carlists and lift the siege helped to keep up the morale.

But before the liberator came, the besieged were to know misery, fear, and hunger. Horse meat, cats, and even rats saved many from starvation. Some would steal down to the river at night, and with the aid of lanterns, scoop up the fish killed by the detonation of the more powerful bombs. Don Miguel writes that it was a sad Christmas in Bilbao that year.

However, the children continued their games of war. In the midst of this suffering, even while the bombs rained death and destruction, they invented new games of playing at soldiers. One of the favorite sports was a sort of bowling game played *con tablones de la "Batería de la Muerte."* The purpose was, apparently, to knock down imaginary soldiers with make-believe "death artillery." "The little rascals," writes Unamuno, "were beside themselves, taking the perils of war as a game. The arrival and departure of troops, columns of soldiers marching by, the ships coming in with their pilot-houses all darkened, the shots,

[6] A *romería* is a combination of a religious pilgrimage, usually to some shrine, a picnic with folk dances, and a street fair.

people rushing back and forth, and especially the constant blowing of the bugles along the streets of the town, all of this over-excited their baby souls and made them all eyes, ears, and legs, so that they over-flowed with life." [7]

Then came a temporary truce. Hostilities ended and the young people emerged from their homes, where they had taken shelter from the bombs, like sunshine after rain. The girls gaily jumped rope in the streets and some even ventured out to communicate with an occasional stray soldier from the besieging forces. Again the town was united in joy and relief. This lasted only a few days before the killing was resumed with redoubled energy. At last came the dawn of May 2, 1874, when the liberal forces actually arrived to substantiate the many rumors, and the Carlists withdrew. The siege was over for Bilbao, the killing stopped, and once more the people had white bread to eat. May second was a thrice-eventful date for Spain, Don Miguel later recalled: May 2, 1808, when Napoleon's troops committed the deliberate massacre of thousands of Spaniards, a date immortalized in Goya's painting; May 2, 1866, when the liberals under General Prim rebelled against Queen Isabel; and May 2, 1874, when the siege of Bilbao came to an end.

The outstanding event of the siege for Miguel, however, the event to which he repeatedly referred in speeches and essays, occurred one day as he was standing in the mirador of his home. Before his very eyes an enemy bomb fell and exploded on the roof of the house next door. Another lesson in history, it was perhaps this event that awakened his social consciousness. Perhaps it was at this moment that he first actually suffered with his country and felt Spain within him, the feeling which often led him to exclaim, *"Me duele España!"* (Spain hurts me.)

Others in the town would not soon forget the siege of Bilbao, the *sitio*, as it is called in Spanish. Not long afterwards a group of young students considered Bilbao's liberal hotheads organized themselves into a club which they named, El Sitio, in commemoration of the siege of Bilbao.

[7] Unamuno, *Paz en la guerra*, p. 165.

# The Young Owl Opens His Eyes

CHAPTER 5

As AN ADOLESCENT, MIGUEL must have been tall, thin, and awkward. One friend describes him as having deep-set eyes which peered out from "the face of a young owl." This owlish appearance became so accentuated in later years that Spain's national caricaturist, Bagaria, once drew him with the figure of an owl perched about his head. Salvador de Madariaga carries the likeness further by writing, ". . . all this vitality and ever-moving activity of mind is shot through by the absolute immobility of two owlish eyes piercing the darkness of spiritual night."[1]

The mountains which surround the town, though steep and laborious to climb, beckoned to him irresistibly. From the top of Arnótegui he learned to view the shifting tides in nature, the ocean, the clouds, the seasons, and the struggles of men to live in the circumstantial history which passes away leaving only that *intra-historia* within their souls. To the mountain, symbol of the ancestral heart of his *pueblo* (people), the boy and, later, the man ever returned. Drawn to its lofty heights and the broad view of the world below, Miguel would trudge upward with Pedro, Mario and other classmates who often outstripped him in endurance. More and more he was forced to pause for breath while his friends went ahead or waited for him impatiently. This weakness and other traits set him somewhat apart from his fellows. Gradually they were coming to consider him "strange."

[1] Introduction by Salvador de Madariaga to Unamuno, *The Tragic Sense of Life in Men and in Peoples.*

Writing of this period of his life, Unamuno describes the awakening of his mind by his early reading, the lifetime habits he was forming, and the ideas which he was absorbing. Then he adds: "Slowly my body was growing weaker."[2] He was at this time imposing upon his mind the same discipline which he later applied to his body. Recalling an especially heavy tome which he was determined to read, he writes: "However, with strong determination, the same determination which applied later to physical exercises, regenerated my body, I made up my mind to read it all, and I read it."[3]

As is characteristic in individuals of strong personality, Unamuno made his strength out of his weakness. He continued this stern discipline throughout his life to overcome an incipient tendency toward tuberculosis. Long mountain climbs daily, cold showers in winter followed by a quick rub-down with a stiff brush, and the refusal to wear an overcoat even in the coldest winter weather gave him a robust, rugged physique to the end.

After graduating from Don Higinio's *colegio*, Miguel began his secondary education at the local Instituto Vizcaíno. Here it was, in the fourteenth year of his life and during the fourth year of his *bachillerato*, which corresponds roughly to the senior year at a high school in the United States, that Miguel began to unfold. From his reminiscences and from his portrayal of Zabalbide in his first novel, *Paz en la guerra*, there emerges a clear picture of the adolescent Miguel. In his prologue to the second edition Unamuno wrote in 1923: "Here in this book—that is the person I was . . . I gathered together the flower and the fruit of my experience of childhood and youth; here is the echo and, perchance, the perfume of the most deeply-rooted recollections of my life and the life of the people among whom I was born and raised. Here is the revelation which history, and with history, art became for me."[4]

The first books to stir his imagination were the works of Balmes, a Catalán publisher and amateur philosopher, and Donoso Cortés. Recalling the effect of these writers, he exclaimed:

Heavens, how I was stirred when, back there in the fourth year of my *bachillerato*, I read Balmes and Donoso, the only writers on philosophy which I found in my father's library. Through Balmes I learned that there

2 Unamuno, *Obras selectas*, p. 853.
3 *Ibid.*, p. 851.
4 *Ibid.*, p. 319.

was a Kant, a Descartes and a Hegel. I scarcely understood a word of his *Fundamental Philosophy*, one of the weaker of all the weak works of Balmes, but nevertheless, I read it. Sometimes I would fall asleep with the book open. And sometimes, tired and bored, I would amuse myself by catching flies and pinching them . . . All of that business of the old man, Kant, about pure reason and its a priori forms, the formulas that Fichte derives from his $A = A$, Hegel's doctrine about the identity of pure being and pure nothing, were things that produced vertigo in my young and groping mind . . . I preferred philosophy, the poetry of the abstract, to the poetry of the concrete" [5]

". . . for a change I would read a little volume of poems by the same Balmes, another by Mexican authors, romantic and weepy, and the severe and harsh *Araucana*.[6]

These adolescent tastes foreshadowed the course he subsequently followed: from the reason and science of Hegel, which absorbed him as a young man, to philosophy and the affirmation of vital values, as a mature man. Here is a remarkable parallel with the course of one who lived some twenty-five years earlier in Copenhagen, the "mad" Dane, Kierkegaard, who was later to capture Unamuno's imagination.

Balmes first introduced him to Kant and Hegel, and, although at this time he touched only the surface, *la cáscara* (the peeling), their philosophies were to take root in a few years. From the first peelings of Hegel there came forth pulp, (*"de ellas brotó pulpa"*). From Balmes, also, he acquired a taste for mathematics at an age when he did not yet comprehend that "it is madness to try to hold in these equations the infinite complexity of the living world." [7]

From Newton's conception of space as the immensity of God, Miguel obtained his first metaphor. This idea struck a sympathetic chord in his poetic soul. "My soul's breast seemed to swell within me," he wrote later, "forcing me to breathe the air that fills the immense divinity and to contemplate the heavens that reflect it." Henceforth the metaphor was to mark his style, both in speech and writing, while God in Nature, God as Nature, was to reappear as a possibility in his speculations.

But the concept of the paradox, the conflict and the contradiction of life, took root when he came upon it in Donoso's *Essays on Liberalism*: "Those reflected rays of the paradoxical thinking of Maistre, his

[5] *Ibid.*, p. 851.
[6] *Ibid.*, p. 857.
[7] *Ibid.*, p. 852.

teacher, the idea that human reason loves the absurd . . . just think
what an impression that made on a mind just beginning to open its
calix to the light of truth."[8] Already he had grasped the paradox of
the absurd, long before he read of it in Kierkegaard.

But the boy's mind was not steeped solely in such theoretical ab-
stractions. His love of nature, and perhaps the contact with the Basque
poet, Trueba, in Lecuona's studio, set him delving into the history and
legends of his own people. Perhaps Trueba himself introduced him
to the works of the Basque writers, Goizueta, Araquistáin and Vicente
Arana. In his own *Recuerdos de niñez y de mocedad* he confesses that
these authors filled his head with "the names of Aitor, the ancient
patriarch from the land of the Rising Sun: Lecobide, the lord of
Vizcaya, who is said to have fought against the armies of Octavius,
master of the world; Lelo and Zara; Jaun Zuría or Señor Blanco, who
came to the shores of my land from Ireland, and countless other
legendary figures."[9] And Unamuno adds,

I still keep the notebooks of those days, where in a lacrimose style, trying
to imitate *Ossian*, I lamented the fall and decadence of the race, invoked
the sacred tree of Guernica . . . I evoked the august shades of Aitor,
Lecobide and Jaun Zuría, and cursed the black serpent that bored [*horadaba*]
its way through our mountains, dragging its iron rings and belching forth
smoke, bringing corruption to us from beyond the Ebro . . . and whenever
we could we'd go to the mountain even if only to Archanda, to berate the
miserable present and to search for some measure of the liberty of the
primitive *euscaldunes* who died on the cross cursing their assassins, and to
put the blame on Bilbao, poor Bilbao, for much of all of that. Something of
the breath of Rousseauism urged us to lose ourselves in the dense hillsides
of Iturrigorri.[10]

Indeed, young Miguel was so fired with the cause of Basque independence that he wrote an anonymous letter to King Alfonso XII
taking him to task for having signed the law of July 21, 1876, origi-
nated by Cánovas, abolishing the ancient privileges (*fueros*).

Trueba it was who first realized the boy's potentialities and often
talked with him, sometimes on the old stone steps at the end of the
Calle de la Cruz, or perhaps in Lecuona's studio. Miguel never forgot
either the friendship or the verses of the poet.

[8] *Ibid.*, p. 853.
[9] Luis S. Granjel, *Retrato de Unamuno*, p. 67.
[10] *Ibid.*, pp. 67–68.

Cuentos de color de rosa
nos dejaste, amigo Trueba;
su lectura me renueva
la niñez esperanzosa.
Me ciñen rosas del alba
de la vida que he soñado,
y me limpian de pecado,
que es el niño quien nos salva.
Cruzábamos nuestras horas
en las estradas de Abando,
tú con tus cuentos soñando,
tú fuiste, Trueba, el primero
que adivinara mi sino;
Dios te puso en mi camino
cuando rayó mi lucero.
Vuelvo a tu chocholería,
la del Bilbao de mi cuna;
la rueda de la fortuna
vuélvanos el primer día.[11]

Rose-colored stories you left us,
Trueba, my friend;
I read them and relive
my hope-filled childhood.
They girdle me with morning roses
of the life of my dreams;
they cleanse me from sin,
for it is the child who saves us.
Along the Abando roads
we would while away the hours,
you dreaming on your stories;
it was you, Trueba, who first
divined my destiny;
God put you in my pathway
when first I saw the light.
Again I feel the spell of your words,
the spell of Bilbao that cradled me;
if only fortune could return
those early days to us.

A wise and inspiring teacher directed the young minds assembled in the psychology class at the Instituto Vizcaíno. "It was a class in psychology," Unamuno recalled, "and already the mysteries of the spirit had the strongest hold on me, even then, when I was very young, the Sphinx, in whose embrace I hope to die, was beckoning me."[12]

[11] Unamuno, *Cancionero*, pp. 349–350.   [12] Unamuno, *Obras selectas*, p. 864.

Recognizing conflicting ideas as healthy stimulants, the professor often assigned debates in which Miguel displayed a gift for argument. The boys would compose and memorize talks on various topics. One such effort, he recalled, was on the subject "The Divinity of Jesus Christ." "Unfortunately," wrote Unamuno, "I paid too much attention to the ideas." He remembered quoting something about the statement that "if Socrates died like a wise man, Jesus Christ died like a God." [13]

Summing up his years of schooling in Bilbao, Unamuno concluded that "this was the course that brought about the greatest change in my spirit," [14] and wrote that when he was not in school or reading, he was engaged in endless discussions with his classmates. After school hours, often on Sundays, they would climb to the top of Arnótegui and continue the debates begun in class. "And what discussions . . . all about the first beginnings and final end of things." [15]

However, Miguel was not always in the company of others; often he would retire with a book to his favorite spot beneath the shade of the beech trees.

It seems impossible that just a half-hour's distance from Bilbao there still remains that isolated spot at Buya, that hermit-like strip of land with its densely-growing beeches covered with silver bark, and its little running stream; that vestige of majestic virgin primeval forest—I used to go there to purify myself of the upsetting irritations of the town, of the infection from human contact; many a time I have gone there to submerge myself in the shade of the beech trees, to read there among the ferns, lying on the green earth, the soothing pages of the immense *Obermann*, the cradle song of the unfathomable enigma . . . Oh, my Buya! Ah lovely heritage from the dense forests that forged our race.[16]

This early desire to escape from the irritations of the town, "the sadness engendered in him by contemplating objects of human construction as contrasted with the joy he felt when looking at nature's manifestations—a tree, a cloud"—may indeed be "the key to Unamuno's childhood," as Laín Entralgo writes.[17]

*Obermann* by Sénancour here first cast a spell over his sensitive soul, a spell which was to last a lifetime. Fifty years later, identifying

13 *Ibid.*, p. 849.
14 *Ibid.*, p. 850.
15 *Ibid.*, p. 852.
16 *Ibid.*, p. 839.
17 Pedro Laín Entralgo, *La generación del noventa y ocho*, p. 34.

himself with Obermann, he wrote a poem entitled, "Obermann on Top of the Alps":

> Obermann, lying in the short Alpine grass
> Wept, "Ah, if only we had lived!" as he saw
> How the clouds drifted at his feet, while the peace
> Of heaven—tragic silence—filled him with emptiness.
> "Man must die;—perhaps" and dreaming once again
> "But die resisting—and if it is really Nothing
> That awaits us—let us not act for our ill
> And so make Justice of it"—felt himself swoon.[18]

Miguel also discovered and revelled in the sentiment of *Ossian,* like any other young romantic. "I would go off to some shady spot with Ossian in my pocket to repeat his lamentations to the Morven, to Rino and the children of Fingal." [19] When his eyes grew tired of reading, he would sit for hours lost in feeling and thought—in just that order, feeling and thought, for he was to affirm the priority of emotion over intellect in man, the heart over the head, and on this would he build his philosophy. At such times, he took to prayer and even mysticism, contemplating at this early age, the eternal mysteries of the enigmatic sphinx.

When I was fourteen years old, as a result of much reading during long sleepless nights, and my contact with the organization of San Luis Gonzaga, I experienced my first spiritual crisis, the soul's entrance into puberty . . . those were days when I would weep for no reason, when I believed myself the object of a premature mysticism, and I would take pleasure in staying on my knees for long periods of time to torture them.[20]

The culmination of this adolescent crisis he describes as having occurred when he was alone one evening at dusk at the old Jugo homestead in the little village of Ceberio:

One evening, at dusk, I was on the wooden balcony of the farmhouse . . . And I was seized by such an unaccountable anguish that I began to weep without knowing why. It was the first time this had ever happened to me and it was the countryside that in silence whispered life's mystery to my heart.[21]

---

[18] Unamuno, *Cancionero,* p. 58, translated by Joyce Rudd White.
[19] Unamuno, *Obras selectas,* p. 850.
[20] Granjel, *Retrato de Unamuno,* p. 69.
[21] Antonio Sánchez Barbudo, *Estudios sobre Unamuno y Machado,* p. 17.

Tragedy, sadness, and tears in nature, in the spiritual world, and in his society impressed Unamuno permanently. Recalling the first play he ever saw, no doubt in the old Teatro Arriaga, Unamuno was to write, "and I only remember a lady dressed in mourning weeping at the feet of a gentleman wearing slashed trousers and a *valona*. And it is the first, and to date the last time, that I have seen a woman weeping and kneeling at a man's feet." Commenting on this, Laín Entralgo writes: "The preservation of this memory is in itself a window through which to understand the peculiar psychology of Unamuno, the child." [22]

How did he appear to others? Though we have no source of information but his own words, the writer of *Paz en la guerra* attempts an objective description of himself as Pachico Zabalbide:

In his relations with others, he was ordinary, although he was considered something of a serious crank. He talked a lot but it was always as though from within, bothering a lot of people who thought him tiresome and pedantic because he always wanted to monopolize the conversation, stubbornly picking up where he left off whenever he was interrupted. Then, too, they sensed that treating the listener as an abstraction and engrossed within himself, his conversations were nothing more than pretexts for his monologues, and other people mere geometrical shapes, samples of humanity which he treated *sub speciae aeternitatis*. For his part, he was greatly worried about what other people thought about him, for it hurt him if they judged him ill, and he tried hard to be liked and understood by everybody, for he was deeply concerned with the idea that others had of him.[23]

Not only in talking did Miguel find an outlet. He began to express himself in writing; he even started to outline a new system of philosophy. Recalling his youthful efforts which eventually culminated in his masterpiece, *The Tragic Sense of Life in Men and in Peoples*, he described this initial effort as "very symmetrical, bristling with formulas, and just as labyrinthine, as complicated, and as involved as I could make it . . . the result was much too clear. And so it is with me still, the more obscure and complicated I want to make something, the clearer it turns out to be. I never reveal my thinking more clearly than when I am trying to conceal it." [24]

What boy with an owlish expression, a boy who spends much time alone reading, weeping, a prey to religious seizures, a boy who stubbornly monopolizes the conversation and claims to have invented a

---

[22] Laín Entralgo, *La generación del noventa y ocho*, p. 31.
[23] Unamuno, *Paz en la guerra*, p. 62.
[24] Unamuno, *Obras selectas*, p. 853.

new system of philosophy—what boy like this would not be considered "something of a serious crank"? One day one of the boys, Sabas, showed Miguel a picture, "a certain picture," only to see him grow pale and walk away horrified. Then Sabas *knew* he was a crank. About his reactions to such erotic sexual tendencies, sometimes considered natural in adolescents, Don Miguel later wrote:

Regarding the mystery of iniquity, what we used to call doing nasty things, I prefer to pass over in silence. Those boys that led others to evil really terrified me.   I still recall the fiendish laughter of Sabas . . . when he saw me grow pale and turn my eyes away from a certain drawing, filled with fear rather than shame.

His Spanish biographer, Granjel, quotes the foregoing from Unamuno's *Recuerdos de niñez y de mocedad* with the comment that, "This was possibly due not so much to the integrity with which he was living his religious convictions as to the tender attachment to his mother and the early almost preadolescent love that drew him to her who was to be his wife." [25]

[25] Granjel, *Retrato de Unamuno*, p. 74.

# The First Conflict:
# Marriage or the Church

CHAPTER 6

THE YEAR 1879, WHEN MIGUEL was fourteen years old and already beginning to develop in body, mind, and heart, was, indeed, a crucial year in the boy's life. That year, writes Unamuno, he met Concha Lizárraga Ecénarro. Concha was born in Guernica, in the very heart of Vizcaya, where the natural rhythm of peasant life flowed strong and true, where loyalty to tradition and the Church was as unquestioned as life itself. There, beneath the branches of a sturdy, old oak, Carlos VII had sworn to uphold the traditional *fueros* which guaranteed individual rights and privileges. Thenceforth, this tree was regarded as a symbol of these rights, even as the historic Charter Oak in England. All of these loyalties, all of these racial roots were embodied in Concha, and to her Miguel was drawn irresistibly with a force which increased during the twelve long years of courtship, and lasted to the end of their lives together.

Concha and Miguel did actually spend their lives together, for although he writes of meeting her when he was fourteen years old, other evidence indicates that the two had played together before that time in the house on the Calle de la Cruz. According to Felisa Unamuno, their daughter, Concha's parents moved to Bilbao when she was just a child and she used to play with "some cousins of my father's there in the house." Later she was left an orphan and returned to Guernica to live with an uncle and aunt. Unamuno himself writes that this happened when Concha was twelve years old. As she was born on July 25, 1864, the same year as Miguel, he was the same age when she returned to Guernica. One can imagine Claudio and Telesforo Aranzadi, the cousins, Miguel and Concha on the stairs, in the mirador, in front of the church of Los Santos Juanes, and playing perhaps on the old stone steps of the Calle de la Cruz. It seemed natural to couple the two, Miguel and Concha, and long before the age for falling in love it was tacitly understood that they would some day marry. But one day, at some given time Miguel became conscious of Concha; perhaps it was in his fourteenth year. Did it happen in Guernica or in Bilbao? His sonnet "Dulce recuerdo" pinpoints one tingling moment in Bilbao's Arenal and in the church of San Nicolás:

> Te acuerdas? Fue en mañana del otoño
> dulce de nuestra tierra, tan tranquilo,
> en que esparce sus hojas aquel tilo
> que sabes; eras tú verde retoño
> con las trenzas no presas aún en moño
> cuando pasando junto a mí y el filo
> no resistí de tu mirar y asilo
> corrí a buscar al corazón bisoño
> en el cercano templo. De tus labios
> fluía gota a gota una sonrisa
> muda y clara, cual de alma sin resabios
> de amor, pero que está al amor sumisa;
> desde entonces tus ojos astrolabios
> son de mi viaje que en el cielo frisa.[1]
> Bilbao 1910

Do you remember? It happened one morning in the sweet autumn of our homeland, so peaceful, when that *tilo* tree that you know loses its leaves; you were a fresh green sprout with your braids not yet bound when you passed close by me and I could not resist the sharp edge of your glance, and I ran in search of your undisciplined heart to the nearby church. Slowly your lips parted in a clear, mute smile, like a soul inexperienced in love, but one who is submissive to love; since then your eyes have been the astrolabes of my voyage that now nears heaven.

The poet's note on *"tilo"* reads, "It is a *tilo* tree in the Arenal that speaks to the hearts of all good natives of Bilbao." This tree held a special meaning for Unamuno; under its branches he wrote his first

[1] Unamuno, *Rosario de sonetos líricos*, p. 159.

love sonnet to Concha, and its destruction years afterward inspired his poem "Muerte del tilo del Arenal." [2]

Some time after Concha moved back to Guernica, Miguel began to make weekly visits there. He would traverse the fifteen to twenty kilometers over the mountains on foot to see the girl whose eyes overflowed with the joy she carried in her heart, and to imbibe the age old spirit of his race in the shade of the symbolic oak.

But there were many hurdles for Miguel to surmount before marriage; the first and possibly the foremost was economic. Except for a library of Spanish and Spanish-American books, his father, Don Félix, left little or nothing in the way of earthly goods. His uncle, Juan Cruz, disappointed everyone by leaving most of his money to his American manservant, so Doña Salomé opened up a bakery shop to keep the family going, and after his university career Miguel helped by private tutoring. A correspondence between two of Miguel's friends regarding the economic distress of the Unamuno family indicates that the young university student, very much in love but with no permanent employment, was forced to give private lessons as a means of supplementing the family income. It also mentions that there was some opposition to Miguel's marriage. [3]

To these two difficulties may be added one more possible explanation of the delay, namely, Miguel's own hesitation. It was not that he ever faltered in his feeling for Concha, or even remotely considered anyone else. In fact, his constant love for one woman both before and after marriage is an incontrovertible fact, in spite of what certain sensation seekers later tried to imply. His hesitation was caused by a tendency toward mysticism, toward a life devoted entirely to religion. In a letter, written from Salamanca some eighteen years later, he relates an incident which occurred during his early courtship, ". . . One day when I was scarcely more than a child, I had come home from Church and happened to open a Bible. It opened by chance to the passage 'Go and preach the gospel to all nations . . .' It made a deep impression on me; I interpreted it as a command to become a priest." [4] He was very much in love so he tried to put it out of his mind. However, the incident was repeated; once again, after partaking of Holy

[2] Manuel García Blanco, "Don Miguel de Unamuno y sus poesías," in *Acta salmanticense* (Universidad de Salamanca), Vol. VIII (1954), pp. 13–14.

[3] Correspondence between Areílza and Ilundain in Hernán Benítez (ed.), "Cartas inéditas de Miguel de Unamuno y Pedro Jiménez Ilundain," in *Revista de la universidad de Buenos Aires*, Vol. III, No. 9 (January–March 1949).

[4] *Ibid.*, Vol. II, No. 7 (July–September 1948), pp. 74–75.

Communion, and confessing in Church, the Bible opened in his hands
at random, this time to the 9th chapter of St. John. Though Unamuno
does not say to which verse he turned this time, it could have been
the 27th, in which the man, whose eyes had been opened by Jesus,
answered his questioners and said, "I have told you already, and ye
did not hear: wherefore would ye hear it again?" "And even now,"
he writes, after sixteen or eighteen years, "I remember that morning
alone in my room. For a long time the sentence kept repeating itself
inside of me and the memory of those words has stayed with me always. Several times I have told my friends about it explaining it one
way or another, but the incident remains engraved on my heart. And
a year ago when suddenly the old disturbances and restlessness returned, the memory of that strange experience of my youth returned
with redoubled force." [5] Such a coincidence could scarcely fail to
produce a deep impression on a boy naturally inclined toward mysticism. He saw it as an unmistakable sign that he was called to dedicate
his life to the Church. This call conflicted with his love for Concha,
or so it seemed to him, and marked the beginning of a struggle which
was to become so intensified within his own soul that it would color
his entire concept of humanity and finally serve as the foundation upon
which he would build his philosophy.

That "strange incident of his youth," since it occurred when he was
"scarcely more than a child," must have taken place before he went
to the University. However, even after his return to Bilbao in 1884,
during those unsettled years when he was worried by financial difficulties and was dabbling in socialism, he still doubted the wisdom of
married life for himself. During this period he started writing in
earnest and felt sure that he would devote his life to it. Then there
arose the question of whether a home, love, and duties of a family
might interfere with his efforts as a writer. Indeed, the whole question
of celibacy was one of his main concerns, even after he married.

The young Miguel's love for Concha, his doubts and hesitations
concerning himself, are revealed in letters which he wrote continually
during that period to a Basque friend, Arzadún. Of his sweetheart he
wrote, "She is a house plant and I am a domesticated bear. Everything
will turn out for the best. She will finally civilize me and I shall have
someone in whom to take refuge from the stupidity of the world."
And further, "Marriage will be good for my hobbies and my work. I
recall hearing you say that I need a safety valve, and I believe that

5 *Ibid.*, p. 75.

is right." [6] Thus he wrote in favor of his decision, recognizing his need of a safety valve and of a refuge from himself as well as the "stupidities of the world." At the same time he was beset by doubts: "For a long time a stupid egoism made me fear it. I would say to myself 'Goodbye' if I get married. All of the spiritual energy that I expend on her will be lost for my works." But he added, "I've cured myself of this. Moreover, I used to think what all those monsters of ambition and egoism think: So-and-so, and So-and-so—a whole string of enviable men—were celibates. This reads like a confession. And I went even further: More than once there occurred to me the foolhardy idea that if I have children, the attentions and care that I owe them may distract me from the care I owe my ideas." [7] Then Miguel poses a situation in which he would have to choose between his writings and his as yet hypothetical child. His house is burning and he can save either one or the other. Which will he choose? But this is only the result of a poisoned imagination, he concludes, a state of mind which he has overcome. He decides in favor of man as against ideas, the vital as opposed to the intellectual: "Now I believe that to make a man is the most delicate and glorious work of art; because it is not a question of merely producing him and giving him up to the hands of imbecile teachers, [Could he have been thinking of Don Higinio?] and in a world which he does not know." [8]

The significance of the hypothetical situation which Miguel posed bears consideration. First, it involves the necessity of choice. It is a clear-cut question of either/or. Then he chooses for man—existence— to make a man. As he states it elsewhere, "Man's work is to make his own soul." The parallel already noted with Kierkegaard's philosophy is becoming evident. So far it can only be a coincidence, for not until 1900 did Unamuno become acquainted with the Dane. The similarities, both in life and ideologies are many: the father's early influence, the aloofness from crowds, the hostility toward so-called progress, the hesitation to marry, and the reasons therefor. But here comes the divergence; Kierkegaard rejected marriage, gave up his Regina to become a religious writer, while Unamuno married his Concha and became a poet—a poet with intermittent reversions to religious, even priestly, practices.

[6] Hernán Benítez, "La crisis religiosa de Unamuno," in *Revista de la universidad de Buenos Aires,* Vol. III, No. 9 (January–March 1949), p. 22.
[7] *Ibid.,* p. 23.
[8] *Ibid.,* p. 23.

# The Conflict Broadens:
# Head Versus Heart

CHAPTER 7

MIGUEL WAS SIXTEEN WHEN he entered the University of Madrid, just an overnight journey from Vizcaya, but a far different world from that of Arnotégui and the simple heart of the Basque country. Madrid was the intellectual, the brain center, so to speak, of a country whose heart was its isolated regional sections. When the heart conflicts with the brain, there is ferment, struggle, which can often be resolved only in a paradox, an apparent contradiction. Miguel, already intellectually and emotionally awake, was ready to enter this new world where, during the next four years, his personal struggle was to broaden and intensify.

What were the causes of the intellectual ferment into which Miguel came in 1880? In order to understand them, it is necessary to go back some years. When King Fernando VII died in 1833 Romanticism poured into Spain, brought by the many exiles whom Fernando's political dictatorship had driven out of the country. From France and Germany they came, bringing with them a flood of modern European ideas. The romantic drama of the fiery young Duque de Rivas had touched a sympathetic chord in the Spanish temperament and the poetry of Mariano José deLarra had fired the emotions. The philosophy of Kant and Hegel, then at the peak of popularity in Europe, took root, as did the theories of another German philosopher, Karl Christian Friedrich Krause (1781–1832). A philosopher of little note in Germany, and almost unknown in France, Krause developed a system of philosophy based on a reconciliation between faith and reason, between Christianity and the Hegelian system, which became in Spain, as Unamuno himself described it, "the persistence of Catholic mysticism in the bosom of Protestant realism." [1] Sanz del Río, the Spanish educator, introduced the so-called *Krausismo* to the University of Madrid upon his return from Heidelberg in 1845 and for half a century it created rabid adherents and as rabid opponents in Spain. Not until the end of the 19th century did this philosophy subside, when, as Dr. Benítez expresses it, *"iba de capa caída"* (it was on the wane).

Spanish culture is deeply rooted in a tradition which has constantly resisted foreign influences. During the nineteenth century, this resistance was so strong that it split the country not only politically but culturally as well. Resisting all European "progressive" ideas as pernicious to the primitive, peasant soul of Spain, a group of writers prescribed a cure—return to the soil, to the mountain, and to the folkways of the peasants. Few matched such evocative descriptions of the majesty and grandeur of nature as the novelist, Pereda. The life of the sturdy mountaineer around Santander, and that of the fisher-folk of the northern coastal regions depicted by him, urged the preservation of the Catholic, traditional heart of Spain. In the opposite camp was Benito Pérez Galdós whose psychological novels and dramas hailed the scientific method of European progress. Unquestionably the greatest and most popular Spanish novelist of the nineteenth century, Galdós led the forces struggling to break down religious prejudice and clear the way for scientific and cultural advancement.

In the 1880's Alfonso XII, son of Isabel II, was nominal king, while Cánovas and Sagasta vied for power behind the scenes. Into this ferment of philosophical contention and political rivalries, Miguel came, a boy of sixteen, fresh from the sweet-smelling beeches of his beloved Vizcayan forest, with the dust of the mountain paths still upon him.

Madrid held little or none of the usual fascination of the big city for this country boy. His first impression was one of sadness and depression—a feeling which returned each time he had occasion, and

---

[1] Miguel Oromí, *El pensamiento filosófico de Miguel de Unamuno: filosofía existencial de la inmortalidad*, p. 49.

he was to have many, to go to the capital. That first time after a long
sleepless night, probably in a second-class coach, he arrived early one
September morning. As he walked up San Vicente Street it reminded
him of "a hall the morning after a public ball, when the windows are
open to air it out, and it is being swept." "In the early hours of the
morning," he wrote in 1902, "one only sees an occasional thin face,
the picture of misery, with tired eyes, and slaves of judicial fees. It
all looks like an enormous owl that is preparing to go to sleep; those
dawns are like evening sunsets." [2]

He took a room on the top floor of La Casa Astrarena, a large room-
ing house. ". . . I remember the sense of depression that filled me as
I looked down from one of those ridiculously small balconies, up near
the roof, that overlook Ortaleza Street and saw from up there human
ants crawling along Red de San Luis, Montera, and Ortaleza streets
. . . These emotions," wrote Don Miguel in 1902, "are renewed in me
whenever I enter Madrid." [3]

By 1902 the old Astrarena house between the entrances to Fuencarral
and Ortaleza streets had been torn down to be replaced by the "Babel-
like telephone building." Further down Montera Street near the Puerta
del Sol stood the Church of San Luis, on the same corner which is
today occupied by a modern shop with plateglass show windows.
Directly in front of the church, as though in defiance of what it stood
for, was the Ateneo.

Named for the original meaning of the word, "place of wisdom," the
Ateneo was neither the political forum of the ancients, nor the social
club of the British; it was neither a library, nor a school; ". . . it was,
however, a bit of all of these: an institution that combined all of these
aspects which constituted its singular characteristic, and in truth
rendered it the unique home of Spain's spiritual life." [4] To this day
the Ateneo on Calle del Prado maintains a well-catalogued library
with a large reading room, a spacious lounge, and a good-sized auditorium with a stage adequate for theatrical presentations and other
cultural events. It still performs something of its instructional function by offering language classes for its members. It can no longer be
said, however, that it is "a center or school of advanced studies," as it
was in the last years of the nineteenth century. Such teachers as

[2] Prologue by Manuel García Blanco to Unamuno, *Obras completas*, VI, 10.
[3] *Ibid.*, pp. 10–11.
[4] Victoriano García Martí, *El Ateneo de Madrid (1835–1935)*, p. 236.

Menéndez y Pelayo, Pardo Bazán, Bartolomé Cossío, and Ramón y Cajal lectured from "*la tribuna*, where various courses in higher education were given." [5]

The Spanish male is essentially a social being, a club man. He has always liked to foregather, mostly in an informal fashion, in some restaurant or café or, perhaps, a clubhouse, the latter being available only for the more affluent. The *tertulia* may be strictly organized or entirely informal, but strangers never crash its gatherings. The topics of the conversations are sometimes set—poetry, love, and bullfighting were the proscribed subjects of a famous civilian *tertulia* of the eighteenth century—business is often transacted over coffee cups or wine glasses, and it may be that the comfort and warmth of a café are preferable to a cold and cheerless home. Whatever the motive, a Spaniard is faithful to his *tertulia*. Though the Ateneo was a far cry from this, it has been compared to the old *tertulia* of the Fontana de Oro made famous by Pérez Galdós and other literary lights of the eighteenth and nineteenth centuries.

The history of the Ateneo of Madrid has run the gamut of fortune. It was born on November 26, 1835, with the romantic Duque de Rivas its first elected president. Its home was there on Montera Street from that date until 1884 when it moved into its present spacious quarters on the Calle del Prado. Describing the first quarters of the Ateneo, one of its biographers, García Martí, says that the narrow long balcony facing the church across the way was dubbed "*El Wagón*"; "*La Cometa*" was the term used for the gathering place of the young novices; the main parlor, "*La Cacharrería*" where a picture of George Washington looked down from one wall, was the room in which Sanz del Río and other respected members used to gather.

Founded by the romantics just after the death of Fernando VII, the Ateneo was rooted in the liberal tradition. Speaking before the Ateneo in its opening session for the year 1900–1901, Manuel Azaña, the secretary, expressed its function in the following words: "The tradition of the Ateneo may be summed up in the word tolerance . . . a haven for freedom of opinion . . . Its argument is progress, its armor is intellect, its title, personal validity, its aim, freedom." [6]

When the Ateneo moved into its new quarters in January of 1884, King Alfonso XII delivered the inaugural address. Indeed, his son Alfonso XIII, was an honorary member of the club, as have been most

[5] *Ibid.*, p. 193.
[6] Manuel Azaña, *Tres generaciones del Ateneo*, p. 7.

of Spain's great literary men during its lifetime, while such international figures as Sarah Bernhardt, Henri Bergson, and Albert Einstein have spoken from its podium.

The prevailing atmosphere of freely expressed opinions and the debates of the philosophical and political questions of the day naturally called forth strong censure from many quarters. Often referred to as the *blasfemadero de la Calle de Montera* (the seat of blasphemy on Montera Street) it was the center of Spain's ideological struggles. It was here that the pernicious doctrines of *Neokantismo* and *Krausismo* were preached as were the other prevailing "isms" of the 1880's when the boy Miguel first came to Madrid. According to Hernán Benítez, Cánovas del Castillo had made it "an asylum for all verbal rebellions."

Thus they faced each other, the Church of San Luis and the Ateneo, and between them Miguel was to be torn for the next four years in Madrid. There on Montera Street he would begin to wage the battle between religion and science, between the heart and the head, a struggle that was never to be resolved by him, for San Luis and the Ateneo continued to defy each other in him throughout his lifetime.

At first Miguel naturally continued the religious practices of his childhood and the church claimed his allegiance at least during that first year. He had not yet emerged from what Laín Entralgo calls the first stage in the development of his faith, the "sincere and devout faith of boyhood."[7] He frequented the Ateneo only for classes in German, and, perhaps, an occasional lecture by Don José Moreno Nieto, *el gran prestigio ateneístico*, or, perhaps, to hear the popular novelist Pérez Galdós, or maybe even Clarín (Leopoldo Alas) whom he grew to admire and to whom he later wrote extensively regarding his own personal problems.

Most of his time, however, he spent at the University and at the national library. It is a matter of record that on September 28, 1880, the day before his sixteenth birthday, Unamuno wrote in his own handwriting and signed the required request for his admission to the University in the school of philosophy and letters, giving his address as No. 2 Fuencarral Street. General literature, universal history, beginning Greek and metaphysics were his courses that session. Though languages and metaphysics claimed his attention, he was not overly impressed with his professors in these fields. He referred to Don Juan Manuel Ortí y Lara as "my professor, not my *maestro*, of metaphysics,"

[7] Pedro Laín Entralgo, *La generación del noventa y ocho*, p. 65.

and described him as "a poor spirit fossilated in the emptiest sort of
Thomist scholasticism." It was Ortí y Lara, he recalls, who called the
Ateneo the seat of blasphemy, whereupon "the famous Padre Sánchez,
an Andalusian cleric of much charm, who waged the battle against
the leftist paladins who dominated that old Ateneo," answered that
"no fewer blasphemies were uttered in the University, the difference
being that in the Ateneo *se le pasaba al socio el recibo, y en la universidad, la nómina* [the member was presented with a bill, and in
the University with a salary]." [8]

Most university examinations in Spain are oral, or much like the
graduate examinations in the United States, they may consist of a
written thesis or dissertation, as well as an oral examination of the
student by an examining "tribunal." The secretary of the group examining Unamuno after his first university session was Don Marcelino
Menéndez y Pelayo. The greatest historian of Spanish literature, a
veritable encyclopedia of culture, Don Marcelino was to be Miguel's
professor in his senior year, and in 1891 when Unamuno was seeking
the appointment to the chair of Greek at Salamanca, it was Don
Marcelino who gave him the assenting nod. However, Unamuno could
not have been too aware of the great Don Marcelino during those first
examinations, particularly in his roll of recorder. Miguel's first grades
were "good" in literature, "notable" in history, and "outstanding" in
both Greek and metaphysics.

As the University opened even more doors to Unamuno, he became
interested, and finally during his fourth year, almost completely absorbed in Hegel. Possibly those first lessons in German at the Ateneo,
of which he wrote so feelingly, opened this door. "I can still hear the
good man Schutz saying emphatically, *'ein reicher Ritter!'* And what
a thrill it was to attend those first German lessons that I imagined
were to be the magic key that would open up a new world for me!" [9]

Christmas of the year 1880 was a sad one for the boy—his first one
away from home. He would never forget, he wrote,

the tremendous impression of the first Christmas holidays that I spent there
in Madrid, in my sixteenth year. I was used to quiet family Christmases,
without any to-do, when that distant relative who lived alone in Bilbao
would come to spend those days with my family and bring us children a
present. Then I come to this Spanish court and see Christmas celebrated in
the streets, with noise and commotion and drinking, the people in long lines

[8] Prologue by García Blanco to Unamuno, *Obras completas,* VI.
[9] *Ibid.*

going in and out of the cafés, playing *panderos,* and even *almireces* in your ears. And then came a year when I went out too and sounded my *almirez* as though to drown out my adolescent homesickness with noise.[10]

The boy could not forget his beloved *bochito,* Bilbao, nor his mother, and least of all, Concha. "I came to dream, I cannot remember now what dreams, not of glory, no, but dreams of long hours of study in my own native hideaway, my Bilbao, safe in a home of my own with a wife of my own—she who was afterwards, and now after death—is still mine—a home within my maternal home. It was my dream then. My mother and my sweetheart encouraged me from afar, from Vizcaya, in my career."[11]

One can but imagine that first summer vacation at home. Back at the University in the fall of 1881 he continued to study Greek, history and metaphysics, adding a new subject, Latin and Greek literature, and ending his second year that June with the grade of "outstanding" in all four subjects. Before leaving the University he had studied Hebrew, Arabic, and Sanscrit, as well as Spanish history and literature, philosophy, aesthetics, and, in his senior year, critical history of Spanish literature, this last taught by Menéndez y Pelayo. After the first year his grades were all *sobresaliente*—outstanding.

A scholastic transcript does not tell the whole story of a college career. Miguel was going through a great many changes during that period. He changed his address at least twice, once from the Casa Astrarena on Fuencarral, to No. 8 Plaza de Bilbao, and thence in September of 1883 to No. 3 Mesonero Romanos. The usual request for admission to attend his chosen classes this last session was signed not by himself but by one Felipe Zuazagoitia, whose address was Calle del Carmen No. 28.[12] But the more significant change was in his interests and habits, particularly his religious practices. Of his four-year period in Madrid he later wrote: "I spent it refreshing myself in philosophical books of chivalry, by the knights errant of Krausism, and all of their squires."[13] "During his fourth year in Madrid," writes Benítez, "he became Kantized and Hegelized, spending most of his time in swallowing down Krausism, the only thing doled out to the students as philosophy in the like-named school in the *Blasfemadero*

[10] *Ibid.*
[11] *Ibid.*
[12] *Ibid.*
[13] Hernán Benítez, "La crisis religiosa de Unamuno," in *Revista de la universidad de Buenos Aires,* Vol. III, No. 9 (January–March 1949), p. 14.

on Montera Street." [14] So Hegelized was Miguel that he translated, among other German works, the *Logic* by that author.

However, it should not be assumed that Miguel was a student who simply echoed the philosophies of others. On the contrary, he demonstrated a characteristic independence of mind, as one of his professors testifies. Addressing an Ateneo audience some years after Miguel had completed his studies there, Professor Morayta praised him in the following terms: "And guided by his lucky star, he struck out along unchartered paths, anticipating by several decades the existentialism of Heidegger and Jaspers." [15] Morayta was definitely referring to his student days. Had Miguel, perchance, come across something by Kierkegaard and so been introduced to his ideas before 1900, when he wrote that he was discovering the Dane's philosophy? This is possible but extremely doubtful. Morayta testifies to his independence of thought, and it would seem more probable that any similarity in Miguel's and Kierkegaard's ideas at that time was a mere coincidence. Did Heidegger and Jaspers later read Unamuno and so, perhaps, could he not have been the father of modern existentialism? Although this is an unsubstantiated conjecture, it is not altogether illogical. The irrefutable fact stands, however, that Unamuno was an independent existentialist thinker who discovered in Kierkegaard a kindred soul.

After his first year in Madrid, absorbed in a world of books, and in the philosophy "doled out" by the Ateneo, the young student gradually began to abandon the religious rites which had so marked his early childhood. It was a deliberate turning away from the church rather than negligence. For the first time reason was taking priority over emotion.

Miguel's days were not entirely filled with study for he was too ardent an existentialist ever to have become a bookworm. He often spent his Sundays at a dance hall frequented by soldiers and servant girls. This "underworld" café called La Fuente de la Teja, answered a need in the boy, formerly met by his mountain climbing and retreats to La Buya—a need to penetrate beneath the intellect and brain of Spain to her heart and soul. As Gómez de la Serna writes, it was there that he breathed in the aroma of the common people (*"respirando el aroma de lo vernáculo"*).[16] Perhaps, here at La Fuente de la Teja he

14 *Ibid.*, p. 47.
15 Hernán Benítez (ed.), "Cartas inéditas de Miguel de Unamuno y Pedro Jiménez Ilundain," in *Revista de la universidad de Buenos Aires,* Vol. III, No. 9 (January–March 1949), p. 53.
16 Unamuno, *Obras selectas,* p. 1052.

spent those countless hours playing chess to which he refers: "I, during my youth," he says, "had succumbed to the seduction of the tame
and inoffensive mania for chess-playing . . . during my fleeting years
in Madrid, some Sundays I would spend at least ten hours playing
chess. This game . . . came to be a vice for me . . . But as I am, thank
God, a strong-willed man, I succeeded in overcoming it." [17] Before he
finally did conquer this habit, Unamuno adds, he indulged in the game
for two or three hours every afternoon, playing with a little old man
whose identity he never knew. Perhaps Miguel was trying in this way
to quiet the voice of conscience, the voice of the Church.

Attempting to explain Miguel's repeated ruptures with the Catholic
Church, Benítez concludes that in his formative years the boy was
not well-grounded in the Catholic doctrine as based on Saint Thomas,
for good *Tomistas* were scarce. Instead, he took to reading Protestant
writers—Harnack, Schleiermacher, Renan, and Sabatier—more from
curiosity than from "fickleness," and "unfortunately the splashing
spattered all of his works with pellets of Protestant, Jansenist and
Modernist heterodoxy. Not a single one of them escaped the tragic
tainting." [18] Protestantism appealed to his head and Catholicism to his
heart. So identified is Spain with Catholicism that Benítez writes:
". . . Unamuno was a Catholic because he was a Spaniard and anti-
Spanish because he was anti-Catholic. This is the clearest statement
of his inner religious drama." [19]

The climax of his first spiritual crisis occurred in Bilbao, either during or soon after his university career when he passed through the
second stage in the development of his faith, *i.e.*, "in adolescence, crisis
profoundly lived." [20] Such a crisis comes to Pachico Zabalbide in *Paz
en la guerra*. In the novel the boy returns to Bilbao where home ties
and childhood influences are strong and when his uncle pleads with
him in the name of his dead mother to confess and be forgiven, Pachico
agrees. However, he does not give in without spending sleepless nights
during which "he was tormented by the awful mystery of time . . . To
have to pass from yesterday to tomorrow without being able to live
in a whole series of time." The voice of conscience so long muffled
during those days in Madrid, now spoke out clearly, suggesting new
forms of torture. There in the

[17] Unamuno, *Contra esto y aquello*, p. 123.
[18] Benítez, "La crisis religiosa de Unamuno," p. 55.
[19] *Ibid.*, p. 44.
[20] Laín Entralgo, *La generación del noventa y ocho*, p. 65.

dark solitude of night the emotion of death, an actual emotion that made him tremble at the thought of falling asleep, overcome by the realization that some day he would fall asleep, never to awaken. It was a mad fear of *la nada* [nothingness], a fear of finding himself alone in empty time, a mad fear that made him dream with palpitating heart, that, smothered, he was falling, falling in an eternal vacuum, a terrifying fall. Hell terrified him less than *la nada*.[21]

Such torments were unendurable and, at last, he followed his uncle's advice and confessed. The result, however, was far from satisfactory. He reveals his disillusionment in unmistakable terms. The talk with his uncle preceded a sleepless night and the next morning he consulted the priest:

He confined himself to expose to the confessor only the bald facts, without a single detail: that he had certain doubts. He didn't say what doubts; the priest advised him to exercise prudence, talking against reading in general, and recommending relaxation and country life and the Confessions of St. Augustine. "But not the Soliloquies! That is too strong yet." And as Pachico left the confessional, disillusioned with his attempt, he thought to himself, "The poor man must think I haven't read the Soliloquies, or that I am a mere infant." The crisis passed and Pachico once more took up the thread of his ideas, avoiding all conversation with his uncle.[22]

Miguel's young mind, which had been taught to reason at the University, was groping to solve the mystery of death. The mad fear of *la nada* was to haunt him during a large portion of his adult life. He was to plumb the depths of despair in that cry of agony, *El Cristo yacente de Santa Clara* and rise at last to the spiritual heights in that glorious pronouncement of his living faith, *El Cristo de Velázquez.*

[21] Unamuno, *Paz en la guerra*, pp. 61–62.
[22] *Ibid.*, pp. 60–61.

# Waiting on the Mountaintop
## and Facing Realities

CHAPTER 8

RECORD HAS IT THAT ON JUNE
20, 1884, Miguel read his *Tesis Doctoral*, *"Crítica del problema sobre
el origen y prehistoria de la raza vasca,"* consisting of over 13 thousand words. It is an evaluation of all the studies of the problem known
at the time, in which he explains the fallacies of the generally accepted
idea that the Basques are the descendants of the primitive Iberians,
and concludes *"que casi nada sabemos de la cultura prehistórica del
pueblo vasco"* (that we know almost nothing about the prehistoric
culture of the Basques).[1] Among the many authorities examined by
Unamuno, William von Humboldt was one whom he considered most
authentic. Indeed, Unamuno translated a part of Humboldt's *Reises-
kizzen aus Biscaya* into Spanish, and later indicated his desire to
render more of the German's studies on the Basques into his language,
a task subsequently carried out by his cousin. Telesforo Aranzadi. The
contribution of Aranzadi in the anthropological field was probably due
to Unamuno's influence. Miguel's examiners on this final occasion of
his university career, of whom professor Miguel Morayta was one,
passed him with the grade of *sobresaliente*. Free at last to pursue his
dream, Miguel returned to Bilbao, a thoughtful young man of twenty

[1] Unamuno, *Obras completas*, VI, 104.

with a brilliant university career behind him, and a turmoil of conflicting emotions within.

There followed a period of varied activities during which he mingled with the working people of Bilbao and rubbed elbows with the poorest of them in a "miserable little old café," or he wrote socialistic articles for a newspaper which he also helped edit. To meet more practical demands, he did some private tutoring.

There were afternoons with his companions in the candy shop of his uncle Félix Aranzadi: Claudio and Telesforo, Mario Sagárduy, Pedro Eguillor, and another friend, perhaps the same Felipe Zuazagoitia, who signed the university admission form for Miguel that last year in Madrid. Felipe's son, Don Joaquín Zuazagoitia, who was until recently the mayor of Bilbao, and who now lives in peaceful retirement in that city, says, "My father was one of Unamuno's old friends." Don Joaquín himself was one of the many young men who was to come under the influence of Don Miguel in later years and he still recalls many tales of this period in Unamuno's life. Yes, Felipe Zuazagoitia must have been one of the members of that *tertulia* in the shop of the *confitero* Aranzadi on the Calle de la Cruz. Don Joaquín tells that Don Félix, who was lame, was a man of many interests, one of them being an intense fascination for archeological excavations of such things as dolmens, or any other exhumed object from the past. He also enjoyed "baiting" the young men (especially Miguel) just to hear them argue. "Aranzadi was to Unamuno like the cat to the tiger," and Pedro always added his word of wisdom, for Don Joaquín says, "Pedro talked like Socrates."

Then Miguel resumed with vigor the walking habits of his boyhood. A favorite hike was some fifteen kilometers over Pagasarri Mountain to the old Jugo *caserío* (farmhouse) of Ceberio. Here in the *caserío* Arilzabengoa his grandfather, Juan Antonio Jugo, was born and reared. *"Borona amasada en casa, castaña asada a la brasa del hogar . . ."* (Home-made corn bread, chestnuts roasted on the hearth) as he would one day describe it, reminiscing in verses when, in exile in a foreign land, his heart was torn with longing. And he would recall the *"leche de vaca casera"* (milk from the family cow) he drank there as a boy. Then, strengthened by the memory, he would write:

> . . . *y coser la vida entera*
> *sin soñar.*
> *Y gracias a este misterio*
> *de mi abolengo Ceberio,*
> *soportar*
> *del mundo civil el yugo,*
> *pues me diste con mi Jugo*
> *jugo de siempre esperar.*[2]

> and sew up one's whole life
> without dreaming.
> And thanks to this mystery of my
> Ceberio lineage,
> to bear
> the yoke of worldly existence
> for you gave me with my Jugo
> the sap of eternal hope.

The little old house still belongs to Unamuno's children who cling to it probably more for sentimental reasons than any other. It stands high off the ground, leaving room for the *cuadra* where the animals sleep on the ground beneath the house. Running along one side of the house a narrow wooden balcony faces the surrounding mountains—Vargas, Goicogaue, and Mandoya. An inscription over the small doorway to the dark interior reads: "Año de 1783" (the number 3 is almost indiscernible in the worn old stone), below this is the number 133. Inside, the place smells of hay and cow dung; occasionally the braying of Perico, the donkey, can be heard from below. Outside, a little stream divides the property from the open field beyond which leads to the encircling hills. Other *caseríos* dot the little valley, thatched roofs topping their white exteriors. The Gorostiaga family are still its tenants and Martín, the head of the family, relates with pride that Don Miguel attended his father's wedding. In a neighboring *caserío* the Artinabalde's may also recall Unamuno. The young Miguel with two of his favorite walking companions, Pedro Eguillor and Enrique Areílza, would often cross Pagasarri Mountain and spend the day at Ceberio. The house may have been unoccupied then, for the three would batch it and enjoy a meal which Pedro, of recognized culinary abilities, would prepare.

However, the hike which Miguel took most frequently was over the mountain to Guernica. In his soul Miguel knew that he was really waiting, waiting for life, his own life within, to assert itself and show

[2] Unamuno, *Cancionero*, p. 202.

him his way, and waiting to marry Concha. When the restless mood
was strong upon him he would climb to the top of Arnótegui looking
for patience to endure and inspiration to go on. This period in his life
was a time of waiting on a mountaintop.

Missing the evenings he used to spend at the Fuente de la Teja in
Madrid, he began to frequent a café of the same ilk "where the idlers
of the town came to play cards for a cup of coffee." [3] Occasionally he
would join in a game but usually he merely listened to the talk of
these men "of flesh and bone" for he preferred their talk to any newspaper accounts of current wars or politics. The café offered relaxation
from the journalistic enterprise which took up much of his spare time
during the day.

Miguel and his friends, this group of young *impecunes* (penniless
ones) of the town, founded a weekly publication which they called
*La Lucha de Clases*. It was "the first socialistic organ in Bilbao aimed
at creating a revolutionary party." [4] The magazine was literally loaded
with anonymous articles contributed by Miguel. As a result, Unamuno's name carried with it for some time a socialistic stigma. In an
effort to erase this, Benítez writes that his socialism was neither materialistic nor atheistic. However, these were the days of his positivism
*enragé*. Referring to this period, his friend Enrique Areílza, wrote in
a letter dated June 13, 1902, "He has spent his life studying positive
science, which is cold and inexorable, and since it has brought him
neither glory nor tranquility of spirit, he hates it to death, he hates it
all the more because he carries it around within him, it is the grievous
thorn in his faith but from which he will not be able to free himself
because it constitutes the basis of his great knowledge and his worth." [5]
Miguel had come to the third stage in the development of his faith:
"a fleeting scientific optimism in his youth." [6]

His talent lay in writing; he sensed this strongly now and turned
not only to journalism, but to poetry and the novel as well. His
subjects? Bilbao and the Basque language *éuscaro* the subjects he
knew and felt most strongly. He began writing poems during that
last year, 1884, and they appeared from time to time in a Bilbao paper,

[3] Unamuno, *Paz en la guerra*, p. 271.
[4] Hernán Benítez, "La crisis religiosa de Unamuno," in *Revista de la universidad
de Buenos Aires*, Vol. III, No. 9 (January–March 1949), p. 51.
[5] Hernán Benítez (ed.), "Cartas inéditas de Miguel de Unamuno y Pedro
Jiménez Ilundain," in *Revista de la universidad de Buenos Aires*, Vol. III, No. 9
(January–March 1949), p. 139.
[6] Pedro Laín Entralgo, *La generación del noventa y ocho*, p. 65.

*El Noticiero Bilbaíno,* then in two Madrid magazines, *Revista contem-poránea,* and *Revista nueva.* These early efforts, according to Manuel García Blanco,[7] were related to the poet Antonio Trueba. Two of them, both bearing Basque titles; "Udabarria" (Springtime), and "Or kon-pon," were printed in *El Noticiero Bilbaíno* on April 12, 1885 along with a composition by Trueba. Miguel had read them first at a folk-lore festival of Vizcaya and Navarra. His earliest known poem titled "Arbol solitario" (referring to the historic oak of Guernica) appeared in the same paper in 1884.

So deep-rooted was the writer's interest in his native region of Spain that all of his literary efforts of this period, and as late as 1889, were dedicated to it. It is the topic of a series of lectures which he gave in El Sitio in Bilbao. Gradually other magazines began to carry his articles: *La Revista de Vizcaya, El Norte* and *Bilbao Ilustrado.* One of these early articles, "Del elemento alienígena en el idioma Vasco," was even republished in a German philological publication in 1893.

Contrary to what might be expected, Unamuno's purpose in all of his studies on this subject, was to counteract the "misunderstood chauvinistic spirit which has used the disinterested and austere labor of science to promote pretensions and aspirations toward regionalism."[8] As he stated elsewhere with reference to the same subject, "I love our common fatherland with the ideal love of a soul that is looking for harmony, with a love born from reading its history, and I love the *patria de campanario* with a real love searching for the marrow of her soul, with a love that was born with me."[9]

It was during this time that Miguel began making notes for what eventually evolved into his first and longest novel, *Paz en la guerra.* His town, his people, and himself he poured into this book but it was not completed until 1897. Here it was, in the character of Francisco Zabalbide or "Pachico" (nickname for Francisco), that he poured out his intimate doubts and longings. Like Pachico he would resume the habits of his childhood and wander alone across the fields humming a monotonous tune (he never sang when anyone was listening for he couldn't carry a tune), or he would climb to his favorite spot up on the mountain to carry on his interminable ideologue or monologue. And his thoughts would run somewhat as follows: "Always every-

<hr />

[7] Manuel García Blanco, "Don Miguel de Unamuno y sus poesías," in *Acta salmanticense* (Universidad de Salamanca), Vol. VIII (1954).

[8] Prologue by Manuel García Blanco to Unamuno, *Obras completas,* VI, 23.

[9] *Ibid.,* p. 32.

thing new and everything always old in the perpetual change, above
the eternal immortality of things." [10] Or pondering on contradictory
ideas he would reason: "Instead of reaching the conclusion that many
reach: 'you can't be certain of anything,' I concluded that everyone
is right and it is a great pity we cannot manage to understand each
other." [11]

The sweeping view from Arnótegui inspired some of his most profound philosophical thoughts. His physical weakness conquered at last,
he would make the climb almost daily. He was gradually overcoming
another weakness—that gripping terror at the thought of death and
the idea "'all or nothing,' that is the temptation of Lucifer." Seeing
the ceaseless beating of the sea upon the rocks below, he began to
parallel this conflict of nature with the struggle of peoples and races.
Here Unamuno evolved his life's basic philosophy which is the nucleus
of his magnum opus: *The Tragic Sense of Life in Men and in Peoples,*
*i.e.,* this constant struggle is the "clash that produces life." History and
nature were his teachers:

History reveals itself to him [to Pachico Zabalbide], the constant struggle
of peoples, and its purpose, perhaps unattainable, is the real unity of the
human race; a struggle without truce or rest. And then, probing beneath
the spectacle of war, his mind becomes absorbed with the infinite idea of
peace. Water and land, struggling beneath a benevolent sky, effect their
fecund mating, engenderer of life, which the former initiates and the latter
preserves.[12]

Lost in contemplation, removed from the world both physically and
spiritually, Miguel began to conceive of the eternity of the instant:
"He forgets the fateful fleeting hours, and in an instant that stops,
eternal, immobile, contemplating the vast panorama, he senses the
world's depths, its continuity, its unity, the surrender of all its many
parts, and he hears the silent soul of things as it swells with the
harmony and melody of space and time." [13] Viewing the ever-changing,
ever-changeless sky, Miguel would wonder at the "strange feeling of
immobility of the present fleeting instant." [14]

From such conceptions, he would pass to the Divine Being who
made it all. He would feel God controlling nature and *in* nature:

[10] Unamuno, *Paz en la guerra,* p. 272.
[11] Unamuno, *Obras selectas,* p. 851.
[12] Unamuno, *Paz en la guerra,* p. 326.
[13] *Ibid.,* pp. 326–327.
[14] *Ibid.,* p. 270.

And finally, the view of undulating vastness from the heights above seemed like the magnificent spectacle of the respiration of nature sleeping a deep and dreamless sleep. At other times when he felt the powerful rush of wind between sea and sky as it lifted the waves and swept the clouds, he would recall the Spirit of God moving over the waters, and he would imagine that from one moment to the next, the august shadow of the Omnipotent Ancient One might appear, even as He is pictured on Altars, outlined against the clouds, his long flowing vestments floating in the heavens, to raise up new worlds from the submissive waters.[15]

At such moments, Miguel felt himself "thirsting after Truth, not Reason." Feeling the peace from the mystic union with nature he concludes that "peace springs from the struggle to live, the supreme harmony of dissonances; Peace in war itself and beneath war, unending, sustaining it and crowning it. War is to peace what time is to eternity: its ephemeral form. And in peace, Death and Life seem one."[16]

But the elevated mood of the mountain peak must give way to everyday life. So Miguel would return to the world below, armed with renewed faith and energy to fight against "inextinguishable human ignorance, the mother of war." He descended from the mountain determined to "provoke discontent in others, the primary motive of all progress and all good."[17]

As Miguel's love for Concha grew his doubts about marriage vanished. However, before taking such a step he had to find a job. The provincial government of Vizcaya (the Diputación) added a new course in the Basque language to the curriculum of the Instituto Viscaíno and Miguel applied for the position. He was one of five applicants, another of whom was Don Sabino de Arana y Goiri, the man who was to organize the movement to nationalize the language. Of the five, only two were considered. The members of the Diputación were pretty evenly split between the two. The first one considered was "Don Miguel de Unamuno y Jugo," who "naturally occupies the first place" since his is the only university degree indicating a knowledge of literature and philology and especially since "he has received the grade of outstanding in his examinations in Greek (first and second year), Greek and Latin literature, Spanish, Hebrew, Arabic, critical history of Spanish literature and Sanscrit." And Unamuno's supporters added the following in his favor: ". . . the works which Sr. Unamuno

---

[15] *Ibid.*, p. 272.
[16] *Ibid.*, p. 328.
[17] *Ibid.*, p. 329.

has published in the *Revista de Vizcaya* about the Latin element in
the Basque language; the thesis he read for his *doctorado* in which
he made a detailed study of Basque thus having in his very hands a
Basque-Spanish dictionary, both of the spoken language and of the
classic and literary language . . ." as well as ". . . different compositions
of less importance, in prose as well as in verse, written in Basque, and
his participation in the public classes organized by the Basque-Navarese
folklore [society] in this town." [18]

But thanks to Miguel's "lucky star" as Professor Morayta has called
it, the final vote was in favor of the other applicant, Don Resurrección
María de Ascue, who was considered to have "greater conditions of
fitness, not only because of his priestly character which is so appropriate for a teaching career, but because of the competence and satisfaction which he has shown in his knowledge of the Basque language,
as demonstrated by the works he has presented." [19]

The day on which this decision was announced, June 11, 1888,
Miguel was in Madrid taking the competitive examinations for the
position of teacher of logic, psychology and ethics in the same institute
in Bilbao. Here again he was doomed to failure. One can only imagine
the immediate effect of two failures at that time. Writing seventeen
years later about this last failure, and a subsequent one in metaphysics,
Unamuno blamed them largely on his independent spirit. If he felt
any bitterness in 1888, it had all disappeared in 1905 when he wrote:
"But considering my standard at that time and in those subjects, and
considering above all the independence of judgment which was already
my spiritual dowry, I failed, and I was bound to fail . . ." [20]

Far from being discouraged, Miguel decided to seek a university
appointment. For such a position he had to stand a competitive examination. The first time, he appeared as a candidate in the field of
psychology. It was with no lack of self-confidence that he faced
his examiners, but they did not pass him. In fact, Unamuno made
four unsuccessful attempts to secure appointments, as professor of
psychology, logic, ethics, and metaphysics. The explanation lay neither
in lack of knowledge nor in lack of presence of mind. Miguel never
missed a question; he was never at a loss for words. On the contrary,
he was so full of them that he went to the opposite extreme and poured

[18] The secretary's records of the Diputación de Vizcaya, as stated by Don
Manuel García Blanco, in the Prologue to Unamuno, *Obras completas*, VI, 25–26.
[19] *Ibid.*, p. 26.
[20] *Ibid.*, p. 27.

forth a veritable flood of eloquence. He even questioned and argued with his dignified examiners who were the recognized academic authorities of Spain. At first they were pleased, then annoyed and, finally, disgusted with him. These repeated failures of his were common knowledge among his friends. One of them wrote to another that each time Miguel appeared before the

august tribunal, he would calmly draw out the card and start talking: "about this, so-and-so says . . . and so-and-so adds . . ." and he would talk on and on, to the astonishment of those gray-haired professors, before an audience of such learned and distinguished erudition. When his success was beyond doubt, when all he needed to win the appointment was to stop talking, and when the topic was exhausted, he would add with aplomb, "and I say . . ."

Then the friend continued, "The learned professors would admit confidentially to each other, 'He knows more than we do! but how can we entrust young people to this wild man?'" [21]

Not until 1891, when he stood a fifth examination, did he succeed in receiving a university appointment. Two of the members of the board were Don Juan Valera and Don Marcelino Menéndez y Pelayo. The former was the venerable Spanish critic and novelist, and one-time ambassador to Washington; Don Marcelino by that time was the president of the Royal Spanish Academy. In this way Unamuno was appointed to the chair of Greek in the University of Salamanca.

Coincident with the examination for the position in Salamanca, another young Spaniard was being examined for a vacancy at the University of Granada. The two candidates would appear day after day to be questioned in turn, each listening to the other's examination. What was more natural than that they should lunch together afterwards? As they both had a sweet tooth, they would meet again in the afternoon for an ice cream, or sometimes at a certain *horchatería* (restaurant that serves *horchata*, a cold drink) on San Jerónimo Street, and from there go for a stroll in the Retiro Park. During the month of June and on into July Unamuno and Angel Ganivet met in this fashion. Just a year younger than Miguel, Angel was shy and quiet. When he did talk it was generally of the gypsies in his native Granada. Miguel was the talker, however, as usual, and Angel recalled later that once "on the marble-top table of the café you drew me a frog with such finished artistry that I've never been able to forget it; I still

[21] Benítez, "La crisis religiosa de Unamuno," p. 19.

see it looking fixedly at me as though it wanted to eat me up with its bulging eyes." [22]

The examinations over, Miguel and Angel parted, never to meet again. Miguel won his appointment, but Angel lost his and eventually went into the consular service. Unamuno lost track of him entirely until five years later. Then one day a professor in the University of Salamanca, Don José María Segura, who was from Granada, showed him some letters written by Ganivet to a newspaper of that city, *El Defensor de Granada*. Struck with what he thought was a new note in Ganivet's character, Unamuno wrote to his friend of those examination days in Madrid. Ganivet answered and thus began a correspondence that lasted until shortly before Ganivet's mysterious and perhaps tragic death in 1898. As Don Miguel explained, from this correspondence came the idea of exchanging "open and public letters in *El Defensor de Granada*," for the purpose of exposing their ideas on the future of Spain; this correspondence was eventually published under the title, *El porvenir de España*. The concern for Spain, the diagnosis of her problems, with prescriptions for their solutions that comprise this little volume, was to be the theme of the writings of the so-called "generation of 1898." The brilliant incisive novels of Pío Baroja, the sensitive lyrical writings of Azorín, Antonio Machado's colorful feeling for the land and soul of Spain, and the lyrical evocations of Valle-Inclán, all revolve around this concern: Spain, why is she as she is, and what will be her future? Unamuno's cry, that cry he first felt standing there in the mirador of his home when the Carlist bomb destroyed his neighbor's house, "*me duele España*," is the same *amor amargo*, a bittersweet love that these writers all feel for their native land. Of these first two, Ganivet and Unamuno, it was Unamuno who was the *portavoz*, the loudspeaker for this generation, not Ganivet. As Unamuno himself explains, some held that Ganivet influenced him, but, if anything, it was Unamuno who influenced Ganivet. "He was my precursor in death, but I was the older and I had already published my five essays of *En torno al casticismo* when he published his *Idearium español*." [23]

Besides the fruitful friendship with Angel Ganivet, those years of repeated trial and failure, which must have produced some bitter discouragement however unexpressed, were crowded with other salient events in Miguel's life. Two of these occurred in 1889, one when he

[22] Unamuno y Angel Ganivet, *El porvenir de España*, p. 50.
[23] *Ibid.*, preliminary notes by Unamuno.

spoke before an audience in the Ateneo, the other when he visited Paris. Just what was the occasion of his address in the Ateneo that year is not clear. Unamuno later referred to the event and recalled that he had addressed an audience there in the following terms: ". . . My one desire is, not to give you ideas of my own or of others; ideas have little value—but to strike the untouched chords in the psalter of your hearts." [24]

A visit to Italy that year, his first trip outside of Spain, took him not only to Italy, but to France and Switzerland as well. Miguel was then a young man of twenty-five and it was naturally to the celebration of the completion of the Eiffel Tower with its accompanying gay crowd, that he referred in a later mention of the trip. Visitors from many countries paraded along the Champs Élysées and by the bookstalls that line the Seine. As a spectator of that celebration in the year 1889, Miguel, fortunately, could not know that in 1925, some thirty-six years later, he would spend agonizing months in Paris, that the timeless flow of those same waters of the river Seine which now mirrored the carefree throngs around him would then tempt him even as the waters of the river Dwina in Russia tempted Angel Ganivet. However, he did not feel himself one with the carefree throngs. Indeed, the frank and often expressed antagonism which he felt for the French may have begun during this visit. Certain it is that, like Ganivet, he felt keenly the isolation of his people—his *pueblo*—even as a sensitive individual is isolated by the incomprehension of a world of hustling material progress.

However, Miguel could not have felt this too keenly during that first visit abroad for he was going home, back to Vizcaya, to Bilbao, and finally to Guernica, "that most lovely town, sacred home of the Basques," for as he had written in "Agur, arbola bedeinkatube!" "I more than anyone, love you, because in you I have realized my happiest dreams, in you I have spent my happiest hours, and in you is the nest that holds my heart's desire." [25]

[24] Unamuno, *Obras selectas*, p. 209.
[25] Unamuno, *Obras completas*, VI, 209.

# Concepción Lizárraga y Ecénarro de Unamuno

CHAPTER 9

BORN IN GUERNICA, JULY 25, 1864, to a father whose family name was Lizárraga, and to a mother from the family of Ecénarro, Concepción was just two months older than Miguel. Although the possessive "de" was added when she married Unamuno in 1891 at the age of twenty-seven, Concha and Miguel belonged together from the beginning. As children they played together, as a girl she drew him irresistibly, during their long years of courtship she appeared to him in dreams, and as a wife she comforted and mothered him. Her spirit pervades all of his writings, though only two of them, both sonnets, name her directly. Like home-baked bread, Concha was the substance of his life without which he could never ascend the mountain peaks.

What kind of woman was she, this Concha whom Miguel had chosen? Could she understand his intimate struggle in which his exalted mysticism fought with his atheistic pessimism? The picture of Concha is vague as to her appearance, but it leaves no doubt as to her character.

Described as a "pleasant blond with blue eyes,"[1] and, ". . . more

[1] Federico de Onís, "Unamuno íntimo," in "Cursos y conferencias," *Revista del colegio libre de estudios superiores* (Buenos Aires), (July–September 1949), pp. 34–36.

gracious than good-looking . . ." [2] she is also referred to as ". . . better than she was smart . . . more thrifty than rich . . ." Concha was simple and unpretentious; to Miguel's "literary coquetry" she would merely reply that she didn't understand "those things, the jumbled things of a man." [3] A visitor to her Salamancan household described her as "not very tall, and plump, though not very; built on lines more or less, or perhaps slightly taller than her children Felisa, Rafael, Pablo . . ." The same writer quotes the following from a letter written by her son Rafael: "My mother's character, extremely simple, was nevertheless unusually good and comprehending. A person of no intellectual claims, she nonetheless had the intellectual capacity of understanding her husband completely. Words fail me to describe the effect that her death had on my father. I can say without hesitation that wherever the theme of love and extreme tenderness appears in his writings it is largely the inspiration of my blessed mother." [4]

Another description comes from the pen of a Salamancan writer, Don Fernando Iscar Peyrá:

She was a lady . . . who must have been pretty in her youth, with a full face and light complexion, she had a peaceful expression and a slight smile. She was always in love with her Miguel whom I think she considered one of the most mischievous of all of her children, remaining somewhat aloof from the transcendency of his work. Don Miguel, who, as you know, claimed never to have had carnal dealings with any other woman, loved her most tenderly. In the spectacular life of her husband, Doña Concha was always busy about the household tasks. [*Entre bastidores.*] [5]

Indeed Miguel loved her with the idealism of a lover, with the passion of a husband, and with the clean devotion of a son. He refers repeatedly to her in letters to intimate friends, and particularly to one, Arzadún (a Basque with whom he corresponded from 1890, a year before his marriage, until 1920). Miguel was a frequent dreamer; dreams impressed him deeply, especially the ones related to Concha or his family. An early letter to Arzadún tells that he dreamt of the kiss that his bride would give him on the forehead on their wedding

[2] Hernán Benítez (ed.), "Cartas inéditas de Miguel de Unamuno y Pedro Jiménez Ilundain," in *Revista de la universidad de Buenos Aires,* Vol. III, No. 9 (January–March 1949), p. 138.

[3] Hernán Benítez, "La crisis religiosa de Unamuno," in *Revista de la universidad de Buenos Aires,* Vol. III, No. 9 (January–March 1949), p. 18 n.

[4] Rafael Santos Torroella, "Los poetas en su dolor," in *La estafeta literaria* (Madrid), (November 30, 1945), p. 25.

[5] *Ibid.*

night. Another dream, probably sometime before 1891, he related in an unpublished correspondence between two imaginary people, Juana and Enrique. Among this correspondence is a paragraph dedicated to Concepción, his sweetheart: "One night there came to me one of those dark dreams, sad and somber, that I cannot rid myself of, I who by day am naturally happy. I dreamt that I was married, that I had a son, that that son died, and above his waxlike corpse I said to my wife: 'look at our love, it will soon rot; everything ends that way!'" [6]

Unamuno probably never told Concha of this dream. She was like the morning sunshine that dissipates the darkness, and in her presence he was ashamed of being depressed: "In my life of struggle and fighting," he wrote, "in the bedouin-like life of my spirit, I have spread a campaign tent in the midst of the desert. And there I take refuge and refresh myself. And there I am restored by the steady gaze of my wife who brings back the cool breezes of my childhood. Her heart's joy overflows in her eyes, and before her I am ashamed of being sad." [7] In another letter to Arzadún Miguel wrote of Concha and their future life together: "If God does not give them to me (children), it matters not; I shall have ideas as children! And after all, is she not a little boy?! A boy, a real little boy, even her face; that's why I like her! She has the freshness of a little boy. This in the soul and body of a woman, is all that I desire, and I shall have it." [8]

During this period Miguel was seeing Concha regularly, trudging the fifteen kilometers over the mountain roads to Guernica where the "blond with blue eyes" lived close to the primitive heart of Vizcaya in the shadow of the symbolic oak. Near her house, on some Guernica street corner, there was a graven stone on which St. John and a duck swam the ocean from Patmos to reach this hidden village.

> On a street corner of my Guernica
> there is a duck that serves as an eagle
> for St. John, a duck that
> swam here from Patmos, and
> in the stone its deed is immortalized.
> In those bygone youthful days
> of my one and only courtship,
> how earnestly I would contemplate
> the rock-hewn duck that was waiting
> with St. John, there on the

[6] Armando Zubizarreta, *La inserción de Unamuno en el cristianismo: 1897.*
[7] Bernardo Villarrazo, *Miguel de Unamuno: glosa de una vida,* p. 37.
[8] *Ibid.,* pp. 36–37.

> streetcorner, for the eagle that
> should come to take its place.
> But in time I have penetrated its
> profound mystery; as good a duck-like
> eagle as an eagle-like duck.[9]

It must have been a quiet life she led there in her uncle's home. She lived there from the time she was twelve years old until fifteen years later when one cold day in January, the thirty-first it was, in 1891, Miguel walked that mountain path alone for the last time. Fifteen years of living, with some schooling—no more than the usual amount—learning to sew and to cook as all Spanish women do, going to mass every morning and waiting for her Miguel. It was then that her real life began, in the home on the Calle de la Cruz, for it was there, to that room with the mirador, that Miguel first took her to share the bed in which he had slept as a boy, the bed in which she would bear his first child, the bed to which he returned throughout the years to dream again of bygone joys and tears.[10]

It is the mirador on the second floor to the right, [writes Unamuno to Pedro Eguillor] and it opens off of a room to the rear of which there is a bedroom where my soul took shape, where I planned my fights, where I began to give private lessons, where I married my Concha. From there I used to hear in the distance from the other part of the house, echoes of the rosaries that she would tell with my mother and my sister. There in that room with the mirador, my oldest son Fernando, was born: there, years later, on the fiesta day of Our Lady of Begoña—she was watching the people come from Calzados Street—my mother died. Coming to know my one and lasting love, the birth of my eldest son, the death of my mother.[11]

Passing the first impassioned period of romantic love—and impassioned it must have been for this man of flesh and bone, so intense, so sincere that he even thought with his whole body and soul—his love grew gradually into a relationship "in which if the scorching sun does not shine, neither is it ever night." Sexual love he held as the basis of all love. The process of its spiritual flowering through the travail of childbirth to compassion, from concentration on self to imagination for others, and finally to the Creator himself, can be read in the *Tragic Sense of Life in Men and in Peoples,* and it is also clearly

[9] Unamuno, *Cancionero,* p. 201.
[10] Unamuno, "Mi vieja cama," in *Rosario de sonetos líricos.*
[11] Mario Puccini, "Unamuno y D. Pedro Eguillor," in *La Gaceta Regional* (Salamanca), December 31, 1937.

manifest in his own love story. After thirteen years of married life Unamuno wrote in 1904 about Concha: "And then there is my wife, who never causes me a moment's worry, who stays perennially young, who brightens my heart with her constant happiness, and who is my great support and the perfect dawn of my life. Yes, a beautiful dawn; the sun that parches and burns does not shine, but it is never night. Ah, blessed day of my marriage." [12]

Concha had one trait that stood them in good stead. ". . . she knew how to squeeze the last *céntimo* out of a *peseta.*" And this was exactly what had to be done, for children came in quick succession. Seven children were born during the first eleven years of their married life, and two more followed soon after. By 1902 the strain of making ends meet on their scanty salary was revealed in a letter in which Unamuno wrote of having to pay out several thousand *duros* to meet someone else's obligations, adding, "That squeeze of a thousand *duros* has hurt and set me back at least a couple of years. The blow fell just when I was beginning to balance my family budget and straighten out my affairs (having settled some little debts) and just at the birth of my seventh child, a daughter . . . this obliges me to work harder and push the publication of my works . . . and the sad part is that it is to pay for someone else's mistakes and excesses." [13]

Frequent visits of Unamuno's adored sister, Susana, must have added to the financial strain. Although Susana had become a nun, she kept in close touch with Miguel whose spiritual stress must have caused her no little concern. She was his *ángel custodio* (guardian angel) and her letters had a profound influence on this constant vacillation between faith and doubt. Of Susana, Benítez writes, ". . . he would receive a letter from Susana, his dear little sister-nun, who was his weakness, and his frightened heart would stir within him and assert itself against his head, and then goodbye to Lutheran theology. Back he'd go to confession and to communion, to the unutterable joy of his wife and children!" [14]

In 1908 Miguel's older sister, María, moved into his Salamancan household as a permanent addition. She lived there until her death in 1932. Besides being another mouth to feed, María had an unfortunate personality which was a strain on them all. The children clashed with

---

[12] Benítez (ed.), "Cartas inéditas de Miguel de Unamuno y Pedro Jiménez Ilundain," Vol. III, No. 9 (January-March 1949), p. 159.

[13] *Ibid.*, p. 129.

[14] Benítez, "La crisis religiosa de Unamuno," p. 84.

her, and her long standing relations with Miguel came to such a point that all direct communication between them was impossible; any communicating was always done through a third party, and that third party was Concha, Concha the *buena* who got along with everybody.

None but an excellent manager could keep order in such a household and Concha did just that. Unamuno was essentially an orderly man and she ran the house smoothly so that he might maintain the strict routine of his own making—a routine necessary to meet the ever-increasing demands on his time. His students began to turn his home into a classroom, meeting there often for extra lessons in the evenings. They were always welcomed, as were the growing number of visitors who sought him out. Concha's presence was felt if not seen, for she was quiet and unobtrusive, preferring to remain in the background.

The hardest period of all for Concha must have been the six years of Don Miguel's exile when he was first on the island of Fuerteventura in the Canary Islands, then in Paris, and finally in the French border town of Hendaye. Both financially and spiritually she must have had a hard struggle, but she never complained nor did she criticize her husband for his determination to see his voluntary exile through to the bitter end. From Fuerteventura Unamuno wrote: "During all of my political struggle of these last years, my greatest support has been the spiritual integrity of my life companion . . . who has been and is a bulwark and my deepest consolation." [15]

Miguel was always Concha's first and foremost concern; she watched over him as a mother over a child, humoring his whims, cooking his favorite dishes and comforting him in his times of distress. His health had always been one of her husband's preoccupations, and as he grew older it became almost an obsession. Recalls Felisa,

He would get an idea about himself, an ailment of some sort—and he'd be afraid to eat. My mother would say: "Heavens, man, why don't you eat? I'm going to make you an omelet with just one egg." Then she would go into the kitchen and put two eggs in the omelet, saying "He'll never know the difference." When she put the omelet in front of my father he would say: "Bring me a knife." "What do you want with a knife, there's only one egg in there?" "Bring me a knife," he'd repeat. Then he'd cut the omelet in two.

Another time when the family went to be with him in Hendaye they found him quite depressed about his condition. He had gotten the idea that he had cancer of the throat and he wasn't eating a thing. Dr.

---

[15] Luis S. Granjel, *Retrato de Unamuno*, pp. 126–127.

Cañizo, one of Unamuno's best friends on the university faculty, had accompanied the family on this trip.

"I'm going to take you to Bayonne right now and let a good doctor there look you over," he said when he saw my father. We all went along [recalls Felisa]. The doctor there asked Father if he didn't have some spots on his back. "Yes," he answered. "Well, it's from rheumatism," said the doctor. My father had suffered from rheumatic pains previously and thus he was convinced that there was nothing wrong with his throat. When he came out of the office laughing my mother said, "Look at his face, there's nothing the matter with him!" So he got over his scare and began to eat and was quite well again.

Concha visited him when he was in Paris using some lottery ticket money to do so, and during the five years he lived in Hendaye she went to him every summer and took the children, living usually in cramped quarters, for it was enough just to be with him. After one such visit when Unamuno was feeling her absence most acutely, he wrote: "She mended my socks, but they are all holey again, even as the socks of the sorrowful Don Quixote."

The course of Unamuno's religious faith was tortuous and complicated; not so, Concha's. Her faith was simple, unquestioning and true, a bulwark indeed for her tortured Miguel. However heavy her home duties might be, Concha went "every morning at seven or eight o'clock to mass at La Purísima." This is the testimony of Doña Pilar. Is it any wonder that Miguel found in Concha a refuge when politics, friends, reason, and even God seemed to fail him? The following scene from his drama *Soledad* is completely revealing:

Agustín: —do you love me?
Soledad: Do I *love* you—!
Agustín: Say it, say it again that way, with all of your flesh and blood— say it. Do you love me?
Soledad: Agustín, my son!
Agustín: And what do you love me for, my wife?
Soledad: To love you—to dream you—Agustín.
Agustín: And why do you love me, Soledad, why do you love me?
Soledad: Why?
Agustín: Yes, why? Do you know why you love me? You don't answer? Do you know why you love me? Well, I know.
Soledad: Tell me, and then I will know too; I think I love you because I do—Why?
Agustín: Because I have only you—because all others have forsaken me—everyone—everyone—everyone. The hand of God has forsaken me—

Soledad: God's hand, Agustín?

Agustín: No, not God's hand, no! God's hand is your hand, my wife.
God gave it to me and He alone will take it from me—Your
hand, Sol, your hand—(kissing it), my anchor. A mother's
hand—

Soledad: It was—

Agustín: It is, Sol, it is. Every woman's hand is a mother's hand. And
you are my mother, my wife—[16]

Great minds have need of simple souls. Not only did her husband
turn to her, but so did another of Spain's great, the eminent novelist
Countess Pardo Bazán. This extraordinary woman from Galicia had
dared to write of life in the raw as she saw it in the provincial ancestral
homes of northwestern Spain. In bold, strong words she described the
degradation of Spain's fast-disappearing hidalgos in scenes of such
natural realism that they were branded as naturalistic. In *La cuestión
palpitante* Pardo Bazán had indeed pointed out the value of the scientific method used by the Goncourt brothers and Zola in France; hence
she became known as the leader of Spanish naturalism, if such a school
ever existed. A member of the Ateneo in Madrid where she was a
frequent lecturer, she was ever a controversial figure, even a scandal
in the eyes of Spanish Catholicism. Pardo Bazán found in Concha a
true friend. The countess was "*Muy amiga de doña Concha*," and she
came often to visit at the house on Bordadores Street. What common
ground could these two possibly have found for their friendship? The
novelist gave Concha a present that suggests the answer. It was a cook
book. "She gave her a cook book," said Doña Pilar, "for Doña Concha
was a very good cook. Besides Miguel's favorite *lentejas* she liked to
make *arrope* [a dessert of fruit and honey]." Like Concha, Pardo Bazán
was decidedly on the plump side. She knew and liked good food, and
she always found it at Concha's table. She often said that Concha "was
one of the most charming women she had ever known."

If one word could describe Concepción Lizárraga y Ecénarro de
Unamuno, that word would be *buena,* for it was repeated over and
over by Doña Pilar and her family in talking about "Doña Concha,"
as everyone in Salamanca familiarly called her.

The shadow of every great man is cast in a woman's mold and that
of Miguel de Unamuno was Concepción Lizárraga, the blonde from
Guernica. Her husband was the first to proclaim it. "I have put my
Concha," he wrote in later life, "the mother of my children who is the

[16] Unamuno, *Teatro,* pp. 142–143.

symbol of my Spain, of my dreams and of my future, for in these children I shall become eternal, I have also made it a point to put her in one of my recent sonnets and her presence pervades them all."[17]

After some thirty-three years of devotion, Don Miguel "nearing at last the peak of the career which my God has assigned to me" finds comfort in Concha, his *costumbre* (habit).

> *Ahora que voy tocando ya la cumbre*
> *de la carrera que mi Dios me puso*
> *—hila su última vuelta al fin el huso—*
> *Me dan tus ojos su más pura lumbre.*
>
> *Siento en la misión la pesadumbre,*
> *grave carga debe decir: "Acuso!"*
> *Y en esta lucha contra el mar intruso*
> *eres tú, Concha mía, mi costumbre.*
>
> *En la brega se pierde hojas y brotes*
> *y alguna rama de vigor se troncha,*
> *que no en vano dio en vástagos azotes.*
>
> *Pero al alma del alma ni una roncha*
> *tan sólo me rozó, que con tus dotes*
> *eres de ella la concha tú, mi Concha.*[18]

Now as I reach at last the topmost height
of the career my God to me allotted
—even the spindle weaves the final thread that's plotted—
Your eyes suffuse me in their purest light.

The trying task weighs heavily upon me;
the serious charge should speak out: "I accuse!"
and in the fight against the world's abuse
my habit, you, my Concha, still uphold me.

In struggle the leaves and tender shoots are lost
and even a hardy limb may fall along the way.
The youngest tendrils are the storm's sure cost.

But not one welt was hurt or torn away
for 'round my heart of hearts so sorely tossed
your blessings formed a shell, Concha, my stay.

---

[17] Unamuno, *Cómo se hace una novela*, p. 65.
[18] Benítez, "La crisis religiosa de Unamuno," p. 29. *Concha* in Spanish means *shell*.

# The Father

CHAPTER *10*

"WHAT LOVE WAS HIS FOR HIS family, what a wonderful father, what a good husband, and what a loving grandfather,"[1] writes one of Unamuno's friends. There is ample testimony of his love for his children in whom he "hoped to become eternal." He expressed it in his concern for their welfare both physical and spiritual. His tender thoughts of them he put into some of his most beautiful poems.

Concha bore him nine children, of whom six are living today. The first-born, Fernando, came probably in 1893 (in 1959 Felisa gave his age as sixty-six) in the Bilbao home on Calle de la Cruz. Concha went home, not to Guernica but to Bilbao, to be with Doña Salomé, and there in that room with the mirador, there in Miguel's *vieja cama*, she gave him what he most passionately craved: a child, a child to bear his name, and to give him, perchance, immortality.

Unamuno had taken his bride of eight months to Salamanca in September of 1891. That same summer he had finally passed the gruelling examinations in Madrid where for a month and a half he and Angel Ganivet had listened to each other's sessions with the examiners, sipped the cooling *horchata* in that restaurant on San Jerónimo Street, and strolled together the pleasant paths of the Retiro Park. After repeated failures he was at last launched on what would be his lifetime

[1] Manuel Altolaguirre, "Don Miguel de Unamuno," in *Revista hispánica moderna* (New York), (January 1940), p. 10.

career, for it is doubtful if Don Miguel ever seriously considered leaving Salamanca. True, when the chair of philology was added to the curriculum of the University of Madrid in 1899, Unamuno appeared as a candidate before the examining tribunal, but as he himself announced, much to the relief of the other candidates, "I have come to appear before the tribunal because I have a right to take part in these competitive examinations which I have applied for, but I do not plan to take them; I am returning to Salamanca this afternoon. I have come only because one should never fail to practice ones' rights." The foregoing is related by Spain's recognized philological authority, Don Ramón Menéndez Pidal, who was himself a candidate for the position. "I breathed a sigh of relief," adds Don Ramón, "when I heard that." The occasion was the first meeting between these two. Menéndez Pidal describes the incident published in *Cuadernos de la cátedra Miguel de Unamuno,* volume 2.

The meeting took place in the Universidad Central de Madrid on the Calle San Bernardo. Don Eduardo Saavedra was chairman of the examining board and all the candidates had gathered and were nervously waiting, that is, all except Unamuno, "the candidate most feared by them all." Rufino Lanchetas, one of the other candidates, told them not to worry for he knew that Unamuno planned to return to Salamanca that same afternoon, and only a few minutes remained before the time set for the examination. Just as Lanchetas finished talking, there appeared in the entrance of the waiting room the figure of Unamuno, ". . . who, scrutinizing the depths of the hall with his owl-like eyes, walking slowly, advanced absentmindedly toward us. I have never seen such an unwelcomed figure. He greets us as unknown rival candidates. Just to make conversation, Lanchetas says something to him about the rumor that he was quitting . . ." whereupon Unamuno explained his purpose in being there, and relieved them all.[2] Obviously he had no intention of leaving Salamanca then, nor probably at any other time during the remaining forty-five years of his life.

It was with the attitude of complete dedication to whatever Salamanca might hold for him that Unamuno arrived with Concha in September of 1891 to occupy the chair of Greek. Henceforth *Castilla enjuta* was to be his second home. The "rock of his intimate culture" was to be more deeply split and the split would hurt at first for Unamuno missed his *bochito.* The sweet streams and silvery beeches were

[2] Ramón Menéndez Pidal, "Recuerdos referentes a Unamuno," in *Cuadernos de la cátedra Miguel de Unamuno,* II, 5–12.

ever beckoning and throughout the years he would answer the call over and over again. Slowly and surely, however, the golden stones of Salamanca, the "pock-marked craters of the moon" that were Castile, would insinuate themselves into the very marrow of his bones. Once on the train as he was returning from Bilbao in 1910 he caught sight of Orduña, the mountain that stands between these two divergent landscapes of Spain, and wrote: "In Castile Vizcaya comforts me, and in Vizcaya I miss my Castile . . . from your fresh green arms, mother Vizcaya, I go to dry Castile . . ."[3] This same transition he expressed later as follows:

> salí de los sirimiris para subir a Castilla.
> Se me secaron los huesos, mas en sus tuétanos vibran
> las húmedas chireneadas de mi niñez bilbaína.[4]

> I left the sirimiris to go up to Castile.
> My bones dried up, but the damp chireneadas
> of my childhood in Bilbao still vibrate in their marrow.

Unamuno recalled that first momentous arrival in Salamanca when, armed with a letter of introduction from the father of a school friend in Bilbao to Don Pablo Beltrán de Heredia, he and Concha went directly to his home in Salamanca. They were guests in Don Pablo's household for several days so it was here that Don Miguel began to make his first lasting friendships. Slightly younger than the new professor, Don Pablo's son relates that his father helped them to find their first home—the old blue-tiled house whose glassed-in miradores (was it perhaps the mirador that drew them?) still overlook the Campo de San Francisco, and nearby the church that houses la Dolorosa whose heart is still pierced by the seven sharp swords.

It is doubtful whether Don Miguel visited this virgin often in those first years of married life, and if he did, it was no doubt through love of Concha, la buena.

The exact stage of Unamuno's faith at this period is a moot question among his critics for, as has been pointed out, there is a discrepancy between the religious experiences of Pachico of Paz en la guerra and statements that Unamuno made about himself in his personal correspondence and in Recuerdos de niñez y de mocedad. The difference in Pachico's age when certain events occurred in connection with the bombing of Bilbao, his return from the University, and the

[3] Unamuno, "Frente a orduña," in Rosario de sonetos líricos.
[4] Unamuno, Cancionero, p. 149.

date of his mother's death, and Unamuno's known age at these times have thrown confusion into the ranks of the commentators; it seems a matter of minor importance. It is clear, however, that during his student years in Madrid, either after or during the first year, he left off going to mass and soon after his return to Bilbao he underwent a change of some sort, due no doubt to the influence of his mother, which resulted in a resumption of religious practices. A statement Don Miguel made in 1895 in a letter to Leopoldo Alas (Clarín) seems to date this reconversion in 1886 when he was in his twenty-second year. He wrote: "I too have my mystic tendencies, for not in vain have I been attending mass once a day and taking communion every month with true fervor, and not as a matter of form until I was twenty-two years old, and I stopped doing it, I believe, because I took my religion so seriously." In the same letter referring to the plot of a story he planned, Unamuno wrote: "a boy who carries in his soul a profound religious education . . . He loses his faith from his very effort to rationalize it (so it happened to me)." Unamuno's eminent Spanish critic, Señor Antonio Sánchez Barbudo, who cites the foregoing statements from Don Miguel's correspondence, concludes that, "after having lost his faith in Madrid he recovered it at some time, probably upon his return to Bilbao, when he was twenty years old." [5] This conversion, however, is not altogether convincing, either in the character of Pachico, or in Unamuno's own life. Continuing the relation of his plot in Clarín's letter, Unamuno writes: "He is weary and feels that the world is destroying his soul. One day he goes into a church and the dark interior, the lights . . . take him back to the days of his innocence . . . and he finds new faith and he hears mass without being officially a believer." [6] The reader will recall that when Pachico talked to his uncle about his faith, he did so in the name of his dead mother, and it was on the anniversary of his mother's death that Pachico returned to the church and confessed. Although Doña Salomé did not die until 1908, Mr. Sánchez Barbudo is probably correct in assuming that it was due to her influence that Miguel did likewise. If his mother could have such influence over him in Bilbao, surely Concha could have been as strong, if not a stronger, reason for the earnest young husband to conform, at least outwardly, in his new surroundings.

The young couple lived in their first home overlooking the Campo

[5] Antonio Sánchez Barbudo, *Estudios sobre Unamuno y Machado*, p. 21.
[6] *Ibid.*, p. 23.

de San Francisco for only about two years after which they moved to a house on the Plaza de Gabriel y Galán. It was here in this house not far from the *clara carretera de Zamora*, the highway along which Don Miguel would take his daily walks into the country, that their first children were born. Here, facing the old Salamanca bullring which has since been torn down, stands the house which, though it has been remodeled and enlarged, still holds many memories of those early years in Salamanca. Unamuno, the professor, from here began first to fire the minds of his students; Unamuno, the reader, from here first heard the heartbeat of many lands; Unamuno, the writer, began to stir men's souls; and here Unamuno learned the joys and tears of fatherhood.

Five children were born while Concha and Miguel lived in this house; Fernando, Pablo, Raimundo, Salomé, and Felisa. After the birth of the first baby in Bilbao, Doña Salomé came to be with Concha in Salamanca for the birth of the other children. Just before their fourth child was born Mario Sagárduy wrote from Bilbao: "I hear that Doña Salomé is going there sometime in May to take care of Concha and to receive your fourth child (quite a respectable number)." [7] That child was Doña Salomé's own namesake, the daughter so dear to the father heart of Unamuno, the delicate little cripple, who would one day give him his first grandchild, Miguelito. Felisa was the last of the children to be born here. The others, José (Pepe), María, Rafael (baptized Raimundo), and perhaps the youngest, Ramón, were born in the rectoral house on Libreros Street, No. 11. However, if Felisa was right in giving Ramón's age as forty-three in 1959, this would mean that he was born in the house on Bordadores Street.

A man of compassion and love, Unamuno felt instinctively drawn to anything helpless or weak—a blind man or a child—and for his own children how much greater was his tender love and care! In summing up Unamuno's contribution to Spain, one writer says in essence, "He taught us how to be a good husband and father." The evidence of this is in his life and works: "In the background, the laughter of my children; by the cozy warmth of the *camilla*, [work table with place for charcoal brazier underneath] Herodotus offers me rich fruits . . . Before me in her chair she is sewing; gazing a moment into her eyes, I taste the secrets of history, and in the holy

[7] Letter from Mario Sagárduy dated May 31, 1897, in correspondence at Casa Museo Unamuno.

peace within my home, to the tranquil rhythm of quiet breathing, there works within me, like slowly plowing oxen, the sweet silent thought." [8]

Unamuno was a poet and as a poet he knew how to talk with children for he was ever a child himself. Though all of his children were a part of him to help gain for him some earthly immortality, each child was an individual whom he cherished and respected. Sixteen years after his death, María recalled vividly the searching gaze which he would sometimes fix upon one of them, usually when the family were gathered around the table. In a succession of probing questions Unamuno would seek to penetrate his innermost being until the child's one wish was to be released from the grip of his piercing eyes. Felisa tells of his unfailing sense of justice in settling their arguments. "My mother would administer a vigorous slap all around, but my father always said, 'I don't know how this started,' and so refused to punish us. But if he did know, then he punished fairly."

Rafael was the only child with blue eyes. His fair hair and chubby red cheeks gave him a particularly fresh appearance, so that his father fell into the habit of greeting him with, "*Ola, joven incauto y de rostro placentero.*" (Hi there, carefree young man with a pleasant face.) Sometimes his father would simply call out, "*Ola, joven incauto!*" And the child almost as soon as he could talk, would finish the phrase: ". . . *y de rostro placentero.*" A slight speech impediment must have made this most amusing for Unamuno would laugh with delight: "*Sí, sí, eso es!*" Then, growing serious, the father would gaze penetratingly into the child's blue eyes and say: "I wonder where he got those eyes." (*De dónde se habrá sacado esos ojos?*)

On another occasion, when the stirring rhythms of Carducci's poetry were ringing in his soul, Don Miguel, holding his son Pepe between his knees, began reciting the lines in an exaggerated declamatory fashion, whereupon the boy responded in like fashion: "*Sansón, Sansón mató a los filisteos!*" (Samson, Samson, he slew the Philistines!)

It was in the lonely night watches, over the sick bed, or perhaps awaiting the birth of a new child, that the father brooded most tenderly, and such moments brought again the presence of death to his troubled spirit:

> Waiting for sleep there in my bed, like in a tomb;
> in the cradle by my side lay the child, and from

[8] Unamuno, "Dulce silencioso pensamiento," in *Rosario de sonetos líricos.*

yonder in that other room, where the soft green
filtering lamplight outlines three kneeling figures,
comes the murmur of ave-María's.
My mother, my wife, my sister, as though from another
world, the other, the one we hope for. (En el lindero.)
Through the silent rooms where my children, their souls
lost from their limp bodies—lay in deep rest—the
murmurs came filtering through their peaceful breathing,
and without dreaming, I dreamt; am I living or dead?

This poem, "Incidentes Domésticos" from *Poesías 1907* hangs framed in Unamuno's bedroom there on the second floor of the Casa Museo Unamuno, and brings to mind those other lines that could well be the sequel:

I heard there in the darkness in the cradle
a sound that seemed a sigh:
the child was stirring,
he was looking for a new face of sleep.
I stretched out my right hand
that I might touch his body,
and thus assure myself the darkness was
keeping safe in its lap
my child entire,
his form, his weight.
And feeling on my hand
the warm breath from his lips,
almost dreaming, I thought:
no, I am not dead! [9]

Just like their father before them, Don Miguel's children were educated in the tradition of the Catholic Church. They never knew and perhaps never dreamed of their father's intimate struggle for his faith. One has but to visit the Casa Museo Unamuno in Salamanca to see the evidence of it. His library, study, and bedroom are kept as they were during his lifetime there. The bedroom entrance from his study faces the brass-trimmed double bed, the very bed he lay in on that night—so many nights—while the sick child Raimundo, the little hydrocephalus  lay there in the cradle beside him, and Concha, Doña Salomé and María prayed in the room beyond. On the wall by the bed hangs an image of the crucified Christ with the graven letters overhead: INRI. In the wall to the left of the entrance is a niche for holy water, and above this, lying on a cushion, and protected by a

[9] Unamuno, *Poems*, translated by Eleanor Turnbull, p. 141.

glass covering, is a tiny crown of thorns. Encircling the crown are the words: "*Corona hallada en el Jordán por Pascuala de Unamuno el día 14 de abril, de 1868.*" (Crown found by the Jordan by Pascuala de Unamuno on the 14th day of April, 1868.) In the center of the crown is a little scene of the adoration of the shepherds with the inscription: "*Gloria in Excelsis Di*" written above. Pascuala de Unamuno, the sister of Don Miguel's father, his own aunt, and the mother of Don Miguel's mother, his own grandmother! A crown of thorns was His crown, and it was also Don Miguel's.

Unamuno was the first to protect his family from many of his writings that were filled with vacillations and doubts, his struggle between doubt and faith.

His wife and children were so thoroughly Christian that they never read nor, as often happens, did they even know, what their father was turning over in his imagination day and night and scribbling in the piles of notebooks always ready on the table. And they didn't have to consult the *Index* (of books banned by the Catholic Church) to keep from reading his works. Don Miguel himself was the first to protect his children from the heresies in his books. He was the first to include his books in the *Index* before they were published, and so place them beyond the reach of those who were closest to him.[10]

Of the child Raimundo, the father wrote in a letter to Clarín in 1900: "Daily before my eyes I have one (son) of my flesh, and he is handicapped, a poor hydrocephallitic son . . . this one, the little sick one, the idiot, when I gaze on his painful deformity he seems to me more beautiful, better looking, than my other four. And mind you, these others are good looking, and agile, and bright, and happy."[11] Was it this child that inspired the poem, "Mi niño"? The father, watching over his sleeping child, is carried back to his own childhood, back to his infancy, until he feels himself to be again "unborn."

Other letters show the constant concern, the long suffering, the helplessness that he must have felt in watching his beloved child slowly fade away. Raimundo was born in the Casa Unamuno in 1896 and he lived to be six years old. Mario Sagárduy from Bilbao who had been a guest in the home and had seen this struggle, wrote often during the year 1896 inquiring about the baby's condition.

[10] Hernán Benítez, "La crisis religiosa de Unamuno," in *Revista de la universidad de Buenos Aires*, Vol. III, No. 9 (January–March 1949), p. 84.

[11] Hernán Benítez (ed.), "Cartas inéditas de Miguel de Unamuno y Pedro Jiménez Ilundain," in *Revista de la universidad de Buenos Aires*, Vol. II, No. 7 (July–September 1948), p. 51.

They must have known then that Raimundo would never be normal. A few months after his birth, the baby was stricken with meningitis, and by the end of that year he grew noticeably worse. Not until many years later did the family know that Unamuno had made two drawings of Raimundo which he always carried with him in his billfold. He wrote this to his dearly beloved daughter, Salomé, from Hendaye in 1927.[12] The tragedy of this child had a profound influence on Unamuno, a lasting influence, and it may well have been the immediate cause of Unamuno's spiritual experience referred to as his crisis of 1897.

That was the year that their first daughter, Salomé, was born, and Doña Salomé came to be with Concha. The tense spiritual suffering of the father at that time occupied the foreground of his thoughts, hence his fourth child may not have impressed him greatly. In her, however, he was to know much happiness, but again, a happiness tinged with grief. When Salomé was a little girl she was being fitted one day for a new dress when the dressmaker noticed an irregularity in the measurements of her back. In fact it was the dressmaker who first discovered the slight hump which from that time on grew slowly. By the time Salomé was grown she was obviously, though slightly, a hunchback. The curious visitor in Salamanca may hear vague references to a fall when Salomé was a baby. This may perhaps explain the special tenderness her father always showed her. She grew up to marry a young poet who was one of Don Miguel's special admirers, José María Quiroga Plá. It has been said that the young man married Salomé to be associated with Don Miguel, and he simply moved into the home where he continued to live until after his wife's death in 1933. Miguelito, their child, was born in October 1929. Don Miguel received the news of his birth in his exile home in Hendaye, whereupon he made the following entry for his *Cancionero*: "23–X–29. Received telegram that my daughter Salomé has given me my first grandchild, a boy. And there is no more poetry."[13] When Don Miguel walked into his home for the first time in six years he greeted Concha with the question, "Where is he?" "The baby wasn't well that day," remembers Felisa, "and we had taken him up to *la galería*. My father ran quickly up the steps; when he saw the child he gazed at him in silence, and he wept with emotion." From that moment on Miguelito was his pride and joy, the special comfort of his grandfather's old age, for after

---

[12] Armando Zubizarreta, *La inserción de Unamuno en el cristianismo: 1897.*
[13] Unamuno, *Cancionero*, p. 356.

Salomé's death in 1933 Felisa became his adopted mother, if not legally, certainly in spirit.

Salomé lived only four years after Miguel was born, but long enough to act as head of the household when everyone but Concha moved to Madrid in 1931. She was never well after the birth and it may be that the child cost her her life, though some have hinted at tuberculosis as the immediate cause of her death. Today Don Miguel shares a crypt with Salomé in the Salamancan graveyard, and he must have wished it so. Her poet husband felt a deep admiration for his father-in-law— an admiration which he showed by helping to collect and publish many of the scattered articles which Don Miguel was constantly sending to newspapers throughout the Iberian peninsula.

Felisa de Unamuno, Don Miguel's fifth child, leads a quiet busy life in her childhood home. A short, plump figure, with smiling clear brown eyes, dark wavy hair cut short and graying slightly at the temples, she keeps the Casa Museo Unamuno in order, receives visiting strangers who come merely to look, and answers questions of students seeking information for assigned reports. Quick to distinguish between idle curiosity and sincere interest, Felisa will take time to talk with anyone who has a definite purpose. The care of Don Miguel's unedited correspondence, ordered and neatly filed by her hand, is a task to which she has devoted long hours. She returns the true devotion of her father whose memory lives deep within her. Felisa, the child, was once waiting impatiently for some event, it could have been her birthday. The days of waiting dragged by slowly, and she voiced a wish to sleep away the days between. Her father's response was in the poem entitled, "La Niña Felisa":

> —Los días todos que hasta el quince faltan
> quiero pasar dormida,
> para que lleguen antes—
> dijo la niña Felisa;
> y yo que he sido niño:
> —no así lo quieras, no, pobre hija mía,
> pues horas llegarán, ten por seguro,
> en el rápido ocaso de la vida,
> en que esos días muertos añorando
> "¡Si volviera a ser niña!"
> de corazón suspires
> llena de compasión hacia ti misma.[14]

[14] Manuel García Blanco, "Don Miguel de Unamuno y sus poesías," in *Acta salmanticense* (Universidad de Salamanca), VIII (1954), 422–423.

"I'd like to sleep away the days
from now until the fifteenth
to make them pass more quickly,"
said the child Felisa;
and I who was once a child:
"No, don't wish that, poor child of mine,
the day will come, of this I'm sure,
at the swift setting of life's sun
when, longing for those dead days,
'Would I were a child again!'
you'll sigh with all your heart
and full of self-compassion."

"María is the one most like her father," says Federico Cuadrado, and certainly she bears a strong resemblance. She has the same deep-set black eyes, but his profound seriousness is lightened in her by quick flashes of humor. It was María who brought the manuscript of the *Cancionero* to the United States for Don Federico de Onís to edit. When María left Salamanca to come to America in 1946, ten years after her father's death, the home on Bordadores Street was finally broken up. The Unamunos had occupied that house for thirty-two years and many of the townspeople felt that the place should be kept as a monument. A certain R. Aguirre Ibáñez wrote as much in a local newspaper of April 4, 1946. He began his plea by writing, "The house is for rent and María is going to America." Since that year María has taught and studied in the United States, returning frequently to Salamanca where she visits her good friends Paquita Cuadrado and Doña Pilar at No. 4 Bordadores Street.

There was some disagreement about the naming of the eighth child whose birth came soon after the death of the little deformed Raimundo. By this time the household had grown to a total of nine: six children, their parents, and their grandmother, for the latter's presence was required by emergencies of birth, death, and illness. Guests and visitors of the distinguished rector and widely read author added to the hustle and bustle in the old stone house adjoining the University. Under such circumstances it is understandable that before the father realized it his new child had been baptized with the name which was decidedly not of his choosing. Such things as christenings and first communions Don Miguel left to the women of the household anyway; in fact he became more known for his absences from church than for his presence. Thus it happened that when the child was only a few days old Don Miguel heard someone refer to him as Raimundo. "No, no,

he is not to be called Raimundo," he said. A relative had proposed
the name of Rafael. "But he's already been baptized as Raimundo,"
said Doña Salomé. It was too late to change, but the boy was never
called Raimundo; he is Rafael. However, his father always evaded
the issue by using his own pet name for him: Chito. Raimundo by
baptism, Chito to his father, Rafael to his family and friends, he is
Salamanca's eye specialist and lives with his pretty young wife on the
Calle Generalísimo in that town to this day. Low of stature like his
sister Felisa, he still has the ruddy cheeks and speech impediment of
the *joven incauto* (the carefree boy), but thick-lensed glasses and the
slightly balding head proclaim that he is no longer *incauto*. The only
two children living in Salamanca, Rafael and Felisa visit their parents'
graves together every May 15, the anniversary of their mother's death.

Here in the cemetery in the crypt to the left of the entrance a new
stone was added on May 14, 1956. Their brother Pablo, at the age of
sixty-two, shot himself, leaving his wife and five children. On his stone
is inscribed: *"Hágase tu voluntad"* (Thy will be done). Before his own
death, Don Miguel's heart was saddened by Pablo's unhappy marriage.
In 1934, just before Concha's death, he married a girl twenty years
his junior. She was never able to assume the responsibility of a large
family and Pablo, the dentist, sought escape in many ways until finally
there seemed to him only one way out. As a boy and a young man
Pablo was good—so good that his friends dubbed him "San Pablo."
His end must have grieved his brothers and sisters.

The last child was Ramón, *el chico,* who was born in 1916, if Felisa
is correct in giving his age as forty-three in 1959. Ramón is the child
of his parents' old age and as such he must have been very close to
his father's heart for, according to the Mexican writer, Alfonso Reyes,
Unamuno made some drawings of this child. Ramón was caught in the
civil war fighting for the losing side. He escaped afterwards to France,
but not before a shot destroyed the sight of one eye. An unsuccessful
operation in Paris seemed to demoralize him and since then, although
he is back in Madrid, he sees little of his family and friends in
Salamanca.

Fortunately, Unamuno lived to know the comfort and companion-
ship of his first-born son, Fernando. After completing his studies to
become an architect Fernando married and established his permanent
home in nearby Palencia. His father was a frequent visitor there where
he used to love to go to write. A companion on many trips throughout
Spain and Portugal, as were the other boys, Fernando seemed to be

the one his father could most depend upon. When Don Miguel was officially pardoned by Primo de Rivera's government after being taken as a prisoner to the Canary Islands, it was Fernando who went to him there, and when Don Miguel made his triumphal entry back into Spain via Irún, Bilbao, Valladolid, and finally Salamanca, again it was Fernando who was with him all the way. Using his prerogative as the oldest son, Fernando is today concerned with the editing of Unamuno's works as well as the destiny of the old *caserío* of Ceberio near Bilbao. It is Fernando who visits his father's beloved *bochito* and maintains the ties with relatives there. In a letter dated May 29, 1959, Fernando writes to Antonio Lizárraga in Bilbao:

Dear Antonio,
    Martín Gorostiaga and the *peismoco* from Ceberio were here today. They were afraid that the *caserio* of Ceberio was sold to Angel Gorostiaga because he had told them so. I have assured them that that is not true, nor do I think it will be for the time being. Naturally I did not tell him the price that he had told you he would offer me. I also assured Martín that I would do nothing unless he knew it before I signed. I have decided to go to Bilbao this summer to get information on its defects and prices.
    For the moment keep on writing up the receipts in the names of the heirs of Ramón de Gorostiaga. I don't want to decide on selling or on renting without being sure of what is best for us. María is coming this summer. She will land in Algeciras on July 8 and will spend two months in Spain. I think she will go with me to Bilbao.
    I am going to San Sebastián with Mercedes on June 27 to attend the wedding of a niece, Ana María Adamaca.
    Many regards to everybody, and love from your cousin who embraces you.
                                                                 Fernando

In a strong masculine hand, the letter is written on paper with the letterhead in the upper left-hand corner, "Fernando de Unamuno, Arquitecto," and in the right-hand corner, "Teléfono: 1343, Palencia."

These are Unamuno's children, the "children of the flesh" who are perpetuating his name in their own ways. They were proud of that name, even as children, and he loved them for it. One day in the classroom he told the following family incident, a habit of his which doubtless delighted his students:

A foreigner came to the house to see Unamuno. One of the children was playing in the room with them when the following conversation took place:
    Visitor: "What is your name?"
    Child: "Pepe"

Visitor: "What else?"
Child: "Unamuno"
Visitor: "What else?"
Child: "Basta" (That's enough).

Yes, they were proud of that name, and they felt too their father's tenderness and protection which isolated them from the currents of controversy that eddied about him. They also felt his strangeness; the eccentricities which set him apart from other men. With maturity they have come to realize his role as a Spaniard and as a human being, and they take pride in contributing to the ever-growing legend which surrounds their father—the Unamuno legend.

# The Unamuno Legend

CHAPTER *11*

WHAT WAS THE PHYSICAL AP-
pearance of Don Miguel? The adolescent boy who had struggled to
conquer a physical weakness became a stalwart figure, the face of a
"young owl" acquired the wise look of an "old owl," and certain habits
became fixed as personal eccentricities, inseparably associated with
the legend of the grand old man. Innumerable word pictures, many
photographs, several paintings, a caricature, and last, but perhaps
the most impressive of all, a sculptured bust of the man preserve his
physical likeness.

The task of describing a man is difficult, for a human being changes
constantly and escapes description. What is true one moment changes
within the twinkling of an eye. Many writers have attempted the task
of describing Don Miguel. One of these, Salvador de Madariaga,
acutely aware of the difficulty involved, ends his masterful word-
picture thus: "Such is, rather, his photograph. For Unamuno himself
is ever changing."[1]

Beginning with this precaution, the following description is offered
as a composite of the word pictures by five men, who, at different
times during his lifetime, came within the orbit of Don Miguel's disturbing presence. These men are the above-mentioned Salvador de
Madariaga, Julián Marías, Gómez de la Serna, Federico de Onís, all

[1] Introduction by Salvador de Madariaga to Unamuno, *The Tragic Sense of
Life in Men and in Peoples,* p. x.

four Spaniards, and Jean Cassou, a Frenchman who was, however, the son of a Spanish mother, and to whom Unamuno refers as more Spanish than French.

Described by such varying adjectives as "admirable," "original," "genial," "rare," "extravagant," and "paradoxical," Unamuno's appearance left the general impression of strangeness. More specifically, this strangeness was of a priestly nature, the strangeness of one who wishes to be identified as dedicated to a sacerdotal calling, not the staid formality of the Catholic clergy, but rather the ecclesiastical air of an English clergyman or a Welsh divine. There is a striking similarity in physical types between the Basque and the Welsh races and Dr. Madariaga likens Unamuno to a composite group of Welshmen—one in many, a unity under multiplicity.

This general impression was caused by his dress and physical features. Unamuno had a philosophy of clothes, which he expressed in words almost identical with the words of Thomas Carlyle in *Sartor Resartus*. He rebelled against what was uniformly customary, against any pattern which encased or *classified* modern man within a type. He saw all cosmopolitan dress as a negation of man's universality. ". . . I know no creed more foreign to universality, to humanity, rather, than the cosmopolitan creed as in use today. Ones tries, thereby, to arrive at a common man, a 'type' of man . . . a poor unfeathered biped who everywhere dresses by the same model . . . That is to say, the man for the clothes not the clothes for the man . . ." [2] Paraphrasing Christ's words regarding the observance of the Sabbath, Don Miguel believed in "clothes for the man, not man for the clothes." In a day when eccentricities were consciously cultivated by Spanish intellectuals, Unamuno, though he would resist being thus classified, had the knack of adopting those oddities which were most comfortable and, thus, more apt to survive; for instance, he always wore a solid-front vest of his own design. It fastened up the side and on one shoulder, and it fitted in front up to the collar. Thus it eliminated the use of a necktie. As Madariaga puts it, his contempt for the passing world "is shown in the peculiar attire whose blackness invades even that little triangle of white which worldly men leave on their breast for the necktie of frivolity and the decorations of vanity and blending it, leaves but the thinnest rim of white collar to emphasize rather than

---

[2] Unamuno, *Contra esto y aquello,* p. 132.

relieve, the priestly effect of the whole." [3] Upon closer inspection one might catch the outline of a crucifix beneath this vest and notice that the "blackness" of his garb was blue, a dark blue. Don Miguel always wore a blue suit which he proudly called his *uniforme civil*. When one wore out, he would buy another exactly like it so that it always appeared to be the same suit. It was at all times scrupulously clean, thanks, no doubt, to the faithful ministrations of Concha.

He wore, or rather used, a black hat of soft, flexible felt. Indeed, this hat was his "prop" as a cigarette or pipe (Don Miguel never smoked) is for some men. In the heat of a conversation or speech, he would take it off and stuff it into his pocket, only to take it out and put it back on his head, or, instead, if particularly stirred, to hurl it energetically at the nearest target. The low shoes which he wore the year round was another eccentricity of dress because these are never worn in Spain during the winter months. This, then, was his dress both in summer and winter for until the last years of his life he stoutly refused to pamper himself with an overcoat, even in the bitterest weather.

The black hair and beard of his youth eventually changed to iron-grey. His high cheekbones, a high aggressive forehead, bore a ruddy complexion which Madariaga likens to the "colour of the red hematites on which Bilbao . . . is built, and which Bilbao ruthlessly plucks from its very body to exchange for gold in the markets of England." [4] A long, slightly curved nose carried out the owl-like expression of his black eyes that seemed to watch suspiciously from their deep sockets through and around the edges of a pair of spectacles. ". . . two eyes like gimlets eagerly watching the world through spectacles which seem to be purposely pointed at the object like microscopes." [5] The secret of Don Miguel, all his intensity and combativeness, his agonizing doubts and his abiding faith were revealed in those eyes. Their intense gaze into the mystery was, to quote Madariaga again, "the steel axis round which his spirit revolved in desperation, the one fire under his passions and the inspiration of his whole work and life."

Picture, then, this man, a tall bony figure, the head set firmly on his broad shoulders, his hands behind his back, walking resolutely

[3] Introduction by Madariaga to Unamuno, *The Tragic Sense of Life in Men and in Peoples*, p. x.
[4] *Ibid.*
[5] *Ibid.*

ahead over the rough-hewn cobblestones of a Salamancan street or
up a rocky mountain path, all the while carrying on his inexhaustible
monologue, indifferent alike to the station or the understanding of
his companions. One writer likens Don Miguel's indifference to his
listener's station in life, to the same characteristic in Don Quijote who
discoursed before the goatherds even as he did before the Duke and
Duchess. The vehicle of that monologue, his voice like that of "an old
rooster," fell harshly upon his listeners' ears—"the words came out
raspingly, in scanned sequence." His admirers came from all parts of
Europe and America to stumble breathlessly along beside him in their
eagerness to hear what his rasping voice had to say. There is a striking
similarity between the personal habits of Unamuno and those of
Kierkegaard for thus does Lowrie picture the Dane striding along the
streets of Copenhagen.

Unamuno was not an easy subject for a photographer or painter
and not an accommodating model for his sculptor. Any success of
such efforts deserves the special gratitude of posterity. There are
several portraits of Don Miguel by well-known artists. Among these
there is one by the Basque artist Losada, painted in Bilbao in the
spring of 1906 while Unamuno was spending the Easter holidays
there, one by Zuloaga, another Basque, and a third by Gutiérrez
Solano, painted when Unamuno was nearing the end of his life. An
interesting study done by Vázquez Díaz in oils of Unamuno as an old
man hangs on the wall behind his *camilla* in his study at the Casa
Museo Unamuno. In his bedroom at the same house is a drawing by
José Herrero Sánchez entitled "Unamuno en brazos de la muerte."
Losada's portrait hangs in the library, and on another wall in the study
is a rather strange likeness of Miguel, the boy. On entering the place
one is almost overwhelmed with the presence of the man for he is
here in all stages of his life—from the plaster model of his right hand
in a glass case on the library table, to the drawing of his death mask
in the bedroom. Another rather curious portrait hangs in one of the
official halls of the University. The massive conference table speaks
of faculty meetings held where the past rectors of the University look
down from their huge framed portraits around the walls of the hall.
The last in the series of these men whose lives span hundreds of years
is the portrait of "Sr. Don Miguel de Unamuno, 1900 a 1914." Garbed
in the scholastic gown and insignia of rector, his figure is standing
with the right hand resting lightly on a heavily carved table and hold-

ing between thumb and forefinger the staff which signifies the authority of the position. The observer's eye travels upward to the bare head that somehow does not seem to belong to this body. The incongruity is explained by the fact that the portrait was composed from a photograph of Unamuno's head which the artist has painted onto another man's body. As Felisa explains, the work was done in Salamanca while her father was in exile in France.

A lifelike bust of Don Miguel stands today in the quiet stone-paved patio of the Palacio Anaya, the school of Philosophy and Letters of the University of Salamanca, in the turn of the stairway that leads to the second floor gallery. The figure is of heroic size, the head in bronze and the body in stone. It is so lifelike that after dark the students hesitate to pass that way. The first time Unamuno himself saw it in Salamanca he gazed fixedly at it. "How strange to see oneself in bronze," he exclaimed, and turning away, he never looked upon it again, for he never climbed those stairs after its unveiling in 1934. Seeing its plaster cast in Hendaye, he wrote, *"Me vi en yeso, sentí frío, sentí el peso del vacío"* [6] (I saw myself in plaster; I felt cold; I felt the weight of emptiness). The sculpture is the work of Victorio Macho, a sculptor from Palencia, who has since moved to Lima, Peru. To him posterity owes a debt of deep gratitude because, as Benítez says, this piece of sculpture is adjudged, by contemporary artists, one of the most noble in all Europe. Benítez tells, also, the story of its tortured execution in Hendaye during the days of Unamuno's exile there. The old man waged an insistent, though losing battle, with the artist. After many exhausting sessions, Macho thought that it was finished but Don Miguel snatched his instrument from the sculptor's hand and, with a rapid movement so characteristic of him, slashed a cross on the breast of the clay model. Later Don Miguel's daughter, María, asked him: "Why did you do it, papa?" And he replied by raising a forbidding hand, motioning her to silence, and exclaimed only "Ah!" Today, thanks to Victorio Macho's patience, we have this remarkable likeness of Don Miguel.

Thus far, the picture of Unamuno is incomplete. Any art critic knows that the revealing features of great portraiture are the eyes and the hands—the eyes for the spirit and the hands for the body. Only a master can paint the hand which conveys its owner's habits. The artist, Gutiérrez Solano, seems to have captured those busy, thinking

[6] Unamuno, *Cancionero*, p. 368.

fingers which were forever creating things. "He used to make things with his hands" is the finishing touch to the description by Federico de Onís, and there he left it. What a world of meaning lies in these words. He made things with his hands, (surely Professor de Onís intended the creative concept of "hacer," not the vague translation, "to do") and it is precisely at this point in the portrayal of character that the word-picture may excel over the brush, bound as it is by time and space.

Four portraits would be required to show the customary postures of Don Miguel's hands: the writer's hands, the artist's hands, the moulder's hands and the creator's hands. Unamuno as a writer will constitute a chapter in itself. As an artist, he did not escape the desire of most great men to excel; as a moulder he never passed the amateur stage of playing, not with clay, but with bread crumbs; as a creator he never tired of playing God. This last he did by means of a creative art of his own invention which he dignified with an etymologically derived name, "*cocotología*."

Of Don Miguel, the artist, there is all too meager information. Dr. Alfonso Reyes of Mexico, a personal friend and one who walked beside him along the River Tormes, has written a short article on his drawings. Dr. Reyes had in his possession some of these which Unamuno may have given him or which the children may have turned over to him later, knowing of his interest in this aspect of their father. Many in this collection are drawings of people—there is one of Concha, some curious self-portraits, and sometimes merely a hastily-sketched head or a revealing facial expression. Others depict "the designs in rock in churches and cathedrals, faces of animals, or the ecstatic calm of the Castilian countryside." Then there is the one of Ramón, and a likeness of the Mexican poet, Amado Nervo. This last was published in the *Revista moderna* of Mexico. Dr. Reyes describes the picture as a "rapid drawing, skillfully executed during a conversation, in which perhaps the best thing is the hand." [7] There is also a drawing of "*la actriz*." Could this be of Margarita Xirgú, a great star of the Spanish theater, who once acted in one of his plays and to whose performance Unamuno attributed its success? Of a landscape drawing, Dr. Reyes writes "then there is a landscape of little value in itself, but curious as an illustration of certain descriptive phrases which Don Miguel has

[7] Alfonso Reyes, "Unamuno dibujante," in *Simpatías y diferencias* from *Colección de escritores mexicanos*, II, 223.

written in his own handwriting as a commentary on the drawing . . ."
There are drawings of animals. One of "a torture rack with an inscription that recalls the *caprichos* of Goya," other grazing animals, and
"a whole collection of toads and rats intended for a certain *Batra-
comiomaquia* [a study of frog-like vertebrates] which he considered
once." [8] And "finally, the plan of a monogram which he began to trace,
a little daydream of the pen, on the card which acknowledges the
receipt of the *Plano oblicuo.*" [9] Could Don Miguel have succumbed
in this to the whimsy of doodling?

Such is the meager collection of Unamuno's drawings in possession
of the Mexican writer. As works of art, they would never attract
attention. They do, however, constitute an expression of the artist in
the man. His feeling for line rather than color, Dr. Reyes thinks, influenced his preference for the landscape of the river valley rather
than that of the ocean. As he expresses it, Unamuno "finds the de-
signer's certain symmetrical delight in that palpable demonstration of
the greatest of earth's folds, resulting from the gorges that form the
river beds." [10]

Of Don Miguel, the moulder of bread crumbs, there are many witnesses. The ever-increasing stream of visitors to the home of the Salamancan bard was always treated to an unending monologue which
was delivered, when he was not walking, at a table, either in his home
or nearby at the café Novelty in the Plaza Mayor. His listeners may
not remember the words but they never forget the ceaseless activity
of his hands—the fingers working, modeling the nearest available
material which offered itself to their bidding. Crisp loaves of Spanish
bread are abundant and always present on every table. What could
be more natural than that those restless hands should reach for the
convenient bread crumbs? His ceaseless moulding of his *"migas"*
(crumbs) of bread accompanied and emphasized his steady stream of
talk. Even as he used that old felt hat as a prop when outdoors, so
when he lingered at the table, seemingly unwilling and almost unable
to end a conversation, his fingers moulded the bread crumbs into his
now universally famous *migas.*

This activity was, with Unamuno, perfectly instinctive, almost sub-
conscious, but his scientific art of *cocotología* required the complete

[8] *Ibid.*, pp. 224–225.
[9] *Ibid.*, p. 224.
[10] *Ibid.*, p. 225.

concentration of hand and eye. As he watched him once, his friend, Max Grillo asked, "Which is greater, the effort of the fingers or of the eyes?" And Unamuno answered promptly, "Of the eyes."

The process was simple. First he took a piece of paper already cut to measurement and, manipulating it deftly with the tips of three fingers, an expression of extreme effort of will in the eyes, fashioned a perfectly-shaped little figure, or *pajarita*, as he called it. With intense and swift dexterity he would convert a flat piece of paper into three-dimensional figures of varying shapes and sizes. Though he had a repertoire of some eighteen different varieties of *pajaritas*—vultures, eagles, beetles or pigs—it was not the resulting shape that mattered. Half in play, half in earnest, as a man who jokingly tells the truth but reserves the privilege of hiding behind the jest, Unamuno engaged in this diversion. The whole idea lay in the fact that he was the creator of a form derived, not from a solid body, but from a flat surface. To these forms, he, by an act of will, gave spirit, his own spirit. By this process he became for an instant "a creator," if not God himself. On one occasion Don Miguel triumphantly produced a *pajarita* the exact size of a pin's head. Whereupon his friend, Ramón Gómez de la Serna, said: "Now you should try to make a man." Flashing a piercing look at him over the top of his glasses, Unamuno exclaimed, "Never! Not that! That would be too much! Just suppose I succeeded!" [11]

This eccentricity and his rationalized deductions from it provoked such curiosity that he even wrote an exposition on this process and his philosophy concerning it, which he entitled *Notes on a Treatise on Cocotología*. Its success was instantaneous and it brought him more money than all of his writings in Spanish put together. It is included, complete with illustrative drawings, in the first edition of his equally eccentric novel *Amor y pedagogía*. This novel and the accompanying treatise were written during the time when Unamuno was engaged in reading Carlyle. They are obviously influenced by Carlyle's *Sartor Resartus* which Don Miguel quoted freely and whose philosophy of clothes he adapted to his own convenience.

The term, "*cocotología*" Unamuno explained, is derived from "*cocotte*," French for "good time girls," hence "little paper birds" and "*logía*" meaning a treatise, and he added that this definition is omitted from the Larousse dictionary. The importance of the name, he went on to say in a more serious vein—even his jesting was in deadly earnest—cannot be overemphasized for "the name makes the object

[11] Bernardo Villarrazo, *Miguel de Unamuno: glosa de una vida*, p. 75.

and even creates it." Carlyle was right, Don Miguel proceeded, when he put into the mouth of Diogenes Teufelsdrockh the following:

For indeed as Walter Shandy often insisted there is much, nay almost all, in Names. The Name is the earliest garment you wrap around the earth-visiting ME; to which it henceforth cleaves, more tenaciously (for there are Names that have lasted nigh thirty centuries) than the very skin. And now from without, what mystic influences does it not send inwards, even to the centre; especially in those plastic first-times, when the soul is yet infantile, soft, and the invisible seedgrain will grow to be an all-overshadowing tree! Names? Could I unfold the influence of Names, which are the most important of all clothing, I were a second greater Trismegistus. Not only all common Speech, but Science, Poetry itself, is no other, if you consider it, than a right Naming . . . In a very plain sense the Proverb says, *Call one a thief, and he will steal.*[12]

Unamuno quoted from Goethe and Shelley: "He gave man speech and speech created thought which is the measure of the universe (Prometheus Unbound)." The ringing sounds of names, Spanish names of cities which he knew almost as well as he knew himself constitute an entire little poem in his *Cancionero*. It is preceded by a quotation in French verse about the Cid, Ruy Díaz de Bivar, as follows:

> Et tout tremble, Irún, Coimbre,
> Santander, Almodovar
> Si tôt qu' on entend le timbre
> des cymbales de Bivar.

> *Alava, Málaga Cáceres—Játiva Mérida, Córdoba,*
> *Ciudad Rodrigo, Sepúlveda—Ubeda, Arévalo, Frómista*
> *Zumárraga, Salamanca—Turégano, Zaragoza.*
> *Sois nombres de cuerpo entero—libres, propios, los de nómina,*
> *el tuétano intraductible—de nuestra lengua española.*[13]

Such names are indeed the untranslatable marrow of the Spanish language.

Finally, underlining the term *"Cocotología,"* he defined it as "the science that treats of the *pajaritas de papel.*" This led to a sarcastic thrust at science which "may come to be perfect science" and "perfection is attained at the expense of personality."[14] The perfection idea led to God: God is the projection of ourselves, of all of us, therefore, He is our perfection. "Therefore He is the collective I, the uni-

[12] Thomas Carlyle, *Sartor Resartus*, p. 67.
[13] Unamuno, *Cancionero*, p. 101.
[14] Unamuno, *Amor y pedagogía*, p. 259.

versal I, the All-I." [15] Reasoning thus, from the sublime he descended
to the ridiculous, and by means of logic in the form of mathematical
equations and formulas, he proved such absurdities as that the Chinese
tangram, a favorite child's puzzle game, is a descendant of the *pajarita*.
He scorned, also, the *evolucionismo* of Darwinism which holds that
everything comes from something else. ". . . Darwinism . . . which in
its blindness and arrogance holds that the different species extant today have, all of them, all, including the human species, proceeded
from others . . . Seldom has such a heinous error been made." [16] Just
what was the point of these conceptual, these philologically scientific,
antics? Why, to prove the fallibility of reason. He was playing a game
of fighting with himself, with his own intellectuality which so tormented him. Consider the *cocotte,* he added, or the *pajarita de papel,*
and do not fall into the error of trusting to reason. This is sarcasm
again—Don Quijote's "reason of the reasonless" ("*La razón de la sin
razón*").

As an appendix to the whole volume, Don Miguel drew pictures of
the four "genders" of *pajaritas;* neuter, hermaphrodyte, masculine and
feminine. These he followed with a drawing of a sunset as seen by a
*pajarita* and a concluding admonition; "Let us carry on in peace, and
let us drown our pedagogy in love and charity." [17] Thus, the fourth
portrait of Don Miguel must paint him at his favorite game, the game
of playing God.

[15] *Ibid.,* p. 260.
[16] *Ibid.,* p. 270.
[17] *Ibid.,* p. 285.

# To Stir Men's Souls

## CHAPTER 12

BEHIND AND ABOVE THE UNA-
muno legend there was a noble purpose. All of his works, especially
his novels, say that life must have a purpose, otherwise there would
be no life. As his Spanish biographer, Villarrazo, so aptly puts it,
Unamuno seems to be saying,

When we look from within at this tremendous fact that is our life, we soon
realize that it consists basically of a certain dynamic quality. Our life is
never just being [*estar*], simply occupying space. To love always means to
live because of something [*por algo*] or for something [*para algo*]; it is a
*transitive verb*; hence a human life cannot exist without a vital interest that
sustains, constitutes, and organizes this life. The moment this vital interest
becomes completely and finally inactivated, life ceases to be.[1]

Don Miguel adopted personal eccentricities and indulged in rationalistic absurdities to draw attention to himself, and to the writings
into which he had breathed his spirit. In this way he sought to stir
men's souls. In December 1902 he wrote to a friend: "How can I help
it if some people think that I am a sage whose job is to teach useless
information to my countrymen and not . . . (I shall say what I feel)
and not an apostle, or a poet, or a sentient being whose mission is to
agitate men's souls, to wake them up, to instill them with the vital
religious uneasiness concerning the hereafter, to console them for hav-

[1] Bernardo Villarrazo, *Miguel de Unamuno: glosa de una vida*, p. 45.

ing been born, or to persuade my people to persist in their own identity, not in any other." [2] Another desperately sincere young man, Kierkegaard, had written forty-nine years earlier: "I am only a poet who moves men by means of ideas . . . To move, only to move, is what I desire. Oh, may this succeed."

To stir men's souls! Particularly, to stir the souls of his countrymen and to fill them with his own "thirst for immortality" was his avowed goal. The vague desire to awaken his own people from their restless sleep, which had been born within him on a mountaintop in Vizcaya, now had a clearly defined purpose and a specific direction. After dedicating a lifetime to this purpose. Don Miguel, delivering his farewell address at the end of his university career in 1934, said in essence: "I have striven to know my people better, in order that other peoples of the earth may know them better, but especially that 'they may be known to God' . . . and so live in His memory, which is history, the divine thought traced upon our human earth." [3]

Don Miguel repeatedly defined his purpose in words and his entire life was the action whereby it became realized. His utter disregard for the personal security of his position, provided he attained his goal, proves his sincerity. Often he appeared ridiculous, and ridicule is harder to bear than poverty, hatred, or contempt; but though the ridicule wounded him, he faced it as unflinchingly and nobly as did his beloved friend and master, the mad don of La Mancha. The example of this master was always his guide, for as one writer expressed it, Don Miguel lived all of his life with a madman, Don Quijote. At times, when the daily struggle obscured his goal, he would return to the source of his inspiration, to Gredos, to the Peña de Francia, or to Arnótegui, to "wind up his heart springs with the pure air of the mountain peaks."

Unamuno was accused at times of contradicting himself and of talking and writing in riddles. Far from denying it, he rather gloried in it.

It is said the Hellenic characteristic consists in distinguishing, defining, separating. Well, mine is in indefinition and confusion . . . One must confuse, confuse above everything. Confuse sleep with watching, fiction with reality, truth with falsehood; confuse everything in one great Mist. The joke that is not acrid and confusing serves no purpose. The child

[2] Hernán Benítez (ed.), "Cartas inéditas de Miguel de Unamuno y Pedro Jiménez Ilundain," in *Revista de la universidad de Buenos Aires*, Vol. III, No. 9 (January–March 1949), p. 151.
[3] Unamuno, *Obras selectas*, p. 1048.

laughs at tragedy; the old man weeps at comedy . . . for all is one and the same. One must confuse for he who does not is himself confused. My forte is to talk, to produce subtleties, to play with words and terms.[4]

With this purpose in mind, Don Miguel approached every task. He wanted to administer "a poke in the ribs to literature, to philosophy, to sociology, in fine, to life as a whole." Others, after reading his works, have testified to this aim which Unamuno had so clearly defined. "Unamuno didn't want to amuse, nor instruct, nor convince; he wanted two things; to exist for others, to be irreplaceable and unforgettable, to continue living in their memory—this was the first thing; the second, to cause everyone to live restless with longings."[5] This purpose was accomplished by the constant struggle in his life, a struggle which Dr. Madariaga, with accurate perception, defined as a strife between enemy truths; the truth thought and the truth felt.

In August of 1901 Unamuno was given the opportunity to stir the souls of his beloved Basques in Bilbao. He had not visited his *patria chica* (little homeland) for five years and although he had authored the stirring essays, *En torno al casticismo,* and his writings continued to appear in the Madrid papers, Bilbao remembered him only as a native son and a rare one, at that, with his readings and talking and his adolescent mystic seizures. Then he had gone to Madrid where he had made a brilliant university record and come back to apply for a position teaching the Basque language in the local institute. In fact, his name was always associated with any kind of activity connected with Vizcaya's native language, and since Miguel had left Bilbao in 1891 the interest of the town had been more acutely focused on such activities. Rapid growth of commerce and industry had brought the outside world so much closer that life had begun to change. Even as Miguel and his boyhood friends had decried the "black serpent" bringing evil from beyond those hills, so now Bilbao resisted this change. Its resistance found expression in a movement to nationalize the Basque language—*Euskera.* Rallying around their leader, Sabino de Arana, the *Biscaitarras* as they called themselves, had organized a fiesta, the first *Juegos Florales* (flower festival) in the history of Bilbao. Such fiestas are common throughout the Spanish-speaking world where poetry contests are the featured events of the fiestas. All of the

---

[4] Hernán Benítez, "Unamuno y la existencia auténtica," in *Revista de la universidad de Buenos Aires,* Vol. II, No. 7 (July–September 1948), pp. 19–20.

[5] Prologue by Julián Marías to Unamuno, *Obras selectas,* p. xxv.

innate aesthetic feelings of the Hispanic peoples are expressed on these
occasions when the most beautiful girl, the queen of the festival,
presents the highest award—a perfect rose—for the best poem.

Now the enthusiastic *Biskaitarras* organized the *Juegos Florales* to
promote the cause so dear to the heart of old Bilbao. What more
natural than that the main speaker on the program be their own
Miguel who was now rector of Spain's oldest university, and whose
specialty had been that very cause which they were now promoting?
Don Miguel accepted their invitation with alacrity.

It is August 1901 and he is returning once more to Bilbao. As the
train slows down Unamuno feels in his pocket for the bulky speech
which he has so carefully prepared and snatches up his old felt hat
from the seat beside him. Although many of his boyhood friends have
left, he still knows most of the townspeople, and this time he will
make sure that they will remember him. This is his opportunity to
wake them up with confusion and contradiction.

The day of the fiesta dawns as dreary and damp as any day in Bilbao, but the flower-decked floats, carrying the queen and her attend-
ants, dispel the customary mists. By night the fiesta spirit has reached
a fever pitch, and every heart swells with pride and satisfaction in
Bilbao, the center of the Basque country, and with pride in her traditional language and customs. The town fathers, headed by the
mayor, and the families of the lovely young maidens who are the
flower and pride of Bilbao, gather in the Arriaga theater. The queen
and her court are duly arrayed on the stage, the mayor pronounces
his flattering introduction of the guest speaker and Don Miguel appears. Dressed in the garb of a protestant preacher, he walks slowly
and deliberately toward the footlights. He draws his speech from the
pocket of his old blue suit and looks calmly over his audience. The
dramatic events of this occasion are described by a contemporary as
follows:

. . . the theater presents a splendid sight, indicative of that wealth [the
recently acquired riches of Bilbao]. On the stage, the fiesta queen, who is
going to present the flower—the romantic rose of the troubadours of
Provence—to the winning poet, is richly bedecked and surrounded by her
maids of honor . . . In the box seats and orchestra, the plutocrats of Bilbao
are dressed in their best. Seated in groups on the main floor and in the
galleries, the young people who have just joined the new Biskaitarra party,
founded by Sabino de Arana, expect Don Miguel, the high priest of that
race of the millenium, to justify their separatist attitude in the eyes of Spain.
Unamuno, who is one hundred percent Basque, walks slowly toward the

footlights. Tall, broad, strong, wearing a frock coat and a lined waistcoat that reaches up to his collar, he has in his hands the note sheets of his address, which is going to explode like a charge of dynamite. His gestures and clothes are those of a Protestant minister. The speech begins. His voice is measured and calm . . . The first projectiles that he hurls are aimed at the language . . . The separatists that fill the theater protest; it makes no difference. Don Miguel regrets that Menéndez y Pelayo, referring to Trueba, has spoken of Basque poetry as honorable. Poetry that is only honorable is not poetry. And he attacks the customs so exalted by that poet.

He talks to the capitalist of low salaries. To the laborer, of the defects of his work. For the purpose of the speech is that: to leave everybody dissatisfied [que todos queden descontentos]. Finally he hurls his last and worst attack. "El maketo—the Castilian ridiculed by the Basque because he is poor and comes from the interior to make a living—the maketo—he tells them—is more intelligent than you, and since he knows how to talk, he is making a place for himself in your lives, and some fine day your women, like the Sabines, will let themselves be carried off by the Romans." . . . The Biskaitarras want to kill Don Miguel, and in one jump are up on the platform. The parents, the husbands and brothers of the maids of honor, rushed down to save them. The stage is left bare, but Don Miguel standing alone, serene, imperturbable, continues his speech. The theater is empty save for a few faithful ones scattered here and there. The spectacle is over.[6]

Corroborating this account is a statement of the queen herself, la Marquesa Arriluce de Ybarra, who, fifty-eight years later, said: "He [Unamuno] attacked the Basque language, and some people wearing red berets who were up in the gallery [paraíso] came down and tried to get up on the platform, but the other young men prevented them and they didn't get up. Don Miguel continued imperturbably."

The author of the foregoing account, María de Maeztu, goes on to recount an incident which she says occurred the following September. After this "affair" in Bilbao, it was spread abroad that Don Miguel was the avowed enemy of Biskaitarrismo. Consequently he was invited to speak in Valladolid, the heart of old Castile and Vizcaya's bitter rival. Wearing the same costume and in the same manner he appeared in Valladolid's theater and began by quoting the following lines from the poem "A orillas del Duero" by Antonio Machado:

> Miserable Castile
> yesterday the mistress
> wrapped in her rags
> she scorns all she ignores.

[6] Prologue by Manuel García Blanco to Unamuno, Obras completas, VI, 39, 40, 41.

The results are similar to those that occurred in Bilbao. However, Don Manuel García Blanco writes that Don Miguel could not have quoted these lines about Castile since the poem was not published until 1910. He also points out that María de Maeztu's account of Unamuno's Bilbao speech is inaccurate, and he includes that speech in volume six of the *Obras Completas* which he is currently editing in Salamanca.

According to Don Manuel's account, Don Miguel began by expressing his delight at being again in his native town and added: "I owe my spiritual roots to Bilbao; here my mind built its Jacob's ladder of basic ideas to heaven; with frankness I shall pay her back something of what I owe." He remarks on the changes that have taken place while those "heralds of eternity" Pagasarri, Arnótegui, Arráiz, Archanda, remain the same. He contrasts the landscape of Vizcaya and Castile, the one where the ripe "wheat undulates in the sunshine," and the other where the "grave oak stands motionless in the wind . . . From my Vizcaya, from Bilbao, the seed; from my Castilla, from my Salamanca, the fruit." Going back into the past of his *parientes mayores*—the days of the fighting ancestors of the Basques— he recalls the bloody feuds of the old families: Leguizamón, Basuerto, and Zurbarán, and refers to the ruins of the old Zurbarán castle which can still be seen on the heights of Begoña. The struggle of Bilbao has always been between the tiller of the soil and the merchant. Bilbao was founded, he says, in 1300 by Don Diego López de Haro for the express purpose of carrying on foreign trade. Blessed with a natural harbor in the river mouth it has been a supply center for the two Castiles. Passing over discords of the past, Unamuno summarizes them in a statement which he was to repeat many times in his best-known works: "The present is the effort of the past to become the future." After pointing out Bilbao's wealth in natural resources he states that her greatest wealth, nonetheless, is in her sons. "A race forged by sea and mountains, whose strength is agility; above all of little imagination, of a language rich in everyday practical terms, but poor in ideal or abstract terms, short of speech but strong in action . . ." Then Unamuno lists some of Vizcaya's great men: del Cano, the first to go around the world, which, he added, is *not* Vizcaya; Legazpie, who won the Philippines for civilization; Ignacio de Loyola, founder of the Jesuits ". . . a school of cosmopolitanism; the poet, Iparraguirre, who at the age of thirteen left his home as a wandering troubadour to traverse France, England, Switzerland, Portugal, and who landed on the Argentine pampa to carry echoes of the symbolic oak to the *ombú* of that land." Then, says Unamuno, "If we want to make our character count for something, let us stamp it on all around us. Let us act as though we had a plenty and to spare," for the Basque is the last person to live in his own castle and to sing his own praises. Like the British, let us have our empire, an empire without an emperor, diffused and peaceful, not aggressive and warlike. And as a recipe for this spiritual diffusion he admonishes them: "If you don't want to be invaded, invade; if you don't want to be absorbed, absorb; anything rather than draw into your shell and be isolated." And, he continues, let us pass from the *patria chica* to the greatest and the only *patria*, the *patria humana*. "And if a Basque established the company of Jesus, let us, his race, help to establish the Company of Mankind."

Thus Unamuno tried to make them see that their real problem as a part of Spain was *"Para qué España?"*—to help determine the true destiny of Spain on earth. To enclose themselves within their language would be only to defeat this purpose, and although the best language is always ones' own, many peoples go through a transition stage and Vizcaya had reached that stage. "The Basque language is becoming extinct and no human force can avoid its extinction; it is dying a natural death. Let us not grieve for the death of its body; it dies only that its soul may live . . . Bilbao must use the Castilian language and from this language, pronounced and constructed by the different peoples that inhabit vast domains in both worlds, there will emerge, not different tongues, . . . but a super-Castilian, the Spanish language, the Spanish American language, one and varied, flexible and rich, as vast as its domains." A writer, says Unamuno, can be just as truly Basque in Castilian.

Is Trueba any less a Basque than Iparraguirre? . . .
Let us give our language a holy burial and continue to study it as modern science demands, but life is above science . . . Life, above all, concrete life; and life is bringing us the loss of the Basque language.

The rest of Don Miguel's address was a sermon, a sermon in which he preached peaceful coexistence with their neighbors by spiritual interchange. He condemned the "ostentatious display of wealth" in Bilbao where the rapid acquisition of riches had gone to people's heads. "A certain *delirium tremens* in business . . . may carry you to produce a generation of neurotics on the verge of insanity . . . and if life is a dream, it may become a nightmare for you." Riches should be used to acquire culture as they are used by the Yankee millionaires.

"Art will guide you in acquiring well-being . . . No art is healthier, more classic, than that which springs from economic well-being . . . Our idyllic age ended with the crystalline songs of Trueba; let us enter our heroic age with songs of iron . . . Think on life. The women of Vizcaya can be our inspiration." And then he says, "She [Vizcaya] is the Sabine who lets herself be carried off by the Roman."

And now, as this first flower festival ends, let us salute all of the peoples and regions that make up our common historical homeland, Spain, and all of the peoples in both hemispheres who clothe their thoughts in the robust Spanish tongue; let us pray that our Basque race, poured into the great historical Spanish-speaking race, a race in the making, may be the ferment that shall raise it to the great human family, one and supreme; and may art lead our industry and commerce to the conquest of the society of the future, in which all men may commune together in one spirit, and that the earth, free labor, internal justice, perpetual peace, pure faith, life—a work of love, may be the common property of all peoples beneath one ideal heaven of truth, goodness, and beauty.

I have spoken.[7]

Unamuno did not read this speech unmolested. We learn from the commentary of Ramiro de Maeztu that he was interrupted five times by shouts from the gallery: "To Salamanca, to Salamanca!" Each time "Unamuno would sit down with his knees apart, his notes in his hand, and his eyes proudly fixed up above where the battle was waging. Then those of us who appreciated his sincerity would applaud and Unamuno would get up again without any signs of nervousness or haste. The cries would silence him, and again the applause would bring him to his feet."

And the local press reported:

During the course of the peroration, the speaker was interrupted several times by bravos and applause, and when he came to the paragraphs regarding the Basque language, shouts and whistles were heard from the seats in the gallery, which was the cause of skirmishing that interrupted the speech for ten minutes. The speaker, unperturbed, waited for things to calm down, continuing afterwards with his speech, and receiving finally an enthusiastic and unanimous ovation which lasted some time. This part of the program ended with a parade of the queen and her maids of honor which took place in the same manner as before with a repetition of the triumphal march and the ovations.

The press went on to mention the general discussions provoked by

[7] Unamuno, *Obras completas*, VI, 291–307.

the address and added: "Some of Unamuno's friends began soliciting pledges to have a general celebration and to honor him with a banquet." [8]

Sr. Maeztu was correct when he predicted in 1901 that "Bilbao will talk about its first Juegos Florales for a long time. For a long time Spain will talk about the Basque who has struck the bravest Spanish note in these sad times of divisions and misfortunes. Personally I consider that the intellectual history of Vizcaya begins with Unamuno . . ." [9]

In 1958 Señor Villarrazo wrote: "Vizcaya, the generous homeland of Unamuno, will long live in the love and admiration of mankind for having produced her immortal poet, in whose works a whole people is idealized; Miguel de Unamuno, prince of geniuses of the Spanish Basques." [10]

As for Unamuno himself, he felt that his experience in the "Bilbao affair," as he termed it, taught him a great deal. He commented on it repeatedly. Henceforth, Bilbao could not ignore him, for he had succeeded beyond his fondest hopes in stirring them up. The immediate result, of course, was to create enemies and alarm his friends. Hearing of the affair, one friend in Paris wrote Don Miguel urging him not to sacrifice himself thus and tendering sympathy at the storm of protest and criticism which he had provoked. His answer, however, was anything but that of a stricken object of public persecution; it was rather the answer of a man who is boasting over a recent victory. "I do not need consolation—Spain is a country of free speech!"

In December of 1905 he wrote to the same friend: "The affair of the flower festival of four years ago is just this summer bearing fruit." [11] The "fruit" to which he referred was his increased popularity as a speaker and as a writer. This gave him other opportunities to agitate the souls of his countrymen. One of these presented itself during an uprising in Barcelona in the latter part of the year 1905. Barcelona is the capital of Cataluña, a province which constitutes another regional unity within Spain, similar to that of the Basque provinces. The inhabitants have their own language, Catalán, and their cultural tradition and, consequently, present an ever-festering political problem to the central government in Madrid. Their constantly smouldering

[8] Prologue by García Blanco to Unamuno, Obras completas, VI, 41–42.
[9] Unamuno, Obras completas, VI, 308–311.
[10] Villarrazo, Miguel de Unamuno: glosa de una vida, p. 219.
[11] Hernán Benítez (ed.), "Cartas inéditas de Miguel de Unamuno y Pedro Jiménez Ilundain," Vol. III, No. 9 (January–March 1949), p. 177.

antagonism is easily set off by circumstances or incidents which might elsewhere pass unnoticed. Such an uprising occurred at this time and Madrid was forced to quell it by using strong military measures. Seizing this opportunity, Don Miguel published an article on "Today's Crisis in Spanish Patriotism." He quoted parts of his controversial speech in Bilbao and drove home his message of progress, national progress, based on a struggle between opposing factions. He argued that, even as an individual is composed of contradictory selves, so a people is a unity of conflicting sections and that the progress of that people is based on struggle.

Some six years later, recalling his article, he wrote: "The only fruitful unions are those founded not upon difference but upon opposition," and "It is necessary to struggle, to struggle in earnest, and to seek for the unifying solidarity of the combatants in the fight and thanks to the fight itself." [12] He added that the Cataláns and the Basques "would perform a great service to the cause of Spain's progress if, Catalans, as well as Castilians, Basques, and Galicians, would show their opposition to everything which repels them in the other's manner of being, and if each of the different castes would try to impose on the others its concept and sense of life." [13] Because ". . . from this mutual effort to assert one's self, there can spring the collective national conscience. It is each brother's fraternal duty to impose himself on his other brothers, and when he feels himself superior to them . . . he should say 'This is final. Now I shall take command,' and so try to impose his authority although because of it they throw him out of the house." [14] Then he offered the following olive-branch of peace to his own enraged Bilbao "If as I believe, the Basques are the people of Spain with the greatest capacity for true spiritual culture, they will not realize it unless they try to attain it by exercising a conscious effort to impose it on the other people who, with them, live in the Spanish way of life." [15]

Henceforth, his countrymen would listen to Unamuno's words, even if they did not heed them. He had succeeded in drawing attention to himself and to his writings. Whenever August, the month of flower festivals, came he was sure to be swamped with invitations to speak. He always welcomed these opportunities to stir men's souls.

[12] Unamuno, *Ensayos,* VI, 141.
[13] *Ibid.,* pp. 141–142.
[14] *Ibid.,* p. 143.
[15] *Ibid.,* p. 148.

# "I Am My People"

CHAPTER *13*

UNAMUNO WAS PASSIONATELY
Spanish. He took pride in Spain's past and at the same time worked
to spur his people on to a more glorious future, that they might again
take their place among the great nations of the earth. For this purpose
he traveled throughout the Iberian peninsula which, as he expressed
it, was the hand of God tenderly holding His people. As the beloved
is all things to the lover, so was Spain to Don Miguel, and in mystic
language he sang to her his song of songs. Her name upon his tongue
was "a rose of flesh whose fresh cherry hues made his mouth to water."
Her name dissolved upon his tongue made his heart to beat with a
wild joy:

The feeling of your name upon my lips holds such sweet charms, oh land in
which my soul has lived, that your very name is my homeland.

Wet with your saliva, from your tongue, the Spanish tongue, I took bread—
the word—like a young pigeon from the dove. Our tongues met, España,
and I felt the burning coal from the nape of my neck to the depths of my
heart, I bit your lips and tasted the apple of paradise. I faint with ecstasy
that you shall become, España, señora; for I am the father of my people.[1]

In fact he so strongly identified himself with the land and the people
of Spain, that he boldly said, "I am my people." And so he was.

Federico de Onís describes him as ". . . this extraordinary man,

[1] Unamuno, *Cancionero*, p. 386.

refined and savage, modern and medieval, mystic and scientist, with the unction of an apostle and the wisdom of a *pícaro,* in whom all the defects and virtues of the race seem to culminate."[2]

During the scholastic session he was confined to Salamanca by his professorial duties, but in the summers he traveled that he might listen to the heartbeat of his people, that he might awaken them to a sense of their own destiny. He wrote:

> To the rhythm of my strides
> I have measured your paths, España,
> the eternal footsteps of your beggars.
> Now my heart beats out the
> measure of my songs;
> deeper than the ocean,
> the pathways of my nation.[3]

One summer, for example, the summer of 1903, Unamuno went to Andalucía in the south where he spoke at various schools and took part in an attempt to settle a labor dispute, to Almería, to Granada, and then to Galicia in the northwest, and thence to Béjar not far from Salamanca. In this last town he spoke twice on the same day. First to "inaugurate the session of the Béjar industrial school," and secondly, before a meeting of laborers and directors who had been deadlocked in a strike for a month and a half. His efforts must have proved successful for he wrote, "And with such good luck . . . that they instigated the first person to person interview of both factions, after a month and a half of refusing to negotiate . . ."

He never felt so close to his people as when he climbed one of his beloved mountains with friends, or when he visited some especially isolated and backward section of the peninsula such as Las Hurdes. He once wrote an anthropological study of these "backward people living in the wasteland of Las Hurdes," analyzing the reasons for their condition and penetrating their feeling for their *patria chica.* He felt his kinship for even these poor peasants for they too were part of his Spain.

Once on a trip to Mallorca he visited the subterranean lake, the Drach, and gave its exact measurements. He recalled the visit of George Sand and Chopin to the island and added that he was living in the same house in which Rubén Darío, the Central American genius, spent his last days. Musing upon the more distant past, he mentioned

[2] Federico de Onís, "Unamuno profesor," in *Revista hispánica moderna* (New York), (October 1934), p. 78.
[3] Unamuno, *Cancionero,* p. 319.

Spain's medieval sage, Ramón Lull, a Catalán, who lived on the island, where he wrote his mystic novel *Blanquerna* and where he met his violent death. Lull was, Unamuno concluded, the first to use the *lengua vulgar* for philosophy in Spain. Feeling the natural beauties of Mallorca, he ended his essay: ". . . Thanks be to God for his work . . . There where the heavens, the hills and the seas narrate the glory of God, one can understand why Lull should have tried to rationalize all theology, for in that spot art is made reason and reason, art. Fantasy has taken on earthly, visible form, congealed into the flower-covered turret of Mallorca." [4]

Though Don Miguel traveled for a purpose, that he might come to know his country and his countrymen better, he took time to measure the Drach, to recall Ramón Lull and to comment on the "flower-covered turret of Mallorca." No detail was too insignificant to stir his national pride. He had, moreover, a profound scorn for travelers who visit his country not to know it, but simply to say that they have been there. "Travel, yes, travel, but not just to be able to talk about it afterward . . . for this is nothing more than the vanity of the North American upstart, of the New York spice dealer or the Chicago sausage manufacturer." [5]

During the winter of 1903–1904 Unamuno seemed to consider moving to Buenos Aires because of the hostility of the Church. Ilundain, who feared that Spain would not tolerate Don Miguel's heresies much longer, urged him to go. His friend wrote him in February: "If you decide to leave for Buenos Aires, we shall talk before your departure. My opinion is that the advantages of such a change of residence will be greater for you and yours than the inconveniences, although these will not be slight." [6]

The "inconveniences" thus referred to were, no doubt, of an economic nature. That Don Miguel seriously considered the change is possible, though it seems that the slight excuses which he offered to explain his hesitation were an indication of his intention to remain in Spain. "Far from having abandoned the idea of my departure for America," he wrote in April of that year, "I am more and more resolved to go. It no longer depends on me. The presidential elections are holding everything in abeyance." [7] By December he had found other

[4] Unamuno, *Andanzas y visiones españolas*, p. 202.
[5] *Ibid.*, p. 30.
[6] Hernán Benítez (ed.), "Cartas inéditas de Miguel de Unamuno y Pedro Jiménez Ilundain," in *Revista de la universidad de Buenos Aires*, Vol. III, No. 9 (January–March 1949), p. 157.
[7] *Ibid.*, p. 164.

obstacles, even more remote than the wavering fortunes of Spanish politics. "The matter of my trip to Buenos Aires is being held up. I want it, but I fear it . . . I imagine that though there may be full economic prosperity, there is a lot of foolishness going on. There, there is no living rock; it is all flood land, there they admire Ferri, Max Nordau, Le Bon . . . There the intellectuals of the Alcan Library are nourished." Dr. Benítez explains that Max Nordau was a popular democrat, "a hothead," who used *La Nación* of Buenos Aires. "He is the inventor of the *fronterizos* and other humbug." Unamuno heartily scorned him, as he wrote three years later to Nin Frías. At the end of this letter he gave another reason, perhaps the real one, for abandoning the idea completely. Referring to Salamanca, he concluded, "I love this rocky castle in which I live alone among so many people." [8]

Don Miguel loved his "rocky castle," his people and his Spain. Though she might turn away from him in anger, he would stay to fulfill his mission. He would remain to take upon himself the national conscience, to fight the Catholic Church, which he felt retarded her progress and to attack the evils and corruption which he saw in the government.

A favorite part of the peninsula which Don Miguel included in his travels was Portugal. He considered it as another of the divergent expressions of the Hispanic spirit, and was an ardent proponent of a stronger Pan-Hispanism. He came to know the country and its people, its history and its literature. Its contemporary writers were his personal friends with whom he communed both personally and spiritually. One has but to read Unamuno's travel essays, *Por tierras de España y Portugal* (Through Lands of Spain and Portugal), to sense this, and his correspondence with such men as Lanjeira expresses it even more strongly.

The tragic sense of life which was Unamuno's he found to a heightened degree in the Portuguese cult of *el dolor,* and Portugal, the country he described as a woman with her back to Europe and her feet in the ocean, drew him strongly. Among Don Miguel's cherished possessions is a group of small autographed photographs of his Portuguese friends—writers, all of them. He kept them joined together in a little open folder and propped in front of his own published works on a bookshelf in his study. They still stand there in his room in the Casa Museo Unamuno, eloquent witnesses of their community of spirits: A. Herculano, 1909; Oliveira Martins, 1909; João de Deus,

[8] *Ibid.,* p. 168.

1908; Anthero de Quental, 1909; C. Castello Branco, 1908; ———
(indecipherable name) dos Reiz, 1908. And there were others: Eugenio
de Castro, the professor from the University of Coimbra with whom
Unamuno used to delight in reading aloud the poetry of that land;
Guerra Junqueiro, "the greatest living lyric poet of Portugal, and one
of the greatest in the world today;" [9] Teixeira Pascoaes, author of
*Sempre* and *Vida etherea*. Unamuno, who visited Portugal almost every
summer, was twice a guest of Pascoaes at Amarante, the ancestral
home of his birth. Once they climbed together—Unamuno, Pascoaes,
and his father—to the top of Marón looking over the pleasant lands
of the region of Traz-os-Montes that is watered by the river Miño.
"I have stayed with him at his Amarante to watch the night fall, the
beam of light from the Támega, under the arched bridge, and I saw
it under the night sky." [10] It was Pascoaes who led him to read *Amor
de perdição* by Camilo Castello Branco, of which he writes: "This
model of works of passion, very superior, in my judgment, to *Manon
Lescaut . . .*" [11]

Amarante was located in the midst of the rural country of Portugal
which Unamuno considered "father of the heroic Portugal of navi-
gation." [12] Contrasting the Catholicism of the two nations, Unamuno
quoted his friend, Guerra Junqueiro, who once said to him, "The
Spanish Christ is an African Christ; he never descends from the cross
where he is bathed in blood; the Portuguese Christ plays with the
peasants in the fields and sups with them, and only at certain times
when he must fulfill his calling, does he hang from the cross." [13]

Of the historian, Oliveira Martins, Unamuno wrote from Espinho
in July of 1908; "This man is one of my weaknesses. I have learned so
much from his sad book, as he himself calls it!" [14]

In Unamuno's library there is a book entitled *Manuel Lanjeira,
cartas de, Prefácio e cartas de Miguel de Unamuno* (published in
Portugal). Don Miguel's preface and his five letters dated from
August 19, 1908, to March 17, 1911, tell the story of a short intense
friendship with a tragic ending. In Portugal that summer of 1908
Unamuno received the news of his mother's death in Bilbao and he
left abruptly without taking leave of Langeira. Another summer Don

[9] Unamuno, *Por tierras de España y Portugal*, p. 18.
[10] *Ibid.*, p. 26.
[11] *Ibid.*
[12] *Ibid.*, pp. 26–27.
[13] *Ibid.*, p. 32.
[14] *Ibid.*, p. 49.

Miguel returned expressly to visit his friend, a brilliant passionate man, who was struggling to maintain his sanity against the odds of an ignorant and uncomprehending society. Their friendship ended only with the suicide of Lanjeira. His body had scarcely grown cold when there arrived a gift from Unamuno, a copy of his *Rosario de sonetos líricos.* "It was Lanjeira," writes Don Miguel, "who taught me to see the tragic soul of Portugal . . . And he taught me to see not a few of the dark recesses of the human soul . . . It was life that killed him, and by his suicide, he gave life to death."

Of Unamuno's Portuguese friends it was Eugenio Castro with whom he was associated for the longest time. Slightly younger than Don Miguel, Castro first became acquainted with him when he was a professor at the University of Coimbra. He was himself a poet and author of two works, *Belkiss* and *Constança,* and it was poetry that brought them together possibly as early as 1890, though their friendship may have been purely a literary acquaintance in the beginning. It was through Unamuno's influence that the Portuguese professor joined the faculty of the University of Salamanca probably sometime after 1900 which was the year Unamuno became rector. Speaking in 1934 on the occasion of Unamuno's retirement, when he himself was honored with the title of "Doctor Honoris Causa," Castro said he had been Unamuno's "very dear friend for forty-four years." The introductory speaker on this occasion was Don Francisco Maldonado. He spoke of the meaning of *Hispánico* since this fiesta for Unamuno was a *fiesta Hispánica.* "Within Hispania," he said, "Unamuno has taught us to love Portugal." He pointed out that it was Unamuno who had brought Eugenio de Castro to Spain, hence his investiture as Doctor at the hands of Don Miguel must recall to him many treasured experiences of the past.[15]

As an integral part of the Iberian peninsula, Portugal was for Unamuno a part of Hispania, and a part of his people. Unamuno, with the Portuguese, joins their poet João de Deus in his song to the nightingale:

> Your day is born with
> the setting sun, oh nightingale;
> may the light that shines for you
> show me the tomb, oh nightingale.

But it is of the "peaceful tomb wreathed in hope" of Herculano that he dreams.[16]

---

[15] *La Gaceta Regional* (Salamanca), October 2, 1934, p. 2.
[16] Unamuno, *Por tierras de España y Portugal,* p. 61.

# "The Chosen One"

CHAPTER *14*

WHEN GOD MADE MIGUEL DE
Unamuno he left out one ingredient—humility. Instead he gave him
an abundance of preoccupation with self—a characteristic which one
Cuban writer calls his *yoísta* conception of life. Just as the seeds of
Spain's glory and of her decadence were contained in one and the
same cause, her spiritual fervor, so the same trait of character in
Unamuno was his strength and his weakness. His admirers called it
"constitutional sincerity," but his enemies pronounced it "insufferable
egotism."

One of the most frequently told incidents that illustrates this egotism
is the following: in June 1905 Alfonso XIII bestowed upon Unamuno
the Cross of the Order of Alfonso XII in recognition of his literary
contributions. Don Miguel requested an audience with the King in
order to thank him. When his petition was granted he addressed himself to his benefactor in the following terms: "I have requested an
audience before your majesty because you have awarded me the Cross
of Alfonso XII which I deserve," whereupon Alfonso remarked that
his statement was a little strange; all other recipients had insisted that
they were undeserving of such a distinguished honor. "And they were
right," was Don Miguel's rejoinder.[1]

Unamuno seemed to have an inborn resentment toward persons in
positions of power, and his fulminations against the royal power were

[1] "Retrato" by Gómez de la Serna in Unamuno, *Obras selectas*, p. 1058.

common knowledge, not only in Salamanca but throughout Spain, for he often publicized it himself from the *tribuna* (speaker's stand) of the Ateneo in Madrid. "With regard to the Ateneo, it was perhaps Unamuno who had most influence from the *tribuna,* both in and out of that center. Unamuno used that *tribuna* to show those rough edges of disconformity that characterized his personality and his works, and consequently his rectorship, through the Ateneo, was in general, one of rebellion and in this sense somewhat disoriented." So writes Señor García Martí, secretary of the Ateneo during the year that Don Miguel's antimonarchical campaign was at its height. As Alfonso himself was a member of the Ateneo, the situation became acutely embarrassing. The Rector became so outspoken that the King summoned him to the palace to put a quietus on him. Evidently Unamuno had been directing his barbs against the Queen Mother whose royal decree had named him to the rectorship in 1900, for the King is reported to have asked, "Why do you talk against my mother? What has she ever done to you?" Accompanying Unamuno during this interview was the Conde de Romanones, several times minister of public education, and a long-time friend of Don Miguel's. The sequel to the visit in the Ateneo on the following day is better known than the details of the interview itself.

The day after this visit the press made it public and commented unfavorably. In the Ateneo, especially in the disrupted younger group whom Don Miguel always kept inflamed with his fiery language, the visit to the palace, after his incendiary criticism of several nights before, was like a direct blow to Unamuno's personality, and they made him the object of their bitterest censure; the higher-ups finally called a special meeting of all members to demand an explanation from him and to call the Conde to account for his having represented the Ateneo on the royal visit.

As for Romanones, a note from me in the press stopped the movement. With reference to Don Miguel, who at first refused to give any kind of explanation, he had to seek refuge in my office from the excited demonstrations of the extremists, and I kept him safe there. I telephoned the Conde de Romanones who was in congress at the time and he came right away. Together we tried to think up a way to quiet the demonstrations, especially of the younger members who were crowding into the halls and the parlors of the Ateneo and whose shouts we could hear from the secretary's office where we were gathered. Unamuno proposed that he write an explanation and send it to the evening paper, or, if it was too late, to the morning paper, giving the reasons for his visit to the palace. While he was writing at the desk in the president's office, the Conde, who was sitting by my side on the sofa, was showing signs of impatience. Every now and then he would mutter under his breath: "Oh, Don Miguel, Don Miguel of my sins!"

Finally Unamuno read us the article in which there was no mention of any explanation; instead it expressed the stubbornness so characteristic of him. We thought that its publication would produce anything but the desired effect, in fact, the very opposite, and so we decided to announce that Don Miguel would speak the next day, which would, for the time being, give him an opportunity to think about what he would say, and besides, the announcement would calm them down and such was the case. Unamuno, quite upset, left by the exit on Santa Catalina Street, and late that same night, around twelve o'clock, I got a letter from him full of bitterness, asking me to announce the next day that his talk would be postponed on account of his physical and moral condition. Several days passed during which the protests began to subside, and finally Don Miguel appeared on the *tribuna* of the Ateneo and everyone listened respectfully but in complete silence, with no shouting and no applause.[2]

Far from putting a quietus on Don Miguel, this incident merely spurred him on until in 1914, the proud rector of the University of Salamanca lost that position. The reasons given for this step were various and will be gone into in another chapter. His subsequent involvement in politics is sometimes ascribed to a determination to fight Alfonso XIII on all fronts. Unamuno used to say, "I am the real king of 'Las Españas', for my kingdom extends as far as the language of Castile reaches, and as long as it shall last."[3]

Some of Unamuno's friends, often jealous of the attention which was being paid him, were antagonized by his preoccupation with self. A letter written in 1904 by Dr. Enrique Areílza, his Basque friend of younger days, to Señor Ilundain, refers to him in most unflattering terms:

. . . some friends from Salamanca came bringing regards from "The Chosen One." No doubt it is proper for me to call him "The Chosen One." It would be more fitting to call him the "Beneficiary" of the Promised Land. Cases such as Unamuno are not uncommon in Salamanca. There is Santa Teresa, for example, to prove that I'm not lying. Unamuno is a product of Salamanca. "Chosen Ones" grow there just like chick peas grow in Fuentesauco and little turnips in Navarniz. Or could it be the result of a monopoly since Don Miguel has installed there a telephone to communicate with the Heavenly Father? Some day we'll find out. Don Miguel won't die without telling us all about his intimacies with God. For the time being perhaps he doesn't dare, for he mustn't betray the confidence of the Supreme Being, but the thunder will come when the two of them quarrel. And they will surely quarrel. Don Miguel quarrels with everyone. As he becomes

[2] Victoriano García Martí, *El Ateneo de Madrid (1835–1935)*, pp. 267–268.
[3] Fray Albino, "Algo más sobre Unamuno," in *El Español* (Madrid), April 10, 1950.

better acquainted with the Supreme One he will find him dumber and dumber; and then we will hear Don Miguel exclaim, "God is a bore; I am greater than he!" Prepare yourself to witness the coming of the Super God.[4]

Don Miguel's lack of humility, a lack of which he seemed acutely conscious at times, estranged him from another great Spaniard of his day—José Ortega y Gasset. Both were philosophers who sought to lead their *España eterna* to a better way of life but by diametrically opposed paths. Unamuno dedicated his entire life to the way which progressed from the spiritual awakening of his countrymen to a rebirth of a national conscience; Ortega believed that a modernization of the intellectual life of Spain would eventually bring about social advancement.

Ortega y Gasset, who was some twenty years younger than Don Miguel, occupied the chair of philosophy at the Universidad Central in Madrid and had attracted quite a large following from among the young intellectuals. One of his greatest ambitions was to classify and reform the role of the university in modern society. He was fired with an enthusiasm to Europeanize Spain by means of her university system but he needed Unamuno, who was then Rector of the University of Salamanca and an acknowledged leader in literary and educational circles, to head up a national movement. He realized that Don Miguel would never be a follower, so, to secure his support which was so necessary for the success of the plan, Ortega offered him the leadership of the movement. It was the newly formed "Spanish League of Political Education," which he, Ortega, had inaugurated with a stirring speech on March 23, 1914. Appealing to the national conscience he had uttered stirring words for a man of thirty-one years old: "Our generation must concern itself in all conscience, with forethought and organically with the nation's future. In fact, it is necessary to call loudly upon our generation, and if those who are in a position to do so do not answer, then someone—anyone—will have to—I, for example." Soon afterwards Ortega went to see Unamuno in Salamanca. The interview took place in the Café Novelty on the Plaza Mayor. The younger man explained his plan in detail. Unamuno, contrary to his custom, listened without interrupting. The other listeners were surprised at his prolonged silence. As Ortega was nearing the end of his explanation, Don

[4] Hernán Benítez (ed.), "Cartas inéditas de Miguel de Unamuno y Pedro Jiménez Ilundain," in *Revista de la universidad de Buenos Aires*, Vol. III, No. 9 (January–March 1949), pp. 172–173.

Miguel cut in with, "Well, Ortega, what you are proposing in this plan is that I be the head and you the spirit. Well, let me tell you that in my plan I shall always be the Father, Son and Holy Spirit." [5]

The break between the two men thus begun, widened throughout the rest of the older man's lifetime. Only once, writing after Don Miguel's death, Ortega hinted at a reconciliation, thus: "Unamuno from whom I had been estranged for some twenty years, became more friendly toward me in his last days . . . a friendship which does honor to us both." [6]

The antagonism between them was common knowledge. Don Miguel never wrote for any publications which were edited by Ortega. The younger man avoided all possible contact with him. Whenever Unamuno went to Madrid, where Ortega had become the acknowledged leader in intellectual circles, he could not resist the temptation to seek an audience for his monologues. He would join a *tertulia* where, more often than not, Ortega was monopolizing the conversation, and would take the most prominent seat. On such occasions Ortega would immediately leave and go to another gathering place, *el fondo de la Revista.* "I just can't stand anyone who wants to be the only one to talk," he would explain.[7] Unamuno would talk on unperturbed, until 8:30. His friend, Gómez de la Serna, usually among those who welcomed the professor's visits to Madrid, describes his behavior. He would eat early and continue talking until, upon consulting his watch, he found the hour to be 8:30. He would then rise abruptly and, with a hasty goodnight, rush headlong up the stairs "like a delirious old man running from a fire." [8] The habit of retiring at 8:30 was an established routine during his entire lifetime. Ortega called him the "possessed Spaniard" and the *"morabito máximo."*

Unamuno made many enemies among the clergy. Indeed, at one time or another he offended all "the grammarians, stylists, philosophers, theologians, and cultured professionals." However, he seemed to take an especial pleasure in his fight with the Bishop of Salamanca. In him, he saw the representative of the hidebound clergy, the incarnation of religious intolerance which was, and is, the shame of Spain. As rector of the University, Don Miguel should have kept on good terms with

[5] Bernardo Villarrazo, *Miguel de Unamuno: glosa de una vida,* p. 81.
[6] Dr. Agustín Basave, Jr., *Miguel de Unamuno y José Ortega y Gasset: un bosquejo valorativo,* p. 160.
[7] "Retrato" by Gómez de la Serna in Unamuno, *Obras selectas,* p. 1064.
[8] *Ibid.,* p. 1066.

the Bishop who was an influential figure in the church but the battle was a harsh and bitter one in which he added, gloatingly, insult to injury. His *mayúscula gresca* with the Bishop was to be a struggle which ended with his loss of the rectorship and his eventual exile. Unamuno also sought opportunities, often of his own making, to antagonize the entire Spanish clergy. He would attend a meeting of churchmen and loudly maintain that all priests should marry or, at least, propagate themselves in the flesh. If his hearers did not appear to be upset, he would add that he himself should have become a Bishop "in order to express heresies; I express them now and no one takes issue with me; but if I were Bishop . . ." Here he would lick his lips and peer mischievously about him.[9]

Don Miguel seemed to enjoy offending the anticlergy also. Spain was divided into two groups, the clergy and the anticlergy. This last was usually made up of Spanish Reds, called *moscovitas* or *comecuras* (those who eat up the priests). In gatherings of this kind he would piously cross himself and exclaim in a loud voice "Christ be praised." [10]

Unamuno's especially piercing darts were reserved for the Jesuits who, one is told, still cannot stand him. In spite of such behavior, Unamuno had fast friends among the clergy. His frequent visits to the monastery of San Esteban in Salamanca where he sustained long, soul-searching talks with the Dominican fathers is still a source of comment in that town. For some reason, the Dominicans of San Esteban held a special place in Unamuno's heart. The townsfolk always used to say that when Don Miguel got ready to die he would surely send for a Dominican to confess. Even his students commented on his frequent visits and talks with the fathers in the pleasant monastery garden called "Mount Olivet." One priest particularly seemed to stimulate the Rector—El Padre Arintero. One day Father Arintero made some statement about faith and salvation, whereupon Unamuno proposed that the two of them have a series of discussions on the topic. Arintero agreed and their discussions began. A student of Unamuno's writes that all that is known about these discussions is how they ended. The language professor dwelt so insistently on the semantics of their terms that Arintero, thoroughly exasperated, finally exclaimed that he didn't want to waste any more time that way. "What must I do, then, to recover

[9] Hernán Benítez, "Unamuno y la existencia auténtica," in *Revista de la universidad de Buenos Aires*, Vol. II, No. 7 (July–September 1948), p. 18.
[10] *Ibid.*

my faith, to believe?" asked Don Miguel. "Practice," answered Arintero. That was his last word. But thereafter Unamuno attended mass regularly for some time.[11]

The Dominican fathers owned a rustic home which they kept as a retreat some seventeen hundred meters up the Peña de Francia on the border between the provinces of Salamanca and Cáceres, on the way to Las Hurdes. One day Don Miguel asked one of his students (probably a Dominican priest himself) if there was any place where he might go for a few days during the following summer. Young Albino told him about this mountain sanctuary and added that there was a crude little guest house nearby very poorly furnished for pilgrims, but that since it was a question of the rector of the University they would probably let him have the use of a little cell in the monastery if he preferred it. "And the guest house, who's is it?" asked Don Miguel. "It belongs to the sanctuary too," was Albino's answer. "Only I should warn that those who use it can do so only on one condition, and that is that they attend mass on Sundays, a condition laid down only to keep the place from being used merely as a vacation spot." Don Miguel didn't seem to mind for he said he preferred the guest house. That summer he betook himself to the retreat on the mountainside and settled down in the pilgrim quarters. He attended mass regularly for several Sundays until one Sunday when some journalists from Madrid came to visit him. When the last bell for mass tolled, Don Miguel was still strolling about with his company. He was informed that mass had begun, but paid no attention. That evening he was asked if he was planning to leave soon. "Tomorrow morning," he answered quickly.[12]

Subsequently Unamuno frequented the Dominican sanctuary on the Peña de Francia to spend time in meditation and spiritual communion with the fathers there. The story is told of a deep well on the sanctuary grounds where Don Miguel often experimented with the echo of his voice. Leaning down over the edge he would call in a loud voice: "Yo . . .!" He loved to hear that returning echo of his own voice that answered. "Yo . . .!" Once the distinguished orchestra conductor, Leopold Stokowski, is said to have visited the sanctuary and on hearing the story of the echo he experimented in the same way. Amazed at the rich tones that resounded at such length, with watch in hand, he

[11] Fray Albino, "Datos para una biografía," in El Español (Madrid), April 4, 1950.
[12] Ibid.

noted the time span of the echo—fourteen seconds. Another orchestra leader, Ataulfo Argenta, even planned to hold an orchestra practice there.[13]

The friendship with Father Arintero lasted over many years, and although they loved each other, they never fully understood one another. The priest sorrowfully told his friend that he "stubbornly refused to see the light."[14]

Don Miguel's friendship with Father Arintero is still recalled by the San Esteban fathers, where Don Miguel, alas, is often judged by hearsay. Talking with a visitor in one of the cool little interviewing rooms of the monastery, Father Manuel Cuervo said, some twenty-three years after Don Miguel's demise:

Don Miguel's death was a punishment from God! He talked a lot of trash. He was an empty man inside and just wanted to attract attention.
Visitor: "Have you read his writings?"
Cuervo: "No—some of them—I have other things to read that are of more importance to me."

Unamuno once paid a visit to his former student, the Dominican Fray Albino, at the monastery of Santo Domingo Real in Madrid. The priest proudly showed him the monastery's office where their magazine, *La ciencia tomista,* was published. Noticing the number of foreign publications that were around, Don Miguel exclaimed: "This is very good. What you folks need is a little airing out."[15]

His enemies said that he was contradictory and paradoxical but never was a man so consistently true to himself and his purpose in life. "Most of what I fight against in others I fight in myself," he wrote a friend; "hence the bitterness of the attack. When I argue most bitterly to refute others, it is because I am refuting my own arguments. Like Job, we are all children of contradiction."[16] So he consistently "went when others were coming and came when others were going."[17]

[13] Fr. Guillermo Fraile, D. P. in *La Gaceta Regional* (Salamanca), February 24, 1959.
[14] *Ibid.*
[15] Fray Albino, "Algo más sobre Unamuno," in *El Español* (Madrid), April 10, 1950.
[16] Benítez, "Unamuno y la existencia auténtica," p. 14.
[17] *Ibid.*, p. 15.

# Which I Am I?

CHAPTER *15*

WHAT COULD NOT ROBERT Louis Stevenson do with the divided self of Unamuno? He could not create another Dr. Jekyll and Mr. Hyde, for the one did not possess the man and drive out the other; rather, the angel and the devil co-existed in Don Miguel, making him one irreplaceable individual, unique and alone in his time, but more *out* of his time. A man with an insatiable thirst for life, eternal life, both here and hereafter, he also felt the pull of the past. "I am not a modern man," he wrote to Ilundain, ". . . civilization and science are repugnant to me . . . to the *savants* and the *sages*, and to all the science of specialists I prefer rather the wisdom of *Ecclesiastes*, of the *Imitation of Christ*, of those who feel deeply." [1]

Asked once if he could have chosen his time to be born, which period he would have chosen, Unamuno answered: "In the Middle Ages, or during the French Revolution." From his antagonism to modern civilization came his horror of all classification. Perhaps it came also from his fear of losing his identity; his "I" once classified along with other "I's" might dissolve into nothing. "I don't want to be pigeon-holed," was one of his most frequently repeated statements. He was indeed, "a man of struggle, struggling with himself,

[1] Hernán Benítez (ed.), "Cartas inéditas de Miguel de Unamuno y Pedro Jiménez Ilundain," in *Revista de la universidad de Buenos Aires*, Vol. III, No. 9 (January–March 1949), p. 151.

with his people, and against his people, a hostile man, a man of civil
war, a leader without a party, a solitary man, exiled, savage, a voice
in the wilderness, provocative, vain, deceitful, paradoxical, irrecon-
cilable, sworn enemy of the 'no-thing,' who is drawn and devoured by
it, torn between life and death, at once killed and revived, invincible
and ever vanquished." [2] One adjective in this quotation should be
modified, *engañoso*. Unamuno was not "deceitful," he was, rather,
"deceiving." He did not try to deceive, but his uncomprehending
countrymen were deceived because he so obviously showed them his
Cain and his Abel, his devil and his angel, the protagonist and the
adversary in one. Such a man at times inevitably appeared ridiculous,
not only to others, but to himself: "There is one terrible ridicule and
that is self-ridicule. It is my reason ridiculing my faith and scorning
it. And this is where I turn to my Don Quijote that I may learn to
face ridicule and conquer it, and possibly it is a ridicule, which—who
knows!—perhaps he never knew." [3]

A most accurate and masterful summary of Don Miguel's dualism,
the one penned by Benítez, is hard to surpass. In ringing phrases like
Unamuno's beloved Carlyle's, he writes:

Seldom has a person felt human dualism so frequently. Few men have
delved so deeply into the mystery of man. When this world has ended, if
God should wish to show the angels a perfect specimen of the renowned
biped that ruled the earth and should try to have them understand the
struggle of conflicting needs [*aporías*], the mystery of contradictions and
the whirlwind of paradoxes that make up the human heart, with its fears
and its phobias, its dreams of soaring to the stars and its grotesque taste for
wallowing in the excresence of the rottenest rot, he would show them Don
Miguel, that rare mixture of seraphim and demon, atheist and believer, at
once tragic and taciturn, that paradox of flesh and bone who while living
set all of Europe agog, and now that he's dead and buried, has whole books
and libraries written about him. [4]

Unamuno himself, probed, dissected, and questioned in a vain effort
to decide "Which I am I?" He wrote,

Our innermost thoughts are woven with intimate contradictions . . . For you
can't join in a civil war unless you can see both sides of the question; and
unless you can feel your adversary's right—because you carry him within

[2] "Retrato" by Jean Cassou in Unamuno, *Cómo se hace una novela*, p. 22.
[3] Hernán Benítez, "Unamuno y la existencia auténtica," in *Revista de la
universidad de Buenos Aires*, Vol. II, No. 7 (July–September 1948), p. 15.
[4] Hernán Benítez, "La crisis religiosa de Unamuno," in *Revista de la universidad
de Buenos Aires*, Vol. III, No. 9 (January–March 1949), p. 31.

yourself—you cannot feel your own. Contradictions? Paradoxes? The Gospels are full of them, not to mention Paul's Epistles, Paul the formidable dialetic philosopher, the man who like Job, was made up of intimate contradictions. Christ arose in him—whom He knew not in the flesh—the Christ who saying that he had brought peace, and repeating peace, said, "Think not that I am come to bring peace on earth; I came not to bring peace, but a sword. For I am come to set a man at variance against his father, and the daughter against her mother, and the daughter-in-law against her mother-in-law. And a man's foes shall be they of his own household." Matthew 10:34-36. And again: "I am come to bring fire on earth; and what will I, if it be already kindled?" Luke 12:49. This is the right and this is the left, the tragic, the dialectical and controversial play of contradictions.[5]

This struggle, this dissension within himself was the basis from which sprang faith, life; it was, therefore a necessary struggle for him. "I am the center of my universe, the center of the universe and in my supreme agony, I cry with Michelet: 'My self, they are carrying off my self!! . . . Each man is worth more than all humanity . . . I do not want peace between my heart and my head, between my faith and my reason; rather I want them to fight with each other." [6]

Eccentric? Yes. Childish? At times. Ridiculous? Alas, he was all of these. But viewed in the light of his purpose, and reviewed from the vantage point of his achievement, his human weaknesses give strength, his fears imply courage—for the individual is valid, without need to dissimulate longer, and machines count for nothing beside the smallest of us! One man is worth the whole universe, and each man is irreplaceable for, as he wrote,

There is no other "I" in the world! Here is a thought we should never forget, and especially when we are dismayed over having to disappear some day, and they come at us with all that rubbish about being an atom in the universe, and that without us the stars follow in their course and that good will prevail without our help, and that it is conceit to imagine that all of this immense fabrication was made for our own benefit. There is no other "I" in the world. Each one of us is unique and without substitute. There is no other "I" in the world! Each one of us is absolute. If there is a God who has made and maintains the world, He has made it and maintains it for me. There is no other "I"! There may be others greater or lesser, better or worse, but there is no other I. I am something entirely new, an eternity of the past is come together in me, and from me there springs an eternity of the future. There is no other I. This is the only solid basis for love among men, for neither is there any other you than you, nor any other he than he.[7]

[5] Unamuno, La ciudad de Henoc: comentario 1933, pp. 81, 82.
[6] Francisco Ichaso, Defensa del hombre, p. 13.
[7] Bernardo Villarrazo, Miguel de Unamuno: glosa de una vida, pp. 179-180.

This thought gave added urgency to his quest. Others had found an answer, or seemed to, and he listed some of them:

"I know who I am," says Don Quijote,
"And dreams are only dreams," Segismundo.
"I die because I die not," thus Teresa
Ship of fire in this world of ours, this mundo!
"Like a club . . ." Loyola, you were wrong,
Don Juan: "The credit time is long!" [8]

Unamuno's quest, this quest for himself, led to the quest for God, through suffering and bitterness:

"Our Father who art . . . what art thou?
My life is thy being, not thy stay;
Let my will be thine, oh Master,
Take me, at last, in thine own way.
I am joyful too, though sadness fill me,
Ill, though well and still persisting
Thou didst form my soul of contradictions,
Mysterious, 'twixt being and existing.
Our Father who art—I would be;
That which flows disappears—to flow
That which lives never lasts—to grow
Disappearing, never lasting—but to live.
But, alas, remaining, everlasting
things have bitterness to give. [9]

Unamuno was his own double—his angel and his devil, but more than this, he was multiple, a society within himself. He was an unending revelation of his different selves to himself. To Oliver Wendell Holmes' three Johns in *The Autocrat of the Breakfast Table*: the man that I think I am, the man that you think I am, and the man that God knows I am, Unamuno added a fourth, the man that I want to become. It is by this fourth "I," the "I" whom I earnestly strive to be, that I am finally judged. Conscious of his multiplicity, his different and warring selves, he constantly strove to answer the question: "Which I am I?" A man so determined on being himself must search for the answer to this question, as unsolvable as it is necessary. He must continue the search, a search so absorbing that at times, like one who fails to see the forest for the trees, he loses all consciousness of self and with a start of horror, senses again his old fear of *la nada*. "I

[8] Unamuno, *Cancionero*, p. 246.
[9] *Ibid.*, p. 50.

believe that divine wisdom is so deep within us that we shall never discover it," he wrote to Ilundain. The feeling that one experiences for an instant, perhaps, on gazing at one's image in a mirror was constantly recurring to Unamuno, for he wrote, "And this is why I cannot gaze for long into a mirror for suddenly my eyes are lost in those eyes, in their own image, and when I look upon my own gaze, my being seems to flow away from me, back to my unconscious state, to the past, to the no-thing." [10]

The same sensations recurred as he struggled to be himself in his writings: "The Unamuno of my legend, of my novel, the product of my friendly I, my enemy I and the rest, my friends and my enemies, this Unamuno gives me life and death, he creates and destroys me, he holds me up and lets me down. He is my agony. Am I what I believe I am, or what I am thought to be? Even now these very lines become a confession to my I unknown and unknowable; unknown and unknowable to myself. Even now I am making the legend in which I am to be buried." [11]

So he struggled to make his legend, the Unamuno legend, in which he was buried to live ever after!

[10] Unamuno, *Cómo se hace una novela,* p. 71.
[11] *Ibid.,* p. 71.

# *They Knew Him Well*

CHAPTER  *16*

". . . IN THE MIDST OF ALL OF this I feel a certain strange sensation of loneliness and abandonment. At times I seem to be all alone, while others are mere shadows, spectres that move and talk . . ." [1] Thus wrote the man who was scarcely, if ever, alone, father of an ever-growing family, professor and rector of a famous university, author, and, to many, a friend, for he gave himself completely to them all. "Give yourself to everything [*date a todo*]," was a vital part of his message, and in every human relationship he struggled to achieve the sincere, the perfect giving of himself, so that he stood revealed to everyone. In every work, in every letter, in every conversation, his aim was absolute sincerity, for he had an unquenchable *sed de sinceridad* (thirst after sincerity). To Clarín he wrote: "I wish that this could be what it cannot be, absolute . . ." [2]

Such a man is inevitably defenseless for, alas, there are those who do not repay in kind. Countless lives touched his, hence many knew him well—lifelong friends of his childhood: Pedro Eguillor, Mario Sagárduy, Enrique Areílza, and others; friends from other lands who knew him first in his works and were drawn by him, some even to his rocky castle of Salamanca: Professor Warner Fite from Princeton,

[1] Hernán Benítez (ed.), "Cartas inéditas de Miguel de Unamuno y Pedro Jiménez Ilundain," in *Revista de la universidad de Buenos Aires,* Vol. II, No. 7 (July–September 1948), p. 86.
[2] Unamuno, *Epistolario a Clarín,* p. 104.

Professor Everett Ward Olmsted, from Cornell, J. Crawford Flitch, the English translator of *The Tragic Sense of Life*, Jacques Chevalier, Jean Cassou, Waldo Frank, and others; literary friends of his own "generation of '98" in Spain, and last, but by no means least, the companions of his daily life who worked, lived, and communed with him in Salamanca. Many of these are known mainly through correspondence. There is a particularly revealing correspondence with three Basque friends, two of whom, Enrique Areílza and Juan Barco, had grown up with him in Bilbao. Jiménez Ilundain from Navarra was also a Basque, but their paths did not cross until 1897. The devious course of the relations of these three men with Unamuno can be traced in a correspondence which lasted over a period of twenty-five years. Though there are frequent revelations of pettiness and jealousy, there is an underlying element of loyalty, of personal interest, and keen perception which marks some of the letters as valuable epistolary literature. However, what makes them particularly pertinent is their witness to Unamuno's preoccupation with the spiritual growth of his fellow man as well as to his capacity for friendship. Many of the letters also reveal him more completely, not only as a man, but as a writer, for Don Miguel could never for an instant divorce himself from his literary productions. He would often outline an entire book, an essay, or a play in a letter to one of these men, conceived only in his imagination where it was doomed to lie stillborn. Indeed, Unamuno's pen could hardly have produced everything its owner wished even if he had lived a thousand years.

The correspondence between Don Miguel and Ilundain furnishes a particularly rich source of information. After Ilundain's death in Buenos Aires on April 19, 1943, at the age of seventy-seven years, his family made this correspondence available and it was published, annotated by Professor Benítez, in the *Revista de la Universidad de Buenos Aires*. Appearing in the 1948 and 1949 issues of this quarterly, the letters run from 1897 through December 12, 1922—twenty-five of Don Miguel's best years.

Ilundain became interested in Unamuno after reading his first novel *Paz en la guerra* in 1897. He felt immediately drawn to its author; the two had other ties besides their common racial background. His first letter, dated from Callarta in 1897, was that of an admiring reader to an established novelist and is devoted almost entirely to enthusiastic remarks about the novel and an interest in the author, whose basic concerns coincide with his own. "I too am the son of a *choco-*

134 THE LONE HERETIC

*latero,*" he wrote. He is referring to the character of Ignacio in the novel who is the son of the chocolate dealer whose corner store is the scene of those presiege *tertulias.* He is a friend of Zabalbide into whose character Unamuno has woven so many of his own experiences and feelings. Don Miguel was plainly flattered and lost little time in answering the letter. He saw in Ilundain a man of perception who, although a business man, concerned primarily with making money and providing for his family, admitted that beneath his materialistic activities he felt the call of the spirit. Much of the correspondence dealt with Ilundain's spiritual position.

Ilundain became such an admirer of Unamuno that he went to Bilbao to make the acquaintance of his two other close friends. He attended their *tertulias,* where they read and discussed Don Miguel's works. Thereafter, the three exchanged letters in which the common topic was their interest in Unamuno. Through this correspondence some of Don Miguel's most intimate conflicts are revealed.

Both Ilundain and Areílza were confessed atheists but became Catholics before they died. Unamuno who "struggled" for words, as did Jacob with the angel in the desert, died without abjuring a single heresy. Ilundain, in a letter dated from Paris, September 20, 1905, refuted Don Miguel's attempt to prove the existence of God based on the need for God. "As an atheist," wrote Ilundain, "I feel no need to believe in God. You too have been an atheist." [3] A letter from Areílza to Ilundain explained Unamuno's thinking on the subject. "Like Tolstoi, he [Unamuno] supposed to have reached God by way of reflection, by the heart, denying that reason is capable of perceiving him." [4]

In the same letter Areílza evinced a concern for Unamuno's reputation as a writer. Commenting on his habit of thinking aloud, he wrote, "Consequently, his conversation‾ is so pleasant and ingenious that I doubt seriously if anyone in Spain surpasses him. He should by all means go to Madrid, so that they may know him personally and not form a mistaken idea of his importance, as might well happen with those who base their judgment only on such strange works as *Amor y pedagogía.* Not to mention the economic problem, which ever present, would be more easily resolved." [5] Obviously, these three friends followed Unamuno's varying fortunes with proprietary eyes

[3] Benítez (ed.), "Cartas inéditas de Miguel de Unamuno y Pedro Jiménez Ilundain," Vol. III, No. 9 (January–March 1949), pp. 173–174.

[4] *Ibid.,* p. 139.

[5] *Ibid.,* pp. 140–141.

and were no doubt among the avowed *unamunófilos* who rallied around his standard. "As the Tyrians [6] and the Trojans in their day fought a whole Iliad over the corpse of Patroclus, so there has been waged around Unamuno, and there is still being waged, a whole literary storm. In one camp, the Unamuno partisans raise their hero's banner to the skies. In the other, the Unamuno haters treat the poor man scandalously and dare to brand as a heretic and an excommunicant one whom they have never even read." [7] The circumstances to which Areílza referred occurred after Don Miguel's death, but these friends were undoubtedly his first standard bearers.

A rift in the friendship seems to have occurred during the year 1902 which is commented upon in a letter from Ilundain. By this time Ilundain had met Unamuno who had visited him at his own home in Callarta, where they had walked and talked together. At some time during that year Barco visited Unamuno in Salamanca. The topic of their conversation is not specified; it may have been upon some philosophical point. At any rate, Don Miguel must have hurt Barco in some way. Bitter words passed between them which led to an argument. Unamuno emerged the victor. Then, Barco, defending himself by pointing to Don Miguel's numerous enemies, declared, as a parting thrust, that Ilundain, the ever-faithful, admiring friend, had also turned against him. The thrust went home and Unamuno was truly heartsore. Soon after Barco's visit, Unamuno received a letter from Ilundain quoting Areílza as having said that "Unamuno . . . always settles his doubts by believing what is most convenient for him." Since the recent quarrel with Barco was fresh in his mind, Don Miguel naturally attributed this quotation to Barco. Ilundain subsequently cleared up this point and affirmed his own friendship. Unamuno accepted the explanation and the rift was closed.

Even if these three faithful friends were jealous of him at times, they were also jealous for him and anxious that Bilbao should appreciate her author-son. Unamuno, spending his summer there in 1905 after the "Bilbao affair," had been completely ignored by the press. The reason, as Areílza wrote to Ilundain, was that shortly before "in Madrid he talked to a group of journalists and treated them horribly." [8]

---

[6] The Achaeans and the Trojans fought over Patroclus' body in the *Iliad*.

[7] Hernán Benítez, "Unamuno y la existencia auténtica," in *Revista de la universidad de Buenos Aires*, Vol. II, No. 7 (July–September 1948), p. 15.

[8] Benítez (ed.), "Cartas inéditas de Miguel de Unamuno y Pedro Jiménez Ilundain," Vol. III, No. 9 (January–March 1949), p. 175 n.

Unamuno is revealed in these letters as a man who tried to tell
nothing but the truth. He interpreted sincerity as being a constant
confession of himself. As Benítez states it, "Unamuno unamunizes himself by unamuno-ing, that is by tearing out his very insides, by a
constant process of making himself over." He added, "How perfectly
this fits into the existentialist fashion." [9]

When Don Miguel and Concha arrived in Salamanca in 1891 they
were befriended by the family of Don Pablo Beltrán de Heredia with
whom they spent those first few days. There were young people in
the family whose friendship was to prove longlasting. The son, Pablo,
Jr., was a *contertuliano* with Don Miguel in the Casino until that fateful day, the last time that Don Miguel joined his old associates there
to be told that he was not welcome. A daughter in the family was
godmother at the baptism of Unamuno's second child, Pablo.

Among the first friends he made at the University was Don Luis
Maldonado Ocampo who later became rector. "A man of letters and
of refinement," he proved a true friend in spite of differences of opinion which inevitably occurred in almost all of Don Miguel's relationships. Don Luis' son, Professor Francisco Maldonado, testified to this
friendship forty-three years later when, speaking on the occasion of
Unamuno's retirement when the University honored him with the title
of *Rector Vitalicio* (Rector for Life) he said, "The deceased professor
and rector of this university, Don Luis Maldonado . . . with energetic
eloquence preached against the political persecution carried on against
Don Miguel de Unamuno, with whom he did not see eye to eye, but
of whom he was a dear friend and fervent admirer." [10]

It was Don Luis who in 1894 prologued a collection of poems entitled, *Querellas del ciego de robliza,* and his name will always be
linked with Unamuno's in Salamanca, since it was for him that the
poet wrote the first version of his immortal ode "Salamanca." With the
poem Unamuno wrote the following letter dated June 6, 1904:

My dear Maldonado: I am keeping my promise. You will receive this the
same day on which you enter your forty-fifth year, which I hope will be
prosperous and happy. May you double that number and may I live to see
it. Forty-four is a beautiful age. And now to honor you on such a day the

[9] Benítez, "Unamuno y la existencia auténtica," p. 82. The writer has no further
information regarding Barco. The son of Enrique Areílza, José María de Areílza,
was the Spanish Ambassador to the United States, 1954–1960. A street in Bilbao
is named for his father.
[10] *La Gaceta Regional* (Salamanca), October 2, 1934, p. 2.

only thing I can think of is to send you what I composed yesterday praising our Salamanca.[11]

Seventeen years after Don Miguel's death this pean in praise of the city that stands as a "forest of stone that history carved from the heart of mother earth" was set to music by Joaquín Rodrigo and sung as a cantata on the occasion of the VIIth centenary of the founding of the University. In stately metaphors it sings to the tall grove of towers that stands as dark immobile foliage against the sky, even as the dark foliage of the Castilian oak stands motionless in the wind. He saw the golden grain in the fields of Armiño undulate as do the golden stones where, when evening dies, peace sleeps in the furrows. Peace and hope, and memories that ripened through the years in the ancient halls, sleep in calm repose. Oh Salamanca, among your golden stones the students learn to love while your encircling fields yield sweet fruits—and when I die, my golden Salamanca, remember me. And when the setting sun inflames the secular gold that cradles you, with your speech, herald of the eternal, say that I have existed.

On a warm spring day there were two men walking along a dusty lane that led through a field of undulating green grain. The lane was bordered with bright red poppies and blue *tomillo* among which were scattered bushes of yellow broom. The land lay flat around them. Beyond the field they could see an occasional oak tree with its stiffly rounded dark foliage as fixed and motionless as a child's picture of a little tree. The two men were walking rapidly toward the misty mountain range ahead. Though the land was flat, they seemed to be walking on top of a huge ball completely enveloped by a spherical sky that was almost close enough to touch. It enveloped even the mountain range in front while in every other direction both land and sky curved downward together over the edge of the horizon. Though the lane was wide enough to accommodate them together, they were not walking side by side; one, the taller, was going ahead in long determined strides, while the short chubby one took quick little steps that forced him to break into an occasional run to keep from falling behind. Both men were carrying suitcases and both were hatless. As he hurried to keep within hearing distance of Don Miguel's croaking voice that never stopped, the short one shifted his suitcase from one pudgy hand to another. Little beads of perspiration stood on his high forehead that

[11] Manuel García Blanco, "Don Miguel de Unamuno y sus poesías," in *Acta salmanticense* (Universidad de Salamanca), Vol. VIII (1954), p. 51.

met a receding hairline. Stray strands of hair stood up in disarray on his round dome of a head. The little man's face was lined in pleasant smiling lines, and his whole round figure bespoke an inner goodness. He was smiling now in spite of the physical effort the circumstances required. The little man's name was Don Agustín del Cañizo. He had occupied the chair of pathology on the medical faculty of the University of Salamanca since 1905. He and Don Miguel had become almost inseparable. In him Don Miguel had found an attentive listener, a friend whose utter goodness he could trust, as unpretentious and comfortable as an old shoe, yet a man of sound learning and intellectual curiosity. And over and above all of this, Don Agustín loved Spain—the country and the people—as did Unamuno himself.

While Don Agustín struggled with his suitcase he thought of his pleasant *finca*—his little farmhouse in Béjar where they were going now, and the little mountain river where the two would take a dip in the cool waters. Then perhaps they would climb up to the Dominican monastery on the Peña de Francia and forget the immediate worries of everyday living to meditate on God, the nature of God, and man's destiny hereafter. The two often went to Béjar together for, as rector of the University, Unamuno was responsible for the administration of the public schools and the appointment of the teachers throughout the province of Salamanca. Both of the men liked to walk and they always walked from the station to the *finca*, but this was the first time they had had to carry their own suitcases for there was a little old man that usually performed this service. On this occasion, however, when the *viejito* took their bags he had asked in a sly fashion: "And who is going to pay me for this?" "Go on," they said, "nobody is going to pay you for anything." And they started off bravely with their bags. By now they were regretting their rashness, and when a chicken vendor overtook them and offered them a lift they accepted with alacrity. Thus, like Don Quijote and Sancho, they arrived in Béjar. As they were dismounting they heard the chicken vendor inquire of an on-looker: "Who in the world are these two? They've been telling me that one of them was a doctor, and the other, a university professor!" "Oh they are harmless. They've just got a lot of curiosity!" (*Nada, si por ver, no más—unos inocentes.*)[12]

Don Agustín had become the Unamuno's family doctor and spent much time in the *casa rectoral* on Libreros Street. Felisa recalls Don

[12] Incident related to the writer by Felisa Unamuno.

Agustín's pouring over German medical magazines with her father which together they translated into Spanish. Sometimes Don Agustín would ask rhetorically after reading an involved technical description of a case; "And what happened to the patient? Alas, he died!" At which the two would laugh heartily together.

A family man like Don Miguel, Don Agustín lived in Salamanca for twenty-six years during which time, as Professor J. Estella wrote, he lived "close to one of the greatest Spaniards of all time, near Don Miguel de Unamuno, shoulder to shoulder in the University, in the street, in an austere home life, and in the simple diversions of their leisure time; like brothers they followed *la escondida senda* [the hidden pathway] in the eternally marked footsteps of Fray Luis . . . "[12]

There are many photographs of Don Miguel and Don Agustín together that testify to their friendship, and there is one inscribed "Professor Cañizo in the monastery on the Peña de Francia, accompanied by his intimate friends, D. Miguel de Unamuno and Don Antonio Trías (Year of 1924)." That was just before Don Miguel's six-year exile during which Don Agustín visited him in Hendaye where his old friend was ill and discouraged.

In 1931 when Unamuno was in Madrid, Don Agustín took a professorship at the Universidad Central there where he taught until he retired in 1946. The testimonies of his contributions written at that time and published together stress two outstanding qualities: one, his *bondad* (his *humanity*), the other, his friendship with Unamuno; in addition, they stress the basic constribution he made to the development of dedicated doctors in Spain. If Don Agustín had been on the University faculty at Salamanca when that body voted for Don Miguel's dismissal, surely one voice would have been raised in his defense. On the occasion of the good doctor's retirement in 1946 one testimony in his honor was read as follows: "Don Agustín knew real sorrow . . . on the death of his friend Unamuno." [14] Doctor Cañizo learned much from Don Miguel, for he used Unamuno's own words in his own last lesson: "For the purpose of life is to create a soul." [15]

Another long-time associate of Unamuno's in Salamanca was a man dubbed by the local paper as "a republican, socialist doctor"; "a man of rare and interesting complexity," "of radical ideas in politics and

[13] *Libro homenaje al profesor don Agustín del Cañizo con motivo de su jubilación*, pp. 62–63.
[14] *Ibid.*, p. 27.
[15] *Ibid.*

ultra-radical agrarian ideas." [16] He was Don Filiberto Villalobos whose tombstone stands today a few feet from Unamuno's crypt in the Salamancan cemetery. The kind-hearted doctor who ministered to the medical needs of the sisters in several of the local convents was also active in educational circles for he rose to the position of minister of public education. However, his one absorbing interest was agrarian reform, a movement which he headed in Spain. A familiar sight in front of the Café Novelty in the Plaza Mayor was that of Don Miguel and Don Filiberto sitting at a table talking, or walking around the cloistered arcade of the plaza—talking, or standing together on a street corner—talking, always talking. In Don Filiberto again Unamuno had picked a man described as "good," "loyal," "capable of great sacrifice and of unlimited generosity." [17]

Another familiar sight was Don Miguel leading his blind friend, Cándido Rodríguez Pinilla. Cándido was the bachelor brother of a successful doctor of Salamanca, this latter the father of a large family of children that were constantly in and out of the Unamuno home. Though Unamuno knew Dr. Rodríguez Pinilla and his family well (the two families once spent a summer vacation together in Portugal), it was the blind man with whom he had most in common. Intimate glimpses of Unamuno and his relationships with Don Luis Maldonado, Cándido, and others, are afforded by letters written by another man who came to know Don Miguel very well during the period from 1901 to 1903.

Fragments of this correspondence have been published by the University of Salamanca in the *Cuadernos de la cátedra Miguel de Unamuno,* Vol. I–III, 1948, and signed with the initial "M." Some of the letters are to the writer's father in Granada, others probably to his wife. One letter reveals that "M" may have stood for Manuel, and the careful reader might guess that Manuel was a journalist assigned to Salamanca during those years. M's own relationship with the University Rector is as interesting, if not more interesting than anything else. At first M is completely indifferent, then, through daily contact— sessions sometimes lasting as long as five or six hours at a time—hikes along the Carretera de Zamora, or to the nearby town of Alba, conversations over coffee cups in the Plaza Mayor, visits at Unamuno's own home and in the homes of Maldonado or the blind man, his feelings change from indifference to antagonism, curiosity, defiance, and

[16] Name of paper withheld upon request.
[17] *Ibid.*

finally admiration. Beginning with the first letter, and running through nearly every one there are references to "the blind friend of Unamuno," "the blind man of Alba," "the *tertulia* of the blind man and Unamuno."

On November 10, 1901, M writes about hiking along the Zamora road with Maldonado, the blind man, a journalist, and Unamuno, "with Unamuno talking as we walked . . . We arrived [at Alba] a little before dark and spent the whole time talking with Unamuno . . . Finally to the drug store [*botica*], the only place to meet anyone in this village, where I found Unamuno preaching, and another journalist from Madrid, a certain Castell; the rest of us played the role of listeners." [18]

A few days earlier, November 6, 1901, he had written: "I went out again headed toward the Rector's house, and when I turned the corner, I almost ran headlong into him 'body, soul, spectacles, and umbrella'." What followed was a description of what most of his visits with Don Miguel turned out to be: M accompanied U to a café where U took coffee while M and others gathered around, among them, Maldonado. Then the three, U, M, and Maldonado, with a fourth who was a doctor-photographer "went to take the air on a road which I understand is the Zamora road." The conversation must have turned to politics, for M adds that the three others were "long-tailed democrats and republicans, or monarchists, I wasn't quite sure. Back we went to walk in circles around the well (*dar vueltas a la noria* [19]), I mean around the Plaza, and by this time I had had enough, and so we broke up." [20]

November 28, 1901: this time M writes, "Unamuno dominated the conversation but I managed to get a rise out of him, and I found out his secret, his plan . . . he intends to be no less than a Spanish Luther! . . . I contradict him or point out his mistakes, as the case may be, and I think this gets me further than going into him or avoiding him like the plague, which is the way they treat him here." [21]

About Maldonado, M writes: ". . . he is quite a pianist, and besides, a representative to the Cortes (the Spanish Congress). The blind man is very fond of music. Now for Unamuno, music is just a noise that says nothing to him . . . Tomorrow afternoon," he adds, "I have

---

[18] *Cuadernos de la cátedra Miguel de Unamuno*, II, 16–17.

[19] In Spain the blindfolded mules draw water by describing a wide circle around the axis of a lever to which they are hitched. The lever turns a wheel in a perpendicular plane with buckets fastened to the spokes, thus lifting and pouring the water as the wheel rotates.

[20] *Cuadernos de la cátedra Miguel de Unamuno*, II, 16.

[21] *Ibid.*, pp. 17–18.

agreed to go with the blind man to see Unamuno, who has been in bed with a fever since last night." [22]

December 4, 1901: "You probably think that yesterday went by without the Unamuno lecture, well, you're mistaken . . . so here I am, a confidant of our Luther, who, if he errs, I believe it is in good faith and from his misdirected antagonisms and exaggerations, for he has a good noble heart, and high ideals . . ." [23]

He describes Don Luis Maldonado as "a stout, short, young man, alert, over-refined and polite, married to a native Salamancan girl (*una charra de Salamanca*) who is very pretty . . . rich, a farmer, related to all the best people; an ex-delegate to congress (*diputado*) and professor of law: he's not like the people of Salamanca, although he is so pompous and obsequious that he must have some *charra* blood in him. He too is devoted to literature, he writes *charro* stories and has good connections. Very polite to me." [24]

Don Miguel obviously took a decided interest in M. He would read him long passages from *Tabaré* which he said was the best piece of Spanish-American literature ever written, or he would read from his own translation of Carlyle which he was working on at that time. M's father became worried about the influence this man was having over his son, and his son answered: "In your letter today you maintain that Unamuno is crazy, with strange ideas, which I do not deny; but I do deny that his are any stranger than mine, the difference being that I keep them to myself and he proclaims them aloud." [25] M's friends must have waged quite a campaign against Unamuno for he writes: "You know, I believe you have all ganged up against poor Unamuno who has never done anything to any of you." And referring to a third party, M adds: "You should see how wrought up he gets, and how angrily he talks about him [*i.e.*, about Unamuno] and even against me, for the sin of being in his company! . . . And do you know what you gain by all of this? You make me want to be with him that much more, to see if he really is crazy." [26]

And this was the case, for on December 12, M wrote: ". . . while I was in the café waiting for Maldonado, Unamuno came in, invited me to take a walk and there I went, accompanied also by the *médico* [possibly Dr. Rodríguez Pinilla, Cándido's brother], and do you know how long the session lasted? Well, no less than six hours by the

[22] *Ibid.*, p. 18.          [23] *Ibid.*, p. 19.
[24] *Ibid.*, p. 21.          [25] *Ibid.*
[26] *Ibid.*, p. 22.

clock." By now it seems that Unamuno had an inkling that M's family disapproved of him for M writes:

. . . he must have guessed the campaign that you are carrying on against him because he explained the reason for his carryings on [*la razón de sus sinrazones*], the why of his foolishness and crazy doings, the deliberate purpose, so he says, which he has set for himself by making himself appear eccentric and crazy, and that is to make himself known, to make people talk, to run everyone else crazy, so that in that way, once he has prepared the way . . . he can make himself heard and will not pass unnoticed.

This time M writes that he left Unamuno, "with my head pounding." [27]

M's family were not the only ones concerned over this friendship. It seems that the Bishop of Salamanca, at that time Father Cámara, of the Augustinian order, may also have been worried, for he began to seek M out, and on one occasion took him to La Flecha, Fray Luis' famous old country place, and one of Don Miguel's favorite haunts.

Then a visit of Unamuno's to Granada produced a new turn of events. While there Don Miguel became acquainted with M's father who was completely won over. In fact, so complete was the conquest that in September of 1903 M wrote to him: ". . . but you make me tremble for fear you are undergoing a serious mental disturbance . . . for that business of being so Unamuno-ized, much more so than I, from what I gather, is a grave and alarming symptom . . ." [28]

Unamuno and his friend M discovered a common interest which is mentioned only slightly in a letter written by the former to his friend in 1902. The Rector writes of having found two old tablets and offers to draw pictures of them to send to M. Of one of the tablets Unamuno wrote: "It looks to me like something Roman, and I am inclined to think that the markings on the other are not letters but numbers; that they are *tarjas* [ancient Spanish copper coin] from some accounts, some system of accounting on slates." [29] On the twenty-ninth of the same month Unamuno wrote that he was sending M "the three tracings and one drawing done with every care and a great deal of work, because it is necessary to get the paper exactly parallel with the slate, and to look closely for the reflection of the shadow in order to be able to distinguish the markings." [30] This interest in ancient excavations harks back to Unamuno's boyhood days in Bilbao where Don Félix

[27] *Ibid.*, pp. 22–23.
[28] *Ibid.*, p. 27.
[29] *Ibid.*, p. 30.
[30] *Ibid.*, p. 31.

Aranzadi talked of such things in his candy shop on the Calle de la Cruz.

As the patterns on the old Roman tablets emerged through the paper where Don Miguel looked for their markings, so the pattern of his life emerges woven around his family, his work, and his friends. Unless Unamuno was out of town, his favorite haunts outside of his home were the University, and the Plaza Mayor, or perhaps he might be found in the Campo de San Francisco watching the autumn leaves fall as he communed with Cándido who taught him how to listen, he, Don Miguel, who was always listened to; and how to see—the blind man taught him this. "He took me there many times, my soul's brother, Cándido Pinilla, the seeing blind man, to hear the nightingale. To hear the nightingale that sang among the cloistered trees, to hear, above all, the nightingale that sang within us. And to see! He, the blind man, would take me, his *Lazarillo,* to see! [*lazarillo*—leader of the blind] And we would see! We would see beyond the future, that which is beyond all that is to be, and that is what was before everything that has come and gone, what is underneath and above that which is passing, that which enfolds it, the august, eternal form." [31]

The memory of those hours with Cándido in the Campo de San Francisco comforted Don Miguel when, alone, an exile, he watched the autumn leaves falling in the little Parisian park where the statues of Washington and Lafayette are shaking hands. ". . . there, close by in the chapel of the Veracruz, the Dolorosa of Corral eternalizes the expression of superhuman sorrow" . . . in the Virgin whose

heart is pierced by seven swords . . . And when one emerges from the whirlwind of gilded volutes, how different is that calm that comes as one watches the golden leaves falling and whirling among the faded flowers on the ground, the golden leaves of the golden autumn of the Salamanca of gold . . .

Cándido, my friend, the leaves must be falling now in that park of our nightingales. Have you been there to hear them fall? The Dolorosa of the Veracruz hears them falling too . . . And I dream on the future of our Spain and on dreaming the dream of final freedom . . . beneath the sky that lights and warms the soil where lie our dead. Dead? . . . Lafayette and Washington are not dead. Neither are Columbus, nor Fray Luis, nor the commoner Maldonado, nor Father Cámara. And this, thanks to the theater that is history. And in this theater they have invented a surgical anesthesia for the soul, is it not so, dear Cándido?" [32]

[31] Unamuno, "De Fuerteventura a París," in *Nuevo Mundo* (Madrid), September 1924), p. 91.
[32] *Ibid.*, pp. 92–93.

There in the Campo de San Francisco it was the blind man who taught him that surgical anesthesia which he used when the time was come. But the time was not yet, not here in Salamanca where his soul lived its fill of the sweet and the bitter of life.

Should one fail to find him there, or in any other of his favorite haunts in the town, then one could be sure that Don Miguel had left the golden stones of Salamanca behind to "wind up the springs of his heart" with the fresh mountain air—either at Béjar, the Peña de Francia, at Gredos, or perhaps he might be found weekending at the country place of Don José María de Onís. During the early 1900's when Unamuno was in the throes of writing some of his most profound essays and novels, Don José held the position of librarian at the University. He came to know the writing Rector intimately and collaborated on much of his bibliography. One of Don José's sons, Federico, a student at the University, was destined to immortalize the spirit of Don Miguel, that indomitable, fascinating spirit of the Spanish people, in the United States. No Hispanic scholar who studied at Columbia University within the last half century could have failed to feel the fire of that spirit which has inspired both teachers and students of Spanish in many a classroom throughout the length and breadth of these United States. Don Federico de Onís, one of today's most outstanding Hispanic scholars, has taught, written and edited over a period of more than fifty years, while his wife, Harriet de Onís, who collaborates closely with him, is an artist in her own right. Her English translations of outstanding Spanish writings from both sides of the Atlantic are matchless reproductions of content, feeling and beauty.[33]

Back in those early days when Don Miguel was rector, Don José María de Onís owned a country *dehesa* in a rustic community some twenty kilometers from Salamanca. La Granja, as it was called, was located in a primitive setting where the peasants, or *charros* of the province still wore their traditional, colorful dress which today is only a special costume in the cities and towns. The persistence in these folkways and dress of old Castile, of her traditional fiestas and dances,

---

[33] Federico is not the first de Onís to promote friendship between Spain and the United States. His great great grandfather, Don Luis de Onís, was ambassador to the United States from his country during the presidency of Thomas Jefferson, as the unpublished correspondence between these two testifies. Aware of the contribution which the editing and publishing of such correspondence would make in the field of international relations, Don Carlos de Onís (Don Federico's brother) has already prepared the groundwork for such a publication. It is awaiting only the proper collaboration from this side of the Atlantic.

had a strong attraction for Don Miguel and for many others who visited La Granja. Here at La Granja he could see and hear and touch the soul of that Spain which he thought was to be the salvation of the country, the balm of her injured feelings, and the fountain from which her future renaissance would come; this was the salvation prescribed by many of the writers of the generation of 1898. Unamuno, who was the loudspeaker for that generation, here sounded one of the notes that is still echoing in the works of Azorín, Pío Baroja, Antonio Machado, and even Valle-Inclán.

A vivid description of the *dehesa*, La Granja, and Don Miguel's first visit there comes from the pen of Don Federico himself, who, in 1891, was a boy of five when he made the acquaintance of Unamuno, the young professor of twenty-six, newly arrived in Salamanca from Bilbao.

My family owned several *dehesas*, one of them named "La Granja," [The Farm] which was near the town of Garcihernández, a league from Alba de Tormes. It was so named because it had been a farm belonging to the fathers of the order of Saint Jerome in Alba. One could still see that the forester's house, where we used to stay, was made inside the house and chapel of the priests, for the old stone walls and arches were still standing. The old folks preserved traditions from the times of the priests, traditions which they had heard from their parents and the oak tree that grew the best acorns was still called the Prior's oak.[34]

One day, [writes Don Federico] my father said: "Tomorrow we are going to La Granja with Unamuno." It was the first time I had ever heard that name, as strange to me as to everybody else; but I didn't ask who he was for with a child's sense for language by which he effortlessly learns new words every day, I simply thought that it was a new word for me preceded by the article *un*, like *alumno* or something similar, so I awaited the following day full of curiosity to find out what the *amunos* were like.

When he came I saw that he really was a man, but different from others. His physical appearance, gestures, and manners were not like those of the Salamancans; his voice was louder and his expression more open and frank. At that time he had a thick, black beard, but it was short; the same aquiline nose and owlish eyes. What impressed me most of all, as it must have impressed everyone, was that he wore no coat when everybody else was wearing a cape or overcoat, for it was in the fall. Then too, he was wearing low shoes, as in summer, not high shoes, and a soft, black hat, while all the professors or men of the middle class were wearing hard tops—or derby hats. That flexible hat he was wearing was round and of a soft material so that he could fold it up and stick it in his pocket. At other

[34] Federico de Onís, "Mi primer recuerdo de Unamuno," in *Strenae: estudios de filología e historia dedicados al profesor Manuel García Blanco*, p. 375.

times he would throw it up in the air and leave it just anywhere. Neither
was he wearing a necktie and his chest was covered by a waistcoat that
reached up to his neck line. He wore a solid blue suit and looked clean
and well dressed.[35]

Professor de Onís goes on to recall his impression of Unamuno's
physical strength and agility. The party set out from Salamanca on
foot one cold, sunny morning. When they had crossed the old bridge
on the Santa María road, they met the mule-drawn wagon that had
been sent to pick them up. As was customary, it had a protective
covering on top and a rug on the floor of the body with chairs inside.
Unamuno, he writes, refused to get in and sit down with the rest of
the party; instead, he jumped up and sat on the rear end of the wagon
with his feet hanging over. When they had gone along in this fashion
for some distance, Don Miguel jumped off and told the others to go
ahead and he would catch up with them. They proceeded slowly and
after a while, Unamuno appeared running at full speed and jumped
back up on the wagon.

At last they came in sight of the primitive little Castilian community
of La Granja along the banks of the Almar River, a tributary of the
Tormes. From the grove of oak trees on the overlooking hillside one
could see it all—the open fields covered in thyme (*tomillo*), called the
*tomillar*, the grove of ash trees, the little plaza with its white and
black poplar trees surrounded by the old, stone wall, and the hill tops
in the distance, each having its own particular name.

During the next several days of that visit, Unamuno seemed possessed with the desire to see everything, making it hard for the five-
year old to keep up with this strange but fascinating person. In the
evenings they would sit in the open doorways and watch the homecoming calves and oxen waiting to be called by name to eat from
their trough. They saw the flocks of sheep returning over the old
bridge while the thrush sought nesting places in the nearby poplars
and across the evening sky flew the bitterns crying raucously what
sounded like "*a dormir!*" (to sleep).

All of these sights and sounds, added to the hooting of the owls
in the ash trees and accompanied by the nightly chorus of frogs and
crickets—the sights and sounds of Old Castile—made such a profound
impression on the young professor from the land of the Basques that
they became an integral part of him forever thereafter. He listened
to the *charro* songs, watched their folk dances and, naturally for him,

[35] *Ibid.*, p. 376.

kept up a steady stream of talk. However, he was listening also, for
Federico saw him occasionally note down a word or phrase that struck
his ear, expressions which he was to incorporate into his prolific
writings.

Then, of course, the boy Federico, never forgot the little paper dolls
with which Unamuno entertained the children, the *pajaritas de papel*,
theme of his popular treatise on *cocotología*. And, Federico concludes
his reminiscent sketch, "I could see that he had the closest understanding with an old shepherd, old Uncle Claudio, who didn't know
how to read but who had a great deal of wisdom and a sense of humor
that I too admired." [36]

[36] *Ibid.*, p. 378.

# Through Doubt to Faith

> While I live, oh Lord, give me doubt
> and pure faith when I die.[1]

CHAPTER *17*

MIGUEL DE UNAMUNO HAS been called at once "the greatest heretic of modern times"[2] and "the greatest Christian of the last part of the nineteenth and the first part of the twentieth centuries."[3] God alone knows exactly where the truth lies between these two extremes. He has been claimed and proclaimed by many groups which are limited not by boundaries of geography, but rather by boundaries of the spirit. To these he reveals his dualism, his contradictory, many-faceted self, revolving ever about the central problem, that of immortality, hence, God, whose function is to insure for man that everlasting life to which he aspires. Religions are man-made to answer the spiritual needs of different races which must create a satisfactory God. Now the nature of God matters little, for man's image of him necessarily varies. He may be pictured as an old man with a long grey beard, a warrior God as of the Hebrews, or God, the Conscience of the Universe, according to man's needs. What does matter is man's longing for immortality and the faith with which he believes in it.

Living in a world that requires a form and substance for religion and in a country traditionally steeped in the dogma of the Catholic

[1] Unamuno, *Poems*, translated by Eleanor Turnbull, p. 40.
[2] By P. Antonio de Pildáin y Zapiáin, in *Ecclesia*, October 12, 1953.
[3] By Armando Zubizarreta in "Diario," in *Mercurio Peruano* (Lima), (April 1957), p. 188.

Church, Unamuno was naturally expected to take a stand regarding this religion. Such a stand for such a man was obviously impossible. Deep in his roots, buried in preceding generations and before the dawn of consciousness in childhood, his nature was conditioned to Catholicism, yet with the dawn of that consciousness, from the moment when the individual, Miguel de Unamuno, took over, he began to see that there are many paths to spiritual progress, that man-made dogma holds no option on heaven. As a young man he had concluded that *all* are right, the pity being that they cannot come to an understanding. Religion for him revolved around the one and only important problem of man, his immortality, and since this is man's primary concern, Unamuno's every thought and action is permeated with it. Consequently it is impossible to consider any aspect of the man apart from his religion; it was his ever present preoccupation both as a person and as a writer. One can, however, extract from his writings specific statements about his religion, some of them made in response to direct questions—pressured pronouncements—for Catholic Spain demanded them. It is dangerous, however, to draw any conclusions from such statements of his, and only after a careful weighing of his life and works as a whole, should any be drawn.

There is one man who has attempted this: Dr. Hernán Benítez of the University of Buenos Aires. Considering that Dr. Benítez is himself a Catholic priest, his *La crisis religiosa de Unamuno*, is a remarkably unprejudiced appraisal of Don Miguel's religion, his religion *sui generis*, as Dr. Benítez terms it. To quote him further, Dr. Benítez writes that Unamuno's religion seems to spring from negation and from atheism. He concludes, however, by claiming Unamuno for the Catholic Church, in spite of the fact that Don Miguel died without recanting his heresy. The struggle between the heart and the head he makes synonymous with a struggle between Catholicism and Protestantism, at the same time warning that a man who speaks in paradoxes usually means the opposite of what he says: "Quite frequently, Unamuno says what he means exactly backwards. And what he means can only be discovered by the person who has the sense of 'life' which is a mixture of humor and gravity, of teasing and being in earnest, of tragedy and farce, of defamation and definition. He who reads him without this sense will go mad or be outraged, or what is worse, he will take him at his word, which is to understand him exactly backwards." [4] Like Kierkegaard, he was a desperate man, and a desperate man says the opposite of what he means.

Although all of Unamuno's writings may be considered religious, some of them bear more directly on the question than others. These are written either as answers to demands—pressured pronouncements— or as spontaneous outpourings of his deeply religious nature. In the first category, statements written under pressure, belongs his essay, *Mi religión* (1907). A Chilean once wrote and asked Don Miguel just what his religious views were and he answered with the essay, for the question was echoed by a whole nation. Later, during his exile in Paris, came his spontaneous religious expression, *La agonía del cristianismo,* which he related directly with Spengler's *Der Untergang des Abenlandes.* The appearance of this work, written originally in Spanish but published in the French translation of Jean Cassou and retranslated later by Unamuno himself into Spanish, brought forth a general outcry of criticism and vituperation from the Spanish clergy. The lack of understanding and downright ignorance of some of these protestors are epitomized in one priest who objected loudly that Christianity was by no means on its death-bed, and pointed a finger of accusation toward the man who dared write such heresy. Now *agonía* in Spanish has different meanings: *agonía* in the sense of deep distress or soul struggle, and *agonía* meaning the death pangs of the moribund. As Don Miguel subsequently pointed out, this priest's interpretation of *La agonía del cristianismo* as the death of Christianity revealed that he had not even read the book that he was pretending to criticize.

Then there is that desperate poem, *El Cristo yacente de Santa Clara,* the cry of a soul whose hope of salvation is buried in a Christ of dirt and clay—*"tierra, tierra, tierra"*—the cry of one who is confronted with the horror of *la nada.* A refutation of this is that spiritual outpouring of faith, the long religious poem, *El Cristo de Velázquez.* This is perhaps the most beautiful lyrical expression of spiritual faith in the Spanish language.

*San Manuel, bueno mártir* is a short story in which may be seen the religious dilemma of the author himself. It is the dramatic presentation of the same struggle between belief and unbelief, focused in a humble village priest who comforts his people by inspiring in them

---

[4] Hernán Benítez, "Unamuno y la existencia auténtica," in *Revista de la universidad de Buenos Aires,* Vol. II, No. 7 (July–September 1948), p. 19.

the faith he cannot share. Conceived, no doubt, when his faith was locked in a losing battle with his doubt, it should not be taken as a definitive statement of Don Miguel's conclusions on the matter. There remains, of course, his most purely philosophical work, *The Tragic Sense of Life in Men and in Peoples*, based on the premise of man's thirst for immortality. It has been called Unamuno's unanecdoted autobiography.

Religion was the subject of a great deal of his correspondence with his boyhood friends, and it constituted the central topic of correspondence with a certain Nin Frías, an Uruguayan writer with whom Unamuno exchanged letters dating roughly from 1900 to 1920. Uppermost in these letters is the concern for Spanish America and the religion of the Spanish-American countries.

Such are the sources of Unamuno's stated religious views. They must be weighed, however, in the light of the aforementioned warnings, as well as in the light of his practices and habits.

Unamuno was a practicing Catholic with certain periodic breaks which were the outward sign of his inner conflict. The core of his beliefs may be found stated briefly and sincerely in his letters to Jiménez Ilundain. This trusted friend wanted to know Unamuno's beliefs, and as a friend he had a right to ask for them. Writing from Paris on April 25, 1905, he put the question, "What do you mean by the word 'God'?" And Unamuno answered directly and simply: ". . . by God, I mean just what most Christians mean: a personal Being, conscious, infinite, and eternal, who rules the universe. He is its Conscience . . . I believe that the universe has an end, a spiritual, ethical end." The statement is preceded by an unequivocal denial of two frequent accusations: "I am neither an atheist nor a pantheist." [5] Thus, in a letter to an intimate friend, and that one a self-confessed atheist, he states simply and sincerely that he believes in the God of the Christians, in God, the Conscience of the universe, a universe with a spiritual and ethical end. He is not an atheist nor a pantheist. But the question of Unamuno's religion is not that simple. For every such statement of conviction one can find somewhere among his writings what appears to be a direct contradiction. In 1934, two years before his death, Unamuno wrote: "I believe that the world has no end . . . it is we humans who give it a meaning and an end that it does not

[5] Hernán Benítez (ed.), "Cartas inéditas de Miguel de Unamuno y de Pedro Jiménez Ilundain," in *Revista de la universidad de Buenos Aires*, Vol. III, No. 9 (January–March 1949), pp. 171–172.

have . . ." [6] This statement was made in an article written for the publication *Ahora* (Madrid, December 25, 1934), not in a personal letter to a trusted friend. Does it *really* contradict what he wrote to his friend in 1905: "I believe that the universe has an end, a spiritual, ethical end"? For obvious reasons Spanish critics are today attempting to support the Church in its condemnation of Unamuno, hence they cull from his writings those statements which, taken alone, easily prove him a heretic, a disbeliever. Nowhere is Unamuno more discredited today than in his own country. As a young Peruvian scholar wrote in 1957: ". . . there is beginning to appear a wave of passion which threatens to obscure the figure of Don Miguel even more." [7]

That he was a Christian Unamuno stoutly maintained, and consistently, but as for being a Catholic, this he refused to affirm. Perhaps the nearest he ever came to accepting verbally that denomination was when he lightly tossed off an answer to a curious visitor—Unamuno had no patience with *turistas*. When one such prying foreigner asked him about his religion, he answered promptly: "Here in Spain we are all Catholics, even the atheists." Now the Catholic Church assumes the right to define a Christian, hence this self-assumed option on Christianity; not a Catholic, ergo, not a Christian. In spite of attempts of such supporters as Benítez, Catholic Spain has refused to accept Unamuno within the fold. And herein lies the crux of the situation. As he explains in *Mi religión y otros ensayos,* Christ is the measuring line for Christianity and all other dogma is superfluous. Christianity's purpose is to save men's souls for immortality, not to bring better health or better government, nor yet to spread culture. When Christianity under Constantine became Romanized it acquired this worldly aspect and against this social Christianity Unamuno's revulsion knew no bounds. Against "duty" and "justice," two concepts which, with the coming of canonical law, have been introduced into Christianity and are entirely foreign to it, he contrasts "grace" and "sacrifice" which partake of its intimate nature.

What did Unamuno believe about sin and forgiveness? Sin there is—the original sin—and forgiveness God grants freely to all. It is from the idea of original sin that there emerges an inevitable contradiction, the paradox of Christianity. This original sin, Unamuno believed, is the propagation of the flesh. The true, the perfect Christian, must be celibate, and only a celibate can be infallible. However,

[6] Antonio Sánchez Barbudo, *Estudios sobre Unamuno y Machado,* p. 18.
[7] Zubizarreta, "Diario," in *Mercurio Peruano* (Lima), (April 1957).

propagation is necessary for the persistence of the human race. Herein lies "the most terrible part of the agony of Christianity"[8] (*agonía,* remember, he uses to mean conflict, struggle). By way of illustration, Unamuno says that "Paul was a great Christian who did not know woman, and thanks to his continence, he engendered through Christ Jesus in the Gospel, not sons of the flesh, but sons of God, sons of freedom, not of slavery."[9]

He frequently quoted other exemplary Christians, celibate Christians, especially his model, both spiritually and physically, Saint Ignatius of Loyola, and another Spanish priest, Father Jacinto. The latter, a priest of the early 1900's, made a notorious break with the Catholic Church. As Unamuno held reason to be in conflict with life, the head versus the heart, so he held the body and its propagation in the flesh to be in conflict with the spirit. Man's salvation consists in the continuation of life, immortal life.

There are, according to Unamuno, several possibilities of immortality (he would let none escape him): two of them were immortality of the individual, and immortality in one's children. Writing of these two kinds of children, those of the flesh and those of the spirit, he asked: "By which ones will we be saved? Those of the flesh in the resurrection of the flesh [the immortality of the flesh was one he insistently harped upon] or by those of the spirit in the immortality of the soul? Are these not perhaps two contradictory forms of perpetuity?"[10]

Indeed, for one who held that "Virility must be economized"[11] and who as the father of nine children led the fullest possible life in the flesh, the contradiction and consequent conflicts were inevitable. In an effort to conciliate these two contradictory ways of life—the mortal and the spiritual—Don Miguel hit upon a "middle course," really a necessary compromise: "But we can take the world to the cloister . . . and in the midst of the world we can keep the spirit of the cloister."[12] This compromise he attempted to live in a most uncompromising manner. There were periods when, perhaps in order to *economizar virilidad* and to strengthen his spiritual life, Don Miguel would betake himself to San Esteban or the Dominican hostelry on the Peña de Francia, there to mingle with the holy fathers, and join them in their devotions, to say nothing of stirring them up by preaching the propagation in the flesh and thus "taking the world to the cloister."

[8] Unamuno, *La agonía del cristianismo,* p. 126.
[9] *Ibid.,* p. 107.        [10] *Ibid.,* p. 102.
[11] *Ibid.,* p. 106.       [12] *Ibid.,* p. 140.

Torn between the spirit and the flesh, Don Miguel was also torn between Catholicism and Protestantism. Dr. Benítez sees his adult life, the forty-five years in Salamanca (1891–1936) as falling into two periods which coincide with his readings first of Protestant and later of Catholic writers. In the first period (1891–1925) Protestant authors claimed a large part of his attention; during the latter years of his life (1928–1936) Don Miguel felt strongly "the Christian influence of his childhood," and turned more to reading St. Augustine and Clemente Alejandrino. It was during his so-called Protestant period that Unamuno wrote most of his best-known religious works—*La vida de Don Quijote y Sancho, Del sentimiento trágico de la vida, La agonía del cristianismo* and *El Cristo de Velázquez*. To the last period belongs the *Cancionero*. In writing of this Catholic period, Dr. Benítez refers to the "Christian" sentiment of his childhood, whereas in reference to his Protestant years the term "Christian" does not appear. Then as though excusing Don Miguel's lack of enthusiasm for Catholicism even in the last period, Benítez explains that "Catholic orthodoxy found only a tired heart." [13]

Although Unamuno rebelled against any classification, religious or secular, Protestant thinking claimed his attention during the longest period of his adult years, if not most of his sincere convictions. With almost savage vehemence, Unamuno wrote about Catholicism to Ilundain in 1901: "It pains me to see how Christianity is blamed for the pagan element that became a part of it to produce this monstrous hybrid that we call Catholicism." [14] And again in 1902 he wrote that he believed Protestantism could save Spain and added, "the person who says this is one who—prays every night . . ." [15] Gradually, as Don Miguel grew older, his utterances against the established church of his country lost some of their vehemence, though in 1905 he still saw Catholicism as an obstacle to the unification of Spain. Pointing to the political policies of the Catholic Church, he affirmed that, always against national strength in empires, Catholicism consistently encouraged regionalism. The separatist spirit of the Basques known as *biskaitarismo*, "is suffering from what we call the reactionary spirit, but it would be simple to call it the Catholic spirit." [16]

[13] Hernán Benítez, "La crisis religiosa de Unamuno," in *Revista de la universidad de Buenos Aires*, Vol. III, No. 9 (January–March 1949), p. 82.

[14] Benítez (ed.), "Cartas inéditas de Miguel de Unamuno y Pedro Jiménez Ilundain," Vol. III, No. 9 (January–March 1949), p. 118.

[15] *Ibid.*, p. 149.

[16] Unamuno, "La crisis actual del patriotismo español," in *Ensayos*, VI, 152.

He lashed out not only against Spanish Catholicism, but against French Catholicism as well, and praised "that vital and austere minority, the grandchildren of the Huguenots who are the salt of the French religious life," as well as "those noble, profound and saintly Jansenists," [17] whose leader, Pascal, he consistently cites as one of his spiritual brothers.

Unamuno was likewise concerned with Spain's erstwhile possessions in America and their religious tendencies. He felt that they lacked a profound religious expression which, however, need not be in the form of Catholicism. ". . . friendly relations with Spain should by no means indicate the conservation of the Catholic ideal." [18] And again this anti-Catholicism is taken as reason to denounce him as anti-Christian; commenting on the foregoing statement, Miranda writing on "El Pensamiento de Unamuno sobre Hispanoamérica" adds, ". . . The vague sort of Christianity which he advocates, helplessly antidogmatic, antitheological, and—a supremely tragic paradox—anti-Christian, had petered out." [19]

Unamuno, unclassified and unclassifiable, recoiled from dogmatism wherever he found it, among Protestants as well as Catholics, and thus he wrote to the priest, Nin Frías: "Christianity is the goal but stripped of all save Jesus alone." And three years later: "We may cease to be Catholic, we shall cease being Catholic in the orthodox sense of the Roman Church." [20]

However, by 1906, Don Miguel, the existentialist, who had been living his theories with his own characteristic intensity, arrived at last at another compromise. He wrote Nin Frías that he believed a universal Christianity, based on both Catholicism and Protestantism, was in the process of evolving, and in this process both faiths would have to concede something.

Although Unamuno did seemingly turn to the Catholic Church in his later years, the extreme measures implemented by that Church in the Inquisition always rankled deep within him. On March 27, 1928, he wrote a poem voicing a plea for God's mercy on Spain for her "bonfires of the inquisition" that turned love into hatred and the cross into

[17] Unamuno, *Contra esto y aquello,* p. 81.
[18] Angel Alvarez de Miranda, "El pensamiento de Unamuno sobre Hispanoamérica," in *Cuadernos hispanoamericanos* (Madrid), Vol. 13 (January–February 1950), p. 68.
[19] *Ibid.*
[20] Benítez, "La crisis religiosa de Unamuno," p. 71.

a hammer. He called the poem a "patriotic confession of contrition." [21]

The lot of an anti-Catholic in Spain has ever been anything but a happy one. Even the redoubtable Rector of Salamanca began to feel the effects. Who would read the books of a heretic, books that had been banned by the Church, and how would that writer meet the demands of a large family? Was he ceding a point in the struggle, was it in recognition of the strength of the Catholic tradition, or was he at the time truly convinced that Protestantism was not for Spain? Whatever the reason, he penned the following on November 11, 1910, to his American correspondent, Nin Frías: "And that Protestantism is not for us who think in a Latin tongue." [22] Remember, however, a desperate man says things "backwards." Spain and Spanish America would follow the course that history had in store for them, but as for himself, Unamuno followed his own star, "patterning his spiritual course after an erotic hybridization of Protestantism and Catholicism," [23] as Dr. Benítez puts it. Whatever his religion, he found in it, at times, the satisfaction of the ascetic, the near mystic, who like the true mystic, Santa Teresa, seeks God within himself: ". . . rather than searching for one's self, it is better to search for God within one's self." [24] But unlike the sixteenth-century mystic, this twentieth-century existentialist did not lose himself; rather he found himself in God: "God is myself, infinite and eternal . . . for thou art more I than I myself." [25]

The reader will recall the crisis which the adolescent Miguel lived through in Bilbao, an experience which marked the second stage in the development of Unamuno's faith. There followed the years of devotion to science and his socialistic writings of young manhood, the period termed by Laín Entralgo as the third stage in that development. In 1897 after living in Salamanca for six years, before his appointment to the rectorship and one year after the birth of Raimundo, his third child, the little hydrocephallitic, Unamuno suffered the most violent spiritual crisis up to this time. The "discovery" of this crisis is attributed to Señor Sánchez Barbudo, professor at the University of Wisconsin and an eminent Hispanist.

In his book *Estudio sobre Unamuno y Machado* (1959) Professor Sánchez Barbudo gives the details of this crisis as revealed by an

[21] Unamuno, *Cancionero*, p. 37.
[22] Benítez, "La crisis religiosa de Unamuno," p. 71.
[23] *Ibid.*, p. 69.
[24] Unamuno, *Andanzas y visiones españolas*, p. 13.
[25] *Ibid.*

article Pedro Corominas wrote in 1938 based on a letter received by him from Unamuno some fifty years before:

In one letter he explained the crisis to me as a thunderous explosion that struck him one beautiful night. For hours he had been unable to sleep and was tossing restlessly on the marital bed while his wife listened to him . . . Suddenly he was seized by an inconsolable weeping. Then his poor wife, her fear overcome by compassion, held him tenderly in her arms saying: "What is it, my son?" The next day Unamuno left everything and shut himself up in the convent of the Dominican monks in Salamanca where he stayed for three days. Some years later he showed me the convent and the place where he spent those first hours praying, with his face to the wall.[26]

This spiritual crisis had a profound and lasting effect on Unamuno. He referred repeatedly to it in letters to friends and described it in some detail several years later. Even Professor Sánchez Barbudo who refers somewhat flippantly to earlier crises as "chateaubrianesque" concedes his sincerity. He writes:

That Unamuno had at least tried, by his crisis, to recover his faith, he himself indicates in several passages of his letters . . .
Hence, those who accuse him of never really having determined to believe, do not do him justice.

He adds, however, that although after 1900 Unamuno's philosophy of doubt and faith became established, this did not indicate that he had found faith in God and in his personal salvation, as Julián Marías believed, and as "could be actually deduced from some pages from Unamuno." On the contrary, submits Sánchez Barbudo, it seems rather to indicate "that he had no faith at all," and that all of his play with ideas and meanings of words was simply a cover-up "to deceive himself by forgetting that he had been unable to believe." [27]

When Professor Sánchez Barbudo wrote the foregoing he had not read the almost day by day account that Don Miguel wrote for a period of at least one month and probably longer, immediately following this crisis. Before 1957 the only notice of the existence of such a diary was the following reference made to it by Unamuno himself in a letter to Juan Arzadún. On October 30, 1897, he wrote:

But all of this is very long, too long to relate, and perhaps some day I'll let you have the notebooks in which I have been writing down for the past seven months, everything that comes to my mind, whatever I think and feel and discover within myself.

[26] Sánchez Barbudo, *Estudios sobre Unamuno y Machado*, p. 44.
[27] *Ibid.*, p. 46.

I am working from within and inwardly directed more than ever, but I believe that it is my duty to reserve my innermost thoughts, to avoid all exhibitionary airs, to shy away from those who have mere idle curiosity, and not to allow the most treasured part of my experience to be dissipated by publicizing it.

And Unamuno adds: "This darned literary profession fills us with vanity and robs us of our innermost being. Always before the footlights!" [28]

The notebooks that Don Miguel was referring to were lost track of until twenty-one years after his death. Then one day in 1957 a young scholar from Lima, Perú, whose Basque ancestry is patent in his name— Zubizarreta—was going through some of Don Miguel's papers in one of the files of the Casa Museo Unamuno. Studying on a scholarship from Lima, Armando was at the time preparing his doctor's thesis on the topic *Unamuno en su nivola* and while working on this he was living in the Casa Museo Unamuno. By chance his eye fell upon three small notebooks in black oilcloth covering hidden between some papers. On the first page of each one there was a tiny cross. The handwriting was unmistakably Unamuno's; the daily entries were of varying lengths beginning in April 1897. Fortunately, Armando knew their significance. Several days later a fourth notebook, covered and marked in the same fashion, showed up. The last entry of this fourth book was May 28, 1897.[29]

A postcard written to Unamuno by one Leopoldo Gutiérrez, dated January 4, 1898, acknowledges the receipt of five notebooks. Gutiérrez refers to the five books again in a letter to Unamuno from Bilbao dated January 12, 1901. The fifth notebook is mentioned by Unamuno himself in some prefatory notes, hence its existence is established and the search for it still goes on. Although Dr. Zubizarreta has made known his discovery, and described to some extent the contents of the diary, he reports that: "It is lamentable that the text of our discovery must remain unpublished until the research in connection with it is completed, and until its significance can be determined, as the publication of such an important document requires." Unamuno's children, possessors of the document, are considering its future publication.[30]

With reference to Professor Sánchez Barbudo's conclusion regarding Unamuno, Dr. Zubizarreta writes: "Unless he (Unamuno) is taken seriously, I do not believe that further work based on the articles of

[28] Zubizarreta, "Diario," in *Mercurio Peruano* (Lima), (April 1957), p. 182.
[29] *Ibid.*
[30] *Ibid.*, p. 184.

Professor Sánchez Barbudo is possible. There is no work before his . . .
[he makes one exception [31]] that has not been profoundly injured by
his conclusions." [32] He adds that Dr. Sánchez Barbudo has placed
Unamuno's sincerity in doubt, calling him a "radical atheist" and referring to some of his works as mere "rehash." "To avoid hasty and
unsubstantiated judgments," he warns "I point to the existence of this
valuable diary." [33]

Dr. Zubizarreta's pamphlet on "La inserción de Unamuno en el
cristianismo: 1897" is probably the most correct and carefully docu-
mented account of the events leading up to Unamuno's crisis, for he
has the diary as a valuable source. The "beautiful night" which Unamuno mentions in his letter to Corominas, and the critical days spent
in San Esteban, occurred probably just before March 3, 1897. On that
day Father Juan José Lecanda, writing from Alcalá de Henares,
answered a letter of Unamuno's and invited him to spend Holy Week
with him. On March 31 Leopoldo Gutiérrez also wrote to Unamuno
from Bilbao stating that a week before he had received Unamuno's
letter with *"la confesión."* The author of *La inserción de Unamuno en
el cristianismo* concludes that Don Miguel probably started his diary
in Alcalá de Henares a few days before April 14, returning to Salamanca around April 20.

What Don Miguel wrote in that diary consisted of ". . . reflections
of different content, of quite varied subject matter, of different
lengths, many quotations, meditations, at times more explicit than
others, in different tones, but always quite clear . . . all of it full of
a profound intimacy, it gives the impression of a rich storehouse like
the *Pensées* of Pascal." [34] Dr. Zubizarreta specifies further: "in the
diary . . . we learn the why of his estrangement from the Catholic
faith; the permanent thread of a hidden faith; his fear of a 'renown
conversion,' the discords between *entregastas,* mestizos, and neo-
Catholics; the silence of God . . . near the doors on the threshold of
the Catholic Church, having read the Protestant theologians, he defines
clearly the errors of the spirit of the Reformation." [35] Indicating the
harsh self-criticism and the fear of pseudo mysticism that runs through
the contents, the diary's discoverer refers to Unamuno's "apostolic
mission" and submits that "He is the greatest Christian of the latter

[31] Chapter on Unamuno in David García Bacca, *Nueve grandes filósofos
contemporáneos y sus temas.*
[32] Zubizarreta, "Diario," in *Mercurio Peruano* (Lima), (April 1957), p. 185.
[33] *Ibid.,* p. 184.          [34] *Ibid.,* p. 186.          [35] *Ibid.,* p. 187.

part of the nineteenth and the first part of the twentieth centuries." [36]

During the early part of the crisis, the violence of that first explosion had such an effect on Unamuno's behavior that friends were actually concerned for his sanity. Letters that he received from his old friend Mario Sagárduy during 1896 and 1897 indicate that for some time prior to the explosion, Unamuno had had premonitions of the crisis— that there was a precrisis period, designated by Zubizarreta as the "anteroom" of his Christian insertion of 1897 (as he terms the crisis) and which he fixes in the years of 1895 and 1896. Unamuno's age at this time was thirty-one–thirty-two; "possibly they were in some way related, by the loving, symbolic imagination of Don Miguel, with the life of Christ," writes Zubizarreta, an idea which he bases on references from the diary in book one, page eighty, and book two, pages ninety-six to ninety-eight. An undated letter from Mario filed with Unamuno's correspondence for the year 1896 reads:

Dear Miguel . . . I have been wondering this afternoon what kind of a spiritual crisis it could have been to bring about such an enormous change in your life that you only write letters and don't read. Either you are ill, which I do not believe, for I've just seen you really strong, and I think you had become accustomed to your strictly regimented life, or, judging that things are not panning out very well for you, you have gone into a horrible mental attitude. I cannot understand the reason for that withdrawal, which I hope will be temporary.

I consider you too big a person to resort to an unjustified escape, foolish even for you, and no matter what reasons your imagination may have suggested. And I say unjustified and foolish supposing that you might be motivated by the belief that you have failed, for without vanity or, blind selfishness, you know yourself well enough as we all know ourselves more or less, to be perfectly aware of the fact that you have never been more vigorous, nor stronger, nor better intellectually, and to make some comparisons, not petulantly, between your level and that of so many poor fish ("percebe") that are writing in our country . . . You have not only fulfilled all expectations, you have reached that point that only the chosen reach . . .

I don't know whether what I am saying is simply a lot of nonsense that has no bearing on the case, for it may be that your crisis has other causes, and that you hope and I believe it would be better provided it is not serious, that your crisis is caused by illness, not by disgust.

Other letters inquire solicitously after Raimundo's health. In one of them Mario writes, possibly by way of encouragement to his friend's literary career: "If Santander has its Pereda, we have Unamuno."

[36] *Ibid.*, p. 188.

On January 20, 1897, he makes a hopeless reference to the sick child: "It is a calamity about Raimundo. I had hoped for better news. Evidently the recovery is slow."

Mario refers again to the crisis in his letter of April 5, 1897, after the storm had broken:

In a conversation I had with Arriola I found out in part what brought on this spiritual crisis that you told me about. He knows something of what might have motivated it, from letters from his friend Orbe.

For your good, and for the good of many of us who have learned a lot from you I hope that this withdrawal of yours will be only a passing one and so it should be . . .

Many of those who did not know Unamuno personally thought that his "antics" were largely a play for notoriety, and some of his severest critics still hold this view. Such an attitude naturally caused Unamuno a great deal of suffering. He expressed his feelings about this in a now famous letter to the writer Clarín (Leopoldo Alas). At that time Clarín was an established critic and author but not an intimate friend of Unamuno. He had criticized the younger man's *Tres ensayos* in a newspaper article which prompted this letter. Writing of intimate details to such a person, Unamuno attempted an objective approach, using the third person in referring to himself. Following are certain pertinent portions of the letter.

Unamuno is a victim of himself, an *heantonmoronmenos* . . . He spends his life trying to be what he is not and without succeeding . . . When Unamuno says and repeats that one must live for history it is because he desperately longs to live in history, and even when his better side may point out to him the wisdom of it, his worst side pulls him. [In the opposite direction?] Here St. Paul's words apply: "I do not the good that I would, but the evil I would not do." But at the same time it pains him that the changes and attitudes that come from his heart are attributed to the sole motive of a desire for notoriety . . . Unamuno is aggressive and he has the misfortune of scorning too many things (now much less than formerly).[37]

The letter went on to confess that he was an intellectual and that

his anti-intellectuality was even more intellectual. And he would suffer and suffer deeply. After he passed through a crisis during which he shed tears more than once and which would have been pure hell without a wife and children . . . he truly believed he had recaptured his childhood faith, and without really believing, he resumed his religious practices, plunging into

[37] Unamuno, *Obras selectas,* pp. 904–905.

the most routine devotions in order to expose himself to the suggestions of his own childhood. The entire household rejoiced, he saw his mother happy again (she is the only restraining influence that keeps him from writing many things that he thinks); his sister recently out of the convent because of illness, went to live with him, until having recovered, she again took the vow. But he suspected that it was all false . . .[38]

Some years after that crisis, Don Miguel described it in more detail. His own feelings, he wrote, were those of horror that occur

when the idea of death lays hold of us . . . the crisis came upon me violently and suddenly, although today I seem to see its progress in my writings. Its explosion took me by surprise. Then I took refuge in my soul's childhood and I understood the secluded life, when my wife came to me when she saw me weeping and exclaimed: "My son!" That was when she called me son, son. My refuge lay in return to practices that might evoke my earliest childhood, somewhat melancholy, but serene. And even now I still have a feeling that comfort is truth.[39]

Concha offered him comfort in his hour of need and as a drowning man, he grasped it in desperation. Not until he could relive it in memory did he begin to understand, as Kierkegaard understood, that "The good for you is truth." After the storm came the calm and a period of redoubled activity and well-being. The concern of his intimate friends, of Areílza and others, their concern, sometimes a bit scornful, appears in their letters. Dr. Areílza wrote to Ilundain in 1902 and referred to their friend's misfortunes a little cold-bloodedly. He mentioned Unamuno's financial difficulties, the disappointment of getting nothing from his uncle's estate, his slight success as a novelist, and the crowning blow, the birth of a handicapped child. Then it was that he suffered, wrote Areílza, "the frightful crisis that sent him to the threshold of the Holy Eucharist, almost a pathological case." More than concern, the letter evinces jealousy, the jealousy of an unsuccessful writer for the successful author and professor.

Ilundain, on the other hand, expressed the affectionate concern of a sincere friend: ". . . don't ever forget that there is within you a Dominican friar," he warned. "Unless you quickly and completely dominate your mystico-religious temperament, it will finally drive you completely mad." He questioned the wisdom of so much preoccupation with "the hereafter," and advised a little of the *joie de vivre*. To

[38] *Ibid.*, p. 906.
[39] Benítez (ed.), "Cartas inéditas de Miguel de Unamuno y Pedro Jiménez Ilundain," Vol. II, No. 7 (July–September 1948), p. 67.

this Don Miguel answered: "I tell you . . . that I thirst for eternity, and without that nothing else matters. I need that, *I need it!*"[40]

The year 1898 seems to have passed in relative calm, spiritually speaking. It was in January of that year that he had described the first violent crisis. Then a letter in December to the same person contains premonitions of another: "But in the midst of all of this I feel a certain strange sensation of loneliness and abandonment. At times I seem to be all alone while others are mere shadows, spectres that move and talk, I am convinced that I am passing through the real crisis of my life . . ."[41]

With what violence this one broke, or whether it dissipated itself in the minutiae of a busy professor's activities is not revealed, but it seems probable that the storms subsided in frequency as well as in violence. He seemed to be entering into Laín Entralgo's fourth and last stage in the development of his faith, that of ". . . an intimate, agnostic religiosity, more adaptable to song than to theological expression, a doubting agony, and that suffering and antidogmatic Christianity which are testified to in *Mi religión, La fe, El sentimiento trágico, La agonía del cristianismo,* and *San Manuel, bueno mártir.*"[42] Gradually Unamuno was beginning to sound beneath the surface waves, to the steady ebb and flow of the ocean tide, feeling for that intra-history beneath the passing circumstance. In 1904 he wrote: "In the ups and downs of my life, I seem to have come into a period of plenitude, of peace and serenity which coincides with perfect bodily health. Inner peace, the strongest foundation for outer combat. And so I am dedicating myself to the stirring up of spirits, to the awakening of consciences. Gradually I am killing my egoism or my egocentricity, and I seek to perpetuate myself by pouring myself into others. Everything else is added unto me."[43]

Gradually Don Miguel was mustering his inner forces for the "outer combat," a combat which he must have felt coming, and which, when it did come, made all his other vicissitudes seem as naught.

Perhaps the highest expression of Unamuno's spiritual vacillations are epitomized in the following poem, a cry of longing and wonder-

[40] *Ibid.,* Vol. III, No. 9 (January–March 1949), p. 135.
[41] *Ibid.,* Vol. II, No. 7 (July–September 1948), pp. 86–87.
[42] Pedro Laín Entralgo, *La generación del noventa y ocho,* p. 65.
[43] Benítez (ed.), "Cartas inéditas de Miguel de Unamuno y Pedro Jiménez Ilundain," Vol. III, No. 9 (January–March 1949), p. 164.

ment expressed in metaphors that resound with the profound music
of poetry:

> *Fantasma de mi pecho dolorido;*
> *proyección de mi espíritu al remoto*
> *más allá de las últimas estrellas;*
> *sueño de la congoja;*
> *Padre, Hijo del alma;*
> *Oh Tú, a quien negamos afirmando*
> *y negando afirmamos,*
> *dinos si eres!*
> *Quiero verte, Señor, y morir luego . . .*[44]

> Phantom of my suffering breast;
> projection of my spirit to the remote
> beyond the last stars;
> dream of anguish;
> Father, Son of my soul;
> Ah Thou, whom we deny affirming,
> whom denying we affirm,
> tell us whether you exist!
> I long to see you, Lord, and die then . . .

[44] Unamuno, *Poesías*, in Miguel Oromí, *El pensamiento filosófico de Unamuno:
filosofía existencial de la inmortalidad*, p. 148.

# The Professor

You, as you pass, your very self must sow,
not looking back, not looking on death's strife,
lest the past weigh upon the path to go.

In you no movement, in the furrows life
whose breathing passes not as clouds but rife
with works, whose reaping is the self you sow.[1]

CHAPTER 18

FEDERICO SAT IN THE MIDDLE of the classroom. He was wearing his overcoat and would have liked to remain wrapped to the ears in his woolen scarf, but scorned to do so. Gloves, too, would have felt good to his aching fingers as he buried them deeper in his pockets. He shivered as he glanced through the frost-covered windowpane, a shiver not altogether from the cold for something like anticipation stirred him. The other students were huddled on their chairs; some, in groups, were talking in hushed undertones and others sat alone, leafing through their Xenophons. The class would start in five minutes and all the students knew that as the cathedral bell tolled eight-thirty, Don Miguel, the professor, would stride into the room, plant himself squarely before them and—but from that point on none tried to predict what would happen. They were entering the second week of the new semester. This was a class in first year Greek, and as yet no mention had been made of a grammar text, but every student had a copy of Xenophon. During those first days when the professor's rasping voice had begun to read aloud the stirring lines, first in Greek and then in the Spanish translation, they assumed that he was simply giving them an introductory glimpse of the language as they would probably come to know it in the future,

[1] Unamuno, *Poems*, translated by Eleanor Turnbull, p. 153.

after the stern grammatical exercises which, no doubt, lay ahead for them. Surely today, Monday of the second week, the grammar grind would begin.

One more minute left. The old clock on the wall ticked loudly and the huddled groups of students moved to break up. The cathedral bell struck—one, two for the half-hour and then the eight steady strokes. Federico counted them, and even as he counted, he heard the steps on the stone-paved patio below. Worn smooth, those stones, and Don Miguel loved every one of them for they imparted love rather than learning. This patio was austere, forbidding and cold to many but as Don Miguel remembered the blessed Fray Luis de León who had pondered there on the mysteries of Job and the Prince of Peace he seemed not to feel the cold breath of Gredos. Here, Cervantes too had found temporary peace to which he had longed to return that he might "dream with you the dream of life, dream the life that is eternal and never die." [2] Here in Salamanca, Don Miguel, the new-born Don Quijote, longed to live forever, to live in his students whose expectant faces were waiting for him even now. And he must stir them, must make them feel his restless spirit and must impart to them that thirst for life so strong within him. This was his chance for immortality, perhaps his only chance. As that feeling possessed him, he entered the classroom. He burst in like steam escaping from a boiling kettle. The steam poured from him as he strode forward. Before he could reach the dais he began: "Years after you have left the benches of my classroom, most of you will have forgotten the doctrines which I may teach you, but you will never forget me." [3] And Federico de Onís never did! Many years later in America, remembering Unamuno and this Greek class, he wrote: "The most extraordinary thing about Unamuno's class . . . was the impact of ideas in all of their fullness, colored with the feelings which men of this temperament lend them, so stirring and vivifying the young souls which they touched as to produce spiritual crises of the healthiest and richest nature." [4] He had begun the class on the first day by reading to them a short selection from Xenophon which he translated into Spanish. Then he explained the alphabet, pronouncing each letter carefully, and he reread the selection picking out and explaining the pronouns. The second day, using the same selection, he

[2] Unamuno, *Obras selectas.*
[3] Unamuno, *Contra esto y aquello*, p. 140.
[4] Federico de Onís, "Unamuno profesor," in *Revista hispánica moderna* (New York), (October 1934), p. 78.

had called their attention to the forms of the words and their interrela-
tionships, keeping always the thought of the entire passage before
them. It was always very orderly, very clear.

That period from eight-thirty to ten passed quickly. Indeed, the
whole year passed and not once did the Professor mention grammar.
Yet by the end of the year the students were reading Greek, and what
pleased Don Miguel even more, they were thinking and arguing
heatedly among themselves. Often they would not have noticed that
the period was over if the beadle had not put his head in the door to
say, "Señor professor, it's time." The Professor would stop as abruptly
as he had started, sometimes even in the middle of a sentence.

Unamuno had taught only Greek during his first years at the University. Then in 1900 he had been named rector of the University of
Salamanca by the royal decree of the Queen Mother dated on October
26. General dissatisfaction with the administration of Mamés Esperabé
who had filled that position since 1869 and was no longer able to
maintain peace among the fractious faculty was hinted as the reason.
Heresay has it that after Unamuno's first faculty meeting there was no
doubt in anyone's mind as to who would run the University, and the
students knew they had a philosopher rector when he said in his first
formal speech inaugurating the session of 1900–1901, "The present is
the effort of the past to become the future, and what does not look to
tomorrow should stay in the lost yesterday."

Besides the new rectoral responsibilities, Unamuno had acquired the
chair of comparative philology in Latin and Spanish, and his hands
were definitely full. Fortunately his new position brought new living
quarters as well, and the Unamunos moved into the rectoral home
adjoining the University on Libreros Street. He installed the office in
the large hall on the first floor of his home from which he had a
private door leading to the University.

Don Miguel enjoyed philology even more than Greek. The class
lasted only one hour. The students used their dictionaries in the classroom where they analyzed selections of neo-Latin literature in verse and
in prose, for Unamuno did not force the students to study outside the
classroom. Books and materials were expensive, and many a poor student learned much from the Professor. There were others, alas, of
whom the opposite must be said, but the Professor was comprehending even of those. One such, a lazy boy, who had scarcely opened a
book, asked for an interview with Don Miguel just before examination

time. Evidently Unamuno conducted at least a part of his examinations orally, as is the custom of most professors in Spain, and interested visitors were also welcomed, for the boy said:

"Look, Don Miguel, I take my examination tomorrow. *Naturally,* I don't know a word, and I find it quite right that you should fail me; but I want to ask you a favor. My father is coming to Salamanca just to attend my examinations. The poor man believes that I am a true Hellenist. I wouldn't want to disillusion him and for that purpose I have come to ask you to call on me for a lesson we agree upon, and which I will learn like a parrot tonight. Afterward, you ask me other questions: I won't [be able to] answer, you fail me in all justice—and I can tell my father that I was confused?"

The plan struck don Miguel as ingenious, and intending perhaps not to question the boy any further, he benevolently agreed to examine him on a set subject: lesson seventeen, for example. The time to examine the boy comes, and Don Miguel says:
"Let's see, now, recite for me—lesson seventeen?"
The student shrugs his shoulders and says evasively:
"I don't know it."
For a moment Unamuno checks his memory—yes, without doubt, it was lesson seventeen they agreed on. Nevertheless, timidly and kindly, he asks in a low voice:
"Wasn't it number seventeen?"
The boy answers:
"Yes, sir, but since my father didn't come—" [5]

As the foregoing incident actually happened the unnamed student is surely one among the many who never forgot his professor of Greek. Another who recalls Don Miguel as a teacher writes that often he would get to the University in the mornings at eight-fifteen to spend the fifteen minutes before class talking to the students as he promenaded slowly around the second floor corridor of the patio. He would either talk familiarly with them or read some article he was currently writing, but he would brook no interruptions and few questions, for Don Miguel always demanded complete attention. If the session proved interesting he would sometimes resume it in the same place after class. [6]

One day in Greek class a boy was translating the passage from Acts of the Apostles in which Paul talked in Athens about the resurrection of the dead. The student must have made some gesture of disbelief for

[5] Bernardo Villarrazo, *Miguel de Unamuno: glosa de una vida,* pp. 71–72.
[6] Fray Albino, "Datos para una biografía," in *El Español* (Madrid), April 4, 1950.

Unamuno asked him: "Don't you believe such things?" "Not I," was the answer. "Well, I do," retorted Don Miguel, and the translation proceeded.[7]

The Professor did not try to undermine the faith of those young students; he seemed at times to go out of his way to strengthen it. On another occasion the students noted that a distinguished-looking gentleman was awaiting the Professor as he left the classroom. On the following day their curiosity was satisfied, for Don Miguel told them in class that he and Señor Azzati, a *diputado radical,* had visited the cloisters of the old cathedral together where Unamuno had commented on some figures carved on one of the old tombs: "That figure in the center represents Christ, the Savior."

"But, maestro," exclaimed Azzati, "do you believe in Christ?"

"I do," answered Don Miguel, "and you?"

"I don't," said the *diputado.*

"And for what reason, may I ask?" questioned the Professor. The answer was: "Just because I don't."

"Ah, well," replied Don Miguel, "if that reason convinces you!"

The Professor reported this with a gesture of scorn for the *señor diputado,* and added that only idiots, not men who think, are unconcerned about religion, about the problem of eternity.[8]

Unamuno, the professor, was never disassociated from Unamuno, the father, or from Unamuno, the writer. One day he read to his class an article he had just completed for *La Nación* in Buenos Aires, and he prefaced it by saying: "My little girl ran into my office the other day and asked: 'Papa, how many horns does an earthquake have?'" The article he read must have been as far-fetched and as disconnected as his daughter's question, for at the end Don Miguel said: "After reading this article, there is surely someone who will say: 'There is no doubt about it; Don Miguel is crazy.' And I was never saner than I am now. I get good money for these articles."[9]

A favorite topic of his in the classroom was Socrates and the owl and the children who tormented the owl. He would say: "The owl is wise, he can see at night. Children are foolish."

Once he outlined to the students an idea of his for a play. It was the plot for *La venda* which was eventually written and produced in Salamanca: a blind woman regains her sight after an operation, but she cannot find her way home—not until she replaces her bandage

---

[7] *Ibid.*          [8] *Ibid.*          [9] *Ibid.*

(*venda*). Then, with the help of her little stick, she goes straight home. "The bandage over the eyes of reason," he concluded, "is so that we may see better." [10]

Unamuno's rectoral duties covered a variety of activities. He acted as a school superintendent for the entire province of Salamanca which carried him to Alba, Béjar, and other neighboring towns where he was called on not only to appoint the teachers and supervise the proper administration of the federal schools, but to speak on many occasions and to enter into numerous community activities. The welfare of his own university students was his constant concern, and the students gave him no little worry for, as is common in European and Latin American countries, they often intervened actively in local politics. In the year 1903 some of the Salamancan students had intervened too actively, and what began as a fracas with the mounted *guardia civil* ended in tragedy for two of the boys. The commotion took place on the street between the University and the entrance to the cathedral. Hearing the noise, two students leaned from the second floor windows to watch. In the turmoil, during which a student was killed in the street, a stray shot also struck and killed one of the two boys at the windows. The other watcher was Federico de Onís. A policeman on horseback had come into the patio of the University and was about to urge his horse up the stone steps to the second floor when Don Miguel placed himself in front of the horse and, with arms stretched wide, shouted: "I am the rector." The policeman got no further, though he retorted insultingly: "You think you are God Almighty!"

But the Rector didn't spend all of his time fighting the local police. Administrative details and an ever-growing correspondence kept him busy in his office. Often he would go straight home from his classes to answer letters which came daily from all parts of Europe and America. Each letter received a careful answer in his own handwriting. The Rector had little use for a secretary nor did he ever use a typewriter. Such second-hand methods seemed to him to be tawdry and artificial. His own hand must hold the pen that traced his spirit's indelible portrait upon the pages of history. History, he thought, is God's dream of man on earth, and the present, this struggle of the past to become the future, must be engraved in words of fire, living words. Thus pondering one day, the Professor almost flung himself back across the patio and rushed headlong into his office. He went

[10] *Ibid.*

172                                    THE LONE HERETIC

straight to his desk and began to answer, one by one, the pile of letters
stacked neatly before him. They were from France, from Argentina,
from Mexico, and some, written in English, even from the United
States. Each he answered in the language of the writer, for Don Miguel
knew many tongues.

The last letter he wrote this morning was to his revered old professor, González Garbín. Now blind, Professor González Garbín still
taught at the Universidad Central in Madrid. His letter to his former
student echoed the cry of grief from all Spanish hearts which were
shocked by the tragic suicide of Angel Ganivet with whom Don Miguel
had felt such a close kinship during those anxious days spent in Madrid
while he waited for his first university appointment. Professor González Garbín had taught Ganivet, as well as Unamuno, and his letter
expressed the sorrow of a father for a beloved son.

This letter still fresh in his memory, Don Miguel took up his pen to
write his daily contribution to the Madrid *La España moderna*. Rarely,
if ever, did his works refer directly to his occupation as a professor
and rector at Salamanca. Today, as he sat musing upon the great
teachers who had stirred his soul in his youth, the image of another
beloved professor, Don Lázaro Bardón, came to his mind, recalling
the touch of that beneficent spirit whose influence still worked within
him. Then he remembered another sincere teacher whom he had
learned to revere long ago through his works—Walt Whitman, that
great North American. These two, Bardón and Whitman, had been
completely serious and sincere and, perhaps, therein lay the secret of
their power. Unamuno recalled that he himself had often been accused
of being too serious. Feeling his kinship with these completely sincere
men, he began to write his article entitled "Concerning a letter from
a teacher."

"I have written a great deal, but it may be that if my name is remembered," he wrote, "my spirit, or that part of the common spirit
which has been entrusted to me, will continue to live, after I am dead,
thanks to that obscure and patient work of one being on another,
thanks to my students scattered throughout Spain and outside of
Spain . . . In my class I have always tried . . . by means of that method
of teaching, to awaken my students' spirits and impart to them an
appreciation of the serious, the profound and the classical . . ." He
continued writing about "that silent labor of teachers who pour our
souls into it." [11] He had tried to be like Don Lázaro Bardón who "was

[11] Unamuno, *Contra esto y aquello*, pp. 138–139.

not a professor of Greek, but a real man, and he will never fade from my memory." Indeed, the personal man, not the professor of Greek or of philology, impressed himself upon his students with every gesture and tone of voice.

As Don Miguel ceased writing, he became aware that the outer office was filling with people. He could hear their anxious feet shuffling on the stone floor. He rose and flung open the door. The interviews started, most of them one-sided for, as usual, Don Miguel *llevó la batuta* (held the baton). The visitors disposed of, he once more closed the door and went back to his desk. From the drawer he took some scribbled sheets of an article which he had started the day before. This he must finish in order to get it in the noon mail to Buenos Aires. He wrote two articles daily; this one for *La Nación* in the Argentine capital and the other for the Madrid newspaper. He wrote swiftly and steadily, rarely stopping to reread. As he finished the second article, he signed his name and carefully affixed the place, Salamanca, and the date, November 4, 1904. Thus ended the morning routine but never did he cease his teaching for he was as much a teacher as a man—the time or place mattered not. "Every man," he once wrote, "should be warrior, priest, and teacher and there is nothing worse than to separate these three functions . . ." [12] The teacher in Unamuno was not the least part of him.

There were some among his students who were as eager to learn as he had been in his youth. They were not content to sit at the master's feet for only one hour a day. Among them the boy, Federico de Onís, perhaps already dreaming of America, had expressed a desire to learn English. "Of course," exclaimed Don Miguel heartily when he knew of this, "we will read English at my home tonight." So Federico, with the other boys, had started coming to his house every evening. Don Miguel would take turns with them reading aloud and discussing the masterpieces of English literature, for he believed enthusiastically in what has been hailed since as the "modern" Great Books system. What method of teaching languages could be more "direct" than Don Miguel's?

Unamuno's teaching was not limited to languages and those who came to learn from him were not all students at the University. One evening a young priest visited him in his home. He was deeply troubled by the conflict of his heart with his reason. The source of his disturbance, as he revealed, was the influence of Nietzsche. He was

[12] Unamuno, *Andanzas y visiones españolas*, p. 177.

caught in the "claws" of this philosopher, as Don Miguel put it when he described him later. Into his hands, Unamuno placed copies of such writers as Sabatier, Harnack, Hatch, and, also, of another thinker, Loisy—a French priest who had been excommunicated for preaching a National Religion—with whom he had become only recently acquainted. Ilundain had introduced him to Loisy's ideas and Don Miguel had requested his friend to send him the principal works of this author. Ilundain had sent them and Unamuno, finding them good, had given one to the young priest. The seed must have fallen on fertile ground for writing of it later to Ilundain, Unamuno said that besides being accused of stirring up a revolution in the spirits of the young, "I am even accused of having perverted priests . . . beginning with him [the one caught in Nietzsche's clutches]. I have come to be looked upon as the spiritual director of several young priests who feel the Catholic faith slipping from them." [13]

As a professor, Unamuno had other duties which carried him to Madrid, to the Ateneo, the brain center of Spain. He evidently enjoyed this part of his work as much as, and probably more than, his administrative responsibilities. He was often called upon to address an assembly of scholars at the Ateneo. In his first speech, delivered there on November 13, 1899, after he had already held his professorship in Salamanca for eight years, he evidently felt that he had been slighted, for his opening remarks clearly indicated this. In order that they might not think he considered this occasion to be too important, he read them something he had already written, something from "my unpublished works." With these preliminaries, he launched into his favorite topic; reason versus faith, taking Nicodemus' questioning of Jesus as the point of departure. "Economics furnishes the mainspring of life and religion furnishes the motive for living. The motive for living, this is everything." As always, he came to the "final cause," of which he said, "to achieve it constitutes the essence of all religion . . . What is the purpose of the whole universe?" he asked. "Such is the enigma of the Sphinx; he who fails to solve it, one way or another, is swallowed up . . . When reason tells me there is no transcendent purpose, faith answers that there must be one, and since there must be one, there shall be one. For faith is not so much creating what we did not see, as creating what we do not see. Only faith creates." [14]

[13] Hernán Benítez (ed.), "Cartas inéditas de Miguel de Unamuno y Pedro Jiménez Ilundain," in *Revista de la universidad de Buenos Aires*, Vol. III, No. 9 (January–March 1949), p. 165.
[14] Unamuno, *Obras selectas*, pp. 879–880.

PLATE I. Don Miguel among his books at No. 4 Bordadores Street. *Courtesy of Cándido Ansede, Salamanca.*

PLATE II.  The mirador (top right) of the Unamuno home in Bilbao,
and the old Jugo farmhouse in Ceberio, across the mountains from Bilbao.

PLATE III.   Unamuno as a boy.   *Courtesy of Fotógrafo Ansede, Salamanca.*

PLATE IV.  Unamuno—college days.
*Courtesy of Fotógrafo Ansede, Salamanca.*

PLATE V.　Unamuno, the professor.
*Courtesy of Fotógrafo Ansede, Salamanca.*

The Southern home of Don Miguel and Concha in Salamanca, overlooking San Francisco Park.

PLATE VII. Photographs of Unamuno's Portuguese friends, on the bookshelf of his study at the Casa Rectoral, Salamanca. *Courtesy of Foto Guzmán Gombau, Salamanca.*

PLATE VIII. Don Miguel's study in the Casa Rectoral, and a collection of his paper creat (*pajaritas de papel*) displayed on its wall. *Courtesy of Foto Guzmán Gombau, Salama*

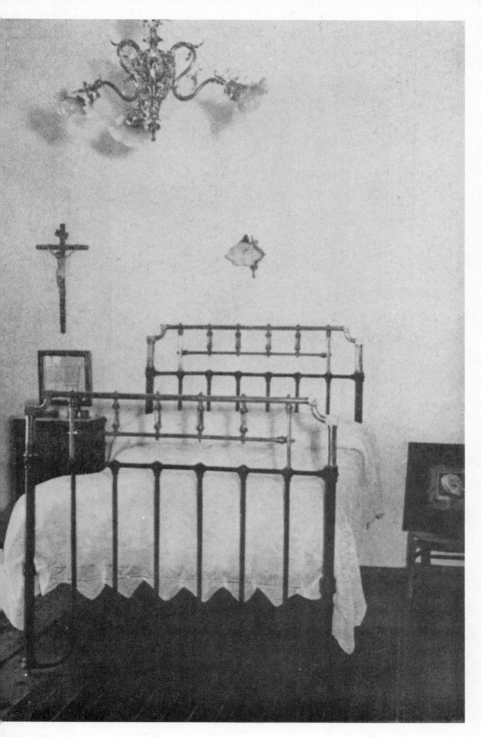

PLATE IX. Unamuno's bedroom. *Courtesy of Foto Guzmán Gombau, Salamanca.*

PLATE X. Unamuno at foot of stone stairway
leading from University patio, Salamanca.
*Courtesy of Fotógrafo Ansede, Salamanca.*

PLATE XI. Portrait of Unamuno, the Rector.
For this portrait, which was painted during
the years of exile, the artist added Don
Miguel's head to a body modeled by another.
*Courtesy of Foto Guzmán Gombau, Salamanca.*

EL S.D. MIGUEL DE UNAMUNO 1900-1914

PLATE XII. Hotel Broca, where Unamuno roomed during his exile in Hendaye, France; and Ursulas Street in Salamanca, leading from Unamuno's home to San Francisco Park.

PLATE XIII. The exile: above, in Hendaye (in his favorite position for reading), and, below, at St. Jean de Lux. *Courtesy of Cándido Ansede, Salamanca.*

PLATE XIV. On the left, Felisa and Rafael de Unamuno in Salamanca in 1959, and on the right, Don Miguel and Miguelito. *Courtesy of Cándido Ansede, Salamanca.*

PLATE XV. Felisa de Unamuno and Doña Pilar Cuadrado in the garden at No. 4 Bordadores Street, 1959.

PLATE XVI.   Miguel de Unamuno y Jugo.
*Courtesy of Cándido Ansede, Salamanca.*

Sometimes Unamuno drew upon his experiences as a professor and as an administrator to furnish subjects for his writings. Two short sketches which are included in *El espejo de la muerte*, "The Diamond of Villasola" and "Why Be That Way?" reflect circumstances which had parallels in his own life. "The Diamond of Villasola" is the story of a teacher who made the mistake of using his students for his own glory. Obviously Don Miguel was examining his true motives for teaching. In the sketch a brilliant student, the diamond, was a complete failure and his teacher, who had felt a personal pride in his brilliance, had not realized "that it may be more feasible to extract light from the potential heat stored within the black lumps of coal, than to snatch life-giving heat from the diamond's light which is merely a borrowed, reflected light." [15] In "Why Be That Way?" Unamuno wrote with pity and scorn of a man who was known among his friends as an "easy mark." He lends money readily but is never repaid, for he considers it too delicate a matter ever to remind his debtors of their duty. He was undoubtedly describing himself and an unhappy incident which occurred during the early years of his rectorship.

Sometime early in 1902 a deficit of 12,000 duros was discovered in the funds of the Liberal Arts School. Over a period of fifteen years, the money had been leaking gradually into the pocket of the *Oficial Primero*. At once, the Rector had authorized an advance payment of 5,000 pesetas to cover the deficit. As soon as the guilty man was identified, Unamuno summoned him to his office. In a letter to Ilundain in which he does not mention the man's name, he wrote, "I tried to straighten him out. I called him to the office. I gave him a time limit." Instead of trying to repay his debts, the man left town only to be arrested in Madrid. He was returned to Salamanca and was finally put in jail. Unamuno had trusted him to the extent of 5,000 pesetas of the University's funds and had to replace this amount from his own meager earnings. This was more than he earned in two years and made it necessary for him to redouble his literary efforts.[16]

These sketches and, in fact, all his other works were directed to the reader who must be awakened. It has been said that Unamuno made all of Spain his classroom, but since his material was life itself, the walls of his classroom have extended to include the whole world.

[15] Unamuno, *El espejo de la muerte*, p. 106.
[16] Benítez (ed.), "Cartas inéditas de Miguel de Unamuno y Pedro Jiménez Ilundain," Vol. III, No. 9 (January–March 1949), p. 129.

# The Reader

CHAPTER *19*

SHORTLY BEFORE HIS DEATH
Don Miguel bequeathed his library of four thousand volumes to the
University of Salamanca. In 1946, ten years after his death, this institution turned over a part of the Casa Rectoral at number eleven
Libreros Street to Don Miguel's children. That same year they moved
from the house on Bordadores Street into this house occupying all but
the first floor whose spacious reception hall was reserved for the University's use. Here on the second floor of the Casa Museo Unamuno
they installed his library, his study, and their parents' bedroom just
as they had been during his lifetime, and here lives Felisa Unamuno,
the loving guardian of her father's books. "All of this," writes Don
Manuel García Blanco in the *Cuadernos de la cátedra Miguel de Unamuno,* "is the property of Don Miguel's children." [1] Blazoned in stone
above the entrance of the building are the combined symbols of Castile
and León—castles for the one, and lions for the other. Within, hanging on the stone wall opposite the entrance, is a heavy tapestry em-
broidered in medieval heraldry, a cold and formal greeting indeed.
The steep stone stairway that leads from the left to the second floor

[1] *Cuadernos de la cátedra Miguel de Unamuno,* Vol. I. However, the whims of
a dictator government are unpredictable. Moreover, the antagonism of the Spanish
ecclesiastical forces as demonstrated in their repeated condemnation of Unamuno's
works, as well as of the memorial exercises planned for him by the University in
1953, render this a somewhat insecure security.

is equally cold and forbidding, but once one is past the bare reception room at the top of the steps and into Don Miguel's library, the chill of impersonality ends. The spirit of the man breathes forth from the somewhat heterogeneous profusion of books and photographs that line the four walls of this room. An old-fashioned wicker-bottomed chair rocks gently in the cool spring breeze that comes from the open window behind it, and the newly sprouted leaves on the old grapevine that entwines the iron railing outside speaks of new life. The round wooden arms of the rocker seem to say: "He was reading here just now and has just passed through that door on your right into his study." We hesitate to disturb him and our attention is caught by a glass case on the long heavy table in the center of the room. Reality intrudes itself when we realize that the plaster cast of that right hand within the case, its strong rather fleshy fingers extending from the hand that rests palm down is Unamuno's writing hand that has been idle these twenty-three years.

With that hand he wrote the scrawled lines that hang on the wall to the left of the entrance. They are framed on a yellow printed greeting from the Jefe del Centro Provincial de Telégrafos of Salamanca to the Director de la Gaceta Regional. The greeting is dated "Salamanca, August 21, 1931." On it Unamuno wrote the following:

(1) In 1901, thirty years ago, I came to inaugurate the session as rector, and I did it, as was the custom, in the name of S. M. [His Majesty] the King.
(2) And I continued inaugurating sessions for thirteen consecutive years, except the one of 1904, twenty-seven years ago, which [blurred] to inaugurate it.
(3) Culture is one and universal, unity is imperial, and universality is etymologically equivalent to catholicity.
(4) It is that Spain which we are continuing.
(5) On the coat of arms of this house are featured lions and castles and that is because this region was half Leonese and half Castilian. Leonese was spoken at the gates of this city and both dialects were fused here.

The centuries drop away while in one's mind beats the ballad rhythm of the lines

> Castellanos y leoneses
> tienen grandes divisiones . . .

A sense of timelessness possesses one and all is wrapped in silence. The clock on the mantel above the fireplace across the room has stopped. Its hands mark the hour of ten-thirty. A somewhat unfamiliar Unamuno looks down from the large oil painting that hangs just above it. It is the work of Zuloaga, Unamuno's Basque compatriot. The man it portrays is more suave and polished than the observer's idea of Don Miguel, but the eyes have his piercing intensity.

On either side of the clock are framed hand-written poems by Unamuno. The one on the right evokes the man in his timeless immortality:

> By the fire my son
> was reading *Quentin Durward;*
> I too read it thus in years gone by
> and thus my grandchildren
> will have occasion to read it some day.
> And thus Quentin lives even as we
> his readers live today.

Here in this room are the books read by Don Miguel, the pages he fingered and turned and turned again to savor the spirits of those who had written. Many of them he knew in their lifetimes, as the countless photographs along the shelves bear witness. There is one of Unamuno himself with two of his students, Federico de Onís and another whose name is not clear. It bears the date "Salamanca, 26 de mayo, 1905." On the same shelf are some honorary medals with a photograph of the recipient; one of them is from "Albert, Roi des Belges" next to a large medal from "The Hispanic Society of America, 1907." Clearly discernible on this one is the following inscription: "Blessed are those whom genius has inspired. They are like stars. They rise and set. They have the worship of the world but no repose."

One of the underlying qualities of genius is energy, and of energy Unamuno seemed to possess an inexhaustible supply which allowed him no repose. Here in this library are the seeds that took root within his fertile spirit to blossom in the multiplicity of works that flourished in his life and writings. Written in ten or more different languages his books touch on practically every field of knowledge. Indeed, as one of his critics writes, "He seems to have read everything of importance in philosophy and history, ancient and modern."[2]

Since, as Don Miguel himself wrote, "Each man can be judged by his favorite books,"[3] and since there has probably never been another writer whose readings were so completely integrated into his life and works, Unamuno's tremendous reading scope renders the biographer's

---

[2] Miguel Romera-Navarro, *Miguel de Unamuno,* p. 31.
[3] Unamuno, *Obras selectas,* p. 860.

task well nigh insurmountable. However, one can feel the spirits of these many writers working in his spirit, for they are reflected in his many-faceted self, and therein lies his originality. Once he was accused of writing what already had been written, and he countered by saying that originality consists in the manner of presentation, rather than the substance of a thought. Though he often used quotations in his books, Don Miguel expressed himself not only on the subject matter, but also on the purpose of his reading. He was concerned primarily with achieving immortality if possible, and sought in other authors a confirmation of an existence after death. However, like all scholars, he often read simply to gain information, to satisfy his insatiable curiosity. "This, my incurable plurilaterality of attention, this spirit of curiosity about everything that happens everywhere, made me learn . . ." [4]

But Unamuno did not limit himself to the cloistered world of books in his search for information. He often went out into the everyday life of his people and preferred to take part in events rather than read the newspaper accounts of them. During World War I he came across an editorial which stated that one must live from day to day. He exclaimed impatiently "No, no, none of this living from day to day; one must live for the centuries." [5] Neither did he limit his reading to one interest at a time. According to him, a good reader should be reading in varied fields at once. On one occasion he himself was in the process of reading Xenophon, Tacitus, a German work on Christianity, a history by "the great North American historian, Parkman," and the correspondence of Flaubert. In 1933 Don Miguel was subscribing to a Greek newspaper, *Eleuteron Bema* from Athens, primarily to read the column of one Fortunio.

Sometimes he sought information that he might use it as a weapon, even as a soldier uses arms to do battle. In 1902 he wrote that he was studying "positive science" in order to combat it, as did Renan and Strauss. Science was his avowed and challenged enemy and there were no lengths to which he would not go in order to fight it more effectively. This is a revealing fact, for he declared that a man fights hardest against his twin brother because he sees himself in his adversary and because he carries his adversary always within himself. In every Cain there dwells an Abel and vice versa. So strongly did Unamuno feel this that the topic is constantly recurring throughout his writings. He devoted a novel and a play to this subject. He also offered

[4] Unamuno, *Contra esto y aquello*, p. 59.
[5] Unamuno, *Andanzas y visiones españolas*, p. 150.

it as an explanation of his bitterest attacks against his political enemies.
Unamuno detested and fought the hard cold works of science, he hated
and wrote against sociology, because the two were strongly entrenched
within himself. He also read that he might make of his knowledge a
weapon against himself.

Throughout his long life Unamuno returned to reread those authors
whom he had discovered as a boy in his father's modest library. They
were his oldest friends and he would turn again and again to the same
passages in those books. This repetition was, he felt, a form of immortality. But the biographer who goes to Unamuno's books in search of
those markings of a favorite passage which so often reveals the reader's
personality, is doomed to disappointment. The same quality in him
which made him exclaim "I will not be classified" led Don Miguel to
avoid ever marking his books. "It has been said," he wrote, "that one
of the best methods of knowing a person is by the passages which he
underlines . . ." Therefore he never underlined a passage "in order to
remove any footholds for those who may read them later in an effort
to judge me." [6] This, however, was a useless precaution because these
passages are found, almost verbatim, in his own writings.

Of his father's books, there were three authors, Donoso Cortés,
Jaime Balmes and Sénancour, whom he continually reread and quoted.
If one book could be named as the one which most influenced his
character, that would surely be *Obermann* by Sénancour. This source
of inspiration was one which remained with him always, drawing him
constantly to the mountaintops. Sometime in 1911 Don Miguel, in the
company of Jacques Chevalier, Maurice Legendre, and others, went
on a mountain-climbing excursion up the Peña de Francia. Resting
peacefully on its lofty heights, they fell to recalling favorite passages
of literature inspired by the surrounding view. His French companions
recited passages from Leconte de Lisle. Don Miguel once more recalled
his *Obermann*: "There on the peak, enveloped in silence, I dreamed of
all those I could have become but did not become so that I might be
the one that I am . . . and remembered my *Obermann*, my intimate
*Obermann*, this formidable book, almost unique in French literature,
which fed the profound nostalgias of my youth and even of my maturity . . . that unfortunate and obscure Sénancour, of whom I have made
almost a breviary. In this unequalled book is revealed to us the
tragedy of the mountain . . ." There follows a long quotation in which
Senancour speaks of "an impenetrable mystery." "I have felt it, I

6 Unamuno, *Contra esto y aquello*, p. 64.

have felt it thus," exclaims Unamuno, "on the peak of the Peña de Francia, in the kingdom of silence; I have felt the immobility in the midst of changes, eternity beneath time. I have sounded the depths of the sea of life . . . *Obermann* is a soul, a vast, eternal soul like that of the mountain." [7]

*Obermann's* spell only grew stronger with the passing of the years, whereas Unamuno outgrew that of Balmes, the Catalán priest-philosopher from Vich. However, on the celebration of this author's birthday, Don Miguel confessed that Balmes had served as much as, if not more than, any other writer to awaken his philosophical curiosity, in spite of his poor interpretation of Kant, Hegel, Fichte, and Schelling.

Don Miguel stated that he had almost made a breviary of *Obermann*. In like manner, he turned daily to that primary source of inspiration for all Christians, the Bible. The epistles of Paul he knew practically by heart. He used them as a basis for his philosophy, as a source of inspiration for countless essays, and as a shield and a sword in life's struggle.

One of the most valuable documentations of Unamuno's readings, one which helps to pinpoint certain periods in his development is his correspondence with Clarín, whom he had heard lecture at the Ateneo during his student days in Madrid. These letters date from May 28, 1895, to May 10, 1900, and are written, some from Bilbao and others from Salamanca, to Oviedo where Clarín was teaching at the Instituto de Oviedo. On April 3, 1900, he wrote:

The enormous amount of philosophy that I devoured when I was preparing for my *Oposiciones* [this places it as the period immediately preceding and including 1891] . . . is now bearing fruit. And, by the way, the matter is of little importance but I recall that I quoted Bergson some two years ago, though I don't remember where. Now [1900] I am much concerned with religious studies, the great *Dogmengeschichte* of Harnack opened broad horizons for me; now I am studying the latest evolutions of Lutheran theory with Ritschl at the head. It is difficult for me to feel Kant, though we may come to comprehend him, because we haven't gone beyond Luther . . . And here, except for Canalejas the Elder, Protestant theory has held no interest. We are lucky to be acquainted with Renan. Perhaps now someone will begin to acquire a taste for Sabatier (not the one of San Francisco, but the other one), Menegoz, the two Revilles, et cetera. And the ones who know the least about all of that are the priests. It is pitiful to read those who pass for the best, Father Ceferino . . .[8]

[7] Unamuno, *Andanzas y visiones españolas,* pp. 25–26.
[8] Unamuno, *Epistolario a Clarín,* p. 82.

This letter reflects all too clearly the circumscribed readings of his compatriots and explains in part why he read so few contemporary Spanish authors. When one of his Argentine readers questioned the fact that Don Miguel scarcely ever mentioned any of these writers in his daily article in *La Nación*, he answered with some scorn that he rarely read them because he knew them so well and, he asked, why read what he already knew? He criticized the widespread frivolity and superficiality of his compatriots. Of these he excepted only the poet Díez-Canedo from such censure and gave as his reason this writer's high moral character which he believed lent much to his writing. Consistently he looked for the man behind the idea rather than the idea itself. In writing of Kant, Hegel, or Schopenhauer, it was always the man Kant, the man Hegel, or the man Schopenhauer, rather than the philosopher with whom he was concerned. Hence he recommended the correspondence of Flaubert rather than his novels.

Clarín himself was an exception to his lack of predilection for his Spanish contemporaries, and even in his case it was during his younger years only that Unamuno read this author. Addressing him in a letter May 9, 1900, Don Miguel wrote: "You have been, in large part, one of the educators of my mind. When I was still a young man of twenty or twenty-one years old, back in Bilbao, how often have I not discussed you and things of yours!" [9]

One other author can be said to have influenced the life and philosophy of Unamuno perhaps as much as *Obermann* and the Bible: Soren Kierkegaard. In the letter to Clarín of April 3 Unamuno wrote: "Now that I can translate Danish-Norwegian or Norse-Danish I am going to dive into that theologian and thinker Kierkegaard, the principal source of Ibsen." He mentions Brandes' book on Ibsen, "which is where I began to learn Danish (a very easy task, since I know German and English.)" [10] Actually it was in 1902 that Don Miguel really discovered the mad Dane, and so strong was the affinity of these two that he wrote of having taught himself Danish "in order to read above all one man, Kierkegaard." [11] In the works of this writer Unamuno recognized his own thirst for immortality and his own infinite God who was beyond man's understanding and hence must be accepted on faith alone. In him he saw too the paradox of Cain within Abel.

Unamuno read carefully and critically other great religious writers— Spinoza, Pascal, Phillips Brooks, and countless others—struggling al-

[9] *Ibid.*, p. 84.        [10] *Ibid.*, p. 82.
[11] Unamuno, *Contra esto y aquello*, p. 59.

ways to absorb the personality of the writer into his own. It was in this sense that he often referred to "eating" books. They were as well digested as any food and nourished his mind and soul, where their authors lived again in him. As though consciously trying to make them come alive, he would repeat their thoughts and refer to them familiarly as "Blaise" Pascal, "Felipe" Brooks, or "Guillermo" James. As he, Miguel de Unamuno, struggled to live in posterity, so he made others exist in him and take on new meanings and hence new life.

In selecting foreign authors to read, he would usually pick the ones least-known outside of their own countries and, as already noted, he even went so far as to learn a new language in order to know a man whose ideas caught his imagination. The French philosopher Jacques Chevalier described him as *"Ce grand Europeen, qui a appris toutes les langues de l'Europe pour lire dans le texte Pascal, Shakespeare et Leopardi, Goethe, Kierkegaard et Dostoievsky . . ."* [12]

After reading Wordsworth, Unamuno wrote, "I must confess that one of the things most influential in making me saturate myself with Wordsworth is that he is rarely quoted outside of England, and above all, that the French, who know English literature, feel a certain aversion to him." [13] Unamuno was prejudiced against all things French, especially French Catholicism and French philosophy, although he had a deep admiration for Pascal and Rousseau. Of all the Frenchmen whom he despised, Voltaire produced in him such a bitter revulsion that he seldom even mentioned his name. Unamuno's repeated harsh statements against his northern neighbors caused Ilundain to question his motives. Whereupon, in an impulsive but sincere confession, he wrote Ilundain that he was really jealous of the importance given the French by the world at large. He was fighting for Spain and was jealous for his own people.

Among the authors of romance literature, Unamuno preferred Cervantes and the Spanish mystics. He read the Italian poet, Carducci, and the works of Spanish Americans like Juan Zorrilla de San Martín, Domingo Faustino Sarmiento and José Asunción Silva. Lamenting the suicide of the Colombian poet, Silva, he attempted to explain the tragedy partially by the poet's reading. Silva probably read Schopenhauer, Taine, and Baudelaire, he conjectured, to the exclusion of the nine-

[12] From a speech delivered by Jacques Chevalier at the University of Grenoble, 1934, when Unamuno was awarded, *in absentia*, the degree of *Docteur "Honoris Causa"* by that institution, in *Cuadernos de la cátedra Miguel de Unamuno*, I, 11.
[13] Unamuno, *Contra esto y aquello*, p. 59.

teenth century English lyricists. "And it was a pity," he concluded, "because certainly if he had known them . . . so superior in comparison to French lyric poetry, fundamentally logical, sensual, and cold, he would have found other tones." [14] Unamuno knew and admired especially the English lyric poets of the nineteenth century: Cowper, Burns, Wordsworth, Shelley, Lord Byron, Tennyson, Swinburne, Thomson, Keats, Christina Rossetti, and the Brownings. Browning, he said, entertained him even though he found him a little confusing. He also knew well the literature of the United States and admired profoundly the North American poet, Walt Whitman.

Unamuno took his concept of life from the great thinkers of all nations and from all forms of literature. He held their ideas, one by one, up to the brilliance of his own critical mind, like a jeweler who examines a diamond for flaws, before he absorbed them into his intimate being. And when "the books are hushed, and the spirits of the poets, the thinkers, and the scholars are sleeping," his moving hand writes their fears, their doubts, their faith blended in his own soul's crucible.

[14] *Ibid.*, p. 38.

# The Writer

"The writing hand moves on . . ."

CHAPTER 20

It is nighttime in my study.
Profound solitude; I hear the beating
in my heart's troubled breast
—it feels alone, the mark, the victim of my mind—
and I hear my blood
whose low murmur
fills the silence.
It is as though the liquid
thread of depside fell deep.
Here, at night, alone, this is my study;
the books are hushed;
my oil lamp sheds its
peaceful glow upon my pad,
like the sanctuary's glow;
the books are hushed;
the spirits of the poets, the thinkers
and the scholars are sleeping.
Death seems to hover over
me with cunning mien.
I turn from time to time
lest it lurk there,
in the darkness I search
for its tenuous shadow.
Angina, youth and such
come to my mind; I reached
the age of forty, two years since.

The fear that silence holds
*it* for me now is overpowering;
silence and shadows
and I think: "Perhaps
when moments hence they come
announcing supper
my body pale and cold
will greet them.
—The thing I was, this that waits—
like those books, stiff and still,
the blood ceased flowing,
freezing in the veins,
my breast quiet at last,
bathed in the gentle oil's warm light,
funereal lamp."
I tremble to end these lines
lest they become strange testament
or rather mysterious foreboding
of the shadowy beyond
that longing for the
life eternal dictates now.
I end them and yet live.

He penned these lines on New Year's eve sitting here at this table
in this room just off the library. Even now they hang framed above
his empty chair on the wall where he turned to search for the visitor
that finally came on New Year's eve of 1936. Unamuno's large,
straight-armed chair, its back and seat of heavy Spanish leather, faces
the square *camilla* where he worked. This is a sturdy table of wood
built around a wooden frame below, whose rounded center hole still
holds at times a copper brasier with fresh glowing coals to warm the
feet, or, failing these, a small electric stove that serves the same purpose. Heavy dark blue curtains draped around the square *camilla* hide
this device. Facing his chair on the opposite side is a similar chair for
the visitor. On the table top is an old, worn, black folder containing
a blotter and some personal papers. In the center is a thick piece of
glass on which stands a glass inkwell, a penholder that contains a
polished section of bamboo, a seal with the initials, M. de U., a small
black lacquer Japanese box divided into four compartments holding
among other knicknacks a tiny stamp of the Virgin; in a wooden file
box there is another hollowed out bamboo section neatly corked at
the end, a large wooden letter opener, some old envelopes and a picture postcard of the cathedral at Huesca. Another large black folder
lies across the table in front of the opposite chair. In it are several

letters to Don Miguel, one from a Señor Gill in Cataluña congratulating Unamuno on a talk he made in 1931 on the Catalán problem, and some photographs of his famous *pajaritas*. Outside the open window on the left Unamuno's famous grapevine winds its gnarled old trunk among the balcony's iron railings as it wends its persistent way around the outside of the building. Both its age and its persistence inspire respect, but it is Unamuno's poem, "La parra de mi balcón" (The grapevine on my balcony) that makes it famous.

From the painting on the wall directly behind Don Miguel's chair Unamuno, the real Unamuno as he must have been, bespectacled and hatted, looks constantly down over his own shoulder as he writes at his *camilla*. The artist, Vázquez Díaz, in 1920 caught the spirit in the body of the man.

On the wall to the left of the window is a small photograph of the Unamuno family just below a painting by an anonymous artist. Beyond the window is one of Don Miguel's own paintings that dates from those early days when he studied art with Lecuona in Bilbao. It is a tavern scene of two men drinking at a table. Below this is a photograph of Don Miguel and Concha taken in Salamanca and dated January 31, 1916. Most of the wall space opposite the library door is occupied by an open bookstand with five shelves containing all of his own published works and their translated editions. In the little open folder before his works are the photographs of his six Portuguese author friends, another of the Argentine author-president, Sarmiento, and a peculiar object of interest, a strange, small roundish formation. Is it? Yes, it looks like a petrified human embryo or brain. Beside it in a little album are more photographs, all of Don Miguel, ranging from boyhood to old age, with many empty spaces where the pictures have been removed. A silver plaque mounted on wood hangs on the wall to the left of this stand. It reads:

Al "Dr." D. Miguel de Unamuno
La Sociedad "El Sitio"
Bilbao
5 de septiembre
de 1908.

It was that summer that he was summoned from Portugal on the death of his mother—the same summer that he delivered that nostalgic speech at El Sitio, recalling the Bilbao of his boyhood. A fitting souvenir, this plaque, for his study.

To the right is the door leading into the bedroom, and there on the wall just left of the door hangs a large glassed-in wooden case in which are mounted some dozen or more of Don Miguel's animal-shaped *pajaritas* and three of his own pencilled sketches, one a profile view of Concha. On either side of this are two more of his poems, and above is the strangest and most arresting of all the Unamuno likenesses. It pictures him, a boy of some twelve or thirteen. The shape of the head is triangular, with the chin an inverted apex, the head is over-sized, the ears sit out at an unnatural angle, and the eyes reflect an impenetrable brooding. The expression of the mouth and chin is willful, even sulky, while the shapely etched eyebrows above the straight prominent nose are the only indications of strength in the overall impression of weakness. One could almost imagine it to be Raimundo if the little hydrocephallitic had lived. Surely this could not be Unamuno the writer!

To picture the man, Don Miguel, as a writer, is one thing. To write a criticism of his works is quite another. However, the man and his writings are so closely intertwined that the task of differentiation is impossible. For him, the word was life, and the writer became his works, while in turn he was recreated by them. Don Miguel was to his writing as a person who sits between two mirrors is to the infinite number of images reflected in them—an unending series of self images. To produce these images and thus attain immortality in space, as well as in time, was the impelling desire which drove him to write. When he wrote to Ilundain concerning his desire for immortality, underlining syllable by syllable, *lo ne-ce-si-to* (I need it), he was writing with the earnestness of a man who would not leave a single stone unturned in his struggle to achieve it, and writing was, for him, a most important stone.

This "use" of his writings for a personal end Don Miguel frankly admits: "We, the writers, are those who, for our use and satisfaction, create heroes, and there would be no egoism if there were no literature . . . To be a hero is to be sung!"[1] A word picture of one's self, he says, impresses itself more strongly upon the reader than any photograph, and this is what Unamuno tries to do: to live in his readers.

> When you think me quite dead
> I shall tremble in your hands
> I leave you herein my soul—book,

[1] Unamuno, *El espejo de la muerte,* p. 153.

> Man, the real world,
> When all of you vibrates,
> It is I, reader, who vibrates in you.[2]

Now this intense self-interest was founded on life, springing from self-compassion and increasing into an ever-widening circle which finally encompassed others. This love for others forced him to action for others, to influence them by his writings. As Marías puts it, "the personal being cannot be impersonal—and the personal being loves, thus he acted upon others, and his writings were prompted by love."[3] And who were these people whom he felt impelled to move? First and foremost, his people, his *pueblo*—Spain. Though Unamuno's scope and interests were universal, he believed in strong nationalism; universality through a strong individuality. Outside of these, there are only vague generalities. And just as with individuals, so "A nation needs to conceive the idea of why it exists; it must feel its ideal of acquiring consciousness of itself; and this consciousness is incarnated in a political organization."[4]

Yet another reason, at once incidental and practical, wedded Don Miguel to his pen, a reason of which he repeatedly and somewhat apologetically reminds the reader—the financial reason. In the midst of a short story where he seems a bit hard pressed for a subject—is it any wonder that a harassed rector and constant writer should betray occasional lags?—Don Miguel inserted the following: "(Do not forget that I am a university professor, and that thereby my children eat, although sometimes they lunch on a lost story.)"[5] The fact that the Spanish-American publication to which he contributed paid him better than the Spanish press explained, in part, his copious writings for the former: "Although I and my children do not eat from what my pen produces, we sup from it, and aside from the fact that over there, on the other side of the ocean, my work is much better recompensed, they allow me much more liberty and in addition, the public responds more."[6] And again ". . . I, who in what concerns my pen, live more

[2] Prologue by Julián Marías to Unamuno, *Obras selectas.*
[3] *Ibid.*
[4] Hernán Benítez (ed.), "Cartas inéditas de Miguel de Unamuno y Pedro Jiménez Ilundain," in *Revista de la universidad de Buenos Aires,* Vol. III, No. 9 (January–March 1949), p. 117.
[5] Unamuno, *El espejo de la muerte,* p. 154.
[6] Angel Alvarez de Miranda, "El pensamiento de Unamuno sobre Hispanoamérica," in *Cuadernos hispanoamericanos* (Madrid), No. 13 (January–February 1950), p. 53.

off of America than Europe . . ." [7] And to Ilundain in 1901 he wrote:
". . . for in addition to being more rewarding financially, that public
wins me over . . ."

Don Miguel's thoughts flowed smoothly and swiftly, in bold handwriting, as his nimble fingers guided the pen across the waiting
*cuartillas*. And once on paper, they were rarely reread on the spot, and
never rewritten. Yet, paradoxically, he was not an improvisor, for he
was not given to sudden inspiration. His thoughts were rehearsed time
and again, examined as carefully as a stonecutter examines a precious
gem, and held up to the penetrating light of conversation, for it was
by means of his constant monologue that he first processed them.
"Unamuno perfected his works in contact with others. It was his way
of thinking." [8] Thus writes Professor de Onís, and it was thus that
Unamuno "made" his literature. During his daily walks he was never
alone, and he was forever trying out his ideas on his listening companions. How many an unsuspecting visitor has been the carbon for
the rough copy of a book, an essay, a poem, perhaps! His lectures and
public addresses, often read, for he was not a natural orator, had likewise passed the test, either of a conversation, or his other processing
method, a personal letter. Don Miguel's correspondence reads like an
intimate conversation in which the nuclei of his works appear repeatedly amended, explained, and criticized. Occasionally an idea or plot
is revealed which never saw the light of publication, as in the letter
written to Ilundain from Salamanca on December 23, 1898. Relating
in detail the plot of a play on which he said he was working, he
explained that it was "the conflict in a spirit which wishes to grow
without succeeding, between the attraction of glory and the love of
inner peace." Then quoting the very lines with which he planned to
end the play, he exclaimed, "It is the divine embrace of love and
death, the embrace of peace in the agony of death . . . Peace, peace,
peace!" [9] And writing to the same friend in 1904, Unamuno gave him
a summary of another essay which was in the making: "Now I am
preparing another on forgiveness, maintaining that the only just thing
is forgiveness. If all men would convince themselves that there is
another life and that all of us will be saved and will enjoy eternal

[7] Unamuno, *Contra esto y aquello,* p. 60.
[8] Federico de Onís, "Unamuno íntimo," in "Cursos y conferencias," *Revista del
colegio libre de estudios superiores* (Buenos Aires), (July–September 1949), p. 252.
[9] Benítez (ed.), "Cartas inéditas de Miguel de Unamuno y Pedro Jiménez
Ilundain," Vol. II, No. 7 (July–September 1948), p. 85.

bliss, no matter how we live, we would be better. The certitude of final pardon takes us further away from sin more than the fear of punishment. Belief in hell has made many sinners." [10]

Writing from Salamanca in March 1898, he gave Ilundain a sketch of another essay: "My very dear friend:—It is a condemnation [an essay titled *El reinado social de Jesús* on which he was working at the time] of war and militarism and all the barbaric sentiments which national exclusivism engenders . . . The superman of which poor Nietzsche dreamed, is nothing more than the Christian who is not fashioned." [11]

The nucleus of Unamuno's best known work, *The Tragic Sense of Life in Men and in Peoples,* first conceived by him as an essay titled *Tratado del amor de Dios,* is obvious in the following letter which he wrote on December 7, 1902, nine years before the first partial publication of that masterpiece:

Spinoza, in proposition VII of Part III of his *Etica* says: *Conatus quo unaquaeque res in suo esse perseverare conatur, nihil est praeter ipsius rei actualem essentiam.* Yes, the effort with which each thing tries to preserve its existence is its very essence. If I were convinced, as I am of a mathematical proposition, that the day of my death marks the end of my individual conscience, if under the ruins heaped up by my reason, no vestige of faith in the immortality of the soul remained to me, my spiritual life would have died . . . And I must proclaim what Kierkegaard calls irrationalism. Not only does one end up by believing what suits him, as you say, but it should be this way, and only peoples of faith persist. [12]

Still working on his *Tratado del amor de Dios* which was eagerly awaited by Ilundain, Areílza and Barco, Unamuno, in a letter dated 1904, further developed his theme of *The Tragic Sense of Life*:

. . . with logical arguments one comes to nothing more than the idea of God, not to God himself. And that idea is a hypothesis, and as such a hypothesis very slight, since what cannot be explained without Him, cannot be explained with Him either. Neither in science nor in metaphysics is God necessary. But I believe in Him because I have personal *experience* of Him, because I feel Him working and living in me. [13]

Unamuno "made" his literature carefully, talking it, thinking it, until he was ready to write it. As for the references to the ideas of other

[10] *Ibid.,* Vol. III, No. 9 (January–March 1949), p. 165.
[11] *Ibid.,* Vol. II, No. 7 (July–September 1948), p. 173.
[12] *Ibid.,* Vol. III, No. 9 (January–March 1949), pp. 146–147.
[13] *Ibid.,* p. 172.

authors with which his writings are replete, except where he uses
quotation marks, they often appear redressed, for he clearly stated
that he turned them over and over again in his mind until they became "his own flesh," hence they flowed naturally and inevitably from
his pen: "Unamuno reads something (not much now) he meditates
more, he reflects, and then what he has made his own flesh pours
forth of itself."[14] Since he never took notes he usually depended entirely on memory: "But as I am wont to do, I read books without
taking notes, and then I think back through them and let them rest
and finally I write what comes from me without remembering in what
form I read it."[15] Thus in the process, all thoughts became his own,
for they proceeded directly from his innermost soul, from "the entrails
of the soul," as he often said. The forms in which he clothed them were
varied: short stories, novels, essays, plays, literary criticism, and poems.
He even planned to write a volume of sermons, an idea possibly taken
from Kierkegaard's example. Besides these, he made numerous translations—from Hegel in his student days, to Seneca, Spengler, and
Carlyle.

One may well ask, what was Unamuno?—an essayist, a novelist, a
poet, or a philosopher? The question has been answered in as many
different ways by different critics, but all agree that first and foremost
he was a man who lived to the full extent of human possibilities, who
felt and expressed a man's overwhelming desire for immortality, and
who so lived that should that immortal life not exist, it would be
an injustice.

Exactly which genre was his best medium is a matter of opinion;
the novel, says Julián Marías; poetry, says Romera-Navarro; the essay,
says a third. Should Don Miguel be called down to settle the question,
he would probably stamp his feet in a fury, toss his old felt hat to the
ground and exclaim: "I will not be classified!" But before he disappeared he just might grin appreciatively at Dr. Romera-Navarro for
in his heart he always wanted to be a poet. He wrote: ". . . *pero al
morir quisiera, ya que tengo alguna ambición, que dijeren de mí: fue
todo un poeta!*" (. . . but since I do have some ambition, when I die
I would like for people to say of me: "He was a real poet!")[16]

[14] Unamuno, *Obras selectas*, p. 908.
[15] Hernán Benítez, "La crisis religiosa de Unamuno," in *Revista de la universidad de Buenos Aires*, Vol. III, No. 9 (January–March 1949), p. 57.
[16] Letter to Clarín written in Salamanca, March 3, 1900, in Unamuno,
*Epistolario a Clarín*, p. 83.

He never wanted to be a critic; throughout his writings one finds scattered deprecatory remarks concerning critics. He looks upon them as men who, for lack of ideas of their own, spend their energies analyzing and evaluating other men's ideas. Critics, he wrote, quoting Schopenhauer, are "those who think in order to write," not those who "write because they have thought." [17] Don Miguel's friends frequently suggested to him that he should undertake more literary criticism. To Clarín, Unamuno admitted that he lacked the courage to tell "the truth about our holy ones," especially the popular novelist, Pérez Galdós, and his own professor, the respected Don Marcelino Menéndez y Pelayo. At the time—in the 1900's—Don Miguel was temporarily at odds with the playwright, Echegaray, and he feared that should he, Unamuno, write the truth about Echegaray's plays, his motives would surely be misunderstood. Hence he wrote infrequently and usually disparagingly about his countrymen, exercising his keenest critical faculties upon the writers of Spanish America. Don Miguel's place in the hall of fame is certainly not among the literary critics.

Unamuno regarded the philosopher with almost as much scorn as he regarded the critic, for, as he explained, the philosopher's task of systematizing is limited by reason. The philosopher, like the mathematician, must classify and arrange thoughts according to logic. Unamuno scorned any idea that he had evolved a system—*that,* he said, is the task of any scholar who wishes to arrange my ideas in order. And so it was, for Miguel Oromí, a Spanish Jesuit scholar, has written a systematic presentation of Don Miguel's philosophical ideas. In 1933, just three years before Don Miguel died, some of his friends urged him to write one more work, to be entitled *Summa Philosophiae Unamunianae,* and submit it as an entry for the Nobel prize. But the Grand Old Man retorted: "As for my philosophy, let some other dyed-in-the-wool Unamunist write it, since I am not one. I may be an ego, but I am not an egoist. My philosophy? Bah! They would first have to raise the bibliographic scaffolding and stay on it, for that is the work of erudites." [18] Neither is it among the world's philosophers that he will rest. And as for his plays, they are few and negligible as drama, for it was not the dramatic situation that primarily intrigued him.

Then among the essayists or novelists, perhaps, he will be found. But hold, there is an unusual stir among the poets. Their age old dis-

[17] Unamuno, *Contra esto y aquello,* p. 19.
[18] *Hernán Benítez,* "Unamuno y la existencia auténtica," in *Revista de la universidad de Buenos Aires,* Vol. II, No. 7 (July–September 1948), p. 34.

pute has broken out again, stirred up by a new arrival who insists that all artistic literature is poetry, be it novel, essay, or actual verse. Poetry, he says, is the mingling of essence and form, even as a liquid takes the shape of its container. Thought, the essence, and words, the style, must be indiscernibly combined. Art, he maintains, is produced by man as an expression of his search for immortality, hence he, one Miguel de Unamuno, is an artist, thus, a poet. Well, the dispute has been in progress for some years now, and in spite of the fact that Byron and Keats are incensed that such an owlish, awkward fellow should presume to take a seat beside them, and others even insist on sending him below to "exchange paradoxes with Shaw," as some writer puts it, it seems that by virtue of his metaphors, he may be allowed to stay in the poet's corner. But, is classification so vital? Must he be classified who so violently resisted all classification for himself? And he resisted it not without reason, for Don Miguel belongs in a class by himself.

Whatever came from his pen, whether novel, essay, play or poem, it was always Don Miguel who emerged, whether in a direct, intimate passage injected like a photograph in the midst of a page, such as, "I, who as the hero of my story, am also professor of Greek . . ."[19] or a parallel situation like the scene from *Amor y pedagogía* in which the wife, in answer to the despairing cry of her husband, comforts him in her arms and calls him "my son." Also, lest the reader, carried on by his interest in the novel, forget the author, a lengthy prologue, sometimes as meaty as the book itself, precedes the whole. Take the following passages from the prologue to this same novel:

In the background of this work there pulsates in effect a certain aggressive and discontent-fomenting spirit.[20]

He seems fatally drawn by the unholy desire to perturb the reader rather than to entertain him, and above all to make fun of those who do not understand the joke.[21]

We cannot explain the fact that being a professor of Greek literature he should take so much care never to mention such literature.[22]

Indeed, all of Don Miguel's prologues should be read, and though he rarely altered a new edition, he never lost the opportunity to insert another prologue, bringing the reader up to date with himself, so to

---

[19] Unamuno, *El espejo de la muerte*, p. 152.
[20] Unamuno, *Amor y pedagogía*, p. 9.
[21] *Ibid.*, p. 10.                    [22] *Ibid.*, p. 11.

speak. In the case of his poems, a favorite device was to insert an explanatory comment in the manner of Saint John of the Cross. Never was an autobiography so clearly apparent in an author's writings. Especially distinct are the agonizing events of his exile years, for it was then that he became truly desperate in every sense of the word. Even in those rare works that seem devoid of such personal reminders, he is inevitably present, for as he explains elsewhere: "Who am I? . . . one of my characters, one of my creatures, one of my agonizers . . ." [23] So obsessed did he become with his identity, the idea of fusing himself with his characters, that he began to feel that they, his creatures to whom he was God, were molding and controlling him. The strange powers of the fictional character over his creator he discussed at length in *The Life of Don Quijote and Sancho According to Miguel de Cervantes Suavedra and Commented by Miguel de Unamuno,* leading up to it with the remark, "unless it be that the hero makes his maker . . . And who made me, then?" he questions, ". . . the hero of my story. Yes, I am none other than a phantasy of the hero of my story." [24] In the novel, *Niebla* (Mist), Augusto Pérez, like the mechanical monster that turns upon his creator to destroy him, like Frankenstein, pays a visit to Don Miguel's study in Salamanca, there to taunt him with the fact that he too must eventually die. ". . . He who creates, creates himself, and he who creates himself dies. You shall die, Don Miguel, you shall die and all who think me shall die. Well, then, let us die." [25]

In this manner Don Miguel struggled that his spirit might live again in the spirits of his readers. Whether or not he has achieved immortality in life beyond the grave, that immortality which none can know and live to tell it, there is no questioning the fact that this immortality in the spirits of others is his. Immortality and God as its source, throughout a lifetime of almost constant writing on nearly every conceivable subject and in as many literary forms as are known to man, this was Unamuno's one idea. It gives finality and unity to all of his writings, coordinating them into a complete whole, rendering them homogeneous in their variety, one in many. The inevitable result is repetition with a certain monotony. However, life itself, and perhaps even eternity is but repetition, as Unamuno and Kierkegaard both said. Wrote Don Miguel: "I am of those who believe that repetition is the only effective thing in life, since life itself is only repetition."

23 Unamuno, *Obras selectas,* p. 1055.
24 Unamuno, *El espejo de la muerte,* p. 157.
25 Unamuno, *Niebla,* p. 289.

Most deep thinkers who have sounded the meaning of life are given
to repeating one idea, as Don Miguel points out:

If one looks well, he will observe that the writers and thinkers who have
left the deepest mark on the human spirit have been in general, men of
very few but very profound and deep-rooted ideas, and that their works
revolve around a few, a very few, fundamental ideas, although these concepts are comprehensive. And there was a reason why Saint Thomas taught
that, as one ascends in the scale of intelligence, one understands the universe
with fewer ideas, until he comes to God, who sees it in one alone: the idea
of himself.

And he concludes: "I have resolved, therefore, always to reduce my
concepts to a few ideas, hence a tendency toward a certain monotony
and repetition of concepts." [26] This repetition he not only made no
effort to avoid, but rather cultivated consciously, often using exactly
the same words, at different times on different occasions, as though
seeking that "eternal return" here and now.

The aspect of his basic idea which impressed itself upon him most
profoundly was life at last, eternal life, the only peace, as a result of
struggle, the constant struggle between the head and the heart—peace
then, from war and in war itself. Hence the paradoxical title of his
first and favorite novel, his "favorite child" as he called *Paz en la
guerra*. Don Miguel used this title, *Peace in War*, for several works
as well as for a part of his long poem, *El Cristo de Velázquez*. In a
short sketch, "Paz en la guerra" which appears in the collection, *La
ciudad de Henoc*, he reminds the reader that he is writing in 1933,
thirty-six years after the publication in 1897 of his novel with the same
title. He begins the sketch with the closing paragraph of the novel, a
paragraph of such profound and beautiful meaning that it bears quoting here: "Only within the embrace of peace that is true and deep
can war be understood and justified; from here we can pledge our
sacred vows to do battle for truth, the only lasting comfort; from here
we determine to convert war into holy work. We must search for
peace only in war itself, in its very being; peace in war itself." [27]

The idea of God is accepted by most heirs of the Western tradition
as well as by peoples of the East. Tons of paper have been covered
with millions of words attempting to express His idea but they do not
necessarily render their authors great. In order to take root and stand
the test of time an idea must be clothed in artistry. Artistry of style

[26] Unamuno, *Contra esto y aquello*, p. 46.
[27] Unamuno, *La ciudad de Henoc: comentario 1933*, p. 80.

is the writer's tool, and in great art, the idea, or content, must be indistinguishable from style. The process of self-penetration and reve- lation is of all processes, the most intimate. Hence the extreme intimacy of Unamuno's literary style. He speaks directly to the reader; his writing is a conversation between *tú* and *yo*. Quickened by imagina- tion, his "conversations" sparkle with figures of speech; the paradox in his prose, the metaphor in his verse. Always his own best critic, Don Miguel keynoted his own writing when he diagnosed the illness of civilization and Christianity as *la contradicción íntima*.[28] Intimacy and contradiction are the keynotes upon which his active imagination plays, thereby relieving the monotony of repetition.

Imagination is at once paradoxical and truth-revealing, and Don Miguel laments the lack of it in Spain.

. . . among these people . . . imagination bores and irritates. They can hardly stand imagination's most genuine product, the paradox.[29]

. . . thinking is a function of the imagination, and observing is too.[30]

Whence comes intolerance if not from the lack of imagination? A person is intolerant . . . because he cannot put himself in the other person's place and see things as he would see them. The great dramatist feels the opposite sides of a question with equal force; the author of a dialogued argument presents first one side of a question and then the other. The greatest imaginations have always belonged to those who have been able to see the basis of truth that lies in the most contradictory ideas. Dogmatic persons are so because of imaginative poverty. A wealth of imagination leads a man to contradict himself in the eyes of the poor in imagination.[31]

*Los dogmáticos* were the targets of his sharpest darts, consequently it was the dogmatism of the Catholic Church that inspired his most outspoken attacks. Going, himself, to the opposite extreme, he rarely penned an unqualified statement. Indeed, throughout his writings there is one word which appears with unprecedented frequency: the little word "perhaps." This *acaso* reflects perfectly his youthful conclusion that remained with him to the end: "everyone has reason." Delving further into the realm of imagination to show its coincidence with tolerance, Unamuno defines it as "the faculty of creating images, and imagination is, in general, the faculty of bringing vividly to mind, as though it were real, that which is not real, and of putting one's self in

[28] Unamuno, *La agonía del cristianismo*, p. 216.
[29] Unamuno, *Contra esto y aquello*, p. 39.
[30] *Ibid.*, p. 40.          [31] *Ibid.*

the other person's place and of seeing things as he would see them . . ." [32]

The Spanish theme of life as a dream is also a product of the imagination: "For the person of imagination, life is a dream, and it is a dream for him because the dream is life, because his ideas take on the reality of living things. The imaginative person dreams, he reproduces, he reconstructs, he appropriates unto himself what he sees and he is enterprising." [33]

The discerning reader will readily see that Unamuno's style was always molded to the nature of the content, as in the ensuing paradox that fits the contradiction between Christianity and civilization: "Christianity destroys western civilization and vice versa. And so they live, destroying each other." [34] The paradox he defines in the following passage so typical of his intimate, personal style; "And I, as the hero and a professor of Greek, know the etymological meaning of that word, *paradox*: from the preposition *para* which indicates laterality, that which goes sideways or is sidetracked, and *doxa,* opinion, and I know that there is hardly any difference between paradox and heresy . . ." [35] His conception of "intrahistory," the spiritual tradition of a people, as opposed to circumstantial events, he expressed in the simple paradox of "the life that passes" and "the life that remains." And again the idea of unity in disunity: "I shall not tire of saying that it is our discords that bind men together, and the intimate discords within each one of us that make us whole and lend unity to our lives, the contradictions of our innermost discords. And, like Don Quijote, it is only in order to die that we finally make peace with ourselves." [36]

Thinking in paradoxes, Unamuno clothed his poetic expressions in imaginative metaphors, fusing the spiritual and the physical worlds in verses that sometimes reached majestic beauty. Such flashes of inspiration he showered generously on his friends, and a personal letter might contain such an offering as the little poem entitled simply, "The sun is setting."

> *En brazos de la tarde el sol se acuesta*
> *en las encinas*
> *que en rebaño apretado lo recogen*
> *con sus copas tranquilas.*

[32] *Ibid.,* p. 39.
[33] *Ibid.,* p. 41.
[34] Unamuno, *La agonía del cristianismo,* p. 206.
[35] Unamuno, *El espejo de la muerte,* p. 156.
[36] Unamuno, *La agonía del cristianismo,* p. 27.

*Las nubes se arrebolan*
*y a la luz apagada, la campiña*
*de pudor se reviste,*
*y desnuda la tierra, recogida,*
*se abraza al cielo.*

*Sobre los surcos*
*se oye el susurro del amor eterno*
*y despliega sus alas*
*en redor el misterio.*

*Es la hora de la siembra,*
*la del recuerdo*
*que lleva en sus entrañas*
*el porvenir entero.*

*Es la hora del amor, la de dar hijos*
*es la hora de vivir, de darse al cielo.*[37]

Wrapped in the arms of evening, the sun
lies down among the oaks
that in close-pressed herd, enfold it
in their tranquil tops.

The clouds turn red
and in the fading light, the landscape
veils itself in modesty
while the earth, naked, unto herself,
embraces the sky.

Across the furrowed earth comes
the whisper of love eternal
and mystery, over it all
spreads out her wings.

It is the time for sowing,
time for remembering,
that in its very being
holds all that is to come.

It is the time for loving, for bearing children,
it is the time for living, for giving oneself to the sky.

"For one metaphor," Unamuno once said, "I would give all the syllogisms, and the corresponding *ergos* which the whole scholastic verbiage can tack on to them; the metaphor teaches me more and enlightens me more, but above all it is by the metaphor that I warm myself, and imagination only works where there is fire."[38] The basic

[37] Max Grillo, "Conversando con Unamuno," in *Revista de América* (Bogotá, Colombia), Vol. IV, No. 10 (October 1945), pp. 55–56.

[38] "Retrato" by Gómez de la Serna in Unamuno, *Obras selectas*, p. 1052.

contradictions of Unamuno's thinking and his struggle to express them
in metaphors inevitably produced poetry, metaphysical poetry of an
intimate lyrical nature wherein thought and feeling are mingled in a
contrapuntal imaginative style which externalized the evolution of his
own soul and hence *was*, and *is*, Unamuno:

> The faces of truth—how many!
> What an infinite universe of words—
> mirror of humanity—
> I struggle to express, lest one be lost . . .
> Oh hand of God unyielding!
> Of God? No, rather hand of chance.
> Sealed up source
> of rhythm and style,
> prison and refuge
> of freedom unsuspecting,
> well of contradiction where "yes"
> and "no" incomplete,
> resurrected to give life
> produce a song.[39]

In poetry the metaphor, in prose the paradox, both products of his
fertile imagination, relieve what might otherwise be a monotonous
repetition of a few basic ideas, and characterize his intimate style of
writing and talking. But Unamuno's style is marked by another quality
which makes it peculiarly his own. He had a special knack for con-
cretizing the abstract. This habit of fusing the spiritual with the
material lends clarity and vividness to his thoughts. When asked how
he found time to accomplish so much, Don Miguel replied that his
working hours were made up of "cubic hours." His thinking was done,
he often explained, with "body and soul," and his beliefs penetrated
to the very "bones of his soul." Someone once made a slighting remark
about Unamuno as an insignificant author who lived in a "little, unim-
portant" Spanish town. This was his eloquent reply:

And now, my dear Mr. M. B. L., what do you want me to say to your
catty and insidious insinuations about the fact that I write from this old,
little, this little and not seldom maligned city of Salamanca, which you
do not know? . . . You need not pride yourself, sir, on living at the foot
of the highest mountain, or beside the greatest river in the world, for
unless you carry around a mountain of thoughts in your head, or a river
of feelings in your heart, it will profit you little, if it profit you at all.[40]

[39] Unamuno, *Cancionero*, pp. 395–396.
[40] Unamuno, *Andanzas y visiones españolas*, pp. 96–97.

Mountains and rivers of thoughts and feelings he carried within him, and the slightest stimulation from without would cause his brimming cup to spill over in expression. And the stimulation? Anything which stirred his sensitive sensory and extrasensory organs, for he seemed at times abundantly supplied with both. However, there is one exception to his "sensitiveness" and perhaps this is the place to mention it. It has been said of Don Miguel, as a man and as a poet, that he had no music in him. He himself wrote, ". . . of the musician I have less than a little." He did not play any musical instrument, he could not carry a tune and nowhere is there record of his having attended a concert. Yet a strong sense of rhythm pervades his poetry, and music he heard constantly, a music from within, silent and ineffable. He was responsive to stimuli from without, the stimuli of Nature. Nature was his music. His was the music of the spheres heard by Fray Luis de León when Salinas, the blind musician, plucked the strings of his lyre; he could hear an eternal symphony in great cathedral bells. His daughter, María, tells of his interview with the Spanish guitarist, Andrés Segovia. The great musician came to Salamanca to play for Don Miguel, but instead of listening to his music, Unamuno proceeded to sketch with nervous fingers a picture of the artist with his guitar. It was the sight of the artist using the instrument of his art with the feeling of a master that moved Don Miguel rather than the echo of the guitar. It must be that this man who was so much spirit, in the solitude of which he has written so eloquently, heard, or rather, felt within him the great harmonies of the "glorious, eternal symphony."

Don Miguel did not consider himself a real story writer, for he often extracted his stories from "something which seen or heard had struck his imagination, or perhaps it would come from deep within him." [41] And his stories in turn served as pretexts for his own observations. "For the hero of my story it is but a pretext for more or less ingenious observations, flights of imagination, paradoxes, etc., etc." [42] Continuing with his theories on the short story, Unamuno added that since life has no solution, neither should the story have one, or else, the writer might offer two possible endings for the reader's choice. A current happening, a poem, a novel written by someone else so frequently furnished the pretext for his own writings that Unamuno's enemies accused him of lacking originality. Pointing out that not even Shakespeare was original, he wrote in his letter to Clarín that originality ". . .

---

[41] Unamuno, *El espejo de la muerte*, p. 154.
[42] *Ibid.*

can never create something from nothing." [43] Indeed, paradoxically enough, perhaps Unamuno's most original creation was his personal commentary on that greatest of all novels, *Life of Don Quijote and Sancho According to Miguel de Cervantes Saavedra and Commented by Miguel de Unamuno.* And how he gloried in his name, Miguel. Spain had produced two great men so named—the first, Miguel de Cervantes, the second, Miguel de Unamuno! Don Miguel considered this his most original work, for he wrote to Ilundain: "I believe I have succeeded in producing my most personal work by commenting another's work. Of course," he added, "Cervantes' text gives me an excuse for all sorts of flights, and it is only a pretext for me to pour forth all of my own thought and feeling." [44] Indeed, the writing of this work so absorbed him that he wrote little else for six months before that letter to Ilundain in December, 1904. "I have never been so utterly absorbed in a work before, nor do I think I have ever put so much of myself into anything, such passion, such vehemence, and my very soul, as I am pouring into my new work . . ." he wrote.

Through Don Miguel's personal correspondence runs the consciousness of his role in the evolution of Hispanic civilization. The idea that his influence is felt and will continue to grow outside the borders of his peninsular country appears repeatedly, even as Spain's first Don Miguel expresses the same idea in the immortal dialogues between Don Quijote and Sancho. Perhaps this self-confidence inspired his imperviousness toward criticism, and the boldness of his attacks which so scandalized some of his compatriots. He wrote publicly against the Parisian scientist, LeDantec, as "the great scientific saint of the University of Paris before whom all of Europe bent kneeling." [45] And he referred to Nietzsche as a "calumniator" who "calumniated Socrates and Christ, and who wanted to be a Socrates and a Christ. His free slandering of Christ and Christianity has only been accepted by those who are profoundly ignorant of what Christ is and what he signifies, and who have never taken the trouble to read the contents of the Gospels." [46]

Perhaps the occasion on which Don Miguel most boldly defied convention and practically begged for the denunciation of Spain's intellectuals was in 1914. During one of his "religious seizures" and partly to

[43] Unamuno, *Obras selectas,* p. 908.
[44] Benítez (ed.), "Cartas inéditas de Miguel de Unamuno y Pedro Jiménez Ilundain," Vol. III, No. 9 (January–March 1949), p. 167.
[45] Benítez, "Unamuno y la existencia auténtica," Vol. II, No. 7 (July–September 1948), p. 16.
[46] *Ibid.,* p. 17.

redeem himself for having written the blasphemous *El Cristo yacente de Santa Clara*, he composed the most typical outpouring of his religious faith, *El Cristo de Velázquez*. Appearing unannounced in the Ateneo in Madrid, the very stronghold of rationalistic anticlericalism, Don Miguel with priestly mien and in apostolic vein recited the entire poem aloud while his audience sat, too stunned to protest. He continued "for hours praying to Christ—shocking, as can be imagined, the pontiffs and priests of that sanctuary of liberalism, that emporium of anticlericalism."[47] This time the "religious seizure" lasted several months for during holy week of the same year he retired to the monastery at Silos "to a sacred, spiritual retreat in company with the monks. He carried his poem. And, surrounded by the Benedictines, he proceeded to read it aloud, commenting unctuously and tearfully the while, and exhorting them to spiritual exercises, he exhorting them rather than they him, much to the profit, no doubt, of the holy ecclesiasts."[48]

But Don Miguel remained impervious to criticism. "I am more and more talked about," he wrote to Ilundain, "that is what I need. My books are beginning to be read, especially in my own town, in Bilbao, where once I was almost unknown."[49] This was just what he wanted, and besides he was becoming so used to stirring up controversies that he had begun to believe he bore a charmed life. Commenting to Ilundain on a recent article of his in which he attacked the regional narrowness of *catalanismo* and *bizcaitarrismo* (movements to popularize the use of the Catalán and Basque languages), he added "I don't know whether or not it will cause a scandal, for I'm becoming accustomed to getting by with anything I say."[50]

During those postgraduate years in Bilbao, Unamuno had begun to write articles which appeared in the socialistic periodical, *La Lucha de Clases* which he coedited with a group of other young hotheads of the town. These expressions may be discounted as the bubblings from a pot in which the real stew is beginning to boil, for, at the same time he was gathering information for his magnum opus, *Paz en la guerra*. For twelve long years the pot continued to simmer. Courtship and marriage, the process of preparing for his Academy examinations for a professorship—all of this occurred during what one critic calls

---

[47] Benítez, "La crisis religiosa de Unamuno," p. 25.
[48] *Ibid.*
[49] Benítez (ed.), "Cartas inéditas de Miguel de Unamuno y Pedro Jiménez Ilundain," Vol. III, No. 9 (January–March 1949), p. 177.
[50] *Ibid.*, p. 178.

"those silent years of his life." Unamuno himself refers to the years from 1883 to 1893 as the period when he most avidly "swallowed" as much as possible.[51] Following this period, his works began to appear; 1897, *Paz en la guerra;* 1900, *Tres ensayos;* and in 1902 the novel, *Amor y pedagogía.* This was the period of Carlyle's influence, so evident in the last-named work that one feels the author must have just put down that strange little volume of *Sartor Resartus* to pen the equally strange and fantastic *Amor y pedagogía.* Indeed, he became so absorbed in the Englishman's writings that he translated into Spanish Carlyle's *History of the French Revolution,* following it with a long essay entitled *Maese Pedro* or *Notas sobre Carlyle.* At first few noted Carlyle's influence on Unamuno, though some who did even accused him of plagiarism.[52]

This period from 1897 to 1905 was a time of "gradual transformations of ideological attitude and of literary procedures," as described by one of his critics.[53] Writing in 1898 to Ilundain, Unamuno said, "After a long rest I have resumed my work with more activity than ever." His influence had extended beyond the national borders, for one, Boafoux, a Frenchman, had sought his collaboration in *La Campaña* to be published in Paris. This change of attitude from the intense rationalism and socialism of his youth to the dominance of a vital faith and love and feeling, is reflected in *Amor y pedagogía.* Before its publication Unamuno characteristically wrote of it to Ilundain (May 13, 1903) ". . . it will surprise many of those who thought they had me classified." [54] And more intimately in his first letter written on January 3, 1898, he had recommended the study of the Gospels (*El Evangelio,* the *libro eterno*): ". . . the greatest miracle is to come to believe in its possibility, after having passed through a period of agnostic rationalism . . . Love is faith . . . life is essence and reason mere form." [55]

Although Unamuno never considered himself a philosopher, scorning the latter as a mechanical systematizer of the ideas of the real thinker, he did attempt to write an orderly presentation of his own thought. The task of organizing a systematic philosophy must have been

[51] *Ibid.,* Vol. II, No. 7 (July–September 1948), p. 86.
[52] Carlos Clavería, "Unamuno y Carlyle," in *Cuadernos hispanoamericanos* (Madrid), Vol. 10 (July–August 1949), pp. 51–87.
[53] *Ibid.*
[54] Benítez (ed.), "Cartas inéditas de Miguel de Unamuno y Pedro Jiménez Ilundain," Vol. III, No. 9 (January–March 1949), p. 130.
[55] *Ibid.,* Vol. II, No. 7 (July–September 1948), p. 68.

extremely painful to him, but he was pushed to it by constant queries as well as by the insistence of his closest friends, those friends of his boyhood days in Bilbao, Areílza and Barco, who had witnessed the reversal of his attitude from socialistic concerns to a deeper preoccupation with spiritual matters. Remembering the sincerity and fire of his early journalistic writing, did they doubt, perhaps, the authenticity of his change? They commented frequently upon it among themselves until at last, Ilundain, writing from Paris in 1905, put the question directly: Do you believe in God and, if so, what kind of God is he?

"My next book, *The Treatise on the Love of God,* will answer your last letter," wrote Unamuno in a letter dated in December of the same year. "In it you will see how I feel about God, a more personal, a more human (or anthropomorphic) God, and a God who is more alive than that of Catholic theology, whose God is Aristotelian in Nature." And he added, "I am becoming more and more of a deist!" [56]

This mention of *The Treatise on the Love of God* (*El tratado del amor de Dios*) is the first reference, to this writer's knowledge, to the work which was to appear eventually as *The Tragic Sense of Life in Men and in Peoples,* his one purely philosophical attempt, which has been translated into many different languages. Its composition or rather evolution, lasted over a period of some seven years, assuming that he began writing it in 1905. Just when he decided to change the title, or whether or not it was his decision and not that of the editor of *La España moderna* of Madrid, where it first appeared partially in 1911 under the new title, is of little consequence. Another letter to Ilundain in February of 1906 mentions his working on the *Tratado,* but the curiosity of his three friends had to go unsatisfied until 1911. The years from 1905 to 1912 (this last is the year of its complete appearance in book form) may be considered his most productive. In *The Tragic Sense of Life in Men and in Peoples* (translated into English by J. E. Crawford Flitch in 1921, Macmillan & Co., Inc., London) Unamuno has presented in quasi-philosophical form his ideas, or rather his idea of life, both here and hereafter, the role of God as the source of this hereafter, and man's struggle between reason and faith, faith based on love, in order to create for himself a soul. Beginning with man as the basic concern of all philosophy, he first establishes man's thirst for immortality. The two means whereby man has tried to convince himself that immortality exists for him are, says Unamuno, reason and imagination. The latter he couples with feeling,

[56] *Ibid.,* Vol. III, No. 9 (January–March 1949), p. 178.

the heart, the vital forces in man which preface all theory or logical systems. The position of the Catholic Church, he writes, is Tertullian's *credo quia absurdum*. Following the processes of reason's attempt to assure man of immortality, he demonstrates the skepticism and final despair to which it leads. Likewise, the processes of the heart, without reason, lead to the same conclusion. "But here, in the depths of the abyss, the despair of the heart and of the will and the skepticism of reason meet face to face, and embrace like brothers. And . . . from this embrace . . . the wellspring of life will flow, a life serious and terrible. Skepticism, uncertainty . . . is the foundation upon which the heart's despair must build up its hope." [57] Founded on feeling, from this despairing embrace, the imagination builds for itself hope in the hereafter, which may be "the real truth." "And as regards its truth, the real truth, that which is independent of ourselves, beyond the reach of our logic and of our heart—of this truth who knows aught?" [58] "The reader who follows me further," warns Unamuno at this point, "is now aware that I am about to carry him into the region of the imagination, of imagination not destitute of reason, for without reason nothing subsists, but of imagination founded on feeling." [59] And so it is: from this point on, *The Tragic Sense of Life* proceeds to take man out of his suffering to self-compassion, from self-compassion to love, from love to a conception of the universe, to a universal conscience which is God. And, he concludes, as a true Spaniard, man's symbol of this eternal struggle is Don Quijote who fights continually for spiritual values in a physical world.

The author of this work, although generally considered a paradoxical figure given to abrupt reversals of opinion and a-logical thinking, was remarkably consistent in his writings. His novels, plays, poems and essays are all imaginative elaborations of the thought content of *The Tragic Sense of Life;* it is the trunk from which sprang the branches of the whole tree. There is hardly a single work of his whose germ cannot be found in this book, and none which can be considered in any manner contradictory to it. Had he written only this one work, it would have sufficed to mark him as a profound, original thinker, but his ideas would have been limited to philosophical thinkers. Unamuno was, fortunately, an artist. Hence his ideas flowered into poetry, the poetry of rustling, watching leaves, the poetry of nature that whispers

[57] Unamuno, *The Tragic Sense of Life in Men and in Peoples*, p. 106.
[58] *Ibid.*, p. 131.
[59] *Ibid.*

the eternal mysteries of divine love. This poetic flowering can be found in such works as his *Cancionero* and *Teresa*.

In the opinion of the writer the little volume *Teresa* contains some of the most beautiful lines of poetry ever written in the Spanish language. Unfortunately it is out of print in Spain and was lacking from the collection of Don Miguel's own works in the Casa Museo Unamuno until a friend of Felisa's donated his own copy in May of 1959. Published by Renacimiento in Madrid, 1923, it is subtitled *Rimas de un poeta desconocido presentados y presentado por Miguel de Unamuno*. It is prologued by an article of Rubén Darío's which that poet wrote for *La Nación* in March 1909 entitled "Unamuno, poeta." In *Teresa* Unamuno proved himself equal, if not superior to, the great modernist poets of both Spain and Spanish America, hence it is fitting that the master and creator of that school of poetry should introduce *Teresa* to the reading public. Darío's judgment of Unamuno as a poet is summed up in the following quotations: "He is not, of course, a virtuoso . . . Nor does he give primary importance to form [60] . . . If he could, he would sing only with a music from within that could not be heard from without, like the noise of subterranean fountains whose crystalline sound of waters finds its only repercussion in the hollowed-out cavities of caves sculptured by stalactites . . . He must write easily, for the theories of his strophes, in an order which seems forced, march loosely in poetic procession." Darío calls Unamuno ". . . this newly born and everlasting mystic." He speaks of "the Nordic tones" of his verses "that seem translated from blue-eyed poets," and adds that "certain verses sound like the blows of a hammer." [61]

In the "Presentación" of *Teresa* by Unamuno himself written in Fernando's home in Palencia in 1921, Don Miguel uses the term *meterótica* which he defines as "the metaphysics of love," that is, life and death, or the process of being "un-born." "And if to die is to become 'un-born'," he reasons, "to be born is to 'un-die'." [62]

In this "Presentación" Unamuno writes that the verses of *Teresa* were entrusted to him by a poor young poet, Rafael, who was inspired to write them by the love and death of his sweetheart Teresa, and who himself died of grief soon afterwards. On page 142 one reads the following strophe:

---

[60] One of the main emphases of the "Modernist" poets was on form.
[61] Prologue by Rubén Darío to Unamuno, *Teresa: rimas de un poeta desconocido*, pp. 8–13.
[62] Unamuno, "Desmorir," in *Teresa: rimas de un poeta desconocido*, p. 36.

*Mi Teresa es Española*
*y mi España es teresiana;*
*vive en mi alma siempre sola;*
*mi patria es la del mañana.*

which may be the clue to *Teresa*. The beloved, Teresa, is Spain, who, though dead, is the homeland of tomorrow. Love solves everything, and is the ultimate *raison d'être*. As Rafael hears Teresa say,

Sing to Love, motive for the universe;
sing to Love, the rest is nothing,
and give me eternal life in your verse.[63]

The *Cancionero* is Unamuno's poetic diary and contains "the ultimate core of what concerned him . . .,"[64] to quote Professor de Onís. A veritable poetic unfolding of a mature philosophy (Unamuno began writing the *Cancionero* in 1928), it differs from his other poetry in that he wrote in it almost daily for himself alone. It contains in all 1,700 poems written from 1928 to the last one which he wrote just three days before his death. Speaking at the University of Buenos Aires in 1949, Professor de Onís chose to read from its contents only the following few lines:

I go out into the street,
I go to see what passes by.
I go to hear what remains.

In these lines Don Miguel voices his intimate concern for *lo que queda*, that which remains, the eternal. The *Cancionero* expresses also his desire for physical immortality, the desire "to live again in the same body and soul in which I lived before."[65] It voices his innermost doubts and fears, as well as the abiding faith which is apparent in his life and works. The *Cancionero* takes him through the most critical period of his life, the years of exile in France, and to that period belong some of his greatest and most intimate writings—*La agonía del cristianismo, Cómo se hace una novela,* besides the *Cancionero* itself. Indeed, so intimately are these others woven into his exile experience that they should be discussed in chapters dealing with that period.

[63] Unamuno, *Teresa: rimas de un poeta desconocido,* p. 127.
[64] Federico de Onís, "Unamuno íntimo," in "Cursos y conferencias," *Revista del colegio libre de estudios superiores,* Buenos Aires (July–September 1949), p. 256.
[65] *Ibid.,* p. 257.

Edited by Professor de Onís, the *Cancionero* was published in 1953 by Editorial Losada, S. A., in Buenos Aires, Argentina. The strict censorship in Spain may explain this for the *Indice de libros prohibidos* is still extant in that country. Although its very name, *Index of Forbidden Books,* indicates strict control, it does not necessarily follow that the books included therein are not read. Repeated queries for specific information about the workings of the Index directed to individuals now residing under Franco's dictatorship have gone unanswered. Dr. Benítez, the critic-priest of the University of Buenos Aires, expresses his approval of it when he writes of *La agonía del cristianismo*: ". . . (included now, and rightly so, in the *Index of Forbidden Books,* as is also its elder brother, *The Tragic Sense of Life*) . . ."[66]

However, this censorial institution may function, it does indicate the disapproval of certain powerful religious and probably political dignitaries as well. In a Catholic country where Church and state are traditionally interrelated, it follows that the reading public of these books is limited. The censorship against Don Miguel, however, instituted first against his writings, gradually became so vehement that it went beyond the literary mark and was finally directed against his person, resulting at last in his exile, the climax and perhaps the *raison d'être* of Don Miguel's earthly mission.

[66] Benítez, "La crisis religiosa de Unamuno," p. 67.

# The Gathering Storm

CHAPTER  *21*

UNAMUNO ENDED THE EXQUI-
site little volume *Teresa* with explanatory notes and a *despedida*
(farewell). The latter he wrote in Palencia in mid-September of 1923.
As he wrote it, a pair of lovers in intimate colloquy passed by his
window and he wondered: "Could they know that a military dictatorship has just been set up in Spain?" [1] He also referred to the "newspaper articles in which I am trying to bring to life the history of my
troubled Spain," and to his poems ". . . fruits of her hours, as these
are of my era . . . and I assure you, readers, that they are both currents of one and the same poetry. For I too . . . have my *meterótica*,
from which I make my *metapolítica*." [2]

For years Unamuno had been attacking everything within the
Spanish state that tended to retard her progress toward what he en-
visioned as her glorious future. His whole life had been devoted to
awakening the souls of his countrymen that they might be stirred into
action. He used every means at his disposal; his writings, his frequent
speeches and even his celebrated monologues for this purpose. As an
important literary figure and rector of Spain's oldest university, he
had succeeded in drawing attention to himself and to the battle he
was waging.

His declaration of war had been made at the flower festival in Bil-

[1] Unamuno, *Teresa: rimas de un poeta desconocido*, p. 226.
[2] *Ibid.*, pp. 226–227.

bao in 1901. There he was fighting the pride of the Basques in Vizcaya
which kept them from working together with the other provinces of
Spain for the national welfare. After the Bilbao affair, Ilundain wrote
him to this effect: "Don't sacrifice yourself by going around telling too
many truths. Is it worth it? After all, remember that Spain and Vizcaya
are not the whole world." In reply Don Miguel boasted of the "freedom
of thought" in Spain. In the same letter he voiced the hope that Spain
would cease to be Catholic before France, and that such works as
Weizäcker's book on religion in the United States should help to free
Spain from Catholic dogmatism. Filled with good spirits and self-
confidence he continued: "I feel that I am beginning to mature [He
was then thirty-seven years old]. Physically my hair and beard are
turning grey and I am gaining more weight than I would like. I weigh
seventy-eight kilos! I already have six children. Spiritually, I am beginning to see smooth sailing. I feel able to carry out my plans, all
of them literary. I'm in the middle of writing a novel [*Amor y
pedagogía*]. I am preparing *New Essays* and other things." [3]

In this same letter there appears the first reference to the struggle
he waged with the powerful Bishop of Soria for over fourteen years,
a struggle which was to be an important factor in his eventual loss
of the rectorship. Mentioning the "long-standing affair I have been
carrying on with the Bishop of Soria," he added, "I want to see who
is more stubborn; whether the Bishop or the Vizcayan" (This comparison of himself with a Vizcayan recalls Don Quijote's fight with the
redoubtable native of Vizcaya). "What really has me somewhat worried is this matter of the rectorship—What I will not consider is resigning." Then, envisioning the future as already past, he planned to
turn the whole experience to a literary purpose; "When I leave here
(three or four years from now, if I don't move to Madrid before this),
I shall write my memoirs with what I have learned from this position." [4]
Evidently Unamuno was seriously considering only a short period in
Salamanca with the idea of transferring his residence to Madrid, probably to devote his whole time to the Universidad Central, where he
did teach for some years by commuting from Salamanca. Nevertheless,
the idea of resigning in the midst of the struggle and thus admitting
defeat could scarcely have entered his head. On the contrary, the very

[3] Hernán Benítez (ed.), "Cartas inéditas de Miguel de Unamuno y Pedro
Jiménez Ilundain," in *Revista de la universidad de Buenos Aires*, Vol. III, No. 9
(January–March 1949), pp. 108–109.
[4] *Ibid.*, p. 109.

fact that the struggle revolved around his position at the University,
no doubt, kept him from going to Madrid.

At the close of 1903, he wrote Ilundain, the Bishop of Salamanca
tried to condemn Unamuno's books and have him deposed as rector,
but without success. "We exchange frequent letters; and foreseeing
that if he carried out his threat we would have a regular family brawl
(*Electra*) here—and a lot he'd gain by that!—I have armed myself
with the battle-book I should carry into the lists." [5] Knowing himself
so well, he foresaw that if the Bishop should not renew the attack, he
would provoke him to it. "Now I'm waiting for the next step;" and,
he predicted "I know I'll end up that way. After those threats and
insults, provoked by what I said at a banquet here, my *Comments on
Life* in the *Imparcial* must have riled the good Bishop quite a bit . . .
I myself doubted that the *suedo* and colorless *El Imparcial* would
accept them. After one of those articles in *El Imparcial*, *El Siglo
Futuro* was practically demanding that I should be shot and in Congress Nocedal has bemoaned the fact that I am still rector, 'since I am
a bad Spaniard'." He concluded imperturbably, "I shall continue my
work."

Unamuno had by now sounded the calm depths beneath the ebb
and flow of circumstances. In April 1904 he wrote optimistically in a
letter "And so I am continuing to expend my energies and give of
myself and so I hope to enrich myself because I am sowing myself.
Only he who gives himself is his own possessor. And I am happy.
This fall I shall publish my lectures in one volume under the title
*Lay Sermons* or simply *Sermons*, although such a title may provoke
stupid comments." [6] The *Sermons*, however, never materialized. Nevertheless, he was like the sea captain who, seeing the storm gathering
far off, makes fast the rigging, battens down the hatches, and prepares
to face it head-on, knowing that his bark is sea-worthy. He knew the
real struggle was yet to come, for he wrote to Ilundain, "All that I
have written, said, and done is only a prologue to what I have yet to
write, to say, and to do." A sense of knowing his own destiny has
crept in, but he faces the storm without flinching and steers his bark
directly into it. From this time on he attacks even the King, at first,
cautiously, with veiled references to the "sad symptoms of anarchy
which seem to be consuming Spain, this anarchy that stems from high

[5] *Ibid.*, p. 162.
[6] *Ibid.*, p. 163.

up—from very high up," [7] and eventually with no precaution whatsoever.

The Church and state had long been locked in a despairing embrace of dissention and struggle—the Cain and Abel of the Hispanic family, each necessary to the other but warring constantly. Don Miguel had openly attacked the dogmatism of the Catholic Church but when he began to meddle in the affairs of state and hurl invectives at the government he could no longer be ignored. Had he limited his criticism to one or the other, he might have escaped unscathed, but his open fight with both caused them to turn on him, like quarreling lion mates, united against a common enemy. Not until 1914 did the storm break and the wonder is that it waited so long. Only the influence and the stamina of a man such as Unamuno could have held it in abeyance for almost an entire decade. So strong was his hold on the *pueblo* that both Church and state feared him.

He continued his habit of visiting monasteries and towns throughout Spain to carry on "mystic activities" and to preach chastity and spiritual devotion to the clergy. Into these sermons he incorporated "some fierce pronouncements against monarchists, separatists, liberals, Europeanizers." [8] Still the sword of Damocles did not fall!

Finally, Unamuno could stand the suspense no longer. Since his enemies were too timid to act and because he felt that the outcome was inevitable, he took the initiative and forced their hands. The occasion presented itself at a gathering in the Lion D'Or in Bilbao. Whether his talk was planned or impromptu—it may have gathered momentum on the spot—it turned out to be a veritable philippic against the King, Alfonso XIII and his Prime Minister, the Count of Romanones. His delivery must have been dramatic. Accompanied by a circle of listeners, he probably began his usual monologue, his fingers nervously rolling the breadcrumbs and scattering them on the tablecloth. Slowly his own words kindled the smouldering fire and he became more vehement. The King he paints as "envious" and "unconscious" and Romanones, for using the King, he denounces as "apprehendable." By this time he has pushed back his chair. His fingers no longer twirl the breadcrumbs. He has drawn his old hat from his

---

[7] Unamuno, *Ensayos*, VI, 132. This appeared in an article entitled "La crisis actual de patriotismo español" written as a commentary on the government's use of military force to subdue an uprising which occurred in Barcelona in 1905.

[8] Hernán Benítez, "La crisis religiosa de Unamuno," in *Revista de la universidad de Buenos Aires*, Vol. III, No. 9 (January–March 1949), p. 26 n.

pocket and has ensconced it precariously on the back of his head. His owl-like eyes dart fire and he holds his audience within the circle of his gold-rimmed spectacles. Probably, men at the near-by tables listened spellbound. Who was there that day? At Unamuno's own table, no doubt, was Enrique Areílza who later described the scene in a letter to Ilundain. Certainly, there must have been in the room a friend of Romanones who would carry the story straight to the ears of the one for whom it was intended. He paused to savor this moment, an instant in eternity. Raising his voice, he repeated that the King was envious and Romanones, the most powerful man in the land was, *presidiable* (should be thrown into prison). At this point he swept off his hat and hurled it to the floor. In the shocked silence all eyes followed it, the hat he had thrown down like a challenging gauntlet which could not be ignored. A stir broke the spell. Some had risen to go while the rest murmured in awed undertones. Thus in the summer of 1914 began what Unamuno termed his "major battle." Henceforth he was not to know "a single day of peace."

Nor was there peace in Europe. The year was 1914 and already "the lights were beginning to go out all over the world." In the faraway town of Sarajevo an archduke was murdered and the First World War began. Spanish opinion was divided between the Germanophiles and those who sympathized with the allies. Don Eduardo Dato was the immediate head of the government in Madrid and leader of the conservatives, the Germanophiles. Unamuno, from the first, espoused the allied cause. His attitude was energetic, vibrant, and decided. He saw immediately that the imperialistic politics of the Kaiser threatened the freedom of Europe. So convinced was he of this that he carried on a regular campaign, writing articles, speaking, and promoting public manifestations in favor of the allies; in fact, as his biographer, Villarrazo, puts it, the government wanted "to reduce him to silence," with the result that he raised his voice all the higher. It was then that a group of his friends instigated his candidacy for a senatorship with the drastic results which are detailed further on in this chapter.

However, the year 1914 had begun auspiciously for the Rector. On January 8 the Ateneo of Madrid honored him with a banquet at which he read his poem entitled *Refinos*. On the following day he read before that body a lecture on education of which his home town paper carried a report on January 10. Titled "Public Education Judged by Unamuno," it said his entire address criticized public education as "a sterilizer of students." He blamed the undisciplined student conflicts and strikes on the university professors and, the report added, ". . . he held that there is no substitute for the teaching of religion." Unamuno lashed out at the lack of interest in religion in the universities, and the suppression of the old schools of theology. He ended by saying: "I believe we are emerging from the barbarism of the other side of the mountains, but we must struggle to avoid falling into that of the Modern School." [9]

An article in the paper for January 15 reveals that Unamuno had recently supported a measure whereby university rectors were automatically eliminated from representing their own universities in the senate. The passage of this measure naturally ruled out Don Miguel himself and focused attention on Don Luis Maldonado for that position. The article expressed the hope, however, that Don Miguel might still occupy a seat in the senate possibly as a representative of the province of Málaga so that he might continue his educational campaign in that highest government body in the land.

It should be noted here that Unamuno's thrusts at state-controlled education (*educación laica*) must have rankled in the soul of the current minister of education, Bergamín, the man directly responsible for ordering Unamuno's dismissal from the rectorship in August of that same year, and the whole question of the University's senatorial representative stirred up a hornet's nest in Salamanca. One of the local papers of March 21 refers to the *pleito* (argument) in the University over the elections and the resignation of one, Mondelo, from the presidency of the voting session. Unamuno himself finally presided and Don Luis Maldonado was elected, as reported in the same paper of Monday, March 23. But subsequent events proved that this *pleito* in the University was far from settled. Not until the edition of August 31 is there further reference to the situation. Then on page two a single-columned article is headed "Unamuno's Dismissal." It states that *The Gaceta of Madrid* received in Salamanca on that day publicized a royal decree providing for the cessation of Don Miguel de Unamuno from the rectorship of the University of Salamanca. According to the paper, a reporter interviewed Unamuno and was told that the first official notice he, Don Miguel, had received of his dismissal was when he read the royal decree. The article quotes Unamuno as saying that he was ignorant of the cause or the pretexts to which his dismissal could be attributed since he had had no letter or official communi-

[9] Name of paper withheld upon request.

cation with the minister of education for two months and had himself
returned from Portugal just twenty-four hours before.

The next day the paper carried a full-page headline on page one as
follows: "Announcement of the schools of medicine and science. Dismissal of Señor Unamuno." The article stated that the violent and
unprecedented dismissal of the University rector, Don Miguel de Unamuno, had been announced the preceding day and on this date, the
suppression of the schools of medicine and science. It hinted that
"someone" seemed anxious to try Salamanca's patience, and added that
when the rumor circulated late the day before that the minister of
public education had expressed his intention of suppressing the above
mentioned schools and moving them to Valladolid on the charge that
they were not functioning normally, Salamanca prepared her defense.
All of page one carried the story of that defense. Protests from the
University were conveyed by "El Senador Maldonado," and telegrams
were sent to Salamanca's representative in the Cortes, Señor Pérez
Oliva. The *Ayuntamiento* met and agreed to send a telegram to Madrid
protesting the matter of the University schools and that body also
discussed whether it would be fitting for the *Ayuntamiento* to inform
the government that they wished the illustrious thinker, Don Miguel
de Unamuno, to continue in his position of leader as rector in the
University, "mainly on account of his prestige," (*por su prestigio
mismo*). However, the resulting telegram referred only to the matter
of the schools. The *Ayuntamiento* stayed in session until four A.M.
awaiting an answer from Madrid!

Column three of the same page carries a story headlined: "Unamuno's
Dismissal. An account of what happened." It begins with a copy of a
document regarding regulations for admission of foreign students to
Spanish universities, which document had been issued by Ruiz Jiménez
from San Sebastián on September 20, 1913. Then follows a copy of a
letter from Bergamín to Unamuno dated July 9, 1914, requesting an
explanation of an accusation made in congress by one Señor Portela
that Unamuno had validated an academic degree issued in Bogotá,
Colombia. This in turn is followed by Unamuno's answering letter of
July 13, 1914. In it the Rector explained the conditions of his accused
action and pointed out their perfect conformance with the declaration
issued the preceding year. Furthermore, he pointed out that besides
the Colombian student in question, Manuel José Casas y Manrique,
there was in the University at that time a Cuban student, Domingo
Nicolás Nazabal y del Castaño, and, he added, "The thing seemed

to me perfectly legal and in conformity with that Royal decree." More-over, in his letter, Unamuno offered to send Bergamín the record of both foreign students. His tone is courteous, clear, and to the point; it leaves no doubt as to the absolute legality of his action in the case.

As the same paper reported, all of Salamanca's *tertulias* were buzzing with the question; one group had drawn up a protesting message which was circulating for ever increasing numbers of signatures during most of the night. It was a telegram destined for "Señor Presidente del Consejo de Ministros." The message, together with sheets of accom-panying signatures, was displayed in many café windows. It informed this "most excellent señor" that spontaneous representatives of all social classes addressed His Excellency to express their profound surprise and deep displeasure. Furthermore, it stated bluntly that the action which was not justified in the eyes of the nation and which was seem-ingly based on hidden motives would appear to be an act of vengeance or some political maneuver unless the government satisfied the public and annulled its legal procedures by reinstating in the rectorship of the University the "illustrious thinker, the one best fitted . . . to exercise the duties of such an important position." The message was dated August 31, 1914, and the list of signatures, too many to be printed, was headed by that of "Cándido R. Pinilla, writer."

An article on page three of the same day's paper, Tuesday, Septem-ber 1, 1914, reports that a telephone communication with Madrid denies the intention of moving the university schools in question, but simply "correcting certain negligencies in them."

However, on page two Bergamín is again cited as having recon-firmed what he had told reporters about the causes which motivated Unamuno's dismissal and which would bring about the suppression of the school of medicine. Bergamín mentioned the many abnormalities in the examinations in medicine at Salamanca. He was quoted as say-ing that things were badly neglected, laboratories were needed, the clinics were not conducted under proper conditions, and even the classes were taught with a lamentable number of interruptions "so that the students come up for examinations without knowing a word."

Regarding Unamuno, again Bergamín is reported to have said that the "Gaceta" will publish the "recourse" for his dismissal, that he feels no enmity toward him and recognizes his merits. Bergamín then praised the current vice rector, Don Salvador Cuesta Martín "who has been appointed rector to replace Señor Unamuno."

The foregoing account clarifies only one thing: Bergamín had ordered the irretrievable dismissal of Unamuno from the rectorship. The people of Salamanca were right: his motives were hidden or, as the message declared, *inconfesables* (nonconfessable).

Although the first official notice Don Miguel received of his dismissal was the royal decree that appeared in the paper, he had, according to Felisa, received unofficial notice of it while he was vacationing in Portugal that summer. However, she points out that instead of going to Madrid to protest it, he dismissed it with a shrug saying, "Well, let them dismiss me," and returned to Salamanca where he read the official notice. Obviously he knew that such a step was in the wind and had a pretty good idea of the reasons behind it.

Further documentation regarding the facts in the case which this biographer was allowed to read by the kindness of Professor Don Manuel García Blanco, include a chronological list of Unamuno's official positions with the University of Salamanca from 1891 when he was first appointed to the chair of Greek, until 1934, the year of his "Retirement as professor upon reaching the age of seventy, and his continuation as 'Lifetime Rector' at which time the 'Chair Miguel de Unamuno' was created in the University, and his name was given to the National Institute of Secondary Education in Bilbao."

The entry concerning the case in point reads:

"1914 He leaves the Rectorship upon Royal Order of August 20."

There is also the typed copy of a letter from Don Miguel to "Señor Director" of a local newspaper including some "Notes" which Unamuno explains he sent for publication to a Madrid daily, and which were returned to him unpublished with the excuse of "I don't know what business about a neutrality law" and about action which the government could take against the paper if the notes were made public. The "Notes" contained Unamuno's own explanation of events. In essence they read as follows:

REASONS FOR DISMISSAL

1st. The first notice I received was a notice I read in a local paper [*En la pizarra de un diario*]. That is to say, that I have been treated with absolutely no consideration. I have been thrown out like a dog. And the Minister called himself a friend of mine and when I went to see him at the beginning of the year he offered me unsolicited by me a seat in the Senate, saying that he needed me there to back some of his plans which he explained to me in part and which, I must confess, did not seem bad.

2nd. To this moment I am in ignorance of the true motives for my dismissal although I suspect them.

3rd. The first publicly announced pretext is that I made rigorous application of the Royal decree of Señor Ruiz Jiménez regarding the validity of foreign bachelor degrees; if this were examined carefully it would be found that I was dismissed for complying with the order in every detail.

4th. The second pretext which my ex-friend and most correct dismissor, Señor Bergamín, has cited has been the deficiencies in the instruction in this university's School of Medicine, and this one is even more absurd. No one has denounced them more than I nor called more loudly for their remedy, which was the duty of the Ministry.

. . . I even requested a review and inspection of the clinical facilities by that Ministry.

But this affair is one which Salamanca, I feel certain, will know how to air in its own good time.

There follows a reiteration of his complaints of the methods of his summary dismissal by one who had only a few months before spontaneously offered him a seat in the senate for his collaboration.

The Salamanca paper did print these "Notes" in the edition marked "year XXX no. 9.278."

After reading the foregoing charges, defenses and countercharges, one may well ask, why was Don Miguel dismissed? When the question was put to Don Manuel García Blanco by this writer, his answer was: "The Madrid government asked Unamuno to support as the University's candidate to the senate someone who was not even connected with the institution. Unamuno refused on those very grounds. Then they offered to make him a senator if he would resign as rector.[10] Unamuno refused to give up the University, saying that he was not interested in the senatorship. Therefore, he was dismissed." This seems quite simple, as immediate causes usually do seem, but friends and acquaintances from elsewhere who judged events on a larger scale saw things otherwise. Besides his dismissal order, for which Bergamín was the instrument of the Crown, a ridiculous sentence was passed on Unamuno, one which does not seem to have been taken seriously enough even to be mentioned on the local scene; Unamuno was sentenced to sixteen years in the penitentiary! All of Spain was shocked and if his European friends did not come to his defense it was because they were giving their attention to the greater conflict of World War I. As Areílza keenly observed: "Now . . . the political leaders of Salamanca and their friends in the cloister . . . looked for a stupid pretext

[10] The University faculty members were supposed to elect their own senator.

(the pretext of degrees) and took advantage of the war that dominates everything, to push him out." [11] They must have known, even as the sentence was uttered, how impossible it would be to carry out. Unamuno was far too influential and popular. He was pardoned and one day appeared in the *palacio del Conde Romanones,* as they called the Ateneo. His unexpected appearance in the gallery brought forth a volley of whistles from the floor, but he only grinned happily, protected by the very man he had insulted. Nevertheless, he could not regain his position as rector and returned to Salamanca, a mere professor, there to take up his battle once more.

His homecoming was a humiliating one and especially so for Concha and the family, for it involved moving from the Casa Rectoral to a new home, the home at Number 4 Bordadores Street, where fortunately for them, Doña Pilar Cuadrado with her two children, Paquita and Federico, received them with sympathy and understanding.

Friends and scholars have given various interpretations of his demotion but all of them agree that it was due to his outspoken criticism of the Church and state. Unamuno's critic, Romera-Navarro, writes that the cause was "his journalistic campaigns, independent of all political parties, and aimed against the evils and abuses from which the nation suffered, his aggressiveness and independence . . . and . . . his attack on the Spanish Crown." [12]

Unamuno did not take his demotion sitting down. As was to be expected, he used every opportunity to strike back at his enemies. Furthermore, he may have been disappointed that the prison sentence had not been carried out. Had this been the case, the Spanish people who always side with the incarcerated would instinctively have been sympathetic to him. As the case stood, he was free and little attention was being paid him. In the years that followed Don Miguel was like a man in a blind rage who deals blows into empty space, even as Don Quijote charged the homing sheep, mistaking them for enemies. Areílza wrote of his behaviour as follows: "Since his demotion, Don Miguel has run off at the mouth in private and in public, much to the satisfaction and joy of his enemies. I believe that he will not occupy the position of rector under the circumstances, and moreover, if he persists in his querulousness, he will be completely ignored by any possible form of government. Don Miguel *tira al zorro.*" [13] Later, writ-

---

[11] Areílza in a letter quoted in Benítez, "La crisis religiosa de Unamuno," p. 26.
[12] Miguel Romera-Navarro, *Miguel de Unamuno,* Introduction.
[13] Areílza in a letter quoted in Benítez, "La crisis religiosa de Unamuno," p. 27 n.

ing of that summer, Unamuno expressed his hatred of politics and especially the politicians of Madrid, who "In their search for future electors, are forced to defend rather than amend their self-admitted mistakes." [14]

During this summer of 1914, it may have been immediately following his dismissal, Don Miguel retired to the peaceful Monastery of Silos. There he dedicated long hours of meditation and work to the writing of his greatest religious poem, *The Christ of Velázquez*, which is a reaffirmation of his faith. He deliberately blocked out the turmoil in his life to concentrate upon the meaning of Christ's agony on the cross. Eleanor Turnbull's exquisite translation offers a rare opportunity for the English reader to live with Unamuno during those weeks in the quiet Monastery. In spite of this deep religious experience he was to write later from the Island of Mallorca "I believe that the worst enemies of religion are the priests." [15]

After his return from the cloistered world at the Monastery Unamuno was caught up in the chaos which existed within the Spanish state. A revolutionary movement was begun upon the resignation of his enemy, the Conde de Romanones, in 1916. The political parties and the national legislative body, the Cortes, demanded constitutional reforms. A general strike of the railway workers had to be settled by military measures. The officials of the telegraph system went out on strike shortly thereafter. There was a clash between the civil and military authorities in Barcelona. Finally, King Alfonso, threatening abdication, dissolved the Cortes.

The general election of 1920 showed that the Spanish people would no longer tolerate just any kind of government. At this time Unamuno was nominated to represent Bilbao and Madrid in the Cortes. His mounting popularity carried him into the company of those "envious" and "scheming" politicians whom he had so lately berated. Dr. Areílza wrote that the sight of Don Miguel "in the company of those not so rich politicians like Lerroux" moved him to pity because there was too great a contrast between the "magnificent attire and jewels" of the politicians and Unamuno's "poor, old jacket and his ever-increasing and trying poverty." "I presume," he concluded in his letter to Ilundain,

[14] Unamuno, "El estilo nuevo," in *La ciudad de Henoc: comentario 1933*, p. 142.
[15] Unamuno, *Andanzas y visiones españolas*, p. 177. Though this essay is signed "Mallorca 1906," other essays in the same volume indicate that Unamuno was in Mallorca in 1916 and his references to the war clearly indicate the First World War, thus pointing to the obvious fact that the year 1906 is an error and should be 1916.

"that when his rage against the monarch is over, he will return to his mania for the hereafter and things of the other life where there must surely be better recompense than in this one." [16] He was defeated in the municipal elections, however, and thus was saved from any part in the turbulence which followed.

After the fiasco of this, his first political involvement, he was gradually drawn back into the current of administrative duties at the University; sometime during the following year he was elected Dean of the School of Philosophy and Letters by that body and on the heels of that the University faculty proposed successfully his appointment as vice rector of the University. [17]

Then, on March 8, 1921, Eduardo Dato, the Prime Minister, was murdered in Madrid. The antimonarchical movement and the unrest in Catalonia swept the Spanish state on inevitably to the dictatorship of Primo de Rivera. In 1923 Primo seized power, with the consent of the King, and declared the country to be in a state of war. He ordered a censorship of the press and forbade all public assemblies for political purposes. Again the King disbanded the Cortes and, in its place, the government set up a committee to serve in an advisory capacity.

Don Miguel now "lost all control" and "raved on, in every sense of the word against the King and the dictator and challenged them in the manner of the knights of old." [18] Since the government suppressed all hostile opinions in the Spanish press, Unamuno used the South American newspapers for his indignant and often offensive criticism of Primo de Rivera and King Alfonso XIII. The storm, which had been gathering its force, finally broke on February 21, 1924, when Don Miguel was ordered into exile.

[16] Benítez, "La crisis religiosa de Unamuno," pp. 26–27.
[17] From Unamuno's official record at the University furnished the writer by Don Manuel García Blanco.
[18] Benítez, "La crisis religiosa de Unamuno," p. 27.

# "Don Quijote on Fuerteventura"

CHAPTER 22

THE SPECIFIC REASONS FOR THE exile of Don Miguel de Unamuno are stated by his most recent Spanish biographer, Bernardo Villarrazo, in the following terms: "His speech in Valladolid and another at the Society El Sitio of Bilbao, together with the publication of a letter of his not written for publication were the immediate causes of his exile on the Island of Fuerteventura. On the 21st of February, 1924, when the dictatorship had been in power only five months, he was notified of the exile order."[1]

The new dictator Primo de Rivera, brought into power by King Alfonso's *coup d'etat* of September 23, 1923, took swift and drastic action against the redoubtable professor. On February 21, 1924, exactly fifty years to the day since he had heard the first bomb explode in his beloved Bilbao, the controversial professor of Greek who had become the "bad man of Salamanca" was taken, penniless and with only the clothing he was wearing at the time, from his home in Salamanca, and thence escorted under military guard to the southern port of Cádiz. His destination was the windswept isle of Fuerteventura, one of the Canary Islands off the coast of Africa. However, there was a delay of seventeen days before he arrived at his island prison. From Unamuno's own pen we have it that he landed there on the 10th of March: "17 days after having snatched me from my home, days which I spent in Cádiz . . . a few hours on Tenerife and 8 days on Las Palmas

[1] Bernardo Villarrazo, *Miguel de Unamuno: glosa de una vida*, p. 233.

de la Gran Canaria." [2] The cause of this delay may have been the usual irregular sailing schedule, or, perhaps, his lack of extra clothing. He seemed to take satisfaction in the thought that, at least, his own money was not being spent to provide for his needs. Unamuno wrote later that he purposely left his home in a destitute condition so as to force the government to care for him and thus protect his own meager savings.

During those days in Cádiz Unamuno had only two visitors, both sent from Madrid for specific purposes which Don Miguel astutely divined and effectively foiled. As he related to his biographer after his return to Salamanca in 1930, one of these visitors, Don Miguel Maeztu, was sent by Martínez Anido, Primo's Chief of Police, whom Unamuno once called an "epileptic." "I know that from the very beginning, they wanted me to escape or to go to the King and ask for 'justice' so that he might do me the favor of granting me a pardon. No, no, no 'favors,' thank you, no pardons. From the first I tried to create for them the conflict of not knowing what to do with me and the responsibility of having to take charge of me and manage me." [3]

As for the second visitor, Señor Aldecoa, he went to offer his services to Don Miguel who told him that he didn't need a thing. Not only did he not need anything, but he handed over to Aldecoa some two thousand pesetas and a fist full of silver saying: "I want to embark without one centime. Let the ones who are making me travel pay. Not I." [4]

One may wonder that Concha was not with him, and indeed she may have proposed to accompany her husband when he took his sudden leave from his dear ones for he wrote later: "I needed solitude, and besides I knew that the real punishment those measly little tyrants wanted to impose on me was to oblige me to spend my money, to deprive me and my children of my scant savings . . . that exile was a kind of confiscation and I decided to make as few expenditures as possible, and even not to pay for them, and that's what I did." [5]

At Las Palmas Unamuno enjoyed a "suspicious freedom" which he took as an invitation to escape. Two acquaintances of his, Tomás Borrás and Ricardo Calvo, stopped off at the island on their way to America and suggested that Unamuno accompany them to Buenos

---

[2] Unamuno, *De Fuerteventura a París*, p. 18.
[3] César González-Ruano, *Miguel de Unamuno*, p. 73.
[4] *Ibid.*
[5] Unamuno, *Cómo se hace una novela*, pp. 101–102.

Aires. However, he tells us that he spent the rest of the days on Las Palmas talking with friends and acquaintances and finally departed thence for Fuerteventura. No sooner had he landed on this island than he learned that influential friends had asked for his pardon. Again Spain was shocked that the grand old man should be so violently treated, and this time protests came, not only from his compatriots, but from powerful friends in France and in America as well.

Four months, almost to a day, Don Miguel remained a prisoner on the island of Fuerteventura—a prisoner, that is, materially speaking. "Stone walls do not a prison make, nor iron bars a cage" for those who exist in the spirit. Napoleon planned a world conquest from St. Helena, and Bolívar dreamed his dream of a free America from an island prison. Even so, the "irreducible" spirit of Don Miguel, here on the rock-bound coast, acquired a new dimension as boundless as the sea. Here it was that he "discovered" the sea. Of this discovery and his other adventures he gave a full account in the little volume *De Fuerteventura a París*. The subtitle states that it is the "Intimate Diary of confinement and exile expressed in sonnets by Miguel de Unamuno." Except for a few poems written before March 10, and others composed in Paris and running through December 21, 1924, its contents constitute a spiritual diary of the few months he spent at Fuerteventura. Outpourings of rage and bitterness against the King and his "royal goose," Primo de Rivera, are intermingled with such exquisite contemplations on the majesty of sea and sky that it is difficult to conceive how they all could have come from one and the same man. Truly he was not one, but many—a society of individuals. The 103 sonnets in the volume are commented upon by Unamuno himself in prose, and each one carefully dated—a sort of thermometer of Don Miguel's spiritual temperature, so to speak. The prologue, a letter to Don Ramón Castaneyra de Puerto Cabras dated Paris, 1925, speaks of the profound impressions and lasting friendships he made during those unhappy days. Surrounded by a closely knit little group of friends, he learned there the virtue of patience, the communion of true fellowship, and the changing changelessness of the sea, as contrasted with his own tragic weaknesses. ". . . that blessed rocky isle where I lived with you . . . friends, all of you, in the unforgettable vigil we kept facing the sea that smiles at our tragic weaknesses." He recalled that "I left that island weeping, and that was because I was leaving with it roots of rock." And, he promised "I shall return in the flesh, for in spirit I am still there." Among that little group of loyal friends was his English

admirer and translator, J. Crawford Flitch. Such intimate contact with
the grand old man marked a turning point in Mr. Flitch's life, for he
wrote afterward to Don Miguel: "I cannot tell you how much I have
gained from my contact with you. I see life from a different point of
view. Yes, I believe I was going to sleep before I reached Fuerteventura; and now I am once more awake." [6]

Writing, reading, playing solitaire, and dreaming of freedom, Unamuno managed to fill the hours that at times dragged by on leaden
feet. He learned the mystery of Time, the difference between the clock
that measures time within each man and the mechanical clock that
binds us all within its twenty-four hours.

> Sangre que es vino en la celeste mesa;
> los siglos son en ti una misma hora
> y en esta hora de los siglos huesa. [7]

> Blood which is wine from the celestial table;
> the centuries are but an hour in you
> and in this hour of centuries a grave.

"Patience and shuffle the cards," cried the voice to Don Quijote in the
Montesinos cave, and it repeated the advice to Don Miguel on
Fuerteventura now.

The arrival of the mail boat always brought news and letters from
home or perhaps a photograph of Concha. His thoughts dwelt in loving tenderness upon this faithful companion and he dedicated two
beautiful sonnets to her. Another faithful friend, Dr. Areílza, wrote
him there offering his services. Areílza had been alarmed by Don
Miguel's open criticism of the dictatorship and had repeatedly warned
him that sooner or later Primo de Rivera would retaliate but Unamuno
had paid no attention to him. During this time, Areílza, in a lecture
given in Bilbao, praised Unamuno's works, thus risking the dictator's
displeasure. That Areílza was anxious for his friend's reputation and
even ashamed for Don Miguel, who continued to hurl invectives at
the government, is evident from a letter which he wrote to Ilundain
about him: "He lost all sense of control, as well as the dignity of a
man who is his enemy's captive; and he has done nothing but write
ugly, rude awkward things, things unworthy of his talent." [8]

[6] From Crawford Flitch to Unamuno, translated by Unamuno in *De Fuerteventura a París*, p. 105.

[7] Unamuno, *De Fuerteventura a París*, p. 84.

[8] Hernán Benítez, "La crisis religiosa de Unamuno," in *Revista de la universidad de Buenos Aires*, Vol. III, No. 9 (January–March 1949), p. 28.

Each day brought letters from unknown friends and sympathizers, and especially from one, a woman who was unusually diligent in protesting the injustice of his punishment. All great men, at some time or another, capture the imagination of "distant admirers." It was inevitable that Don Miguel, who revealed himself so completely in his writings, should be the object of many such attachments. For some time he must have been receiving letters from this Argentine lady, Delfina Molina Vedia de Bastianini, for he wrote of her ". . . she almost had me beside myself with her epistolary persecution." She seems to have been a woman of letters "anxious for her reputation and hoping, perhaps, to unite hers with mine . . ."[9] This remark Unamuno followed by relating an intimate, touching incident with his wife, which he prefaced with the remark that "my wife, although she writes well is not [a woman of letters] . . ."

At last the pardon was granted. Pressure had been brought to bear on Madrid and now a group of influential Frenchmen, headed by M. Dumey, director of the Parisian newspaper *Le Quotidien,* for which Unamuno was a correspondent, planned to send a boat to carry him to France.

Don Miguel was firm in his decision not to return to Spain while she lay bound by the dictator's chains, so not for six, long, agonizing years was he to walk the paths of home again. He preferred loneliness in France to surveillance at home. One may well ask why, if Don Miguel so loved his homeland and his family, and was free to teach in his beloved Salamanca where he would probably have been left unmolested but for his meddling in politics, why then did he voluntarily remain in exile? The answer lies in his self-knowledge, and in his conception of history as the Conscience of the Universe: God. Since history, he held, is the thought of God, to make history is to make God think, to "store up eternity." Consider the following, taken from his *Andanzas y visiones* written in 1916:

It matters not, oh my soul, what you say as long as you express yourself. What are you except a sentence in God's thinking? The thinking of God is history; history is what God thinks, the process of His thinking. And he who lives, one way or another, more or less visibly and audibly in history, however secluded within it he may be, lives in God's thinking, there to remain with thinking in God. And he lives in history who, wishing it or not, consciously or unconsciously, contributes toward making it, every one who has civil consciousness, however hidden or vacillating it may be. Absolute death is unconsciousness.[10]

[9] Unamuno, *Cómo se hace una novela,* p. 103.
[10] Unamuno, *Andanzas y visiones españolas,* p. 216.

Thus Don Miguel explained his meddling in politics, his *meta-política*, as an effort to exist, to affirm his being in this life and in the one hereafter. His friend, Jean Cassou, was right when he wrote "for Unamuno politics is but a way to salvation. A means to defend his person, to affirm it, and to insure that it will live forever in history." [11]

Whether or not Don Miguel's political activities, which he continued to carry on even after his exile, constituted his "great sin" as Benítez writes, they were nonetheless motivated by sincere convictions, which he expressed in the "existentialist lyricism" of the following sonnet written during his island exile:

> *Este cielo una palma es de tu mano,*
> *Señor, que me protege de la muerte*
> *del alma, y la otra palma es este fuerte—*
> *ventura, sosegado y fiel océano.*
>
> *Porque es aquí, Señor, donde me gano*
> *Contigo, y logro la más alta suerte*
> *que es, no ya conocerte sino serte,*
> *ser por ti de mi vida soberano.*
>
> *Pues, qué es sino lo que se llama história,*
> *Señor, tu creativo pensamiento*
> *aquí, en este planeta, vil escoria?*
>
> *La carne, polvo, se la lleva el viento;*
> *y luchando mi lucha por tu gloria*
> *quedarme en ésta, que se queda, siento.*[12]

'Tis but the palm of thy right hand, Lord, this sky.
The other hand, this fortress that protects me,
this blessed ocean stronghold, faithful, calm sea,
watchful guardian of my life's soul, lest it die.

For it is here, my Lord, in searching, that I,
master of my own life, find myself in Thee;
destiny of man, not knowing but to be.
Being Thee I rule my life as from on high.

For what is history but that which Thou hast thought,
Lord, creating on this planet, in thy mind,
the earthly dross, the stuff that comes to naught?

The flesh is but dust that goeth with the wind;
after this agony for Thee that I have fought
I feel secure Thou'lt not my soul rescind.

---

[11] "Retrato" by Jean Cassou in Unamuno, *Cómo se hace una novela*, p. 25.
[12] Unamuno, *De Fuerteventura a París*, pp. 75–76.

For two months Unamuno waited anxiously after he had received the news that his pardon had been granted. The nights brought little sleep and he fell into the habit of walking on the shore, and searching the horizon for signs of a ship. Every night between the hours of 10:30 and midnight he would spend thus, the warm African winds, moist with the salty sea spray, fanning his forehead. No wonder he "discovered" the sea, for there was plenty of time to learn her lessons, time to face his agony of soul and to learn at last, perhaps, humility. ". . . this my new rosary of sonnets is but the intimate diary of my intimate exile. It reflects all the agony . . . of my soul, of my Spanish, my Christian soul . . . some of them [reveal] the discovery I made there, there on Fuerteventura where I discovered the sea." [13]

At last on July first, news came that Unamuno's oldest son, Fernando, with his wife, had arrived on the nearby island of Las Palmas, where they met the group from France, which sailing on the little ship *L'Aiglon*, was headed for Fuerteventura. Did Unamuno know that Delfina Molina Vedia de Bastianini was one of that group? Had she secured the pardon, which she handed to him there on the island of Fuerteventura, from the Spanish government, or had Fernando obtained it and entrusted it to her when they were on Las Palmas? Benítez wrote that "She came with only a noble desire to help Unamuno," but Don Miguel himself wrote: ". . . she came to me in search of emotional excitement of the moving picture type." The moment of their meeting was fraught with high emotion. She handed him the pardon of the Spanish government, and as he took it from her "His features immobile, tears were streaming from his eyes, like tears from the eyes of a statue shaken by a deathlike chill." [14]

How he and Delfina passed the days from July 2 to July 6 is not known. The two must have had long talks together, or perhaps she was content simply to listen. On July 6 she and her daughter left the island and on the ninth *L'Aiglon* sailed smoothly away from the rocky shore of Fuerteventura, bearing with it one who was leaving "roots of rock in the rock." On the eleventh, they reached Las Palmas, and Don Miguel joyfully embraced his two children. Here the little ship *L'Aiglon* bade them adieu, and not until July 21 did they embark for Cherbourg, this time on the *Zeelandia*. The coast of France was visible on July 26, and Unamuno's heart was filled with memories of Concha, for then it was that he wrote that beautiful tribute to her:

[13] *Ibid.*, p. 9.
[14] Benítez, "La crisis religiosa de Unamuno," p. 38 n.

*Ahora que voy tocando ya la cumbre*
*de la carrera que mi Dios me puso . . .*

Now as I reach at last the topmost height
of the career my God to me allotted . . .

Perhaps now he was beginning to realize what life without her would
be. The exile he was facing must have seemed all the more bitter since,
from this point on, it was to be a voluntary absence from her. Recalling in Paris that moment when Concha had cradled him in her arms
like a child, he wrote: "I realized then what God had given me in
this woman, the mother of my children, my virgin mother, whose only
novel is my novel; Concha, my mirror of blessed, divine unconsciousness, my mirror of eternity." [15]

Don Miguel promised to write the complete story of his island exile.
He even intended to call it *Don Quijote en Fuerteventura,* but he
never did. Instead he expressed in the little volume of poems which
he wrote in Paris, *De Fuerteventura a París,* the loneliness he felt
when he walked the shore in the darkness listening to the ceaseless
roar of the breakers, and the bitterness that possessed him because
he, who had devoted his lifetime to working for the welfare of his
beloved Spain, was now an exile from that Spain.

[15] Unamuno, *Cómo se hace una novela,* p. 103.

# The *"Dead Sky"* of Paris

CHAPTER 23

THE *Zeelandia* DOCKED AT Cherbourg the last of August where a multitude of Frenchmen representing the League of Human Rights had gathered to receive the great Spanish rebel. As one Spanish biographer points out, it was not as a poet, a great Christian, or a great philosopher that they honored him, but rather as a man in the role of a great protestor. At the banquet given for him there that night he was described in "somewhat misleading terms of juvenile character." [1]

By September he was in Paris, the heart of that great nation which he had so often scorned, but with a scorn which he had confessed sprang only from jealousy. Now, realizing that he owed to France his liberation, he wrote to Don Ramón Castaneyra in a different key: ". . . my liberation, thanks to the generosity of the noble French nation, which here in Paris is giving me my freedom and dignity . . ." [2]

That letter he probably wrote sitting alone in his little room in the *pension* number 2, Rue Laperouse, located near the Arc de L'Etoile. Despite his gratitude toward "the noble French nation," Paris, for Don Miguel, was a city peopled with artificial beings "who believe that animation and gesticulation pass for true emotion" and he described his room as "a kind of cell" under a "dead sky." Here in Paris despair and the death-wish laid hold on him. For the first time in his long

[1] César González-Ruano, *Miguel de Unamuno*, p. 77.
[2] Unamuno, *De Fuerteventura a París*, Prologue.

years of literary production, no thoughts would come. He would wander like a lost soul among the book stalls along the Seine, the river whose waters now drew him as the waters of the Dwina had fatally drawn his friend, Ganivet, twenty-six years earlier. Indeed, so strong was the temptation to throw himself in that he had to push against the parapet along its edge. Then, spiritually and physically exhausted, he would retrace his steps to his "cell" and lie for hours idle, staring at the ceiling, a prey to thoughts of death and insanity. He felt that reason was perhaps forsaking him altogether. Here there was no Concha to whom he could turn for comfort, no mountains to climb. Instead, he saw only strange faces and the dark waters of the Seine.

Do such feelings seem exaggerated? Certainly Unamuno must have experienced them for he put them in his novel, *Cómo se hace una novela,* which he wrote while in Paris. Some critics of this book have thought so and perhaps there is room for the idea. That exile has produced insanity and even suicide is well-known. The ancient Greeks and Romans, as Benítez points out, often committed suicide when in exile, and only one who has experienced the terrible pangs of home-sickness can really understand what it means for "an exile to feel that gradually, inch by inch, his reason, his feelings, even his memories are fading away, and he is slowly sinking into insanity." [3] Gradually the sufferer "thinks less clearly and loses his appetite for living." [4]

This "loss of appetite for living" is apt to show itself first in a care-lessness toward personal appearance and even cleanliness. So it was with Don Miguel. Recalling the last time he saw Concha when she had darned and washed for him, he would gaze dejectedly at his socks, now as full of holes as were those of the mad don of La Mancha in the Duke's castle. He was too depressed even to change his clothing. Then, realizing, no doubt, that he could, if he chose, go back to his home and loved ones, he would question his own sincerity and wonder if he were play-acting. "But no!" would come the answer, "my part is to play out my life and my truth.".[5] "And now he played the part of an exile," wrote Don Miguel in *Cómo se hace una novela,* that strange mixture of truth and fiction wherein he recounted his experiences in Paris. "Even the careless neglect of my person, my stubborn deter-mination not to change my clothes or don a different suit stems in part

[3] Hernán Benítez, "La crisis religiosa de Unamuno," in *Revista de la universidad de Buenos Aires,* Vol. III, No. 9 (January–March 1949), p. 34.
[4] *Ibid.,* p. 32.
[5] Unamuno, *Cómo se hace una novela,* p. 101.

from the role that I am playing—this, coupled with a slight tendency to stint my pennies which I have always had and which, when I am away from my family and alone, is uncurbed." [6] The idea of looking upon himself as an actor in a play, a character in a novel, finally obsessed him so completely that at last Don Miguel began to write about it. Thus, perhaps, he was saved to live out his novel to the end.

What he wrote, then, was the strangest mixture of objective subjectivity that has ever come from the mind of man. *Cómo se hace una novela* was the tortuous existence of a writer, a man whose very life depended on the act of writing, *in* his writing. In such manner was reality and imagination fused that he seemed unable to distinguish between the two and his "novel" became synonymous with his "life." Truly Don Miguel, by existing, by his very being, was "making" his novel, and so in writing about it he was telling "how a novel is made." First he chose a character, himself, then he selected a name, Unamuno Jugo de la Raza. What followed was an objective account of his hero's actions and reactions; an admission of the death-wish and his horror at the idea of insanity.

U. Jugo de la Raza is unspeakably bored—because now he only lives within himself, in the poor I beneath history, the unhappy man who has not become a novel. [Remember Unamuno's use of "novel" for "life."] And that's why he likes novels. He likes them and seeks them out to live in another, to find eternity in another. At least that's what he thinks, but really he seeks them out in order to find himself, to live in himself, to be himself. Or rather, in order to escape from his unknown and unknowable self, unknowable even to himself. [7]

Then one day his character, wandering as was his habit among the book stalls along the Seine, picks up a book and begins to read. "He has scarcely begun to read it before buying it." He finds that "it fascinates him tremendously, it draws him out of himself and into the character in the novel—the world of an autobiographical confession— a romantic confession—it identifies him with that other one, in fine, it gives him a history." [8]

In the course of his reading, Unamuno Jugo de la Raza, horrified, comes across this sentence: "When the reader comes to the end of this grievous story he will die with me." [9] He feels a recurrence of the old *angina del pecho* from which he had suffered years before, and dropping the book hastily, he makes his way painfully back to his

[6] *Ibid.*, pp. 100–101.

[7] *Ibid.*, p. 73.          [8] *Ibid.*, p. 73–74.          [9] *Ibid.*, p. 74.

room and falls on the bed. There he realizes that on his way home he had felt

tempted to throw myself into the Seine, the mirror. I had to hold on to the parapet. And I remembered other similar temptations of long ago, and that strange being I once imagined, who was born with the death wish and lived with his suicidal tendency for nearly eighty years, killing himself by degrees with thinking, day by day. Is this life? No; I'll read no more from that book—nor from any other; I'll not walk again along the banks of the Seine where books are sold.[10]

But unconsciously, against his will, he is drawn inexorably back to that book. Then "he gazed lovingly at the fatal volume, then at the waters of the Seine, and—he won out! Or was he defeated? He passed on without opening the book, saying to himself: 'I wonder what happens in that story? How does it end?' But he knew that some day he'd be unable to resist and he'd have to get that book and read it out to the end even though he might have to die." [11]

Finally it happens; de la Raza can resist no longer; he returns and buys the book. Back in his room he avidly resumes his reading in bed, and once more he reads the death warning. Impulsively he sets fire to the little volume, and trembling with fear, he falls asleep exhausted. Could it be that he is going insane, he wonders? The fates of other exiles come to his mind successively, Dante, Moses, Saint Paul, Victor Hugo, and Manzini, all of whom "in their enforced absence from their native land learned . . . the meaning of exile from eternity." [12] But no, he is not insane, for how then could he reason to doubt his sanity? Doubt of it is the best proof of it. To be "insane is to lose reason but not truth." Reason, he defines as "the point of accord upon which we all agree," while truth is individual, "personal and incommunicable." Therefore "Reason unites us, while truths separate us." [13] Then, in brackets, he characteristically states the opposite "now it dawns upon me that perhaps it is truth that unites us and reasons are what separate us." [14] Like Don Quijote, who, in the end, regained his reason before dying, Unamuno adds that now he is more serene of spirit, for, when he attacks windmills he recognizes them as such and it is others who think they are giants!

Here he returns to Unamuno Jugo de la Raza, his hero, who has fallen asleep after burning the book. Awakening, he is again beset by

[10] *Ibid.*, p. 75.          [11] *Ibid.*, p. 76.          [12] *Ibid.*, p. 84.
[13] *Ibid.*, p. 85.          [14] *Ibid.*

an overwhelming desire to know how the novel ends. There follow days of endless searching among the book stalls for a volume he knows does not exist. Wherever his gaze falls he sees the waters of the Seine. The unknown ending of the novel gradually becomes synonymous with the fate of Spain. Then come thoughts of *mi Vizcaya* and "the peaceful green of his native countryside, rich with the silent traditions of the ages . . . and the surrounding land would speak to him in the Basque tongue, in the Euskera of his infancy, it would speak to him in soothing trusting babblings of a baby." [15] His childhood friend, the watchmaker, speaking the ancient tongue of his forefathers had once declared "that languages and religions keep us apart," but Unamuno corrects this view with "As though Christ and Buddha didn't say the same things to God, only in different tongues." [16]

At this point in *Cómo se hace una novela* the author's fancy leaves the past in time (time is the real *tragedia*) and projects him into the future. He imagines that eventually he will find another copy of the novel. Then he must decide: to read or not to read? (By now one senses that "reading" is synonymous with "living.") "And why must I die when I finish reading this book, when the character in this autobiography dies? Why am I not meant to outlive myself? To live on and examine my own corpse." [17] But decide he must, and his decision is to read slowly, a word at a time. No, he will not read, but will keep the book within reach for "After all I must die because everybody dies." Then comes the inevitable contradiction: All this about dying is "one of the stupidest things that can be said, the commonest of all the commonplaces, and therefore the most paradoxical of paradoxes." [18]

Here the mind of the writer rebels, and he feels the fear of insanity. Remembering the exiled Manzini's letters to his beloved Judith, he quotes that poet: "they so insisted on calling the poet insane that finally they drove him truly insane; they drove Tasso insane, they committed the suicide of Chatterton and others . . ." This, no doubt, is the idea which inspired Don Miguel to write *La locura del Dr. Montarco.*

Earlier in the book Don Miguel has introduced the idea of insanity which, he points out, according to the Greek term, is to be outside of oneself, or "beside one's self." This, he adds, is analogous with the Latin term *ex-sistere," "Existir."* Hence Jesus was the greatest of all madmen. "Existence is a form of madness . . . The man who is beside

[15] *Ibid.*, p. 93.          [16] *Ibid.*
[17] *Ibid.*, p. 106.
[18] *Ibid.*, p. 107.

himself, who gives himself, who transcends, he is insane. The sacred madness of the cross is none other than this." [19]

In the novel Unamuno Jugo de la Raza is back in the little cell-like room on the Rue Laperouse where he meets his other self, Miguel de Unamuno y Jugo, and there he puts the question: to read or not to read? Then he asks: If he doesn't read the book, will he lose "His will power and his memory, or at any rate, his appetite for life, so that he will forget about the book, the novel, his own life, forget about himself?" Insanity is "another way to die, to die before one's time; that is if there is such a thing as a time to die and if one can die outside of it." [20]

As the reader who has tried to follow this tangled account must realize by now, Cómo se hace una novela is the revelation of a mind and spirit on the brink of insanity, full of penetrating flashes and obscure meanings. Writing the prologue to the Spanish translation from Hendaye in 1927, Don Miguel explained that he wrote it "piecemeal," and would read the "pieces" aloud to his friends, especially to Jean Cassou, who would translate them into French for publication in a local magazine. It appeared first in French, under the title Comment on fait un roman on May 15, 1926, in Mercure de France.

It must have been Jean Cassou who urged Don Miguel to resume his writing in the first place. Thanks to him, perhaps, the desperate Spaniard decided to "read his book slowly," so he resisted the waters of the Seine and lived out his natural life "within himself." That he was ever seriously tempted to do otherwise may be disputed. It remains a moot question. It is a fact, however, that Unamuno was quick to recognize the "death wish" in others. In commenting on the suicide of José Asunción Silva he wrote "There is a fragment in Silva's prose . . . that makes us suspect that perhaps he felt a presentiment of insanity and took his life in order to escape from it." [21] And he frequently stated that suicide, rather than indicating a hatred of life, bespeaks a desire to possess more life, to live in everyone else, and in all places, the thirst for infinity and eternity. If Unamuno saw this in Silva, could he not have seen it in himself?

To Cassou he may have owed his life and his sanity. Son of a Spanish mother, and a man of letters in Paris, Cassou became Don Miguel's guide and translator during the twelve months he spent there. To him Don Miguel entrusted his sonnets for publication, as well as La agonía

19 Ibid., p. 51.
20 Ibid., pp. 115–116.
21 Unamuno, Contra esto y aquello, p. 37.

*del cristianismo,* the other production of his Parisian exile. Although during the first part of his sojourn under the "dead sky" of Paris, Don Miguel lost all of his old desire to write, he slowly resumed his customary habits. However, he abandoned completely all writings he had previously commenced and absolutely refused to write for any Spanish publications on account of the strict censorship in Spain. At least two of his works, therefore, appeared first in French (*Cómo se hace una novela* and *La agonía del cristianismo*) and he himself later translated them into Spanish. Of the first of these two, he writes in the prologue: "I didn't want the original to appear in Spanish for various reasons, first of all, it could not be in Spain where all writings were subject to the most shameful and castrating censorship, a censorship somewhat worse than that of illiterates, of men who hated truth and intelligence." [22] The horror of those days in Paris where he had relived the "sweet pain" of *The Tragic Sense of Life* returned as he prologued the book from Hendaye:

I never again expect to pass through such an intimate, tragic experience. —My whole life weighed me down, my life which was and is my death. There weighed upon me not only my seventy years of individual, physical life; but more, much more than that; the silent tradition of centuries, hidden in the innermost recesses of my soul weighed upon me; ineffable and unconscious prenatal memories pressed down upon me. For our despairing hope of a personal life beyond the tomb is nourished and strengthened by those vague intimations of our roots in the eternity of history.[23]

Gradually Unamuno's life began to fall into something like its customary pattern of walking, talking, talking some more, and then writing. The early mornings he would spend in his room that overlooked the little park where a statue of George Washington was usually drenched in the fine Paris rain. A copious correspondence kept him busy until the eleven-thirty lunch hour. Leaving promptly thereafter, he would walk the long blocks to the Café Rotonde located between the boulevards Montparnasse and Raspail where he arrived around one or one-thirty. There a group of friends was always waiting for him; among them were the Spaniards Eduardo Ortega y Gassett, Esplá the journalist, Luna, and sometimes another great Spanish exile, the novelist Vicente Blasco Ibáñez. This impulsive writer once said to Unamuno: "With your priestly mien, Unamuno, you ought to go to North America to establish a religion and grow rich." Unamuno

[22] Unamuno, *Cómo se hace una novela,* p. 11.
[23] *Ibid.,* p. 10.

answered only with a look of indignation, as might be expected.[24] The
Peruvian writer, Vicente García Calderón, was often one of the group,
as were occasionally Professor Seignobos, Valery Larbaud, his friend
Cassou, Maurice Legendre, and one other who cannot be omitted, a
fruit vendor by the name of Cortes. Cortes ran a fruit store just across
from Unamuno's pension. He had read the *Tragic Sense of Life* and
was a great admirer of Don Miguel's.

Conspicuously absent from the *tertulia* at La Rotonde was the current
idol of Paris, Paul Valéry. These two "greats" did meet, however, when
the Pen Club presented Unamuno as their honored guest at a special
banquet. The "Old Man's" speech on this occasion was a disappointment to Valéry, as well as to the other listeners.

*Don Miguel se leva et, dans un français correct, voire pure, mais auquel
sa voix sans éclat ne donnait ni l'ampleur, ni l'intonation oratoires, parla
avec une sourde émotion de l'Espagne, de son Espagne. On applaudit;
mais la politesse couvrait mal la déception.*[25]

Don Miguel got up and in a very correct, even pure French, but to which
his enthusiastic voice gave neither the volume nor inflexion for oratory,
spoke with deep emotion about Spain, his Spain. There was applause, but
the politeness hardly covered the disappointment.

Valéry avoided Unamuno, who must have felt the slight for one day
he sat down and wrote to him—on July 28, 1925, to be exact—enclos-
ing a poem. But Valéry, who had not read Unamuno's works, and
hence, had no comprehension of his worth, never answered, for time
and his own popularity were pressing. Mlle. Pomés, the French writer
who explains Unamuno's relations with Valéry in *Cuadernos de la
cátedra Miguel de Unamuno*, writes that ". . . *Son abstention lui laissa
une ombre de remords . . . sa mort le frappa.*" (His failure [to write]
left him a shadow of remorse . . . his death shocked him.) After Don
Miguel's death the Frenchman read some of his verse and prose. "*Je
ne me doutais pas . . . qu'il était si grand,*" (I don't doubt but that he
is great) he concluded.[26] The editors of *Cuadernos de la cátedra Miguel
de Unamuno* reproduce in a footnote a statement by Don Miguel to
the effect that Valéry came to his pension and, finding Don Miguel
out, left the following note:

[24] González-Ruano, *Miguel de Unamuno*, p. 80.
[25] Mathilde Pomès in *Cuadernos de la cátedra Miguel de Unamuno*, I, 61.
[26] *Ibid.*, p. 66.

*Vendredi*

*Cher et illustre voisin, muy querido Unamuno, je ne sais pas vous dire en castillan tous mes remerciements pour votre lettre et pour l'honneur de la dédicace. ¡Yo soy vaca! Et je suis desolé de ne pas vous trouver. Mais je reviendrai avec l'espoir de vous dire sans "precission" mais de grand coeur tout ce que je dois decir a usted: Yo no se escribir, muchissimas gracias.*[27]

Friday

Dear, illustrious neighbor, my very dear Unamuno. I know not how to express in Castilian my thanks for your letter and the honor of the poem you dedicated to me. I am a cow [clumsy fellow]! I am sorry not to find you at home. But I shall return in hopes of saying, not as I should but with all my heart, all that I ought to say to you: I don't know how to write. Many thanks.

To return to Don Miguel's daily routine, having arrived at the Café Rotonde, he would hold forth in his customary manner for the next two or three hours talking of many things: astronomy, *cocotología*, and politics, and all to the accompaniment of his nervous rolling of bread-crumbs or making *pajaritas* which were usually retrieved by his friends as souvenirs. On one occasion seated at a nearby table was a typical little Parisian miss made up very much as a *cocotte* herself. After watching for sometime Don Miguel's nimble fingers produce his *pajaritas* she whispered some words to a waiter who repeated the message in like manner to Unamuno. The latter gave no sign and continued talking as he concentrated on his creations. Finally, having made five or six of different shapes and sizes, he carefully signed each one, then raising his eyes to meet those of the interested madamoiselle, he presented them to her gallantly saying only, "Voici, madamoiselle."

Another afternoon the group was joined by a Danish journalist who came looking for the famous Spanish exile. When the waiter had pointed him out the young Dane addressed him in German: "Sprechen Sie deutsch?" They talked for a while in this language, but the young man was not very fluent in German so they talked in French until Unamuno said: "Your long absence from your homeland, sir, seems to have caused you to forget your own tongue. Let us talk in Danish." The journalist was almost moved to tears to find someone familiar with his own language and Don Miguel explained: "I learned the language of your country, my friend, in the books of Kierkegaard, at my little work table in Salamanca." "That is the real Spain," answered the Dane.[28]

[27] *Ibid.*, p. 69.
[28] González-Ruano, *Miguel de Unamuno*, p. 81.

At times the group was treated to samples of the Old Man's terrible temper. One of the party said to him in all good faith: "Don Miguel, forget that critical attitude that you have about politics and the affairs in Spain and you can return to Salamanca."

"Ah! Have you been instructed to say that to me? I know you! Well, just you tell the man that sent you—"

"But, Don Miguel, nobody sent me—"

"Shut up, you rascal!"

"But—"

"Don't 'but' me—Get out of here!" [29]

What revolutionary talk of rebellion against the *ganso real* went on during those afternoons at the Café Rotonde is hard to say. They fed on each other's bitterness and warmed their spirits in fiery invectives. Dr. Areílza from Spain wrote to Ilundain, "He has a host of friends at the Café Rotonde where he pours forth his bitterness. With Blasco Ibáñez and company, he is trying to organize the revolution. But there is so much terror of Communism in Spain that we continue in our role of tame sheep." [30]

Indeed, those must have been turbulent sessions to inspire such thoughts as ". . . my poor Spain, stupified by the cowardly, the most vile, the most uncivil tyranny." [31] And again, recalling that prior to his deportation he had written, ". . . the Royal Goose had less brains than a cricket," he added: "I exaggerated . . . No, he is nothing more than a half wit, a pure and simple fool." [32] "Never has there been a mother so beaten, insulted, so spit upon, ridiculed, and mocked by a son as Spain has been by Primo de Rivera. But, is that a son? Can that thing have a mother?"

At the end of these stormy sessions at La Rotonde, Don Miguel would start the trek back to his pension, accompanied by his companions—this time he would cut through the Luxembourg Gardens to the Pont Saint Michel, cross the Châtelet to Rivoli Street, and thence to the Place de la Concorde up to the Champs Élysées. One by one his friends would leave him until he was left to return alone back to the little Park des États-Unis. Occasionally he would stop to sit awhile on a bench along the avenue and read aloud some of his current invectives.

[29] *Ibid.*, p. 81.
[30] Benítez, "La crisis religiosa de Unamuno," p. 28.
[31] Unamuno, *Cómo se hace una novela*, p. 10.
[32] Unamuno, *De Fuerteventura a París*, p. 57.

Don Miguel received many distinguished visitors at his pension. They all had to climb the narrow stairs to his little room for, as one of them pointed out, the six square meters of the first floor parlor was occupied by a sofa on which a huge doll reclined on a velvet cushion and, asks the visitor, what would Unamuno have done while he received his visitors, put it on the floor, or hold it on his knees? No, he received his callers, from Monsieur Herriot on down, in his tiny bedroom at the top of the stairs. The Old Man would sit on the edge of his bed and offer the only chair to his caller. "And even then it was a miracle that this was available," writes Mathilde Pomés, "Books were piled everywhere. Piles of them stacked on the hearth reached to the mantelpiece and those on the mantelpiece reached to the ceiling."

"There is only one place left," Unamuno said to her, "the ceiling. Stretched on my bed, I float up there as though it were the real sky."[33]

Perhaps it was in this room that he met Briand and Herriot. News from Spain came to him in many ways, besides through the Spanish press. His old friend and enemy, the Count of Romanones, called on him here, as did another old acquaintance, Bugallal, who brought news of the execution of one Lairet, and attempted to explain his own collaboration with the hated Martínez Anido.

The one bright spot in Unamuno's entire Parisian experience was a visit from Concha and children during the Christmas holidays of 1924 which was made possible by a lucky lottery ticket Concha had bought from a poor blind friend. But this was only a short interlude and he soon succumbed to ever-increasing gloom and depression. It was then that he wrote:

> He will come by night when all is sleeping—
> He will come by night with his soft step,
> He will come by night and place his finger
> on the wound—
> He will come as he left, as he has gone
> —the fatal call sounds in the distance—
> he will keep his rendezvous—[34]

In the prologue to *La agonía del cristianismo* Unamuno says that he wrote the work "upon request" expressly to be translated into French by Monsieur Cassou. Second in value only to *The Tragic Sense of Life in Men and in Peoples*, it was written, he says, "while my soul

---

[33] *Cuadernos de la cátedra Miguel de Unamuno*, I, 58.
[34] Antonio Sánchez Barbudo, *Estudios sobre Unamuno y Machado*, p. 119.

was in a critical condition, seized by a veritable spiritual fever, in a nightmare of waiting." The *encargo* (commission), however, was not made by Cassou but by M. P. L. Couchoud. This gentleman was preparing a collection entitled *Christianisme* and it was he who suggested the title, *L'Agonie du Christianisme*. It is a deeply spiritual expression of much the same ideas as were contained in *The Tragic Sense of Life*. Don Miguel attempted to explain the paradox of Christianity. He wrote that the inscription "I am the way, the truth and the life" made him wonder ". . . whether the way and the life are one and the same thing as truth, whether there might not be a contradiction between truth and life, whether it is not truth that kills and life that sustains us in falsehood . . . And herein lies the tragedy. For truth is something collective, social, even civil; the truth is that upon which we all agree, whereby we understand one another. And Christianity is something individual and incommunicable." [35]

The work was completed in Paris, signed and dated December 13, 1924. Other offers came to him but he turned them down—one from *Crítica* in Buenos Aires offered a tempting remuneration for a collaboration. But even the prospect of a considerable financial return could not tempt him, for he never completely shook off his depression in Paris. His emotions were ever near the surface which fact made him unfit for any serious lecturing though he did make a few attempts at the College de France. During one of his lectures the poor old man broke down completely, and the students filed silently from the hall. Afterwards, walking slowly along the street with his host professor, Unamuno, who had said not a word till then, explained that the classroom atmosphere, so reminiscent of his beloved Salamanca and which he missed so desperately, was the cause of his emotion. No, Paris was no place for him; "there is too much history here," he once said. It weighed upon him at every turn and he needed the fresh winds of Gredos.

Finally Unamuno could stand it no longer and so he took flight from the metropolis, the world of society and fashions where he felt alien and alone. He left the "dead" Parisian sky for the mountains overlooking Spain, for his own beloved Basque country that offered him a natural refuge. At the end of August 1925, accompanied by Eduardo Ortega y Gassett, Don Miguel betook himself to the border town of Hendaye.

[35] Unamuno, *La agonía del cristianismo*, p. 23.

# Hendaye – Where Sea
# and Mountains Meet

CHAPTER *24*

AT THE FRENCH BORDER TOWN
of Hendaye the Pyrenees are cut by the meeting of the Bidasoa River
with the Atlantic Ocean. It is a town of mountains and waters and
across the international bridge the Spanish cities of Fuenterrabía, Irún,
and Vera nestle at the feet of ever higher rising peaks crowned by the
majestic Jaizquíbel. On the French side the towns of Bayonne, Urruña,
Saint Jean de Lux and Ondarritz dot the surrounding mountains and
beaches. The promontory of Higuer that projects to form the lovely
natural bay, Unamuno saw as the bridge which linked his two lives,
a silent tongue whose visionary song at evening wove a charm to heal
his wounds:

> *Lengua de tierra del ocaso,*
> *Fuenterrabía, Cabo Higuer;*
> *entre cielos soñado paso,*
> *mi ensalmo del atardecer.*
> *Lengua de tierra de poniente,*
> *vas a bautizarte en la mar;*
> *entre mis vidas verde puente,*
> *ay mis dos vidas de anudar.*
> *Lengua de tierra silenciosa,*
> *bajo el azul cantas visión*

*mi Fuenterrabía piadosa,*
*me estás bizmando el corazón.*[1]

Earthen tongue of setting sun,
Fuentarrabía, Cape Higuer,
in you my evening hymn is sung,
twixt two skys a dreamed illusion.
Earthen tongue of the golden west,
you seek baptism in the ocean,
green bridge twixt my lives, you rest,
blend of my two lives the motion.
Earthen tongue, so silent, singing
songs of vision 'neath the azure,
you, Fuenterrabía, the Godly,
for my heart, the cataplasm.

Here in Hendaye, the Big Bear was the lance that armed him, Don
Miguel, the new-born Don Quijote:

*Ya de noche al abrírseme el cielo*
*en tu cumbre, Jaizquíbel, desnudo*
*repondiendo al clamor de mi anhelo*
*Don Quijote se detiene mudo.*
        *Vestido de estrellas;*
*la Bocina del Norte es su lanza;*
*el Cordel de Santiago a sus huellas*
        *les calza esperanza.*
*Clavileño se está ¡cuán contrista*
*su quietud! Aunque todo él se muera*
*va el hidalgo a la vana conquista*
*de Dios que le espera!* [2]

When the night sky unfolds itself before me
on your highest peak, Jaizquíbel, stark and naked,
in answer to the call of my desiring,
Don Quijote pauses in his course, all silent.
        Bedecked in stars;
the Little Bear his lance is to the northward.
Saint James' Cord sheds hope along his pathway
        round his footsteps.
And motionless stands Clavileño, rending
the heart strings; though he die, all of him,
the knight will go, in vain, to conquer
God who awaits him.

[1] Unamuno, *Cancionero,* pp. 351–352.
[2] *Ibid.,* pp. 121–122.

The natural surroundings recalled those of Bilbao nestled at the mouth of the Nervión flowing to the ocean from the same Pyrenees, and the Basques, though French, were still Basques, the people of that *patria chica* of his childhood. Though Unamuno nursed the memory of that childhood throughout his lifetime, it was here in Hendaye that he strove to submerge himself in it and so find peace in his intimate self, devoid of pretense and play-acting. The sight of Jaizquíbel recalled Arnótegui. The sound of the church bells from Fuenterrabía reminded him, perchance, of the shrine to our Lady of Begoña, while the perfume of the mountain flowers took him back to Ceberio of his childhood. Here he could lie prone upon the ground, his eyelids closed beneath the burning sun, while forgotten memories of glory passed like phantom spectres across the fields of his soul to leave his heart sleeping, his quiet hands waiting there on the green earth while for a time, words were held at bay:

> En tierra, cerrados los párpados,
> mirando al sol; cielo de brasa;
> debajo España, tras los montes;
> en el silencio descansaban
> los 4 labios de mis ojos;
> baño de sangre la mirada;
> el corazón se me dormía;
> quietas las manos esperaban;
> tranquilo el campo verde en torno;
> acechadora la palabra.
> Solemnes, pausados, serenos
> pasaban al paso, pasaban
> los viejos recuerdos de gloria,
> pasaban y nada quedaba.
> Cerrados los ojos, las bocas,
> sin voz ni mirada, fantasmas,
> pasaban a paso de historia,
> espectros del campo del alma.[3]

Prone on the earth, my eyelids closed,
my face toward the sun, the heavens ablaze;
Spain down there, beyond those hills;
in the silence there were resting then
two pairs of lips that were my eyes;
bathed in blood my eyesight was;
sleep was claiming the heart of me;
quiet and still, my hands were waiting;
the green field tranquil all around;

[3] *Ibid.*, p. 180.

> words, for a while, were held at bay;
> then solemnly, slowly, serenely,
> in measured rhythm processing,
> forgotten memories of glory
> passed over me there, leaving nothing.
> The mouths of my eyes were still closed,
> voiceless and blind, phantom spectres
> passed in historical rhythm
> over the fields of my soul.

For lodging Unamuno found a tiny room on the second floor of the little Hotel Broca that faced the railroad station just down the hill. His window opened on a garden overrun with flowers and vines, a little bench beneath an arbor with vegetables growing in orderly rows. Monsieur and Madame Broca treated him well and served him at his solitary table in the little dining room below—yes, here away from the overpowering sense of history that depressed him in Paris, Don Miguel felt

> My freedom of thought
> who in all the world can kill it?
> "the word of God cannot be bound,"
> the wind blows where it wills.[4]

In such an atmosphere Unamuno resumed his readings and his writings with renewed spirit and began the most aggressive struggle of all of his political involvement, an involvement which Armando Zubizarreta calls his *"moral de batalla."* Here too, like Voltaire in Switzerland, Unamuno held court while the world came to him since he could not go to the world, but, unlike Voltaire, he lived in such economic straits that Pablo, his dentist son, had to pay for his lodging. Government and political officials of France and Spain, family, relations and friends from Salamanca and Bilbao, scholars, writers, journalists, and sensation seekers, to say nothing of the local butcher, the baker and the candlestickmaker, as well as tourists and spies, all courted the Grand Old Man, each for a reason of his own. And in the midst of it all, Don Miguel, true to his intimate Don Quijote, did battle in the face of ridicule and built his circumstantial life around his daily routine: reading and writing until noon, a game of *mus* after lunch with his favorite *contertulianos* in the Grand Café off the plaza, and walking along the mountain paths with anyone who would accompany him.

[4] *Ibid.,* p. 364.

Ever since the Spanish *coup d'etat* of September 13, 1923, when Alfonso XIII issued his *manifiesto*, setting up Primo de Rivera's dictatorship, many of its opponents were careful to distinguish between opposition to the dictator and opposition to the King. In fact, most of Unamuno's friends were anxious for him to do likewise, feeling no doubt that the *Directorio* must soon pass, but the Monarchy, never. However, Don Miguel's position in regard to Alfonso antedated the dictatorship by many years and he refused to alter it now. Even when those concerned with his welfare attempted to put conciliatory words in his mouth, he roundly denied them. For example, when the Cuban ambassador to Spain met Unamuno in Paris His Excellency said to him, "I have just come from there, from Spain, and you know what's happening, but I believe we should not confuse the King with the dictatorship," to which Don Miguel answered, "No, they should not be confused, neither should they be separated." Señor Kohly, the ambassador, added: "I have heard that you once said that just as, in the legend, the body of the Cid was mounted on horseback to win one last victory over the Moors, you believe that the King, politically and morally speaking, is a corpse; but that he must be preserved for a last battle against the Pretorians." Don Miguel's answer was, "Yes, I may have said it, then I was mistaken, but you tell him for me, that he must be buried immediately afterwards, not forgiven by virtue of the corpse's deed." [5]

After Primo's fall, when the King was still hanging on prior to his flight from Madrid, Unamuno exclaimed publicly in Irún, "For the watchword 'God, Country, and King' we must substitute 'God, Country, and Law'." [6]

Don Miguel was steadfast in his opposition to the King, as evidenced by spoken and written statements before, after, and during his exile. Here in Hendaye in January of 1928 he wrote that most bitter of all royal attacks in an article titled, "My Personal Quarrel" (*"Mi pleito personal"*). [7] After berating Primo de Rivera and the "epileptic" Martínez Anido, Primo's Chief of Police, he rejected the idea that his "campaign" was motivated by "an individual quarrel of mine with the King or with the pretorian tyranny that he brought to Spain." Since he was given ample opportunity to escape from Fuerteventura, either to

[5] Unamuno, *Dos discursos y dos artículos*, pp. 94–95.
[6] Indalecio Prieto, "La repatriación de Unamuno," in *Acción* (Montevideo), January 7, 1956.
[7] Unamuno, "Mi pleito personal," in *Dos discursos y dos artículos*.

Portugal or to America, he pointed out that his exile was entirely a
matter of his own volition. Then he asked rhetorically: Power! Why
should he seek more power when he already had it? No, the true
motive of this his campaign, his *moral de batalla*, was to acquire renown: "Fame which I continue to increase and enlarge in order to use
the moral and intellectual authority thus gained to free my country
from the most abject, rapacious and brutalizing tyranny, and to chew
the horrible little tyrants to bits—forever—with the mark of historical
reprobates, and at the same time, to save the honor of our Spain in
the eyes of Humanity's conscience." [8]

Recalling a friend's remark that he, Unamuno, could say and do
things impossible for "those who aspired to govern," he exclaimed, "I
don't aspire to govern; I govern!" [9]

"Hate, no!" he continued, "one hates people, not things. And those
objects, those individuals, if they personify anything, it is Spanish
animal force, her infra-humanity, her bestiality." [10]

In spite of such assertions by Unamuno, Don Indalecio Prieto, who
has since been termed a Socialist, *ergo* a collaborator with the dictatorship, wrote that General Mola in his memoirs brags that the
Republicans did not discover a spy while he, Mola, was *General de
Seguridad*; his spy who served in the household of the Republican
president, Manuel Azaña, in Madrid, was even given a position by
the Republicans in Morocco and, states Sr. Prieto, that same spy was
a *contertuliano* with Don Miguel in the Hotel Broca and reported his
innermost thoughts back to Madrid. And, adds Prieto, through that
spy Mola and Berenguer, "head of the government," felt safe knowing
that Unamuno *was attacking Primo and not the Monarchy*.[11] How
could Prieto have thought this? And where did Don Indalecio fit into
the picture? A resident of Bilbao, he had once lost an election to Don
Miguel, but during Unamuno's Hendaye exile, he was apparently sup-
porting the growing adherents of the Republic who rallied around
the Grand Old Man, no doubt in hopes of pulling out a plum for
himself. He frequently visited Unamuno at the Hotel Broca and stuck
to him like a shadow on his triumphal entry into Spain in February
of 1930. His real feelings of jealousy are all too obvious in an article
he wrote in 1956 from his Argentine exile. If, as Don Manuel García
Blanco asserted, Prieto collaborated with the dictatorship of Primo,
he was indeed a turncoat and a dissembler.

[8] *Ibid.*, pp. 13–14.       [9] *Ibid.*, p. 18.       [10] *Ibid.*, pp. 23–24.
[11] *Ibid.* Italics are this author's.

That dictatorship, together with the monarchy that put it into power, kept a close watch on their number one exile for they knew and feared the power of his pen and the fact that the Republicans were focusing their attention more and more on him as a symbol of their growing strength. Unamuno in Hendaye was much too close for comfort and they were determined to lure him away either back on to Spanish territory into their own hands or, with the help of the French authorities, away from the border into France. The policeman, Martínez Anido, was ready to pounce should his prey set foot across the border, and the French authorities were frankly worried lest his presence there upset relations with their southern neighbor. Hence the Republican conspiracies that centered around him were viewed with increasing alarm by both countries. This state of affairs explains why Monsieur Shramek, French Minister of the Interior, invited Don Miguel to leave Hendaye "because," Unamuno wrote, "my presence here could create . . . certain difficulties . . . and in order to avoid any incident that might possibly endanger the friendly relations existing between France and Spain—and to lighten the burden of responsibility on the French authorities." [12] He answered Monsieur Shramek, refusing the "invitation." He wrote, also, to his friend, Monsieur Painlevé, President of the Consejo de Ministros, and to the Spanish Ambassador to France, Sr. Quiñones de León, that he was determined to stay in Hendaye. Neither the French nor the Spanish would let the matter rest there. On September 24 Monsieur Painlevé sent the Prefecto de los Bajos Pirineos from the town of Pau who also tried, but in vain, to persuade Don Miguel to depart.

The French authorities had done everything possible to placate their Spanish neighbors. So far, the controversial professor had done nothing illegal; pardoned by the Spanish government, he was free to come and go and his exile in Hendaye was purely voluntary. In fact, here in Hendaye Unamuno's *moral de batalla* was so aggressive that he became the persecutor rather than the persecuted: "Really—to tell the truth—I have not been much persecuted. I have been the one to persecute," he stated afterward. "When foreign journalists saw poor Primo they would say to me: 'But they say that you are here because you want to be.'

"'No. There is a slight difference; I am not here because I want to be; I am here because he doesn't want me here'." [13]

---

[12] Unamuno, *Cómo se hace una novela*, Prologue, p. 128.
[13] Luis S. Granjel, *Retrato de Unamuno*, p. 313.

As the French had no obligation to protect the toppling monarchical dictatorship in Madrid, the Spaniards took over, but since Don Miguel insisted on remaining in French territory, they had to resort to trickery. The following events Don Miguel described as "a murder mystery campaign." "The abject Spanish policeman commanded by the *versánico* (epileptic) General Severiano Martínez Anido . . . feinting a communist-backed incident . . . the bogeyman . . . and to bring pressure to bear on the French government to place me under arrest."[14] Fortunately, the trick was revealed by Unamuno's friend, Don Juan Cueto, or else it might have worked and Don Miguel might have found himself in jail. The details of this trick Unamuno recounted back in Madrid in 1930 to a packed Ateneo audience. He used it then to make them laugh, though at the time it could not have seemed exactly humorous. Neither are the details quite clear. The whole affair was an attempt on the part of the Spanish authorities to force the French to expel "those frontier men," and Unamuno knew of it through his friend, Juan Cueto, the *jefe de los carabineros* (commander of the riflemen). It seems that Fenol, the policeman (probably on the Spanish side), sent a messenger to a friend's home in Hendaye to buy some toy pistols. This messenger was caught attempting to reenter Spain with a suitcase, presumably full of pistols. Luckily, he was taken by the *carabineros* to their chief, Juan Cueto, who, upon examining the man's papers, noted the address of the Hotel Broca and recognized it as a plot to involve Unamuno. Shortly after this incident, Don Miguel related to his Madrid audience, someone had told the Spanish officer that Unamuno was planning to cross the border, for a good friend of his who bore him a slight resemblance was stopped by a couple of civil guards as he was crossing the frontier from Saint Jean de Lux to Vera.

They tied him and handcuffed him, insulting him and saying:
"At last this accursed old man has fallen into the trap. Let him write, let him write!"
They took him to Vera. As they approached the Vera civil guard, the sergeant who recognized him said:
"Who have you got here?"
"He's fallen, he's fallen."
"Why that's the municipal judge of Lesaca. Turn him loose."

As the result of persistent pressure and a letter from Don Miguel to his personal friend, the lieutenant colonel of the civil guards at San

[14] Unamuno, *Cómo se hace una novela*, p. 12.

Sebastián, the two officers who had captured the innocent victim were dismissed.[15]

Such tactics had the French authorities really worried. Monsieur Shramek made another attempt to entice Unamuno away from Hendaye. This time he wrote to him to say that there was an important letter from the Minister of the Interior (himself!) awaiting him in Pau and he begged Don Miguel to come and get it. This was such an obvious subterfuge that "The Old Fox" answered politely that Monsieur Shramek could very well mail him the letter.

The more pressure they brought to bear on him, the more determined he was to stay. He thoroughly enjoyed giving his monologues to admirers who had come from all over the world to listen to him, the French Basques adored him and from Hendaye he could climb his beloved mountains or wander beside the "changing, changeless" sea which he had "discovered" on Fuerteventura. The beach at Ondarritz was accessible, and sometimes, along the road that follows the Bidasoa he could see the little island of Los Faisanes and go all the way to Biriatú.

Wandering, one day, along a solitary mountain path, he plucked the fateful asphodel, the flower of the dead, the flower which bore his name. The Basques call this asphódelo and it is described as a medicinal plant with long leaves and flowers on stems marked with a horizontal reddish line.[16] Don Miguel explained to Max Grillo that the asfodel was the flower which the ancient Greeks used to dedicate to the dead. Gómez de la Serna writes of it:"Asphodel, that is the mysterious plant which the dead would eat in order to become visible, and so cease to be mere shades."[17] Una is synonymous with asphódelo he further explains, and muno in old Basque means "knoll" or "hill." Miguel means "who like God"; therefore, "Who like God on the hill of the Asphodel." Some add to this his mother's patronymic, as is the Spanish custom, of Jugo (juice) and "with that they added an uncouth sauce to his name of allegorical predestination . . . Unamuno carries the meaning of his name as a literary doom."[18] Death and man's destiny after death had been a life-long preoccupation with him. A professor of Greek, he had a particular interest in the etymology of names, an interest which he shared with Carlyle. He dwelt at length on the mystic significance of

[15] Unamuno, Dos discursos y dos artículos, pp. 117–118.
[16] Max Grillo, "Conversando con Unamuno," in Revista de América (Bogotá, Colombia), Vol. IV, No. 10 (October 1945), p. 52.
[17] Unamuno, Obras·selectas, p. 1051.          [18] Ibid.

his own name and performed astounding feats with it in his work *How to Make a Novel* into which he said he would write "the most intimate experiences of my exile." He selected with careful deliberation, which recalls Don Quijote's process for choosing an appellation for his miserable nag, Rocinante, the name Unamuno Jugo de la Raza for his hero who is, of course, himself. He combined his own with those of his parents. Jugo, he explained, was his mother's patronimic and the name of the old settlement of Galdácano in Vizcaya, the birthplace of his maternal grandfather. Larraza was the baptismal name of his father's mother and means "pasture" in the Basque language.

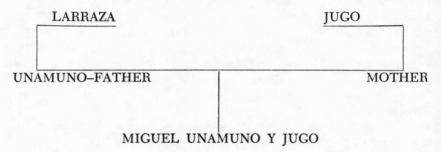

LARRAZA                                                               JUGO

UNAMUNO–FATHER                                                       MOTHER

MIGUEL UNAMUNO Y JUGO

Unamuno wrote to José Bergamín in April 1926: "Am I writing? Little. I am afraid to write. A devil seems to possess me when I take up my pen . . . and I tremble . . . I tremble to think of the man that I could have been, of the ex-future Unamuno, whom I left, abandoned and alone years ago, poor little thing, on a little path of the wind-swept plains of our Spanish history . . ."[19] However, actually he was writing, every day. In fact, he probably never stopped completely for he was still working on *Cómo se hace una novela,* translating his own French version of it into Spanish and writing the prologue for it. Unamuno seemed to be afraid, not of *writing,* but rather of *stopping* writing. This prologue reads as though he felt impelled to continue to "make" his "novel" in order to avoid dying.

But Don Miguel, the redoubtable, was far from dead. It was here in Hendaye that he concentrated all of his physical and spiritual energies to do battle against the moral and political enemies of his *España eterna.* Working with Eduardo Ortega y Gassett, his companion in exile and brother of his one time antagonist, Don José, he penned those "tremendous catalinarians against the dictator, Primo de

[19] Antonio Sánchez Barbudo, *Estudios sobre Unamuno y Machado,* pp. 132–133.

Rivera, full of vehemence and ardor of battle." [20] These were the famous *Hojas libres* (Loose Leaves) to which he himself referred in the Ateneo as follows: "Hojas libres . . . heroic effort of Ortega y Gassett. I was at his side and realize just how much that means." [21] And, writing about them in *Cómo se hace una novela*, Unamuno says, "Under cover of those incidents with the police, I have carried on and continue to carry on my political activities, a sacred political struggle (*la santa política*) here in this frontier corner of my native Basque country, an intimate life of politics turned religion, and religion made politics, a novel of historical eternity." [22]

So intense was his life in Hendaye that one day Unamuno swooned and fell senseless to the ground. The poet, Azorín, who related the incident and who was a frequent visitor of Don Miguel's in Hendaye, may have been there when it happened for he writes: "I judged that his afflictions, his spiritual trials, must have caused the illness, serious indeed, which followed this accident." [23]

It may have been during this illness that his old Salamancan friend, Dr. Cañizo, accompanied Concha and the children to Hendaye. It will be recalled that the sight of his old friend, a visit to a physician in Bayonne, and the never failing cheerfulness of Concha effected a prompt cure. No doubt it was due to Concha's yearly visits that her husband was able to stand the long six-year exile as he did. She always came with some of the children in the summertime when the family would take lodgings wherever they could find them and Don Miguel became for a time the family man he was at heart.

After one of these visits poor Concha was seized by the police and made to spend the night in jail where she slept "with women of common crimes. One poor woman who was there, I don't know whether for infanticide or not, made her bed." [24]

In October of 1926 when Don Miguel had been in Hendaye slightly more than a year, a nephew of Concha's, Antonio Lizárraga, was married in Bilbao. Unamuno wrote inviting Antonio to bring his bride to Hendaye for the honeymoon. The invitation was accepted and the bride and groom spent three days with their notorious relative in the Hotel Broca. "Policemen followed us everywhere," recalls Antonio, who remembers also the daily *tertulias* in the Grand Café where

---

[20] Bernardo Villarrazo, *Miguel de Unamuno: glosa de una vida*, p. 222.
[21] Unamuno, *Dos discursos y dos artículos*, p. 131.
[22] Granjel, *Retrato de Unamuno*, p. 322.     [23] *Ibid.*, p. 323.
[24] Unamuno, *Dos discursos y dos artículos*, p. 138.

Unamuno played an intense game of cards (*mus*) with his favorite
Hendayans. These were the café proprietor himself, Monsieur José
Bidegain—Monsieur Bidegain still runs the café and remembers his
famous client—Ramón Carasatorre who sold raincoats in a little shop
next to the railroad station, and Felipe Arraubarrena, the local butcher.
Another who often made a fourth when the proprietor was busy was
Señor Ramón Viguri, another exile living in the Hotel Broca. In 1931
Viguri was made director of the Spanish Banco Exterior, and in 1936
he was a representative to the Spanish Cortes from the Basque province
of Alava.[25] Once Unamuno was talking to a group of journalists in
Hendaye about his activities and was quoted later as having said:

Here in the solitude I feel more like myself. I prefer to stay here. In the
mornings I work. After lunch I have a game of cards [*mus*] with three of
my best friends in Hendaye, a dealer in woman's clothing, a rubber salesman, and a butcher gentleman. And I like the butcher, for though we
never play for money, he throws himself passionately into the game. That
butcher plays with his whole soul! In my opinion, passion should be the
axis of the spirit. To live passionately is to have the right to live in life.
All else is simply to digest life without dreaming it.[26]

But Unamuno's most constant companion during this period was
probably Ramón Carasatorre, as the townsfolk still testify. In search
of those old associates of Don Miguel's, this writer was directed one
day in June of 1959 to one, Dominique, who lived *sur la route de
Behobie*. Dominique turned out to be a bent old man of kindly face
who was busy working his garden on a hillside against a backdrop of
the Spanish mountains across the Bidasoa. Yes, he recalled Unamuno,
but Don Ramón knew him much better for he used to walk every day
with Don Miguel along the Behobie road. Here the kindly Dominique
called his granddaughter who accompanied the writer to Carasatorre's
shop of household supplies.

Ramón Carasatorre, his pleasant blond wife, and their grown son,
were busy in their large store, the Galleries Lafayette. As it was lunch
time, the amiable Don Ramón directed the visitor to a nearby restaurant where he appeared later, his Basque beret at a jaunty angle on
his slightly graying hair, wearing a spotlessly clean shirt, and tennis
shoes on feet that seemed almost to dance as he walked. Sitting at the
table over a cup of coffee, and later at the store with his family, this

[25] Prieto, "La repatriación de Unamuno."
[26] Manuel Altolaguirre, "Don Miguel de Unamuno," in *Revista hispánica
moderna* (New York), (January 1940), p. 23.

energetic Basque poured forth reminiscences of his old friend, Don Miguel, whom he called *el santo laico* (the lay saint). It was all quite fresh in his mind: the daily walks along the Behobie road parallel to the Bidasoa, sometimes all the way to Biriatou which in Basque means "the end of the road." Here Don Miguel would sit beneath "the tree"—an oak tree—and remark paradoxically: "Here we will make our *principado* (principality, beginning) of Biriatou."

"I will be the sentinel," Ramón would say; ". . . and I with my pen . . ." would answer Don Miguel.

On these walks Don Miguel stubbornly refused to wear a coat until finally the wind became so bitter that "between Doña Concha and me we sold him his first *gabardin*," said Don Ramón. (It may also have been Don Ramón's influence that converted Don Miguel to the use of the convenient Basque beret which he wore then and after his return to Spain.) Along this road was a special farm house he always wanted to see on these daily walks—the *caserío de Moko-Zorrotz*. "And I remember one day," recalled Don Ramón, "that I had a sore foot and didn't feel like walking, but Don Miguel insisted, saying, "No matter, we've got to walk by Moko-Zorrotz!"

"And he was always cracking jokes," said Señora Carasatorre. "Once he came into the store and asked, 'What do you think is the most ferocious of all animals?' 'Which?' we wondered. 'The flea,' said Don Miguel. 'If it were the size of an elephant just imagine what a bite and what a jump it would have!'"

Their son, Pedrito, who was a boy of eight years old in 1928, brought out a treasured photograph of Unamuno inscribed

> To Ramón Carasatorre
> I remember our Hendaye—
> The one of my exile—
> With an embrace—
> Your friend Miguel de Unamuno,
> March 23, 1928

Don Ramón also remembers the games of *mus* played so passionately for a cup of coffee, and when Unamuno won, it was as though he had written books! "He wasn't a good player because he had no malice. Often he would be irritated by what people would say but I could say anything to him and he wouldn't mind. I would often say, 'But you don't know anything about this—about us—you haven't come out of your cocoon in this business of life'."

However, when it came to politics, the salesman of the "articles de menage" was not so knowledgeable. He remembered Sr. Prieto's frequent visits and added that "Don Miguel loved and respected him a great deal. And," he said, "Don Miguel thought they were going to make him president of the republic."

But perhaps Don Ramón was right, for the Republicans did have some such idea. Both Dr. Benítez and another writer, Altolaguirre, allude to such an offer. The former related the circumstances under which the proposition was allegedly made and the latter commented on the absurdity of such an idea. "How absurd Unamuno would have been as president of the Republic! How removed from science were those who proposed it!" [27]

Benítez told the amusing story of a visit Unamuno received from the Republican leaders who were plotting against the dictatorship. Some time in 1931 (it must have been 1930 for Unamuno left for Spain in February 1930) the leaders of what became the Third Republic in Spain paid an official visit to Unamuno in Hendaye. Their purpose was "to offer him nothing less than the leadership of the Republican movement." [28] Don Miguel welcomed them warmly, seated them in a circle, and, when all were supplied with coffee and cigars, he took his place in their midst. As usual, he began his accustomed monologue. He talked so steadily and so long, without giving them an opportunity to put in a word, that before they realized it the time had come for their train to leave. They hurried off without ever mentioning the purpose of their visit. Unamuno wanted none of it, apparently.

Self-centered he may have been but for once he knew his limitations. However strong his wish to "make history" in order to live in the mind of God, he refused to sacrifice Spain to his desire; stronger than any dream for himself was his dream for Spain. On this occasion he showed himself an astute politician. Calling into play all of his powers of attracting and holding attention by his unending flow of talk, he so managed the situation that he was not embarrassed by having to antagonize the very men he was using to destroy the monarchy. At the same time he assured for himself a warm reception into Spain when the dictatorship should finally fall, as well as a welcome by the

[27] Ibid., p. 20.
[28] Hernán Benítez, "La crisis religiosa de Unamuno," in Revista de la universidad de Buenos Aires, Vol. III, No. 9 (January–March 1949), p. 61.

republican government then in the making. When it came to politics, or almost anything else, Unamuno never committed himself. For him politics was but a tool or a "sport," as he also called it. Others might take sides but he wanted freedom to take either or all sides. He once said: "If someone should organize an Unamuno party, I would be the first 'antiunamunista'."

Plots and intrigues brought added renown to the Grand Old Man whose fame at this period reached its peak during his lifetime. Besides politicos, scholars and artists vied with one another for his attention. It was here, the reader will recall, that the sculptor, Victorio Macho, struggled to produce the masterpiece that stands today on the stairway of the Palacio Anaya in Salamanca. Don Ramón pointed out the second floor of a building next to his own store where the stormy sessions between the artist and his subject took place. "Don Miguel couldn't stand it. It made him furious! [Le ponía negro]," he exclaimed. Puzzled as to the reason, he would ask the artist, "But what do you *do* to him?"

Another artist, Juan Echevarría, painted Don Miguel's portrait here which appeared later on the cover of *Dos discursos y dos artículos,* and if Don Ramón is not mistaken, so did a painter named Mezquita for whom Don Miguel sat at the house of Viguri who at that time was a rubber salesman.

Many changes were taking place in Spain during Unamuno's exile and not the least of them for Don Miguel was the death of his lifelong friend, Mario Sagárduy. Mario visited him once in Hendaye bringing his boy, José Ruiz, and the boy never forgot the old man's bitter invectives against Primo de Rivera on that occasion. He recalls him as he stood beside the statue to the war heroes in Hendaye, and held a Spanish newspaper which brought news of some of Primo's festive activities in Madrid. Don Miguel's wrath against Primo was unbridled: "After eating and drinking well, and in the company of pretty girls, he no doubt feels renewed energy to govern this gay Spain; the mouth of that illfated man spreads the foul odor of a prostitute's privy, and with that same impure mouth he dares to take the name of holy Mary." At that moment, recalls José Ruiz, "the church bells tolled the Angelus and Don Miguel uncovered his head exclaiming, 'Pardon, Holy Mother!'"

Mario must have died during 1928, probably in October, for on the nineteenth of that month Don Miguel wrote:

To the Memory of Mario de Sagárduy
> Another bit of me died today;
> the friend of our twin childhood
> ceased his dreaming;
> but I cling to my memories,
> and in the solitude my soul
> seeks a cover for its nakedness.[29]

These lines he wrote for his monumental *Cancionero* which he began in Hendaye in 1928, and which contains some of his innermost
thoughts and emotions, so mirroring his experiences here. On November 11, 1929, he quoted in English a line from William Blake's *King
Edward III*: "Courage, my lord, proceeds from self-dependence!" [30]
He wrote of France, of Spain, of the rivers—the Nervión, the Tormes,
and the Bidasoa. At times the hours, like heavy oxen, dragged slowly
by. At such times the elegance and perfumes of France, France, the
slave of History that lived always in reverse, could not quench his
thirst for his golden Salamanca, and he wrote:

> *Agua del Tormes,*
> *Nieve de Gredos,*
> *Sal de mi tierra,*
> *sol de mi cielo,*
> *pan de la Armuña mollar y prieto,*
> *leche de cabra del llano escueto,*
> *puestas de soles de rosa eterno,*
> *sombra de encina que espeja el Puerto,*
> *cantos de charros,*
> *todo recuerdos;*
> *la carretera de mis paseos*
> *de lazarillo, soñaba el ciego;*
> *balcón de estío ¡ay mis vencejos!*
> *Catedral Vieja, queda lo eterno;*
> *Santo Domingo, reposo inquieto;*
> *Arco la Lapa, fervor obrero;*
> *bancos del aula de mis ensueños;*
> *noches de casa junto al brasero,*
> *duermen los míos, canta el sereno;*
> *siglos de vida que se me fueron.*[31]

> Waters of Tormes,
> snows from the Gredos,
> salt of my homeland,
> sun of my heavens,

[29] Unamuno, *Cancionero*, p. 160.          [30] *Ibid.*, p. 218.
[31] *Ibid.*, p. 151.

soft, dark bread from the plain of Armuña,
milk from the goats of the free, open prairie,
rose-colored sunsets, lasting, eternal,
oak tree shades in the Harbour reflected,
songs of the Charros,
all of them memories;
road that I trod every day with the blind man,
his Lazarillo, sightless, he dreamed it;
ah my black martins, my window in summer;
lasting eternity, the Old Cathedral;
Santo Domingo, a restless tranquility;
Archway of Lapa, workingman's fervor;
desks of the classroom I see in my dream-world;
evenings at home sitting warm by the brasier,
asleep are my loved ones, the night-watchman singing;
æons of living that left me forever.

Here in Hendaye he wrote also all of his *Romancero del destierro* save for the first four poems which he wrote in Paris, impelled no doubt by the idea expressed in the lines:

*Voy clavando los momentos*
*con los clavos del cantar;*
*rosa de infinitos vientos*
*la eternidad al crear.*[32]

Eternity's rose of winds unnumbered
I keep nailing down in song
by creating verses numbered,
nails in time that passes on.

One outstanding event that took place during this Hendaye period was Unamuno's meeting with the German philosopher, Count Keyserling. This gentleman invited Don Miguel to visit him at his hotel in Biarritz. The biographer, González-Ruano, describes the incident as follows:

During one whole afternoon they sat, side by side, looking at one another without understanding each other. Keyserling sees in Unamuno a phenomenon of the race; he interests him, he captivates him, he sees in him a latent symptom of a country's presence, which he approaches with the intuition of Latin prophecy, seeing in him the land of high destiny. Unamuno, on the other hand, sees in Keyserling the traveler, the tourist, the man of the unexpected leap, of the instantaneous interpretation, crafty and surreptitious.[33]

---

[32] *Ibid.*, p. 364.
[33] César González-Ruano, *Miguel de Unamuno*, p. 91.

González-Ruano contrasts the bemonocled, well-groomed, elegant appearance of the German, with the "uniforme civil" worn by the Spaniard who is made uneasy by this unpredictable Keyserling, and concludes that their acquaintance ended there.

It must have been under duress that Don Miguel made that trip to Biarritz for he generally preferred to let the world come to him, and so it did. Maurice Legendre came from Paris, and from the United States came professors Wilfred Beardsley of Goucher College, and Warner Fite of Princeton. Professor Fite came to Hendaye in the summer of 1928 during which time he met Unamuno's wife and wrote that she was "a calm person, limited, rather pretty, who seemed to me admirable." [34] He was later the English translator of Unamuno's novel, *Niebla,* and the author of *Moral Philosophy* which Don Miguel read with pleasure. The correspondence between these two, edited by Manuel García Blanco, reveals that the American introduced Don Miguel to the writing of John Dewey about whom neither was particularly enthusiastic. Professor Fite later sent Don Miguel a copy of *Abraham Lincoln* by Lord Charnwood.

Five years is a long time and no one can know Unamuno's intimate suffering during those many tedious, plowing hours. Here in the solitude of the mountain paths which overlooked Spain he would dream on death whose symbol, the asfodel, he plucked along the way, and it was then that he would feel the presence of God who had created him, as well as the mountains and valleys of his beloved Spain, and he would write: "Reaching beyond myself I find the God of my Spain in this exile experience." [35]

Patiently he waited, for, as he told a young reporter from Bilbao, "I am used to waiting." This must have been on January 29, 1930, because on the preceding evening the 28th of January Primo de Rivera presented the resignation of his government to Alfonso XIII, and in so doing he tolled the bell for the King himself. In desperation, no doubt, Alfonso, among the last of a long line of capitulating European monarchs, called on his military chief (*Jefé del Cuarto Militar*), Lieutenant General Don Dámaso Berenguer, to form an interim government.[36]

---

[34] *Revista hispánica moderna* (January 1957), p. 82.

[35] Unamuno, *Cómo se hace una novela,* p. 151.

[36] This and the following facts regarding Unamuno's triumphal entry into Spain the writer secured from the two Salamanca dailies, *La Gaceta Regional* and one whose name is withheld upon request, in the issues dating from January 29 to February 16, 1930.

But Don Miguel seemed in no hurry to return. When questioned regarding his immediate plans, he replied in essence:

You ask me what I am going to do—well—keep on awaiting the day of justice for everyone. I shall not return until all, absolutely all of the constitutional rights are guaranteed. It will take time to call a meeting of the Cortes and no election campaigns can be considered until every citizen who wants to represent the people has had an opportunity to explain his program. Besides, no professional duty calls me to Spain. The students are asking that some professors who voluntarily abandoned their classes be reinstated, but that does not apply to me; I neither resigned nor abandoned my chair, although the official lie has it that I did so.

On February 21, 1924, my position and salary were suspended and such is still the situation, although my exile sentence was rescinded, and I have not yet been reinstated.

Unamuno continued referring directly to Alfonso:

But the man who must appoint a Minister of Public Education, the one who said, "This will pass, justice will be meted out to all," knows very well the facts in my case and is morally obligated to annul the record which was placed on file without vote [sin resolución], and to see that I receive justice and not favor.

And if I have been delinquent in any other matters, let me be tried and sentenced for it; and I, in my turn, will call for justice toward others.

Spoken authoritatively and "with reason," by a man who has thought long and well, a man who realizes the importance of historical record in humanity's struggle toward ethical and spiritual values. But the taste of victory which was his for the taking finally won out, the call of his España drowned out all else, his head could not restrain his heart, and so it was that some seven days later Don Miguel said to a reporter from La Voz de Guipúzcoa, reclining majestically on his bed in the Hotel Broca as though "prepared to speak at a classical banquet": "I can't say exactly when, but I plan to return. I said recently that I would not do so until all constitutional guarantees were completely reestablished. Today I do not believe that this is necessary because we shall be guaranteed freedom of speech. And besides, we must go back to work with everyone to bring about the total reinstatement of freedom." This change is understandable in the light of interim events in Spain which made his imminent return a foregone conclusion. Berenguer's newly formed government reinstated Unamuno in his university position and it is just possible that he was thinking again of the presidency, for, as Sr. Prieto noted upon his entry into Irún, "his eyes shown with a special gleam when the crowds cried, '¡Viva Unamuno, Viva el presidente de la república'!" [37]

Before leaving Hendaye Unamuno began to receive invitations to speak in Spain; one from the workers of the Ateneo of Gijón in Asturias urged him to make his first public address there, but "this cannot be," Unamuno told the reporter. "If I go anywhere before I go to Madrid, it will be to Bilbao. I have been invited to go through Irún, and I shall do so to send a telegram, the first telegram that I want to send in Spain: a telegram of love and affection to the *majoreros*." Puzzled, the reporter questioned the meaning of *majoreros*. "Yes," explained Don Miguel, "they are the inhabitants of Fuerteventura . . ." and he talked of that island whose arid landscape, so dry and rocky, recalled his Castilian steppes, Castile, where one forgets the present, the recent, which is now so long gone by. Yes, now he has decided to return . . . he'll go to Irún, Bilbao, Salamanca, and Madrid; "and in Madrid to the Ateneo."

"And at the Ateneo, what . . .?"

"To resume the campaign that was being carried on there, especially when the *coup d'etat* came. To ask for justice. The past must not be simply erased for a new beginning." Yes, the record had to be set straight for history.

While the redoubtable Don Miguel was girding his loins to play the lion's part, his home town people were bustling about at a great rate preparatory to receiving his leonese majesty. A local daily of Salamanca announced on February 7 that Unamuno's play, *Tulio Montalbán y Julio Macedo*, would be presented by the Compañía Clásica de Arte Moderno on February 20 in the *Liceo* of Salamanca, while on page six of the same paper there appeared an article announcing his imminent return and giving a long literary eulogy of the ex-rector.

But Unamuno was not to remain an "ex" anything much longer, for the day of his triumph had come. February 10, 1930, dawned cold and rainy. That morning representatives from the Republican and Socialist parties began to arrive at his hotel; groups of politicos from across the border in Irún, from San Sebastián, from Vitoria, from Bilbao, and even from Madrid converged on this little French border town—all of them anxious not only to be the first to welcome the conquering hero back to his native land, but to make a triumphal entry in his company. Among those from Madrid who joined him in Hendaye were Professor

[37] Prieto, "La repatriación de Unamuno."

Jiménez Asúa and the ubiquitous Don Indalecio Prieto. Prieto, by the way, had been included in the new interim government, "a constitutional coalition," along with José Sánchez Guerra, Señor Álvarez, Miguel Villanueva, Señor Alba, Alcalá Zamora, Marcelino Domingo, and Dr. Gregorio Marañón.

But Hendaye could not give up its claim to fame without a fitting farewell. The mayor of that town, the ill-fated Monsieur León Lannepouquet who was to die a miserable death in the Nazi concentration camp of Dachau, presided at a luncheon at the hotel where appropriate words were spoken. As the day progressed the cold winter rain increased and by five P.M., when Don Miguel prepared to take his last walk from Hendaye, this time, however, a one-way walk, the rain was pelting down in sheets so that the Spanish side of the international bridge across the Bidasoa River was hardly distinguishable. However, "nor rain, nor sleet" could deter Don Miguel's fate, as, flanked by Jiménez Asúa and Prieto and followed by a crowd of friends, he and Monsieur Lannepouquet walked solemnly to the center of the bridge that separated the two countries. At this point the French mayor embraced the Spanish professor in the name of France and impulsively cried out, "¡Viva la libertad!" One can but imagine how Don Miguel felt as he expressed his gratitude to "la nación francesa" and took his final leave of that country.

# The Triumphal Entry

CHAPTER 25

FIVE THOUSAND PEOPLE WERE
standing on Spanish soil in the pouring winter rain at five P.M. on that
February 10, 1930. The whole town of Irún, headed by its mayor, plus
delegations from the three Basque provinces, were waiting, eager to
catch a first glimpse of the returning exile. When Unamuno came into
view escorted by an accompanying crowd approaching from the French
side of the international bridge the municipal band of Irún struck up
a tune and firecrackers exploded into the air. Flying the flags of the
Republican and Socialist parties, the waiting throng surged forward
to meet him. Above the shouted "¡Vivas!" the exploding fireworks,
the music and the mob, only snatches of conversations could be
heard—greetings, messages, bravos.[1]

[1] A Madrid reporter, Señor Abeytúa, recorded the following conversation between
Professor Jiménez Asúa and Unamuno which he wrote down in San Sebastián at
one-twenty the following morning, February 11:
    Unamuno: "Ola, dear Asúa!"
    Asúa: "Greetings Don Miguel. You see that these people are ready to
        fight!"
    Unamuno: "Yes, yes."
    Asúa: "Our friend Felipe Sánchez Román asked me to bring you his greet-
        ings because as he was preparing to come the sudden illness of his
        daughter prevented him."
    Unamuno: "Thank you, thank you."
However, Señor Abeytúa, who wrote the foregoing in the early morning hours,
just might have been mistaken; Jiménez Asúa attended the luncheon in Hendaye
and therefore would not have been greeting Don Miguel thus on the bridge.

A procession was quickly formed led by the band, and by Don Miguel's immutable figure flanked by Señores Prieto and Jiménez Asúa, and of course, the mayor of Irún. The Professor's son, Fernando, had come from Palencia and he kept a watchful eye on his father while close on their heels, as close as they could get, came the reporters and the multitude. As they proceeded toward the town this latter increased in volume to such an extent that the procession could make haste but slowly up the Avenida de Francia to the telegraph building on the Paseo de Colón. This was Unamuno's first objective to which he proceeded with customary deliberation to send his first telegram, as intended, while the jostling crowd waited impatiently on the street. Addressed to Don José Castañeira, Punta de Cabras, Fuerteventura, the message read: "My first fraternal greeting upon treading Spanish soil once again, is to the *majoreros* that inhabit that blessed land of Fuerteventura." He sent other messages and received hundreds of them—to be read later in his hotel room—but now he must rejoin the awaiting throng with their flying banners and blowing bugles in a procession that led him by forced marches, amidst an ever-swelling tide of enthusiasm, to the culmination of this nationwide demonstration, to his own Salamanca.

The story of the four days from Monday, February 10, through Thursday, the 13th, reads like the triumphal march of a conquering hero, a hero who savors sweet victory every step of the way yet longs to reach his ultimate goal and receive the crown he knows awaits him. His schedule runs something like this: February 10, Irún—two speeches; February 11, by car to San Sebastián, and thence by train in the afternoon to Bilbao where he spoke three times; [2] February 12 by car to Valladolid where he was met by still other delegations from Salamanca and Madrid and spoke once; February 13th, by car to Salamanca where he was met by Salamancans some of whom went all the way to the adjacent town of Armuña to join in the procession.

Unamuno's homecoming was a cause for rejoicing on the part of practically everyone in that university town; however, there was one person for whom it brought disaster: the University's rector, Don Enrique Esperabé de Arteaga. Indeed, Esperabé must have wished that the blanket of snow which was descending on all of Spain and blocking trains would paralyze all communication and swallow up the slowly but inexorably approaching Don Miguel. The Salamancan *Gaceta Regional* of February 12 printed ominous news: a meeting of

[2] Another entry says he arrived in Bilbao by car.

the University faculty presided over by "the most excellent rector Don Enrique Esperabé de Arteaga" presented a resolution which, however, that gentleman would not allow to be read until plans for Unamuno's reception were discussed. A planning committee consisting of Professors José María Ramos and Manuel Torres had been appointed. There must have been some faculty concern for the control of the students' unbounded enthusiasm since there appears in the same paper of February 12 an appeal for order from the faculty to the students. It reads:

Students! The faculty hopes that when you receive Maestro Unamuno, upon his return from exile to his spiritual home, you will do so with the serenity and good sense that is becoming to true scholarly tradition, and avoid anything in your justifiable rejoicing that might turn the honoring reception into a disorderly demonstration of unruly passions which would place it on a decidedly lower plane and might even cast a shadow over it.

The message is signed by Ramos and Torres, "the commission in charge." This is followed by a "Note from the F.U.E. [Federación Universitaria Escolar—the student organization]." It reads as follows:

Students!
The Committee of the federation urges good sense on the part of all and considers it opportune to notify its members that any extracurricular manifestations will add to the gayety of the reception honoring don Miguel de Unamuno.

L. Pubillones, President.

Esperabé's hour was surely approaching, even as Unamuno's, the difference being that he, Esperabé, was not the man for that hour. But he didn't resign without a struggle. A resolution signed by thirty professors was finally read in that faculty meeting. Professor Prieto Carrasco read it:

1. The University cannot officially honor Unamuno because it is still run by the "academic authorities that represent in it the political spirit that ordered his exile."
2. That the reception with which the University should honor Señor Unamuno is the petition to the most excellent señor, Minister of Public Instruction, that once he is reinstated in his university chair, he be named rector of the University.
3. That the University should receive Señor Unamuno in the University auditorium so that professors and students may hear there his eagerly awaited words.

But Esperabé refused to resign, on the grounds that he would be deserting another group of the faculty. "The only course left is for those professors who wish it, to petition the Minister of Public Instruction for his dismissal," he told them. Following this statement the University officials left, and the professors remained to draft and dispatch a telegram requesting "with all respect, the dismissal of the señor rector." Although Esperabé was supported by a certain number of professors, he resigned, probably on February 13, the day of Unamuno's return, since the notice appeared on the 14th.

While Salamanca was astir with preparations to receive him, the eyes and ears of the rest of the country focused on Unamuno himself who was talking his way back, swept along by the acclaiming mobs of admirers, sensation seekers and, no doubt, a spy or two. The new government still had no president; Sánchez Guerra as president of the Consejo de Ministros was keeping order from his headquarters in Madrid while many turned anxious eyes on the returning exile. There was one who "was a secret spectator," and watched the reception in Irún from an automobile "with drawn curtains." The same figure was seen by another reporter "standing, on top of an automobile with bare head, watching the passing of the procession." He was Don Angel Ossorio y Gallardo. Why was this person reportedly seen in such contradictory attitudes? Surely he could not have been planted by the new government—Prieto, himself a member of that government, was constantly at Unamuno's side. Was Alfonso, the poor forlorn king, concerned over the Professor's popularity? Primo had escaped to Paris where he arrived alone with only two suitcases. Who then was having Don Miguel so surreptitiously watched?

Unaware, perhaps, and certainly careless of whatever hidden motives may have prompted such spying, Don Miguel was swept by the avalanche to meet the many engagements already arranged for him. In Irún these arrangements had been made for him by the Círculo Republicano. Wishing to know the details of these plans one reporter questioned Don Indalecio Prieto as the crowd jostled its way to the headquarters of that organization which was Unamuno's first stopping place:

"Will you speak tonight?"
"No," answered Prieto, "only Don Miguel must speak."
"But you are a significant figure of civic importance, and were always and on every occasion at the head of the dictatorship."
"Yes, but it is necessary to unite our efforts."

By this time the crowd must have been getting out of hand for the figure of Unamuno appeared briefly on the balcony of the Círculo Republicano to enjoin more orderly behaviour. From there he was escorted to the Palace Hotel for dinner. With him, besides Fernando, Jiménez Asúa, and Prieto, were Honorato de Castro, Antonio Sacristán, Alvarez de Burgos, Benito y Roces, Tomás Martínez Bazán, Señor Lezama, editor of the *Libertad* of Bilbao, Mourlane Michena, Alvasorado, and people from Bilbao, Baracaldo, Vitoria, and Logroño.

However, the first audience which Don Miguel addressed after six years' of absence from the country was at the Triquete Ramunchu following dinner that night. The hall was packed to the rafters. Young Anastasio Blanco Elola, as secretary of the sponsoring organization, had to preside. Overwhelmed by the significance of the occasion, as much as by his own inexperience, the young man, by his own admission, was trembling from fright as he mounted to the stage.

I got up, or rather, they got me up on the stage, and I couldn't control my nerves. Don Miguel sat down beside me. While the acclamations for the repatriated man were still resounding, I tried to put together a few coherent sentences in my mind, but when I stood up to speak they left me completely. However, while my knees were still trembling, I began by saying: "Gentlemen and Ladies, Don Miguel de Unamuno . . ." At that moment, Don Miguel grabs me by the arm and orders imperiously: "Have them bring some water!" Those of us who had planned the affair had forgotten bottle and glass required for all speaker's tables.

Here, the young man who addressed the foregoing to Don Indalecio Prieto sometime later, added, "Some may drown in a glass of water, but I was drowning for lack of one. I couldn't speak. Somebody brought the water and I sat down almost unconscious and Unamuno began to perorate." [3] Gradually the flustered young man collected himself. He concentrated on the face of Don Indalecio who was facing him from the front row, and realized that the speaker was waxing lyrical about the Peña de Francia. "I was watching you to see how you reacted to such lyricism, disappointing to those of us who expected something substantially political."

What Unamuno actually said on that momentous occasion was printed in his hometown paper the following day. First he waited calmly for the deafening applause to subside; then he began: "My brothers of Irún: I remember it as though it were yesterday. I was a

[3] Indalecio Prieto, "La repatriación de Unamuno," in *Acción* (Montevideo), January 7, 1956.

boy scarcely ten years old, when I entered into my civil life, into the civil conscience, into my civil majority." Unamuno spoke of the bombs from "the absolutist hosts of Don Carlos de Borbón" that fell on Bilbao on February 21, 1874. Exactly fifty years later on February 20, 1924, "with those absolutist hosts restored, they snatched me from my home to carry me to a desert isle . . ." From there he went on to Paris where "I saw only historical reminders everywhere . . . And I wanted to flee from history." Then he went to Hendaye. "I came to this my Basque country. I saw the ocean once again . . ." And for four years "I have been gazing at the Haya Mountains, whose peaks have clothed themselves in snow, like my head, to greet me." (Much applause here.) He recalled using "my spy glasses, and from there I would follow the flow of the Emalmirea stream to the foot of the Peña de Haya." He told of his walks "along the Bidasoa whose waters circle and mingle with the heroic halls of the sons of France and Spain, waters swollen with historic memories, by the crusade of civil war that blooded them and almost to no avail, for these waters seem doomed to see another civil war." (Ovation here.) Unamuno continued with an account of his exile and criticized harshly the latest events in Spain, interrupted repeatedly by an applause which at the end was completely deafening.[4] This hardly seems the "disappointing lyrical" effusion which Señor Prieto would have us believe.

But to resume Don Indalecio's account as he quotes his friend Anastasio Blanco, as Unamuno was coming to the end of his "cold discourse," "a disturbance broke out up in the gallery[5] at the mention of Primo de Rivera. 'Let him die,' shouted one of the listeners. And a big old fellow from some place in Castile, who was halfway hanging from the roof over the grating there, answered in a stertorous voice, 'Don't let him die, let him live so that he will suffer!' "[6] Señor Prieto identified this fellow as one Ricardo Jiménez, a wine merchant from La Mancha who, like so many other Republicans from all over Spain, had come to Irún to hear Unamuno, "to discover that he wanted to entertain them by talking about the Peña de Aya." As Don Miguel ended his address with the previously quoted words, "we must change the motto 'God, Country, and king,' to 'God, Country, and law,' Señor Prieto got up and went toward Unamuno shouting, 'What's all this about God, Country, and law! Either for the king or against the king!' "

[4] *Ibid.*
[5] *Gallinero,* chicken roost.
[6] Prieto, "La repatriación de Unamuno."

The secretary then called on Don Indalecio to speak, which he did, in spite of the policeman's efforts to silence him. Writing of these events from Argentina in 1953, Señor Prieto seems to imply that although Unamuno was not at that time avowedly Republican, something or someone influenced him to declare himself openly on the Republican side. Señor Prieto's own efforts in that direction, he writes, had no effect on Don Miguel for no one could ever sway him. He adds that it was the influence of the masses, the *masa popular* that won him. "Hence the procedure was to embroil him in the popular Republican whirlwind, since he would not be able to resist the flattery of the masses . . . And his little eyes shown with satisfaction when mobs of his countrymen received him shouting: 'Long live Unamuno! Long live the president of the Spanish Republic!'" Then he adds: "It pleased him in Bilbao to see how the people who years before refused to make him a Republican representative from lack of confidence in his republicanism, and gave the position rather to me, exalted him to the point of proclaiming him future president of the Republic." [7]

But before going to Bilbao Unamuno must have read those hundreds of welcoming telegrams sent to him in Irún. Perhaps he did this late that night, or maybe in the early hours of the following day, February 11, back at the Hotel Palace. One letter from Dr. Gregorio Marañón was read during the program at the Triquete Ramunchu, the Frontón. Decrying the shameless persecution of Unamuno as the greatest sin of the dictatorship, Dr. Marañón wrote: "Nevertheless, it has revealed the true nature of the regime to the entire world and has become the symbol, uniting us all in the cause of justice." Of Unamuno's suffering he wrote: "But the glorious exile can say that the sorrow caused by his absence has been and is beneficial for the homeland. The departure of the dictatorship is like a good sweeping, but the house has been left silent and empty. Unamuno's return will fill it with new and fecund agitations." [8]

Among the messages he may have read alone in his room was one from José Sánchez Guerra greeting him and congratulating him upon his return to the "homeland" and adding the hope that upon the termination of "that shameful act of your estrangement, your noble and beneficent attitude will bring new days of glory to our Spain." [9]

Thus ended Unamuno's first day in Spain; the ones that followed were even more packed with activity. The cold rain of the north had

[7] *Ibid.*
[8] A local Salamancan paper, February 11, 1930.                    [9] *Ibid.*

changed to snow everywhere else. On the 11th, after a busy morning receiving visitors and lunching at the Centro Republicano, his party drove to San Sebastián where a delegation of liberals and Republicans from Bilbao awaited him to extend an invitation to speak that evening in his home town. He refused a similar invitation in San Sebastián and proceeded by train, according to one report, to his beloved *bochito*. Another account has it that he went by car, accompanied, in any case, by Fernando and Señor Prieto.

Bilbao! How his heart must have beat as he approached it, and glimpsed the old familiar drawbridges and the dark sooty houses rising out of the winter's gloom. Seven P.M. it was when they arrived. And this time the home folks were all waiting; even Félix, poor soul, the only one left of his immediate family, was "picketing" the station with his defiant sign pinned on his hat "Don't talk to me about my brother!" The members of the local Círculo Republicano and El Sitio all turned out to receive him. When the car bearing Don Miguel passed the Arenal it stopped for him to alight. Here the gentle spirit of his childhood sweetheart must have filled him with tender memories, memories of that day they met and looked for the first time into each other's eyes, eyes then full of the wonder and awe of young love. Yes, Don Miguel had to pause and walk once again the paths of the Arenal.

He made his way among the expectant throng to the old band-stand—the *kiosko*—and from there delivered his first speech in Bilbao: "I shall always be beside the new generation which is to do away with the dictatorship," said he, and then proceeded to remind them that his last speech at El Sitio had been the "fundamental motive of his exile." After that Prieto too spoke some words, words of eulogy for Don Miguel, but here again as in Irún, the last words.

From the Arenal the party went directly to El Sitio where for the past hour an impatient, eager crowd had been waiting—the Lizárragas, the Sagárduys, the Zuazagoitias, the Areílzas—all the flower of Bilbao's aristocracy. Señor Fatrás, president of the Society, introduced Unamuno here where, as he remarked, Don Miguel made his first and his last speeches in Spain. And Don Miguel began by explaining that last speech. Here it was that on January 5, 1924, "he said that he would not tolerate that they treat him like a recruit."

He returned to Salamanca, he went on to tell them; on February 20 he was indicted and that same day the indictment was legalized, and he received the order for his exile to Fuerteventura. Harking back to his boyhood experience, Unamuno recalled that exactly fifty years earlier, on February 20, he had watched the Carlist bombs falling on Bilbao and added that his exile decree was issued "by the successors of those who hurled those bombs." He told them that later, on May 2, it was not he who had come to Bilbao, but "that other one" who came to preach a new embrace of Vergara. It was that other one, said Unamuno, who had himself declared an adopted son of Bilbao, "my home town," and an adopted son of Guernica, "my wife's home town." Then he went to Salamanca, proceded Don Miguel, where they named him "Doctor Honoris Causa," on account of his honor. The reason was, explained Unamuno, that "my shadow, Miguel's shadow, was chasing the poor little Miguel." [10] This produced loud applause as did his quip about the virtue so much extoled in Spain: honor. When he was on Fuerteventura someone tried to extract a promise from him on his "honor." "Honor?" exploded Don Miguel, "I have no honor. That is a matter for caballeros, and I do not ride a horse. I am an honorable man and on foot."

For the next hour and a half Unamuno reviewed the history of Spain from the times of the Hapsburgs up to the present. He was consciously and purposely fully immersing himself in history, rather than fleeing from it. Once again he wanted to live, to live in history—the dream of God—and by so doing be seen and remembered of God. Yes, perhaps Don Miguel did want to be the president of the new Republic.

After his talk at El Sitio, he attended a dinner celebrating the birth of that republic at the Centro Republicano after which he was called on to speak again. So ended Tuesday, February 11.

On Wednesday, the 12th, he resumed his trek to Valladolid, many kilometers closer to his goal, and this in spite of the snowdrifts that paralyzed most train travel. In Valladolid the crowds were waiting to receive him. His train arrived at six-twenty, P.M. and the station platforms were packed with people who had been waiting for hours. Their applause and welcoming cries followed him all the way to the Hotel Francia. Here again there was a banquet, attended mostly by professors, students, and friends from Salamanca. It lasted from nine-thirty until ten-thirty when he addressed a crowded hall at the local Círculo Republicano where many could find standing room only outside.

By now Unamuno's arrival in Salamanca was so imminent that anything he might have said in Valladolid would have been, or rather was, swallowed up in the frantic wave of predemonstration enthusiasm. On

[10] *Ibid.* The "other one" refers to Miguel Primo de Rivera.

February 13 both of the local papers announced in bold caps the advent of *el maestro ilustre* for one P.M., and both referred to the heavy snowstorm which was still whirling over the chill Castilian steppes. A four-column heading on page three of one of them reads: "*El retorno del maestro ilustre.*" Accompanying the ensuing article is a large photograph of Don Miguel reading in his favorite position—reclining on his bed, in his room at the Hotel Broca. Both dailies voiced the concern of the professors and civil authorities lest the peace and order they enjoined turn to rioting. One carried a separate article entitled "How the City Should Receive Him." It was signed by Cándido R. Pinilla, the blind poet friend of Don Miguel's. He wrote that in Unamuno the students had a master, the laborers a guide, the Salamancan intellectuals a pathfinder and a companion, and all the citizens, without exception, had in him a friend, generous with his words, with his knowledge, and with his teachings. The blind man added that with others Unamuno had fought or had been an ally, and he ended by saying that for over a third of a century Don Miguel's name had been prominent in the history of the city. "Salamanca is Unamuno, and Unamuno is Salamanca."

The complete story of Unamuno's reception in Salamanca is told in the two papers on February 14. Many of the articles are signed "J. S–G," a local journalist. Both dailies fairly crackled with the electric current that had sparked the whole town. One of the front page headlines reads: "*El retorno de Miguel de Unamuno a la ciudad.*" It is subtitled "At last I am at home, among you, in my Salamanca." Beneath these there is an eight by four-inch drawing of the professor's silhouetted figure standing, his hands behind his back, his old familiar hat on his head, and in the background, the cathedral towers. Long before the scheduled hour of his arrival, the crowds had filled the Plaza Mayor, all of Zamora Street leading to the north, along the Paseo de Torres Villarroel, the avenue of the Plaza de Toros, and even out along the Valladolid highway all the way to Armuña where an advance guard of professors and friends were awaiting him. Bus loads of eager students, some even from Madrid, began arriving early. One bus carried a large sign that read: "The Federation of University Students Salute Don Miguel de Unamuno." Groups of workers were carrying flags of their organizations: "The Painters Union," "The Masons," "The Day Laborers." Another bus sign read: "The group from Béjar salutes Don Miguel de Unamuno."

Other eager students on foot stuck their banners in the snow along the highway. When the caravan of some fifty cars which preceded his like a guard of honor—cars from Salamanca, Valladolid, Zamora, and Madrid—came into view there was a movement that ran through the throngs like an electric current. Hats were tossed wildly into the air and "¡Vivas!" resounded over the snowbound countryside. Unable to restrain themselves, so many pressed forward that the entire procession was stopped, and so for some time Don Miguel was detained outside the city limits to receive his first welcome in the open country. Finally the procession resumed its advance, but the progress was so slow that it took more than an hour to travel two kilometers! In view of this situation some of the passengers realized the futility of trying to reach the Plaza Mayor in such fashion. They therefore set out on foot. Those closest to Don Miguel were Don Filiberto Villalobos and, yes again, Don Indalecio Prieto, together with Dr. Población and Señor Carrasco. Others named in the *Gaceta* were Don Enrique Rodríguez Mata, Don Tomás Cortes, and Don José Camón. Fernando, who was his father's chauffeur must, perforce, have stayed behind with the car. So great was the press of the crowd around Don Miguel that a group of students and workers from the labor unions formed a protecting cordon and made their way thus to the central square where the local band was making brave sounds in the *kiosko*. Individuals of all classes greeted him in their own manner. One humble laborer pushed his way through the crowd to hand the Professor a small box. The Professor waved a greeting to a woman leaning from a balcony and she wept for joy. Everywhere as he passed handkerchiefs, hats, and berets went flying into the air. As the journalist describes it, "Old men, teachers, public officials, doctors, merchants, workers, students, professors, servants of business firms, employees, united in one intimate surge of emotion and love for Don Miguel, removed their hats as he passed by and joined in the applause."

Surrounded by the protective cordon the hero at last reached the Plaza Mayor. When he came to the entrance to the Café del Pasaje, Unamuno and his friends somehow made their escape from the crowd and darted into the arcade to the hotel that leads through to Espoz y Mina Street. The crowd interpreted this maneuver to mean that he would enter the Casino by its back entrance and speak to them from the balcony, but instead he headed straight for his home on Bordadores Street, only to find another crowd waiting for him there. But nothing could stop him now. The crowd made way for him and Don Miguel crossed the threshold of his own home again after six years' absence, at two-forty P.M. on February 13, 1930.

"Miguel!" It was Concha's voice which welcomed him and her arms that enfolded him. Then his children, and even María his sister; she was there to greet him too—all of them with "exemplary serenity." When he came to Salomé, the mother of his grandchild, he asked only, "Where is he?" At a sign from her he went hurriedly up the stairs to where the child lay sleeping. He stopped and looked, just looked, then broke into quiet sobbing, the tears of joy running down his cheeks.

In front of the house the crowd of students extended down the Calle de las Ursulas almost to the Campo de San Francisco. The window of Doña Pilar's front room commanded the better view than his own did, and so, at her invitation, he went out on her little balcony to address them. Below a sea of young faces was raised expectantly to his. They had come from Ciudad Real, from Madrid, and one among them, Arthur Wills, was from Cambridge. The signs that they bore must have touched the Professor's heart: "A Unamuno, maestro de maestros, los estudiantes de Ciudad Real," "Viva nuestro maestro Unamuno." Then he said, in essence: "Soon it will be six years since they took me away. I have lived this time believing—I must say it—more in myself than in you. I decided to return and take advantage of what freedom we have—it's not all we want and ask for, but what we do not yet have we will win in due time. (Applause) I don't know about you, but I think I am the same. Fortunately, however, there has arisen a young generation that has taught their teachers and others to be strong men." He spoke of simony—not only in the Church but in the university, where favors, he said, were exchanged for degrees. He told them that the past six years had been years of cowardice on the part of the people and even more cowardice on the part of those who governed. Then Unamuno called for an end to "pronouncements" and added dramatically, "Let the one who caused the last one pay for it!" Directing their attention to the urgency of the present he reminded them that he had to rest for the hard tasks ahead. With a sarcastic reference to the governor, "who is not officially the governor" and who had wanted Unamuno to be received with a simple reception, not with a demonstration, he added that there would be time enough for demonstrations. "And now I am back home" he ended, "in my Salamanca. You can count on me." [11]

[11] *Ibid.* February 16, 1930.

Brave words for the throngs, for the public. But the words he spoke then to his dear ones, and what passed between him and blind Cándido in Ledesma where he spent the evening, is not, nor will it ever be recorded.

As for the students, the dance begun that night in the Casino must needs be resumed the following night, so great was their rejoicing.[12]

[12] *Ibid.*

# Summa Cum Laude

CHAPTER *26*

1930   Professor of History and ancient Castilian language, of Comparative Philology, of Latin and Castilian.

1931   Rector of the University, by Decree of May 22.

1934   Retirement as Professor on reaching his seventieth birthday, and he continues as Lifetime Rector, there being created in the University the "Miguel de Unamuno Chair," and his name being given to the National Institute of Secondary Education in Bilbao.

The foregoing is taken from Don Miguel's official record at the University of Salamanca,[1] indicating that he resumed his professorial duties at that institution, possibly soon after his return in February, but was not officially restored to the rectorship until May of the following year. In a supreme effort to promote unity and restore order, Unamuno opened the University session 1931–1932 with these words:

We shall continue cultivating the history of Spain without regard to name calling and partisanship, for political differences are contingent, temporary, and accidental. Culture is above and beneath governmental forms which cannot alter permanent values. In the name of her Majesty Spain, one, sovereign and universal, I declare open the 1931–32 session of this universal and Spanish University of Salamanca.[2]

But before he resumed the rectorship, there was much to be done,

---

[1] From the typed record shown to the author by Don Manuel García Blanco.

[2] Angel del Río, "Miguel de Unamuno vida y obra," in *Revista hispánica moderna* (October 1934).

for as long as Alfonso occupied the throne Unamuno's campaign was not complete. He had said in Hendaye "I must go to Madrid, and in Madrid to the Ateneo." This he did on May 2, 1930. The date was important—May 2. Things happened to Don Miguel, or Don Miguel made things happen, with a strange recurrence on certain dates, dates of historical significance for Spain: February 21, 1874, the bombing of Bilbao in his boyhood, and February 21, 1924, his exile to Fuerteventura; December 31, when he wrote, "It is night time in my study . . ." and death seemed to lurk in the shadows, and December 31, 1936, the New Year's eve which was yet to come when death would finally claim him; May 2, 1874, the end of the siege of Bilbao, and as he pointed out in *Paz en la guerra,* as well as in his speech at the Ateneo, May 2, 1808, the massacre of the Spanish peasants by Napoleon's troops, and again May 2, 1866, when the Liberals under General Prim rebelled against Queen Isabella. Now, the culmination of his triumphal entry into Spain, he returned finally to Madrid to address again Spain's supreme court of culture, the Ateneo, on May 2, 1930. Fate and Don Miguel seemed to be working hand in hand to realize that "eternal return" in time in his quest for eternity.

The auditorium of the Ateneo on the Calle del Prado was packed that day and Unamuno was in his best form. His audience hung upon his every word and he did with it as he willed; and what he willed was that Alfonso should go. Only then would the campaign—his campaign against the King—begun many years before in this same Ateneo, finally be won. No orator, Unamuno called into play on this occasion all of his histrionic abilities to accomplish his purpose, which he did with such success that the repeated laughter of his hearers bespoke their ridicule, ridicule of Alfonso, and Unamuno knew that victory was his. Telling of the visit he had received from the Conde de Romanones in Paris, Don Miguel imitated the latter's high-pitched voice while he quoted him saying: "No, no, my candidate is the second infante, Don Jaime, the deaf one; a King should be deaf"—Here the audience burst out laughing at Unamuno's voice—but he kept on with: "The bad thing is—and now we pass from the ridiculous to the tragic—that what is happening to the present one is because he is deaf." [3]

First he made them laugh by referring sardonically to the "extraordinary official reception that was afforded me yesterday. I doubt that so much armed force would have been displayed even to guard His Majesty the King, as met me at the station yesterday to protect, or

[3] Unamuno, *Dos discursos y dos artículos,* pp. 89–90.

hide me, and to cut me off." [4] Guessing correctly that it was the King's own doing, he exclaimed: "How little of the little intelligence he ever had is left to that smart ungifted one!" [5]

Poor Alfonso, who even now must have been preparing his ignominious flight into France, nonetheless feared the riots that Unamuno's presence in Madrid might cause. As the speaker told his fascinated listeners, just before he took the train for Madrid, he received from the Rector of the University a communication from the Minister of Public Instruction begging him either to leave the train at the last stop before Madrid, or to "disappear quietly" at the station. Don Miguel put his own interpretation on this message: "I saw the scheme. They said it was on account of Communist elements. That's not true; there are no Communist elements. There are elements among themselves that cry out . . . Their whole purpose was to have something to pardon me for. 'Pardons are insults'," [6] he quoted from the Argentine poet, Mármol, in his incisive verses against the dictator, Juan Manuel Rosas.

As was to be expected, Unamuno disregarded the message completely and was able to boast later that there was no trouble whatsoever. However, Alfonso was taking no chances, hence the armed escort from the station, and when Unamuno addressed an even larger audience two days later, on May 4, at the Europa Theater, police were stationed about to enforce order. Even so, a commotion did break out at one moment but it was soon quelled, and the speaker continued unperturbed as was his wont.

On both of these occasions Unamuno dwelt at length on the defeats and shames of Spain, tracing her history, on the second occasion, from the loss of her colonies to the present. In the Ateneo he dwelt extensively on recent events, particularly on the saga of his exile, always placing the blame on Alfonso, from the loss of Tangier in Africa with its accompanying useless sacrifice of Spaniards in the Moroccan war, to the shooting of a six-year-old boy upon the command of General Trinidad Coello. Summing up the crimes of the King who, he said, received his training as a child at the Casa de Campo [7] by teaching pigs to jump through hoops, he added: "And Cánovas falls, and Ferrer falls, and Dato falls . . . Canalejas . . . Lairet . . . and then comes the terrible effusion of blood at Vera." This last he explained was one of

[4] *Ibid.*, p. 62.   [5] *Ibid.*   [6] *Ibid.*, p. 145.
[7] *Casa de Campo*—private riding grounds for Spanish kings on the outskirts of Madrid.

the many plots to get him and other exiles away from the frontier in Hendaye. Several "poor souls" were led to believe they could start a revolution in Spain. They were arrested and tried, and just before being sentenced a policeman from San Sebastián told them that if they declared that the instigators of the plot had been "so and so, so and so," they would be freed. Since three members of the guardia civil had been killed in the plot, three men must be sentenced to death, although the first military tribunal could not prove their guilt. But as justice must be meted out, they had to die. One of the victims committed suicide by jumping off of a high place "in order to have an effusion of blood." Once Alfonso had defended Spain's death penalty by saying to Unamuno during the famous royal interview when he was accompanied by Romanones, that at least in Spain there was no "effusion of blood," as in France.[8]

Don Miguel also proceeded to blame the King for the shameful way that the Spanish kingdom, having withdrawn from the League of Nations on the pretext that she was not accorded a permanent seat, "had to go back with her ears drooping and her tail between her legs as though begging alms."[9]

He recalled his visit to the King with Romanones. When Sánchez Guerra was president of the ministers' cabinet, Romanones was president of the Ateneo, and when "a member of this latter was the number 7.777, Don Alfonso de Borbón Hapsburgo-Lorena, to all appearances constitutional king of Spain."[10] (Prolonged laughter here.)

Harking back to his own historical involvement and the significance of the other May 2's—1808 and 1874—he continued about himself: "I was brought up during a civil war, and when certain things are mentioned, I bless the civil war; I was reared and cradled in the midst of civil wars."[11]

At this point Don Miguel sat down but continued talking: "I am the words and you the music," he said, and they proved it by applauding. Then he went back to his reference to the adjective, "constitutional" by pointing to the apparent incompatability of the constitutional concept with the Catholic concept. "The two terms seem to create a dilemma, either one or the other. Perhaps today Catholicism may mean the opposite of constitutional."[12]

[8] Unamuno, *Dos discursos y dos artículos*, p. 105.
[9] *Ibid.*, p. 114.
[10] *Ibid.*, p. 63.     [11] *Ibid.*, p. 66.     [12] *Ibid.*, p. 70.

Then returning to his personal experiences in exile, he reiterated his belief in the dignity of the individual and man's power to control his destiny. Someone had written him on Fuerteventura that "there was nothing for it but to resign oneself to reality," to which he answered: "Maybe you believe with Marx, in the doctrine of historical materialism, that things rule men—but I, since I am a strong believer in personalism and believe that it is we men who control things, I'll leave you there with reality and stay here with personality, not mine, but Spain's." (Long applause.)

Yes, Unamuno had appropriated unto himself the personality of Spain, and he did not hesitate to say so now. His work with Don Eduardo Ortega y Gasset on the *Hojas libres,* his own suffering, the humiliation of Concha and much more—all of this, "has saved the dignity of Spain." [13] It was not a question of meeting force with force so that the King might say, "'more soldiers, my army.' Then I, too, would have said: 'I will have my soldiers'." [14]

At this psychological moment when he had already referred to force, Unamuno called upon them, the younger generation, to take the final, the necessary step, to rid Spain of the monarchy: "This generous youth that in the streets destroyed the dictatorship, will destroy this one, the most shameful of all." The answering applause assured him that they would. [15]

"And now," said Unamuno, "allow me, by way of farewell, like one who is going away, to stand again." Here the speaker stood up and his audience followed suit, but he motioned them to be seated, saying, "We will soon, all of us, have to be on our feet." It was after they had obeyed him that he summed up the list of Alfonso's crimes and cried out for justice to Christ himself: "Poor Christ, too; He does not hear, He too is deaf . . . During my six years of exile I have been . . . begging him not to believe that my people are deaf, that when one preaches in the wilderness the rocks hear, and when the rocks hear, it is the rocks that rise up."

In conclusion Unamuno quoted Euripides, leaving his listeners with scorn and fire in their hearts, scorn for the poor person of the King, and fire to take action against him: "Whom the gods would destroy they first drive mad," then he added, "but there is a terrible passage in the Bible, when Jehovah strikes Pharoah, he calls him and because he does not answer, he punishes him. And now God help us to help

[13] *Ibid.,* p. 138.     [14] *Ibid.,* p. 139.     [15] *Ibid.*

Him save this poor land. God save Spain, but with our help: and now—into the street."[16]

Thus incited, into the street they surged to produce such demonstrations against the monarchy that it is a wonder Alfonso didn't take to his heels immediately. Somehow he managed to stay in the country until the following year when he was virtually forced to abdicate and take flight into France. In the meantime the dominant figure was Don Miguel for whose favor all parties vied with one another.

Finally, on April 14, 1931, following the King's departure, the 3rd Republic was officially declared. As was to be expected, the leaders, lost no time in claiming Unamuno for themselves; the Republicans named him representative to the Cortes Constituyentes (Constitutional Convention). This meant he would have to spend most of his time in Madrid, but the prospect of returning to his hermit-like life in a rented room went against the grain. Besides, any large city, and particularly Madrid, always filled him with melancholy—a night or two at the Residencia de Estudiantes, or perhaps at the Casa Velázquez as was his habit when visiting Madrid, yes, but to live again away from his family, no!—So it was that he took a house on Zurbano Street, intending no doubt to move his entire family to the capital, but his plan was not fully materialized. Concha must have sensed that politics was not for Miguel, and as for herself, she refused to have any part of it. Concha did not leave Salamanca but preferred rather to move in with their sons Pablo and Rafael, the dentist and the oculist, who lived on Zamora Street where they maintained offices. Her husband probably regretted his move when this happened, but the die was cast and there was nothing for it but to see it through. The rest of the family seemed eager enough for a change, and so to number forty-nine Zurbano Street they all came—Salomé with her husband and baby, Felisa, María, Ramón, and, of course, Tía María, old and ailing now with tuberculosis, but as dour as ever. Salomé, as the married one, ran the domestic affairs with the help of Felisa, while María, the more studious, enrolled for courses at the Universidad Central.

Without Concha, his guiding star, nothing seemed to go quite right for Don Miguel after this, in spite of the national acclaim that he thoroughly enjoyed. For some reason the house he had taken didn't suit, and another move to number fifty-three on the same street must have been a hardship for such a heterogeneous household. Life in the city irritated him and his constant grumblings and complaints are re-

[16] *Ibid.*, p. 156.

called by Ramón Carasatore who visited the Unamuno household on
Zurbano Street. One particular instance for complaint happened to be
the loss of his pocketbook which was snatched one day by a petty thief
on the streetcar. Then sometime during 1931, Félix passed away,
unlamented, in Bilbao. This necessitated a rather distasteful trip there
to dispose of the quarrelsome brother's miserable effects, for which
Don Miguel could have had no taste. Finally, convinced that he was
a misfit in politics, and unhappy away from Concha, Unamuno gave
up the struggle and went back once more to his real home in Salamanca. Then too, in May of 1931 he had been appointed to the rectorship of the University there, and exactly how he was managing this
responsibility in absentia is a puzzle. He must have been commuting
fairly regularly. So it was that Don Miguel returned to Salamanca, but
Felisa recalls that the children stayed on in Madrid another year.
Concha never returned to the home on Bordadores Street. Where then
did Don Miguel stay in the meantime? Perhaps Salomé's part of the
family returned with him for it is hard to conceive that he would have
been satisfied to leave Miguelito, the child he had come to adore.

These two, big Miguel and little Miguel, were indeed becoming fast
friends. They were together whenever the old man was at home, which
with his return to Salamanca was for longer periods of time. With
increasing age, the old gentleman yielded more frequently to his
natural inclination to work in bed. Miguelito would crawl under the
coverlet at the foot with his toys and picture books and at such times
the grandfather took delight in making *pajaritas* to entertain the boy,
or in drawing strange figures and animals to stimulate the childish
imagination. And Miguelito would invent stories about them which
the old man would write down at his prompting: "This is a donkey
who was so frightened that he pawed up the grass." Or the boy would
say: "Grandfather, you are old. You will die soon." Often the two
would converse on various subjects, usually about words, as children
do, and what a teacher he had to answer those first impulsive questions! [17] Sometimes Miguelito would take the pencil and draw his own
figures which he proudly showed, not to his grandfather, but to his
constant friend and companion, the little finger puppet that María,
his aunt, had made for him. Felisa recalls his devotion and vivid imagination in his relationship to the puppet. It was the morning of the
Día de los Reyes when Spanish children receive the presents the Wise
Men have left in the night. The sages had been particularly generous

---

[17] Unsigned article in *La Gaceta Regional*, December 31, 1938.

that year and Miguelito's presents were piled high. The child took
one look, then held up his puppet friend and showed him each present,
one by one. That done, he took his place at the table with his *guiñol*
and paid no more attention to the presents! One of his aunts decided
one day that *guiñol* needed a bath which she proceeded to administer
while Miguelito looked on. Suddenly the little boy burst into tears,
crying that the soap was getting into *guiñol's* eyes.

The child's laughter and tears mingled with his grandfather's dreams
as the lengthening shadows gathered around the venerable old man.
Is it any wonder that he clung to Miguelito and felt again the stirring
of his own childhood as he watched him romping with Doña Pilar's
grandchildren in the garden? Miguelito was the sunshine of his old
age that flashed fitfully in the darkening gloom.

Death was almost a yearly visitor now in the Unamuno household.
In 1932 Don Miguel's sister, the last of his own generation, was finally
claimed by the disease that had long plagued her. Then in July of
1933 his own daughter, Salomé, died, and Don Miguel clung ever
more tenaciously to his grandchild and to his dreams. This atmosphere
of dreams and comfort in dreams pervades one of Don Miguel's most
revealing stories which he wrote during this period—the penetrating
*San Manuel, bueno mártir*. As Arturo Barea points out in his incisive
essay (published in English by the Yale University Press, 1952), Unamuno seems to have altered his attitude toward *el Pueblo*, the people.
Rather than "wake them up," he prefers to "let them dream for they
really do not want to know the truth, nor would they understand it
if it were explained to them." And as for those who doubt, "many only
dream that they doubt and after all, faith in a dream is better than
no faith at all."

In this atmosphere Don Miguel, nearing his seventieth birthday,
continued to write verses for his intimate *Cancionero*. On March 14,
1933, four months before the death of Salomé, that delicate little
cripple who gave him Miguelito and then faded gradually away, Don
Miguel wrote:

> Ah! the empty silences—to suffer in bitter
> shadows plucking splinters—from the carcass of the soul!
> What searching in this silence—the cradle of the word
> for the truth from a silent God—at the door of his abode.
> The man within waits hopefully—and waiting gives no hope—
> to enter the beyond—to escape from his own nothingness.
> In the essence of a dream—softly breathing the
> breath of infinity—he neither sees nor hears God, he feels him.

The will blind and deaf—clothed in mystic flowers of the ancients,
*volo ergo existo,* dreaming—dreams that he dreams his soul.[18]

There were other grandchildren to help dispel these silences;
Fernando's in Palencia, in whose home Don Miguel was ever a welcome
visitor. There is a photograph of a smiling Don Miguel with four of
his grandchildren, one on each knee—Miguelito and an infant—and
two little girls standing. But such moments were rare for him now,
and even rarer after May 15, 1934.

For some time Concha had been failing noticeably—a childishness
and rejection of her loved ones evinced by her refusal to move to
Madrid or to return to the home on Bordadores Street—was becoming
increasingly evident. Felisa remembers particularly the incident when
her mother dismissed the servant girl on a sudden strange whim and
the following day, finding that the girl had left, she asked why—having
apparently forgotten the episode. A few days later Concha said she
had lost a thousand-peseta bill and accused the servant, Lucía, of
robbery. Fearing that again she might have suffered a lapse of memory,
the children did not accuse Lucía, though she was, of course, dismissed.
"My mother complained that we didn't believe here," said Felisa, "and
we said: 'no, mamá, that's not the reason; it's because you might have
been mistaken.'" Having started to reminisce, Felisa went on to tell of
her mother's last days.

Little by little she was growing worse this way, until one time we were in
Madrid and mother was planning to return to Salamanca the next day with
a friend of hers. Suddenly, she started quarrelling with her friend and
refused to make the trip with her; she only looked at us with a vague
expression on her face. We wanted to call Dr. Cañizo to see her but she
refused. Finally she did return to Salamanca and a few days later she had
the stroke—it was an attack of hemoplegia—which left her half paralyzed.
She lived three months after that. There were days when she would get
up and seem better, but at the end—what agony! She would begin to cry
and my father would be very upset. The doctor said "Don't worry so much,
she's not suffering, it's because of *this,*"

here Felisa motioned toward her head.

"After she died," continued Felisa after a pause, a pause pregnant
with memories of all that happened on that fateful May 15, memories
too sacred to probe, "after she died my father wept a great deal, and
to see my father weeping—! He said that the hardest thing for him
was to see her eyes as they followed his every movement until he went

[18] Unamuno, *Cancionero,* p. 444.

out of the room—and the memory of those eyes! My mother had light brown eyes like all of us have." After another pause Felisa continued: "From that time on my father failed rapidly. My mother had a habit of brushing my father's coat just before he left the house, and I remember that I stopped and brushed him off once just like that and he cried pitifully, remembering—."

They laid Concha, the "blond from Guernica," to rest in a crypt near Salomé in the Salamancan graveyard, and Don Miguel with his own hand wrote the inscription:

Concepción Lizárraga de Unamuno
25 VII 1864            15 V 1934

Fifteen days later on May 30, Don Miguel wrote:

> *After the death of my Concha*
> *(15-V-34)*
> A tender song from beyond the cradle
> reaches me from out of oblivion
> and softly, softly in my ear
> it sings of eternal bliss.
> 'Tis the lost memory
> of my other lost life;
> it says, lest I lose myself:
> go back to your first beginning.[19]

That August when all of Spain was preparing her ultimate homage to Don Miguel, he could think only on her, "the soul of his soul," in whose embrace fire had turned to light, and where he had found the fountain of his life. Then he wrote:

> *El alma de la carne me llevaste,*
> *alma de mi alma,*
> *dejándome vacío y sin contraste*
> *de mortal calma.*
> *Tu alma de carne encarnó en mi linaje,*
> *alma de mi alma,*
> *mi compañera en el terrestre viaje,*
> *de la mano de Dios bajo la palma.*
> *"Y serán dos en una carne sola"*
> *dijo, y formamos los dos*
> *bajo el cielo una sola*
> *del abismo de Dios.*
> *Bien fué tu nombre Concepción,*
> *concha de mi elección!*
> *Me diste tú el espíritu carnal,*

[19] *Ibid.*, p. 449.

*el limpio y casto y puro*
*santo candor de la vida animal*
*libre de todo mal oscuro.*
*En tu regazo, virginal sosiego;*
*en tu regazo*
*donde se me hizo luz el fuego.*
*Fuente de vida hallé en tu abrazo;*
*dentro de tus ojos de saber sereno*
*ví al conocerte que el mundo era bueno;*
*tú me llenaste,*
*y ahora ya huérfano en mi viudez*
*tú, que me guiaste*
*en este pobre suelo,*
*me vuelves, madre, a la final niñez,*
*que me es un cielo.*[20]

You took from me the soul of my flesh,
soul of my soul,
leaving me empty, with death-like calm
cast in the mold.
Incarnate became the soul of your flesh,
soul of my soul,
entwined in my line,
companion of mine on earth's long journey
'neath the palm of God's hand.
"They shall be as one flesh,"
He said, and we two formed one alone
here 'neath the heavens of God's abyss.
Ah, well were you named Conception;
I chose you, shell, for my protection!
You gave me this carnal spirit,
the clean and chaste and pure,
candid spirit of animal life,
free from all dark evil.
Virginal peace in your embrace;
in your embrace
fire turned to light.
A fountain of life I found in your arms.
In the serene wisdom that shone in your eyes,
on knowing you, I saw the whole world was good;
I was filled with you,
and now, orphaned so soon, in my wifeless state,
you who guided me
in this poor land,
as a mother, lead me back
to the last childhood, my heaven.

[20] *Ibid.,* p. 468.

Spain rendered him late her honors: Lifetime Rector of the University, Perpetual Mayor of Salamanca, First Citizen of Honor, and candidate for the Nobel prize for literature. It all happened on this fashion.[21]

In September of 1934 Unamuno was seventy years old, and according to Spanish law, must be retired from his University position. The president of the Republic, Señor Alcalá Zamora, considered waiving this law in Unamuno's case, but decided that "the most exalted should submit to the common law" (El hombre cumbre se somete a la ley común). However, special honors must go to a special citizen. To bestow these honors in a fitting manner the University session 1934–1935 was inaugurated with a ceremony dedicated to Unamuno, during which, according to another tradition, Unamuno would pronounce his "Last Lesson." In order to make the occasion more significant, the Portuguese professor and poet, Eugenio de Castro, brought to the University under the aegis of Unamuno, was to be given an honorary doctorate, thus including the president of the University of Coimbra and other notables from the neighboring Hispanic nation. This rendered the homage to Unamuno a fiesta hispánica and particularly fitting, as Professor Francisco Maldonado said during the ceremonies, since Unamuno had taught Spain "to love Portugal as a part of Hispania."

The ceremonies were set for eleven A.M., on Sunday, September 30, to take place in the University auditorium in the ancient tradition with full academic formalities, such as only an institution of medieval heritage can muster. Dignitaries from Spain and Portugal, visiting scholars from many countries, and former students of the venerable maestro converged on that forest of golden stones that was carved by the hand of history to produce this Salamanca, this "reborn miracle," bathed in metaphysical light, on the banks of the river Tormes.

President Zamora with his secretary, Sánchez Guerra, in the company of others arrived for mass at the church of the Jesuit nuns. At ten A.M. the chief of state (jefe del gobierno) and the minister of the Navy, Señores Samper and Rocha, arrived from Madrid. By eleven A.M. Unamuno, garbed in his black toga and doctor's cape, and flanked by the other dignitaries in similar academic regalia, lined up according to protocol in the vestibule of the University. In the procession were such men as Dr. Gil Robles, Royo Villanova, Casanueva, Dr. Marañón, Antón Oneca, Don Miguel Maura, Don Francisco Camba, and Don Antonio Trías. Members of the press were milling around expectantly,

---

[21] The following account is taken from the two local newspapers, October 2, 1934.

then precisely at eleven, President Zamora entered to be greeted by the awaiting professors. He took his place at the head of the procession by the side of Unamuno and they marched sedately into the auditorium and onto the platform. The sea of faces before them overflowed into the courtyard and beyond the main entrance where hundreds stood together with Fray Luis in the patio of the lower schools (*escuelas menores*) to hear the proceedings over loudspeakers.

Following a long ovation, the participants seated themselves in the following order: To the left of President Zamora were Unamuno, Dr. Duarte Oliveira, rector of the University of Coimbra, and Dr. Eugenio de Castro, with others of the Portuguese contingent. To his right were his own government officials, Samper, Señor Pita Romero, and Don Filiberto Villalobos, then Minister of Education. On the side seats of the lower level were Sánchez Guerra, General Ruiz Trillo of the military forces, the civil governor, Señor Freira, and the mayor, Señor Prieto Carrasco.

The secretary of the University opened the program by reading a decree in which Dr. Castro was declared "Doctor Honoris Causa." Then it was that Professor Francisco Maldonado, the son of Unamuno's old friend and the former rector, Don Luis Maldonado, set the tone for the occasion by speaking on the meaning of Hispanism, and by pointing out Unamuno's lifetime efforts to underline the common traditions of Spain and Portugal. After Unamuno himself had hooded the Portuguese professor, Dr. Castro attested to the years of friendship and common experiences between him and Don Miguel, referring specifically to Unamuno's recent bereavement: "In the very recent past, each of us has suffered similar griefs within our own homes, griefs of such a bitter nature as to leave within our hearts deep wounds that can never be healed." Speaking in his native tongue, Dr. Castro expressed his appreciation at being so honored by the University on the same occasion when she was heaping glory on her "ancient rector and, in the future, her 'rector perpetuo'."

However deeply moved the Grand Old Man may have been by such words, he controlled his emotion and rose majestically to the occasion to read his "Last Lesson." Slowly he got up and walked to the podium "accompanied by the vice rector[22] and several of the professors." As he did so, the audience rose with him and applauded extendedly. With visible efforts to check his feelings the old maestro began his

[22] Don Esteban Madruga.

swan song in these terms: "Companion teachers and disciples, students, everyone." The ensuing speech which he read was packed with his philosophy of language, its relation to time and to the lives of those who use it; this last lesson was the culminating message of a language teacher who had made words the vitalizing force of his existence:

In the beginning was the Word, and the Word is also the end.

The name is the man!

. . . antiquity is the childhood of the nations, and childhood is the antiquity of the soul.

. . . Socrates, like Christ, the Verb, left nothing written; he did not bury himself in writing.

The name, the word, is true action, spoken words are deeds.

. . . the word is action.

*The present is the effort of the past to become the future.*

All of Spain's civilization, all of her economy, her law, her art, her wisdom, and her religion are inextricably woven into the loom of her language, they live and breath in the very marrow of its bones.[23]

This was his farewell to the university he loved, to the students he had inspired, to the dank classrooms he had transformed with the passion of his spirit. And they were loath to let him go. Hence on this occasion, they claimed him for life by bestowing upon him the title of "Rector Vitalicio" of the University of Salamanca.

But before the conferring of this unique title the Lieutenant Mayor of Bilbao read a few remarks, for that town must needs share the limelight with her native son.

The president of the Republic then rose and on him all eyes were fixed. He began by confirming the friendship between Spain and Portugal. He pointed to the many occasions which the two Hispanic nations celebrate together such as the present one when they both honor Unamuno. "Unamuno represents all the potentiality of the Basque spirit converted into tremendous strength," he said, "for to become tremendous it came to flower in Castile, here on the banks of the Tormes." Identifying Unamuno with Spain's Republican government, the president said that he had "struck the necessary note of renovation in the constituent assembly of 1931."

President Zamora then announced the honors which that government now conferred upon him: ". . . the creation of the Chair which shall

23 Unamuno, *Obras selectas*, pp. 1040–1044.

bear the name of Miguel de Unamuno, in which the eminent maestro
will continue his task of teaching, not as a duty to be fulfilled in the
future, but that he may continue to set the example of honest citizen-
ship and to advise the youth with his own peculiar greatness of spirit."

It fell to Don Filiberto Villalobos as Minister of Education to
produce the two official documents for President Zamora's signature.
One declared the retirement of Unamuno in keeping with the law;
the other declared him Lifetime Rector as a nationwide tribute and
created the University chair named for him. It was also announced
that His Excellency was establishing two scholarships for needy students in each of the University schools, two in the secondary school,
and one in the teacher's college. These announcements ended the
ceremony in the University auditorium which was to be followed by
the unveiling of Victorio Macho's sculptured bust of Unamuno in the
School of Philosophy and Letters located in the Palacio Anaya just
across the little plaza from the cathedrals. Headed by the academic
procession, the entire audience transferred itself to that building where
chairs were arranged in the patio facing the speakers at the foot of
the wide stone stairway. The participants here were seated in much
the same order as before. Again the audience overflowed, this time,
packing the entire upstairs gallery around the patio. So much crowded
confusion must have been tiring to the principle figure and it is no
wonder that he said less and less as the day wore on. In fact, he
seems almost lost sight of in the accumulated minutiae of details that
make up the account of the next forty-eight hours' proceedings. It must
have taken some time to move such a crowd from one building to
another, but somehow it was accomplished. The only event in the
Palacio Anaya was the unveiling, but that was preceded by a speech
by Don José Camón of the University faculty. In that address Don
José included a description of the artist's work which is quoted here
because it offers at once an incisive glimpse of the subject's character
and an accurate delineation of a great work of art. The bust im-
mortalizes Don Miguel with

his high sunburnt forehead, tense and pure, whitened by his hair like
stylized wings.

Wings of a nautical bird, sportive wings, with windfilled muscles of steel,
eyebrows where the forehead sweeps downward in a sort of contained
inundation. Tragic eyes, wide open in hollow sockets, not blind but bottom-
less, opened wide like the heavens, and like the heavens too, in infinite,
monotonous amazement. The nose, aquiline, ferocious, a seeker out of

hidden truths, follower of all trails. A nose whose certain soft fleshiness . . .
just saves it from being a beak. And then there is the calamity of the mouth.
A sunken mouth, turned inward from distaste of facile fruits that hang
from every tree. A mouth that receives, like the chalice, the flaming darts
turned ashes from the forehead; a pathetic, moving mouth, antithesis of the
bestial mouth of the gum chewer. Next the chest conceived as an act of
extreme unction. Troubled specimens of matter where the outline of a cross is
vaguely seen. And the arms are folded behind his back. Intrepid? Religious
fear of profaning the sacred signs with which nature surrounds us? [24]

Having looked once upon himself in bronze and felt the cold hand
upon his shoulder, Don Miguel turned away his eyes. It was this,
perhaps, that caused him to say in response to Professor Camón's
description, "Whenever I go up those steps I shall try to look away.
To be in bronze!; a sad thing; better to be in the flesh and in one's
own house." And he meant it, for if Don Manuel García Blanco is
correct, Unamuno never passed that way again. However, his last
words on this occasion bespeak a complete acceptance of himself:
"They have made of me a legend; I give myself to it and may that
legend become whatever God wills. And thank you all."

The burst of applause which followed almost drowned his expression
of appreciation and lasted for several minutes. Victorio Macho's masterpiece, a figure of heroic proportions, was unveiled in the niche at the
turn of the steps where the people stood in long lines to gaze upon it.

It was two P.M. and the *homenaje* continued, like a play that shifts
from scene to scene, while the actors perform their roles against a
changing backdrop. The banquet that followed was held in the main
auditorium of the Palacio Anaya, and given by the University to the
president of the Republic as a part of the celebration, hence Unamuno
was seated at the left of this dignitary. The local paper described it
as a festive scene with pennants displayed from every university in
Spain and Portugal—and a menu prepared by the Novelty restaurant.
It was during the banquet that the announcement of another honor
was made: "The faculty of the school of Philosophy and Letters had
resolved to apply for the Nobel prize for literature for Don Miguel
de Unamuno, as, apparently, a Spanish man of letters is to be selected
this year, and it is hoped that the Republic will support the petition
of the faculty which the University of Salamanca will surely make its
own." [25] According to *La Gaceta Regional* Don Filiberto announced
later to the press that the petition had been presented to the Madrid

---

[24] *La Gaceta Regional* (Salamanca), October 2, 1934.
[25] *Ibid.*

government and that "The government looked favorably upon the project and steps would be taken at the opportune time toward that end." [26]

At four P.M. there came another change in the drama, not just another scene this time, but another act—one which Don Miguel could not have enjoyed for he was anything but a bullfight enthusiast. However, to the bull ring he went, for a photograph of the dignitaries at the Plaza de Toros shows him among those present. The usual fiesta was preceded by musical numbers executed by the military band from Madrid and a group of Portuguese singers.

The third act of the drama, and possibly the one most enjoyed by Unamuno, was the banquet which his former students gave that night at nine in the Restaurant de la Viuda. These "former students" were themselves nearly all college professors and men in responsible civic and political positions. Among them is mentioned one who that year was to occupy Don Miguel's position on the faculty in the language department, Manuel García Blanco; another was Don Carlos de Onís, professor in the institute at Ciudad Rodrigo. Anecdotes were told, autographs were signed and a general good time was in order after the succession of formal ceremonies that had filled the daylight hours.

So end the newspaper accounts of Spain's homage to Unamuno, but his friend, Maurice Legendre, who was in Salamanca for the celebration, describes a ceremony at the *Ayuntamiento* as follows:

. . . thousands of people had come to Salamanca for that apotheosis. A reception was planned to be held in the town hall. The president of the Republic and the minister of Education were present. The famous town square was crowded. The venerable old gentleman, trailing clouds of glory, was expected to appear on the balcony of the town hall at any minute.

After a long wait, which only the patience of a Spaniard would stand, Unamuno appeared and was greeted by a thunderous acclamation. Then he turned casually toward me and our eyes met. I saw that his eyes were filled with tears. Walking over toward me he drew near and said, "You well know that nothing can make me happy now." [27]

Spain knew how to be lavish with her praise, and though in the past she had denied him and turned against him, even as she would again in the future, on this occasion she brought forth the purple robe, placed in his hand the royal palm, and crowned him *Summa Cum Laude*.

---

[26] "*El gobierno acogió el proyecto con mucho cariño y se harán las gestiones oportunas a tal fin,*" *La Gaceta Regional*, October 2, 1934.

[27] Maurice Legendre in *Cuadernos de la cátedra de Miguel de Unamuno*, quoted by Hernán Benítez in "La crisis religiosa de Unamuno," in *Revista de la universidad de Buenos Aires*, Vol. III, No. 9 (January–March 1949), p. 39.

# His Day of Destiny
## October 12, 1936

## CHAPTER 27

THERE WERE TEARS IN HIS EYES
even while the plaudits of the crowd were ringing in his ears, and
they were not easily dispelled by the inept bungling of those who
were steering the Republic's frail bark. Unamuno became ever more
convinced of their inadequacy in the months following his retirement
and, true to his nature, he veered further and further away from any
identification with the Madrid government. As he said to a visiting
writer at this time, "I shall never be with the conqueror." His destiny
was to stand alone, and he never felt this so strongly as when the mob
claimed him. Just nine days before the events of the preceding chapter,
while all of Salamanca was agog with preparations to honor him, Don
Miguel wrote:

> I am my own king, yes, but what of the ministers?
> deaf is their vision, blind their word.
> Life goes on and death does not come,
> and when it does, what have we left?
> A kingdom without a king, worse than a king without a kingdom,
> and Conscience, without foundation, floating.
> You will go forth without eyes, poor words of mine,
> in search of my mouth, turned to dust.
> "I know who I am!" poor Don Quijote,

> infinite knight of his wild fancy!
> While Sancho sleeps, serenely, sans dreaming,
> deaf and blind in the comfortable siesta.
> Poor Oedipus, a prisoner of the Sphynx,
> who snatched out his eyes, once he saw
> the reality of his error, Adam's blame
> for having tasted the fruit of science.
> I am my own king, yes, but what of the ministers?
> deaf is their vision, blind their word.[1]

And seventeen days after his "glorification" Don Miguel wrote:

> It's over—and she's gone! Only mystery
> is reality, and all the rest is nothing;
> and you, what are you and what will you become?
> I wonder what you live for!
> did she die, or did you die with her?
> the star lights up again,
> the dawn fades in the sky
> when the hour has come
> to lose ourselves in the has-been,
> founded in faith.[2]

By the following year, 1935, Unamuno was censuring the Republic more directly. In lines dedicated to the generation of 1931 in which he recalled the noble impulses of the men who forged the liberal constitution during the eighteenth century struggle against France he wrote, "A hundred years have passed and their grandchildren, with broken insignia and broken memory, chink up the crack with another word—revolution! And so the ball of history rolls on—generation of generations!"[3]

Thus revolution came to Spain and with it Fascism and Franco, while the rest of the world awaited its turn to be caught up in the conflagration. Few people entered Spain that were not concerned with that revolution, but one there was—a Dutch Hispanist—who talked with Don Miguel in September of 1936 when Spanish Fascism was in its first triumphant stage. He has quoted Unamuno as follows, "No culture can be born, or grow or prosper under a military regime; it's impossible, impossible. With the military nothing can prosper. They are so many madcaps."[4]

[1] Unamuno, *Cancionero*, p. 473.
[2] *Ibid.*, p. 474.     [3] *Ibid.*, p. 476.
[4] J. Brouwer, "Entrevista del hispanista holandés Dr. J. Brouwer con don Miguel de Unamuno, en el mes de setiembre de 1936," in *Repertorio americano* (San José, Costa Rica), Vol. XXXIII, No. 14 (April 10, 1937), pp. 217–218.

But Franco and Falange were determined to claim the Grand Old Man who may possibly have believed at first that Franco was the saviour of his country. However, Unamuno's close associates knew his bitterness against dictatorships and entered into a conspiracy to keep him quiet. They were successful for a time until the day came when he would be silent no longer, and he cried out in a loud voice for everyone to hear: *"No puedo aguantar más."* (I can stand it no longer.) On that day they left him alone—he stood inevitably alone on his day of destiny.

It happened on October 12, 1936. The patriotic festival of the Hispanic race was being celebrated in the spacious ceremonial hall of the University. It was a formal setting, austere and cold, its walls hung with tapestries. Through the tall windows an iridescent light shimmered falteringly on the amber stones. On the front wall the plump figure of the Caudillo looked down presumptuously from its canopied frame. It was midmorning and they were all there on the presidential dais:

the purple calotte, the amethyst ring and the flashing pectoral cross of the Most Illustrious Doctor Plá y Deniel, Bishop of the Diocese; the lack-lustre robes of the Magistrates; the profuse glitter of military gold braid side by side with the crosses and medals exhibited on presumptuously bulging chests; the morning coat, set off by black satin lapels, of His Excellency the Civil Governor of the Province; and all these surrounded—was it to honour or to overwhelm?—the man whose pride in his incorruptible Spanish conscience was steadfast and straight: Miguel de Unamuno y Jugo, the Rector. . . . To the left and right, on crimson-covered divans, the silk of the doctors' gowns and their mortar-boards with gay tassels in red, yellow, lighter blue, and dark blue, symbolizing Law, Medicine, Letters, and Science . . .[5]

The newspaper account relates that when the presiding officers had been seated the "Bizarre and heroic general Millán Astray" entered to enthusiastic applause. Mrs. Franco then appeared, whereupon Astray went forward to meet her and accompanied her to the platform. There she was given a seat on the right of Unamuno.[6]

It was thus that they were pictured in the local newspaper with Unamuno sitting in the presiding chair. The caption lists all the names except the Rector's. The paper also points out that a public address system carried the speeches to the throng outside, as well as to the

[5] From a typewritten article by Luis Portillo in possession of Federico de Onís, University of Puerto Rico.

[6] From a Salamancan paper, October 13, 1936.

Plaza Mayor. It adds, moreover, that they were radioed to Valladolid and thence transmitted to the Spanish-American countries. Strange that the truth should be so inaccessible today!

The ceremony began when Unamuno arose and pronounced the ritual formula in that thin, clear voice of his. Then he introduced Don José María Ramos Loscertales, himself an ex-rector of the University. He was followed on the program by Father Beltrán de Heredia, Professor Francisco Maldonado and the principal speaker, the poet José Pemán. It was during Professor Maldonado's address that Unamuno became noticeably restive and began to take notes. Although he had previously stated his intentions to keep quiet on this occasion, he seemed to have changed his mind, causing an observant colleague to whisper to his neighbor, "Who knows what will happen now!"

If the professor had been purposely trying to goad the rector to speak, he could not have been more successful. He began by citing the Latin quotation with which a Spaniard had answered Martin Luther on the question of free will. It was *"Hominem tollit qui tollit libertatem."* Next, Maldonado turned to the regional factions in Spain which were so strongly opposed to Franco: the Cataláns and the Basques. These were two industrial, non-conformist factions, he said and therefore imperialistic groups. (Even the reporter felt obliged to soften this statement for he inserted a footnote saying that the speaker was clearly referring only to those Basques and Cataláns who were at the time bearing arms against "the Spanish cause.") Madrid, Bilbao, and Barcelona, said Maldonado, had worked together as a triangle since the time of the San Sebastián pact. Had there been but two economic factors pitted against the rest of the country, they would have destroyed each other, but the triple action was so successful that they had almost realized a third partition of Spain as in the times of Louis XIV and Napoleon. Maldonado thanked the "new Spain" just emerging for the failure of such a partition. He called the Basques and Cataláns, who were, he said, the wealthiest people of Spain and hence greatest in responsibility, "exploiters of the Spanish people and the Spanish name" and accused them of living in a "Paradise of money and high salaries" in the midst of a poverty-stricken, postwar world and at the expense of the rest of the Spaniards. At this point Maldonado added insult to injury by referring to Cataluña and the Basque provinces as "Red Spain," but, he concluded that against Red Spain, against this anti-Spain, there had arisen the Spain of western tradition and of lasting values, the Spain that in terrible circumstances, but circumstances imposing in their grandeur, led by a secular but glorious army, was at the time fighting tirelessly on the very eve of triumph. In terms of glowing oratory the speaker called the current celebration an "ethnical fiesta," a "mystical assembly" of the Hispanic peoples who, within one Church were "transfixed with emotion" as "one divine and happy oracle" speaks to them of their "eternal destiny in history." [7]

Did Pemán's speech follow this as indicated in the local paper? It matters not. What does matter is the dramatic scene which stripped away all restraint to reveal two antagonists in the white heat of passion. General Millán Astray arose unannounced.

With ostentatious humility, he preferred to speak from his own place. His appearance was impressive. The General is thin, of an emaciation which pretends to slimness. He has lost one eye and one arm. His face and his body bear the indelible tatoo of horrible scars. These mutilations and gashes evoke a sinister personality; his angry and rancorous bearing kills any compassion his mutilations might have inspired.

He had been the organizer of the *Tercio*, the Spanish Foreign Legion for operations in Africa; he had been the creator of an iron, inexorable discipline to which the reckless fugitives from other social discipline submitted of their own free will. He had gained those wounds which to many seemed glorious, to some over-exploited, and to all horribly impressive, in those fantastic Moroccan campaigns which had been Spain's bitter nightmare under the regretted aegis of King Alfonso XIII, called "The African" in his day. Yet the unquestionable nimbus which surrounded the figure of the General was due to the gruesome originality, to the mysterious paradox, of his battlecry: "*¡Viva la Muerte!*"—"Long live Death!"

Barely had Millán Astray risen to his feet when his strident voice rang out, as though bursting from that heroic chest bedizened with a galaxy of crosses, the testimonials and rewards of gallantry.

First of all he said that more than one half of all Spaniards were criminals, guilty of armed rebellion and high treason. To remove any ambiguity, he went on to explain that by these rebels and traitors he meant the citizens who were loyal to the Government.

In a sudden flash of intuition, a member of the audience was inspired so as to grasp the faultless logic of a slogan which common minds had thought the product of an epileptic brain. With fervour, he shouted:

"*¡Viva, viva la Muerte!*"—"Long live Death!"

Impervious, the General continued his fiery speech:

"Catalonia and the Basque country—the Basque country and Catalonia—are two cancers in the body of the nation. Fascism, which is Spain's health-bringer, will know how to exterminate them both, cutting into the live, healthy flesh like a resolute surgeon free from false sentimentality. And

[7] This and the foregoing excerpts from Maldonado's speech are from a Salamancan paper, October 13, 1936.

since the healthy flesh is the soil, the diseased flesh the people who dwell on it, Fascism and the Army will eradicate the people and restore the soil to the sacred national realm . . ."

He made a pause and cast a despotic glance over the audience. And he saw that he held them enthralled, hypnotized to a man. Never had any of his harangues so subjugated the will of his listeners. Obviously, he was in his element . . . He had conquered the University! And carried away himself, he continued, blind to the subtle and withering smile of disdain on the lips of the Rector.

"Every Socialist, every Republican, every one of them without exception— and needless to say every Communist—is a rebel against the national Government which will very soon be recognized by the totalitarian States who are aiding us, in spite of France—democratic France—and perfidious England.

"And then, or even sooner, when Franco wants it, and with the help of the gallant Moors who, though they wrecked my body only yesterday, today deserve the gratitude of my soul, for they are fighting for Spain against the Spaniards . . . I mean, the bad Spaniards . . . because they are giving their lives in defense of Spain's sacred religion, as is proved by their attending field mass, escorting the Caudillo, and pinning holy medallions and Sacred Hearts to their burnouses."

The General lost himself in the maze of his own vehement outburst. He hesitated irritated and defiant at the same time. In these straits, an enthusiastic Fascist came to his rescue and shouted:

"¡Arriba España!"

The crowd bowed their heads in resignation. The man went on, un-daunted:

"Spain!"

Mechanically, the crowd responded: "One!"

"Spain!" he repeated.

"Great!" chorused the obedient public.

"Spain!" the Blue Shirt insisted implacably.

"Free!" they all replied, cowed.

There was an obvious lack of warmth and listlessness in these artificially produced responses. Several Blue Shirts rose to their feet as though pushed by invisible springs, and raised their right arms stiffly in the Roman salute. And they hailed the sepia-colored photograph on the front wall:

"Franco!"

The public rose reluctantly and chanted parrot-like:

"Franco! Franco! Franco!"

But Franco's image did not stir. Neither did the Rector.

Don Miguel did not rise to his feet. And the public fell silent and sat down again.

All eyes were fastened in tense anxiety on the noble head, on the pale, serene brow framed by snow-white hair—the uncertain expression of his eyes hidden by the glitter of his spectacles.

Between the fine curve of his nose and the silver of his Quixotic beard, his mouth was twisted in a bitter grimace of undisguised contempt. People began to grow uneasy. A few suddenly felt a recrudescense of their old rancorous abhorrence. Some admired the serene fearlessness of the Master and feared for his safety. The majority were gripped by the voluptuous thrill of imminent tragedy.[8]

Don Miguel rose slowly to his feet. As he did so the Bishop of Salamanca whispered a last-minute desperate warning, but Unamuno, impatient now of all restraint, flung out as though in the grip of this his hour of destiny: *"Es que no puedo aguantar más; no quiero aguantar más!"* (I can't stand any more; I won't stand any more.)[9]

"At times, to be silent, is to lie," his voice was coming in a steady stream now, "for silence is to be interpreted as acquiescence. I could not survive a divorce between my conscience and my word, always well-mated partners.

"I will be brief. Truth is most true when naked, free of embellishments and verbiage.

"I want to comment on the speech—to give it that name—of General Millán Astray who is here among us."

The General stiffened provocatively.

"Let us waive the personal affront implied in the sudden outburst of vituperation against Basques and Cataláns in general. I was born in Bilbao, in the midst of the bombardments of the Second Carlist War. Later, I wedded myself to this city of Salamanca which I love deeply, yet never forgetting my native town. The Bishop, whether he likes it or not, is a Catalán from Barcelona."

He made a pause. Faces had grown pale. The short silence was tense and dramatic. Expectation neared its peak.

"Just now, I heard a necrophilous and senseless cry: 'Long live Death!' To me it sounds the equivalent of 'Muera la Vida!'—'To death with Life!' And I, who have spent my life shaping paradoxes which aroused the uncomprehending anger of the others, I must tell you, as an expert authority, that this outlandish paradox is repellent to me. Since it was proclaimed in homage to the last speaker, I can only explain it to myself by supposing that it was addressed to him, though in an excessive and tortuous form, as a testimonial to his being himself a symbol of death.

"And now, another matter. General Millán Astray is a cripple. Let it be said without any slighting undertone. He is a war invalid. So was Cervantes. But extremes do not make the rule; they escape it. Unfortunately, there are all too many cripples in Spain now. And soon, there will be even more of them if God does not come to our aid. It pains me to think that General Millán Astray should dictate the pattern of mass psychology.

[8] Article by Luis Portillo.

[9] Unamuno is quoted thus by two sources: 1) Dr. J. Brouwer in a typewritten article dated January 1937 in possession of Federico de Onís, University of Puerto Rico, and 2) Pedro Corominas, "El trágico fin de Miguel de Unamuno," in *Ateneo* (1938), No. 157.

"That would be appalling. A cripple who lacks the spiritual greatness of a Cervantes—a man, not a superman, virile and complete, in spite of his mutilations—a cripple, I said, who lacks that loftiness of mind, is wont to seek ominous relief in seeing mutilation around him."

His words rang out crystal clear. The heavy silence gave them resonance.

"General Millán Astray is not one of the select minds, even though he is unpopular, or rather, for that very reason. Because he is unpopular. General Millán Astray would like to create Spain anew—a negative creation—in his own image and likeness. And for that reason he wishes to see Spain crippled as he unwittingly made clear."

At this point General Astray could stand it no longer and shouted wildly: *"Muera la Inteligencia!"*—"To death with Intelligence!"

"No, long live intelligence! To death with bad intellectuals!" corrected Don José María Pemán. A few voices seconded him, many hands were clenched to check an imprudent impulse to applaud the aged Rector. The Blue Shirts felt tempted to become violent, true to totalitarian procedure. But a most unusual realization of their numerical inferiority strangled this impulse at birth. Arguments flared up round the names of academicians who had disappeared or been shot. Irritated "sh's" came from various sides. Some gowned figures had gathered round Don Miguel, some Blue Shirts round their vilified hero.

At last the clamour died down like the sound of surf on the beach, and the groups dispersed. Don Miguel again became visible to the assembly, very erect, his arms folded and his gaze fixed straight ahead, like the statue of a stoic. Once more his word dominated the hall.

"This is the temple of intellect. And I am its high priest. It is you who are profaning its sacred precincts.

"I have always, whatever the proverb may say, been a prophet in my own land. You will win, but you will not convince. You will win, because you possess more than enough brute force, but you will not convince, because to convince means to persuade. And in order to persuade you would need what you lack—reason and right in the struggle. I consider it futile to exhort you to think of Spain. I have finished." [10]

For an instant pandemonium reigned. This was followed by a unanimous silence. With astute presence of mind Don Esteban Madruga, the vice rector, took Unamuno's arm and offered it to Doña Carmen Polo de Franco who, too stunned to protest, walked out of the hall with Don Miguel. Outside a photographer caught them thus surrounded by military Blue Shirts with stiffly raised arms, seemingly pressing toward a waiting automobile. But Unamuno did not enter the waiting car. He did not enter any car for no one invited him. Dignitaries, colleagues, friends, and family, all disappeared in ill-restrained haste—all save one, a local reporter, one Mariano Santiago Cividanes.

[10] Article by Luis Portillo.

As the lone heretic, now truly alone, turned homeward, Cividanes who had no prestige to endanger, walked by his side, and left him at No. 4 Bordadores Street—a lonely place for a lonely man. He could not bear it long. More from habit than reason, he walked the few blocks to the casino to join his *tertulia* friends. They would be in their usual place: in the far left-hand corner of the mezzanine drinking coffee. Both floors of the casino were crowded, and everyone was talking excitedly. Did they fall silent when the serene, hatless figure appeared? He didn't notice for he wasn't thinking about them. Slowly he mounted the steps and made his way toward the customary spot like one in a dream. There were six members of his *tertulia* present: Don Pablo Beltrán, the son of the family that befriended him when he was newly arrived in Salamanca, Don Tomás Marcos Escrivano, the *diputado de Maura,* Don Juan Francisco Díez Rodríguez, director of a normal school, Don Juan Montero, a doctor, and Andrés Hernández. They all knew him well. It was Don Pablo who first spotted the white head as it appeared at the top of the stairs. He gave an involuntary cry of warning, *"Buque en vista"* (Ship Ahoy!), the little group stiffened and everyone in the casino turned to watch this familiar figure suddenly become a strange apparition. The Rector walked deliberately around the mezzanine corridor. Halfway along he paused, one hand on the railing, and looked down on the crowd below, curious to see what was going on. At that moment a voice broke the silence with, *"Mal español!"* Another yelled, *"Afuera!"* (Get out!) Others joined in. Unamuno looked interestedly at them for a second, completely unaware that they were shouting at him. Then he straightened up and walked on toward his group of "friends." Two of them, Don Francisco Díez Rodríguez and Andrés Hernández got up and left. They were applauded by the onlookers. Don Miguel took a seat in the midst of the hostile little group. Don Tomás Marcos broke the embarrassing silence. He said they were sorry about what had happened at the University, but that Don Miguel should not have come to the casino this afternoon. He might get them all into trouble. For some fifteen minutes they all tried to look casual. Don Miguel hardly spoke. Finally Rafael came looking for his father. He took him by the arm and they left together. *"Afuera! Mal español!"* resounded in their ears as they left by the rear exit on Consejo Street and made their solitary way home.

In the meantime news of the morning's occurrence had reached the *Junta* in Burgos and Franco's orders had come. They were inexorable:

if the offense was considered grave enough, the Rector of Salamanca was to be executed without delay. The offense was so considered, but someone who was better advised realized that such an act might fatally injure the prestige of the *Movimiento*.[11] It was never carried out, but that night General Franco's soldiers were on guard before Unamuno's house, and it was thus guarded that Don Miguel lived out the last three months of his life, a prisoner in his own home.

[11] *Ibid.*

# "To Sleep, Perchance to Dream..."

FROM *Summa Cum Laude,* AS they honored him in 1934, to "Throw Him Out," as they defamed him in 1936, was a span of only two years, but in that time the course of those two stars that met in Salamanca sped swiftly on their separate ways; the one to its zenith in the embattled Spanish heavens, the other to its inevitable end beyond the human horizon.

"*Afuera, mal español,*" rang in the old gentleman's ears when he left the casino on the afternoon of October 12, the day of Spain's "Fiesta de la Raza." In stony silence, erect, his bare head up, his hands behind him, he had followed Rafael, still somewhat dazed, down the casino steps, out by the back door and along the few blocks to No. 4 Bordadores Street. There was no Concha to receive him then, only Felisa, María, and Miguelito, too young to understand. Doña Pilar, too, must have heard him—she must have known.

In a dream he submitted to lie down once more upon his bed, to drink the hot chocolate Felisa tendered him, to close his eyes to the failing daylight, and so to dream that he was dreaming. The events of the next three months were all a dream to him.

On October 12 Unamuno's "friends" booed him out of the casino, and two days later, on October 14, his own faculty voted him out of the University. In "Folio 83–86" of the official record of the University of Salamanca there is an entry dated "October 14, 1936" that reads as follows:

. . . the Presidency (Presidencia) has presented the motion which is definitely approved by the Faculty with complete unanimity . . .

Upon unanimously withdrawing their confidence from the present rector, the faculty of the University of Salamanca considers the position vacant, and exercising their right to appoint [*apuntar*] academic authorities propose to the high command for the position of Rector of this University, Professor Don Esteban Madruga Jiménez.

There follow the signatures of those present indicating their "complete unanimity." They are: Andrés Marcos, Ramos Loscertales, Peralta, Francisco Maldonado, Beato y Sala, Bermejo, García Blanco, Rodríguez Aniceto, Sánchez Tejerina, Serrano Serrano, Ramón Retuerto, Rivas, Núñez García, Garrido Sánchez, Pierna Catalá, and Querol.[1] In the presiding chair that day was the dean of the School of Science, Dr. González Calzada. Since the only one in power to call the faculty together was under a close military guard, and had been since the night of October 12, the natural question arises: who called that meeting? When questioned thus twenty-three years later one of the signees answered, "I think there was a phone call from 'high up'." "May I quote you on that?" asked his interviewer. "Oh no," he countered, "I'm not exactly sure." And one, Don Esteban Madruga, the erstwhile vice rector, who on that day assumed the duties of the Rectorship, hastened to point out that he had not been present on that occasion. The reason for his absence is obvious, though it did not altogether explain the satisfied little smile that accompanied this voluntary piece of information. Indeed, Don Esteban conveyed to his interviewer the impression of knowing rather more than he was telling.[2]

In all justice to the sixteen men who signed their consent to the motion which expelled Unamuno from his "Lifetime Rectorship," the political circumstances under which they acted, either voluntarily or

[1] The author was allowed to see and copy the foregoing from the official University record by its rector, Don José María Beltrán de Heredia, nephew of Don Pablo Beltrán de Heredia.

[2] The author had been informed that Don Esteban Madruga, living in 1959 at No. 2 Compañía Street in Salamanca, was in possession of a letter written by Unamuno before his death—a letter none but Señor Madruga had ever read. An interview was arranged with Don Esteban who received his visitor graciously, volunteered some information about events on the day of Unamuno's death, and produced a typewritten copy of the minutes of the faculty meeting on October 14, taken from the official record. When questioned regarding the mentioned letter he declined to produce it on the grounds that it was "personal." However, as the visitor was leaving he said: "Why don't you ask Felisa about it? *She* was the one who brought it to me." Questioned later about this, Felisa said that she had taken from her father to Don Esteban the keys of the University with a letter which she had not read, nor did she have any knowledge of its contents.

under pressure, should be clarified. Since 1934 when the Republican
Government had heaped praises on the head of its distinguished "citizen of honor" upon the occasion of his retirement from active service,
the matter of the Nobel prize had been allowed to remain in abeyance
for lack of sufficient support. The Grand Old Man, true to form, had
begun to turn against the political regime, while on the continent
Nazism, Fascism, and Communism had begun to rear their ugly heads.
It was Spain's misfortune to be the testing ground for these *-isms*
were they might play with their new weapons of war. Hitler and
Mussolini, after signing their unholy pact, sent troops into Spain where
an ambitious young Spanish soldier seized the opportunity to ride on
the crest of their ready-made wave. Reinforced with Moslem troops
from Africa, Francisco Franco Bahamonde, joined forces with German
and Italian soldiers and began a determined campaign against the
Republic. The western allies, in a sort of self-righteous neutralism,
applied sanctions against the beleaguered Madrid government, which
left it a prey to the pretentious masters of Europe. Into this breach
stepped the Russian Communists, along with volunteer companies of
troops from some of the western countries, most of them inspired by
the same sort of idealism that led Byron to die on foreign soil. The
lack of arms, organization, and unity of the Republican cause could
not withstand the modern military tactics of Italian and German
trained soldiers, hence the name of Franco became synonymous with
victory. In October of 1936 this new-born star had himself proclaimed "Head of the Government of the Spanish State and Generalísimo of the armed forces on land, on sea, and in the air." Franco
established his headquarters in Salamanca and was slowly but surely
advancing on Madrid in his struggle against the "red hoards." On the
heels of this proclamation, Don Miguel, the redoubtable rector of
international fame, impelled by his proverbially unbridled passion for
justice and truth, had threatened to sow rebellion in the Caudillo's
own camp. In fact, on October 12 he had done just that in the University auditorium, two days before that faculty meeting.

A serious threat he was, and Franco had not hesitated to curb him,
though of course one might say that Franco's soldiers at his doorstep
were by way of protection. One might say too that the faculty action
was entirely voluntary, and that the Caudillo had no intention of firing
the venerable Rector, as indeed he has been quoted as saying.[3]

[3] Don Manuel García Blanco and the rector, Don José María Beltrán de
Heredia, both quoted Franco to this effect.

The last two years of life were bitter ones for Unamuno, years in which he spent many long empty silences "plucking splinters from the carcass of his soul." Bereft of his Concha and his university duties, a witness to the growing disunity in Spain, he lashed out at the very Republic he helped create and fought a spiritual battle against the whole world. Professor Federico de Onís writes that, in the end, Unamuno was "against Franco or against the revolutionaries of the national movement, whatever it is called, of that there is no doubt whatever." [4]

Although the Republicans tried to keep Unamuno's support by declaring him "citizen of honor of the Republic" in 1935, he did strike out against them, thus lending grounds for the belief that Unamuno sympathized with Franco. However, it is folly to believe that he would have maintained, if he ever really did maintain, a pro-Franco attitude for any length of time, particularly in view of his violent opposition to all forms of dictatorship. Those who knew him well understood that Don Miguel remained true to himself by taking all sides in the struggle for what he termed Spain's *tradición eterna.* He was seeking unity beneath disunity, the calm depths below the stormy waves, peace in war.

Francisco Franco Bahamonde, the rising star of Spain's political heavens, handled Unamuno as the threat to his success that he was. The Rector's last official decree—the message to the universities and academies of the world that was published in the *Gaceta Regional* on October 4, 1936—and on its heels his appeal for Spanish unity that provoked the stormy outbreak in the University auditorium on October 12, drove the Dictator to use force; hence the soldiers before the door to No. 4 Bordadores Street and Franco's troops stationed on the Portuguese border.

From that day until December 31, 1936, Unamuno never took another step outside without that guard, save only for that other guard, the one that bore him to his final resting place on New Year's day. Recalling those gruelling months, Felisa wonders why her father did not try to escape to Portugal. She believes that he could have escaped, but then she wonders: "What would have become of us? Yes, perhaps that is why he didn't do it—it must have been for us." Talking thus Felisa added something further: "One day when my father went to visit his friends the Dominicans at San Esteban a priest told him one

---

[4] Federico de Onís, "Unamuno íntimo," in "Cursos y conferencias," from *Revista del colegio libre de estudios superiores,* Buenos Aires, July–September 1949, p. 259.

of the soldiers had said that if they should see my father getting into
an automobile their orders were to shoot."

The writer was told another incident by a Salamancan who wished
to remain anonymous:

During those three months Don Miguel spent a lot of time writing. I
know that he wrote a letter to a Falangista friend of his who sent it to the
head of Falange here in Salamanca, Francisco Bravo. This man offered to
return the letter to Unamuno who refused it saying, "What do I want with
that letter; I wrote it to be read." Later on the Falange head gave it to a
lawyer here and since then many people have looked for it but it has
never been found.

Franco's desire for the outside world to believe that all was well
between his *Movimiento* and Unamuno is so strong that strict censorship has been applied to all written statements made by Unamuno
after October 12, 1936. This accounts for the mass of rumors and contradictory views concerning Unamuno's final political position. However, Unamuno is reported to have turned over to a visiting Frenchman
a document in which he had made his stand crystal clear. He wrote,

I authorize you to spread it abroad in my name that I am living under
lock and key and that I am surrounded by a frightening mass insanity. I
am surprised that they have not yet shot me. I shall never again walk the
streets of Salamanca. They will carry me out of here only when I am dead.
I have said as much to my bodyguard. I had believed that this *Movimiento*
was one which would save civilization because I believed that it was
operated on a Christian basis. However, I have seen in it the triumph of
militarism to which I am totally and profoundly opposed. These people are
all against intelligence. They are shooting the intellectuals; if they triumph
Spain is going to turn into a country of imbeciles. Occasionally foreign
correspondents visit me. One, a Portuguese, said to me that there is a
great deal of enthusiasm for Franco. Not so. Whatever might have existed
for this regime has disappeared. Only terror is left—a sadistic, cruel,
cynical terror, all the more frightening because it is not the result of
individual excesses, but methodically ordered and organized by the leaders.
And what can I say about all those Germans who are singing *Deutschland
Uber Alles* along the streets of Salamanca?" [5]

[5] G. Alvaro Gallego in *La Voz*, New York, July 25, 1939. Señor Alvaro writes
that Unamuno gave the above-mentioned document to the Frenchman Georges
Sadoul who maintains that he was the last person to interview Don Miguel.
According to Señor Alvaro, Monsieur Sadoul was unable to carry the document
with him into France, hence he hid it in Spain. When that document comes to
light it will be Unamuno's most authentic testimony regarding the Franco
political regime.

Unamuno continued to write poems for his *Cancionero* and remembrances of things past. A letter to his old friend, Pedro Eguillor, in Bilbao, written sometime before his birthday that September, ends with this statement:

This effort that I am making to tear these memories from my innermost I, which are no longer mine, and anything that comes to me from beyond the cradle, from the time of my birth, things that will go with me beyond the grave, frightens me . . . There are so many miserable miseries in the current politics of our Spain! I will soon be seventy-two years old and I would not be afraid to close my eyes if I could close them on a more unclouded, a happier Spain.[6]

The last day, the last word, the last conscious act—it fell to a comparative newcomer on the Salamancan scene to be their only witness. Who was Bartolomé Aragón Gómez? What urgent mission brought him, a soldier at the fighting front, back to Salamanca this New Year's eve? As a young man, Aragón was sent to Italy on a scholarship to study economics, and returned to Spain most favorably impressed with Mussolini and his country. He applied for and took the examination for the professorship in the school of Business at the University of Salamanca where he went at the end of 1934 to teach business and occupy the chair of Civil Law. His first encounter with Unamuno was at a faculty meeting where the Rector caught him impulsively by the lapels and exclaimed, "You won't deny that Mussolini is a common assassin!" "If that is so," the young man answered stoutly, "then we need a common assassin in Spain just as soon as possible." Several months intervened before the young professor had his second meeting with the awful Rector, this time in the school washroom. Don Miguel spoke to him pleasantly enough and invited him to take a walk. "I played up to him and he seemed to like me," admitted Aragón, "so I decided to treat him as an equal." At the outbreak of the Civil War Aragón went to the front as a soldier. That December his presence at the University was required to help examine some of the degree candi-

[6] Mario Puccini, *Amore di Spagna,* quoted in *La Gaceta Regional,* December 31, 1937. In this same letter Unamuno makes reference to another book he planned to write and Puccini, an Italian who met Unamuno in Italy in 1917 when Don Miguel paid his brief visit to the Allied front, and who later visited Salamanca (May–June 1936) mentions *De mis santas campañas* as an unpublished work Unamuno was working on. He states that Unamuno contributed two articles to *un diario madrileño* in April 1936 entitled *De mis santas campañas* and suggests that this may be the title of the work the writer mentions in the quoted letter to Eguillor.

dates. Since Aragón's return from Italy he had written a report of his studies in that country, and some of the professors were urging him to have it published. In fact, that had been the subject of his talk with Don Esteban Madruga on the afternoon of December 31 while the two had coffee together on the Plaza Mayor; Aragón had taken a room temporarily at the Hotel Novelty. It was about the publishing of his report that he had wanted to talk also with Don Miguel, and although Unamuno wasn't receiving visitors at the time, Rafael had made the appointment for him when he had telephoned Unamuno's son that morning.

It was a bitter cold day, and young Aragón turned up his coat collar and buried his hands deep in his pockets as he neared his destination. It was the first time he had ever been to the Rector's home and a slight shiver of apprehension passed over him as he recalled his past encounters with Don Miguel. The maid, Aurelia, answered to his knock and led him to where Unamuno was sitting at his *camilla* in the back room before the window that overlooked the garden below. The old Professor was warming his feet by the electric stove that sat on the floor beneath the curtains. He invited Aragón to occupy the chair facing him. He began the conversation, somehow, and among other things, the talk turned to Ortega y Gasset. For some reason the old gentleman became extremely upset, whereupon Aragón tried to calm him. At one point the younger man thought he noticed a smell of burning, when suddenly Don Miguel swooned and slumped forward on the table. Aragón caught him. He succeeded somehow in getting him to the sofa and it was then that he noticed that one of Don Miguel's shoes was smoking. Skipping the rapid and confused sequence of events which must have followed, Aragón related only that when the doctor arrived, it was a scared Bartolomé that he sent out for medicine.

That night many people came to question the young lawyer-soldier at his hotel. There were so many that finally he refused to see anyone else. One of his visitors had brought the alarming news that the Red radio was broadcasting the story that Unamuno had been poisoned. In a desperate panic of fright he typed a statement of the circumstances of Unamuno's death and gave it to—was it Professor Ramos Loscertales? Aragón did not mention his name. During the sleepless night that followed he had read Unamuno's poem that begins: "It is night time in my study . . ."

On a mind overwrought from having witnessed the death of one of

Spain's great men, the reading of this poem at such a time made an indelible impression. Relating the foregoing events twenty years later, he emphasized the fact by reading aloud that same poem to his visitor. He read it from a small paper-bound book which bore on the cover:

Bartolomé Aragón Gómez
Síntesis de Economía Corporativa
Salamanca
Librería "La Facultad"
de Germán García
1937

Aragón had included the poem in his book along with a photograph of Unamuno taken at La Flecha, and the drawing of his death head by José Herrero Sánchez. Its prologue is a statement written by Professor José María Ramos Loscertales and is entitled "When Miguel de Unamuno Died." [7] Although this prologue has only a circumstantial relation to the contents, it has probably served to sell a goodly number of copies, for in it the Salamancan professor gives the details of Unamuno's death as Aragón told them to him at the time. It is dated January 16, 1937, and appeared first as an article in one of the Salamancan papers. Further details taken from this prologue follow:

Unamuno had been failing physically for the past year and he was perfectly aware of it. I often heard him say: "I shall die like my wife, but more quickly, more quickly." Then, the natural fear of Death made him cover up the feeling of its nearness with an emphatic: "I feel better than ever." These were the words with which he answered the author of this incisive book, on December 31 at four-thirty in the afternoon. Then he sat down at the *camilla* to begin his last monologue:
"Aragón, my friend, I appreciate the fact that you didn't wear the blue shirt, as you did the last time, though I see you are wearing the yoke and the arrows [8] . . . I must say some very harsh things to you and I beg of you

[7] The author visited Bartolomé Aragón at his home at No. 19 on the Calle Zorrilla in Madrid on June 9, 1959, at which time Aragón gave the information contained herein. He talked further of his own work, his interests, and his accomplishments. At the time of the interview he had just returned from a conference of lawyers specializing in economy which had been held in Italy. He was still full of admiration for that country and for Mussolini. Was he working for the *Movimiento*? he was asked. "Well, on the fringes [*al margen*]," he answered. He stressed two things which he had accomplished for Franco's Spain: he had organized the economy of the country and founded the Banco Rural in Madrid. He stated that he preferred war to politics. As for the *Movimiento*, Aragón declared that it was the best thing that had ever happened to Spain. When he spoke of opposing forces his voice rose almost to a shout as he declared repeatedly: "The others were all mistaken!"
[8] Symbol of the Falange.

not to interrupt me. I had said that the Spanish war is no longer a civil war, it is a question of saving western civilization; then General Franco said the same thing and now everyone says it." Here the monologue, closed to this point, broadens along the paths of the historical and archeological past of the nation, of sentimental memories of men of the present, of visions of other peoples; and there is more bitterness and more pain in the comments than acridness or harshness.

Bartolomé Aragón offered D. Miguel de Unamuno a copy of *La Provincia de F. E.* published in Huelva. "I don't want to see it. I don't want to see those magazines of yours, because—how can one go against intelligence?"—"Don Miguel, Falange has called its workers."—"What!"—"Yes, yes, it has done this and they will support it, never you doubt it." Did the amazingly intuitive person that was Don Miguel doubt that? He believed it in his very soul. And he believed it because he wanted it.

When the momentary weakness of his interlocutor made him say: "The truth is, that sometimes I wonder if God has not turned his back on Spain by destroying her best sons," D. Miguel struck the *camilla* loudly with his fist and exclaimed: "That cannot be, Aragón! God cannot turn his back on Spain. Spain will be saved because she must be saved." And—"with his last word he breathed his last" with his face toward God, toward Spain and toward Falange that, grief-stricken, watched him in its arms, in whose arms his remains were carried with a youthful and spontaneous impulse, to the house of God and laid to rest in the harbor of the eyes of his life's companion and in the Father's home.[9]

This ends Aragón's account of the last word, the last conscious look of Don Miguel as it was recounted by Unamuno's erstwhile friend, Professor José María Ramos Loscertales, adherents, both Loscertales and Aragón, of Franco's *Movimiento.* By some strange coincidence Aragón returned from the firing line of a bloody war to the little university town of Salamanca on the banks of the river Tormes to be the only witness of the death of Don Miguel de Unamuno y Jugo, Spain's most influential figure of international fame, who had once brought about the downfall of a monarchy; now in December of 1936 Unamuno is confined under military guard which is ordered to shoot if he tries to escape, and he is feeling "better than ever" as he announces the title of a new book to be called *De mis santas campañas* (From My Holy Campaigns). The Caudillo may well have trembled at the thought of what new campaign Unamuno might have begun had that book ever seen the light of day. By his own confession, Aragón was a thoroughly frightened young soldier who left Salamanca immediately after the funeral on the day following Unamuno's death.

[9] Prologue by José María Ramos Loscertales to Bartolomé Aragón Gómez, *Síntesis de economía corporativa,* pp. 14–15.

Why was Aragón the sole witness of Unamuno's death? Felisa accounts for the absence of the rest of the household: it was New Year's eve; the customary Christmas *Nacimientos* (Nativity Scenes) were still on display, and Felisa in company of a neighbor, had taken Miguelito out to see the sights. María was in Doña Pilar's home helping to care for Paquita who was sick in bed. This left only Aurelia, the maid, who had been with the family almost since the birth of Miguelito. She was busy in the kitchen. Aragón, a *Falangista* who had never come to the house before, stayed only about fifteen minutes, according to Felisa. Aurelia must have let him in and returned to the kitchen, for it was from there that she heard Unamuno cry out (*"dio voces"*). She ran out into the garden, but on seeing Don Miguel talking normally again, returned to her work. "Then Aragón saw my father fall forward and he gave the alarm. When I returned," said Felisa, "they had my father on the sofa. He was dead." María and Doñar Pilar were the ones who heard Aragón call for help and, aided by him, they laid the already unconscious Don Miguel on the sofa. It was Doña Pilar, Concha's dearest friend, who took that noble head to her breast, and in her arms he gave his last long struggling gasp.[10] It was over then, his struggle, for Don Miguel had kept at last his rendezvous with Death.

Word of Don Miguel's death ran through the town like wildfire, and plans for his funeral must have been hastily made. The *Falangistas* asked permission to act as pallbearers the next day (*Pidieron permiso de llevarlo al entierro*). Don Esteban Madruga who had not accompanied Aragón to Don Miguel's home on the afternoon of his death only because he himself was attending a funeral, was greeted by the fatal news when he returned to his own dwelling. The notice of Don Miguel's death and funeral plans were published the next morning in the *Gaceta Regional*. A double column heading on the last page reads:

## Don Miguel de Unamuno Died Yesterday
## His Death Was Sudden

Beneath the well-known picture of Don Miguel taken as he sat on a hilltop at La Flecha overlooking the flatlands along the river below, there are the words: "Facing the country, on the 'windy hilltop,' that was filled with the mystic and tormented spirit, Don Miguel poses, or reposes. Below is outlined, limitless, the Castilian horizon where

[10] These events were related to the author by Doña Pilar Cuadrado and her son, Federico.

the river cradles the poplar trees and roars over the dam, that lulled the evening colloquies of Fray Luis at La Flecha." "It appears," reads the article, "that Unamuno was going about his affairs as usual yesterday, and, around six o'clock in the afternoon he died suddenly without benefit of Science, for he had no warning pain to announce his sudden end . . ." There follows a brief biographical sketch, complete to the item

. . . and about two months ago he ceased in the performance of his Rectorship duties, as the University Faculty unanimously withdrew its vote of confidence.

A universally known writer, his work is copious and has greatly influenced Spanish thinking of the first quarter of the century.

Among his best known works . . .

With the birth of the *Movimiento,* saviour of the Spanish Army against the red tyranny, Señor Unamuno alined himself openly with the *Movimiento,* making statements in which he lashed out against the Marxist government and against the leaders of the popular front that had led Spain into chaos.

The details of his death which followed in the *Gaceta* were obviously secured from Aragón who at that time was cowering in his hotel room at the Novelty, with the additional item, however, that when Aragón notified the family they called in the services of Science and Religion for the "illustrious University professor."

Plans for the funeral were announced as follows: "The funeral for the soul of Don Miguel de Unamuno will be held today at eleven A.M. in the parrochial church of the Purísima Concepción, and the procession with the body [*conducción del cadáver*] at four P.M."

For a land that knows well how to bury her dead, Spain paid slight heed to the passing of one whose shadow still falls over the length and breadth of her, reaching to ever farther corners of the earth.

Representing the University were, the rector, Don Esteban Madruga, and . . . Ramos Loscertales.

Hundreds of people from all classes of society attended the burial.

When the last rites had been said in the home of the deceased, the funeral procession started.

Don Fernando and Don Rafael were at the head.

The parrochial clergy of La Purísima participated.

Carrying the coffin were the Falangistas Don Miguel Fleta, the singer, Victor de la Serna, Don Antonio Obregón and Don Salvador Díaz Ferrer, the Madrid journalists.

Before the convent of the Capuchín Fathers, the pallbearers shifted and the coffin was carried by Don Mariano Rodríguez, national art delegate, and the writers Don Melchor Marín Almagro, and Don Carlos Domínguez.

The ribbons of the casket were carried by the university professors . . . Francisco Maldonado . . . and Don Manuel García Blanco,

while two others carried candles. Led by Don Esteban, the bereaved consisted of the children of the deceased.[11]

The short block from the home along Ursulas Street to the Campo de San Francisco must have seemed long indeed. Then in the sere and windswept park—the little park where Don Miguel and his blind friend, Cándido, were wont to hear the rustle of the rolling dry leaves and the song of the nightingale, the park where Miguel and his Concha had watched the changing seasons from their first mirador in Salamanca, they paused for one long, last look that Salamanca must give to her Don Miguel. The muffled sound of sobs must have mingled strangely with the chill Castilian winds as they filed past his bier in the Campo de San Francisco. For a long while they continued to file by—the old and the young, the high and the low—and that line has lengthened throughout the years to include those who seek somehow to pay tribute to a dauntless soul who dared to think aloud and write his innermost thoughts on life and death and the *tradición eterna* of his Spain. They still go to the little cemetery outside the town. His crypt is in the wall to the left of the entrance; it bears the number 340, *his* number, and on it, beneath the crypt of Salomé are inscribed Don Miguel's own words:

Hide me, Father Eternal, in your breast,
mysterious abode,
I shall sleep there, undone, I shall rest
from the toils of the road.[12]

His spirit, however, is on the mountain top, on Gredos where he asked to be laid, "with the mountain for a pedestal and a mausoleum, to be alone with his land, the land of his dreams, his face toward the rocky, the gigantic Arneal . . ."[13]

Llevad mi cuerpo al maternal y adusto
páramo que se hermana con el cielo.
Llevadlo a la jugosa enjuta roca
que, avara de sus frutos de secano,
tape su polvo mi sedienta boca,
que en sed de amor se ha consumido en vano.
. . .

[11] From *La Gaceta Regional* (Salamanca), January 2, 1937.
[12] Quoted by Hernán Benítez (ed.),"Cartas inéditas de Miguel de Unamuno y Pedro Jiménez Ilundain," in *Revista de la universidad de Buenos Aires*, Vol. III, No. 10 (April–June 1949), p. 533.    [13] *Ibid.*, p. 532.

*Envolvedme en un lienzo de blancura*
*hecho de lino del que riega el Duero*
*y al sol de Gredos luego se depura*
*—soy villano de pie, no caballero—*[14]

Carry my body to the maternal crag on high,
up where the wilderness is sister to the sky.
Take me to the high peaks whose succulent, dry stone
nourishes its sparse fruits for itself alone.
There let its dry earth, long bereft of rain,
cover up my thirsty mouth that thirsts for love in vain.

                    . . .

Wrap me in a coarse linen cloth of whiteness,
woven from the flax that's watered by the Duero,
bleached by the Gredos sun to its purest brightness.
—I'm a rustic man on foot, not a caballero—

[14] Written by Unamuno in France and quoted by Gómez de la Serna in his
"Retrato" in *Obras selectas,* p. 1069.

# EPILOGUE

Unamuno's children and Salamanca continue to pay tribute to the memory of one of Spain's great sons, a Man among men, a Thinker among thinkers, a Seeker after God who feared not, neither did he cease to act, to write, and to speak freely, though it might cost him his life.

As this writer was leaving Salamanca in June 1959, Felisa slipped into her hand her father's death announcement. It is a two- by four-inch folder bordered in black. A picture of the Christ by Velázquez is on the outside, and beneath it are the words:

> For in thee, oh Lord, have I put my trust,
> Thou wilt save me.
>
> David—Psalm 38

On the left, inside page, under a black cross, it reads:

> Miguel de Unamuno y Jugo
> died in Salamanca
> the 31st day of December, 1936
> at 72 years of age
> after receiving spiritual rites
> R. I. P.
> *His family requests a prayer for his soul.*

Enclosed in this folder is a selection from Unamuno's *El Cristo de Velázquez* entitled "The Last Prayer." It begins: "Thou who art silent, oh Christ, to hear us, hear the sobbing in our breasts . . ." And it ends: "Grant me, Lord, that when at last I go hence, lost, to leave this tearful nighttime where dreaming shrivels the heart, I may emerge into the clear, endless day, mine eyes fixed on thy white body, Son of Man, Humanity complete, to the increate light that never dies; mine eyes fixed upon thine eyes, Christ, my vision lost in thee, oh Lord!"

The city that he loved, Salamanca of the golden stones, has commemorated many successive anniversaries of Don Miguel's death by dedicating pages of her local newspapers to articles on Unamuno, poems by him, and photographs of her distinguished author. The two local papers have frequently headed such dedicatory pages on the last day of the year with the last line of Unamuno's Ode to Salamanca: *"Di tú que he sido."* (Say that I have existed.)

The Catholic Church, however, is equally faithful in its efforts to defame Unamuno's memory and to discourage the reading of his works. In 1940 Cardinal Plá y Deniel published a pastoral document advising Catholics not to read his *Tragic Sense of Life in Men and in Peoples,* and in 1953, when the University of Salamanca was planning to honor Unamuno during the seventh centennial celebration of its founding by featuring the dedication of the Casa Museo Unamuno, Bishop Pildáin of the Canary Islands published a pastoral letter which brought about an abrupt alteration in plans. In this document he called Unamuno *"Hereje Máximo."* The Bishop went even further than his predecessor and proscribed not only the *Tragic Sense of Life,* but also the *Agony of Christianity* and the *Life of Don Quixote and Sancho.* The document was published in pamphlet form (sixteen pages.), and distributed throughout Spain and the Vatican only a few days before the University celebration. As a result, the dedication of the Casa Museo Unamuno was soft-pedalled and Unamuno's name was deleted from the program. Moreover, an official visit to Unamuno's grave was abruptly cancelled, but this did not stop many of the visiting scholars from making the trip to the cemetery in the cold autumn rain to carry flowers to his crypt, while many others openly praised him during the ceremonies.[1]

The pamphlet which brought about such drastic changes was full of harsh invectives and ringing denunciations. On the title page it reads:

[1] *Life,* December 21, 1953, pp. 31–32.

D. Miguel de Unamuno
greatest heretic
and
teacher of heresies
by His Excellency, the
Most Reverend
Sr.
D. Antonio de Pildáin y
Zapiáin
Bishop of the Canaries
Pastoral Letter

"Venerable brothers and beloved children" begins the letter, "it is with true astonishment that we have just learned through the daily press, of the homage which is to be rendered to D. Miguel de Unamuno in no less form than the inauguration of the Casa Museo bearing his name, and all of this to celebrate the seventh centenary of the University of Salamanca." Salamanca, proceeds the Bishop, has always been "an exemplary pattern of Catholic universities," after which he lists the names of many great Catholic thinkers who have passed through its halls. The Bishop is shocked that to celebrate such a past, the University has selected "a man whose ideology constitutes the most authentic antithesis of the Salamancan University's characteristic ideology that could be found." And he continues in righteous indignation ". . . a man who . . . calling himself a Christian, has made so bold to publish abroad and insist on denying the most fundamental dogmas of the Catholic religion that one of his most authenticated and objective critics has termed him 'The Greatest Spanish Heretic of Modern Times'." A footnote identifies this critic as one, González Caminero. The Bishop substantiates his statement by listing no less than forty-five of Unamuno's utterances regarding faith and belief in God; he summarizes Unamuno's attitude as the belief that "faith is to want God to exist," "that faith which does not doubt is dead," "that dogma has killed faith," and all of this to prove that "Unamuno perversely denies almost all of the fundamental dogmas of the Catholic religion."

Of Don Miguel himself he writes: ". . . this man, who alienating thousands of Spain's sons from Catholicism," richly deserves González Caminero's criticism of him to the effect that he is "The bitterest enemy of the Catholic faith of his compatriots."

At this point the Bishop's eloquence knows no bounds; he calls upon the shades of the great to rise up and renounce the homage of the celebration and then return in peace to their graves!

He next attacks the three works of Don Miguel already mentioned, the *Life of Don Quixote and Sancho,* the *Tragic Sense of Life,* and the *Agony of Christianity.* Again he quotes Caminero: "In spite of his much vaunted Christianity, His Books Are Full of Heresies, Irreverent Blasphemies, Dirty Profanities, . . ." Not satisfied with this attack, the writer also inveighs against Unamuno's personal library, which was to be housed in the Casa Museo, by citing Menéndez y Pelayo on the lack of originality of Spain's writers, and he adds: take out of Unamuno's books "all of their extravagant and grotesque contents," and they will contain only "the pure unmixed ideas of Kant and Hegel, of Schopenhauer and William James, of Ibsen and Kierkegaard, and especially . . . of Herrmann, Harnack and Ritschl . . ."

Pildáin refers to a pastoral letter written by Señor Cardenal Primado in 1938 when that prelate was Bishop of Salamanca in which he pointed out the ill effects of indiscriminately reading all kinds of books without distinguishing the good from the bad, and he adds that no faithful Catholic should either own or read a book condemned by the Church. "The basis of forbidding the reading of such books is the need for avoiding the danger of perversion," he quotes from the Salamancan Bishop, "who ended that pastoral letter with the following prohibition:

Decree
Declaring that the book *The Tragic Sense of Life* by D. Miguel de Unamuno is forbidden by the general rules of the canonical code.

Bishop Pildáin reiterates this decree and points to the "grave danger" which that and the other books of Unamuno represent.

"Therefore," concludes the Bishop, "we earnestly call upon parents, professors and teachers to forbid and advise young people especially against the reading of works so reprehensible for all who judge them by authentic Catholic criteria."

The foregoing pamphlet was dated September 19, 1953. Most of it was reproduced in *Ecclesia* on Monday, October 12 of the same year, under the heading:

"D. Miguel de Unamuno,
greatest heretic and teacher of heresies,"

with the comment that Pildáin had put his finger on the sore spot. This article published on the Día de la Raza, October 12, exactly seventeen years after that first October 12 when Franco placed Unamuno under military guard, ends with the statement that Unamuno was a "perverse heretic who by his hatred of our religion did more harm than many others . . ." [2]

From the greatest Christian of the first part of our century, to the greatest heretic of modern times, the cycle was complete. As Unamuno himself was torn by an inner struggle, so Spain whose spirit was his own, continues to tear herself apart by plucking from her that which is best and noblest. But she cannot take back what he contributed to the dignity of humanity and freedom of thought—all of Miguel de Unamuno y Jugo, the lone heretic.

[2] From a clipping shown to the author by Don Manuel García Blanco in Salamanca, June 1959.

# BIBLIOGRAPHY

## Selected Works about Miguel de Unamuno

Albino, Fray. "Algo más sobre Unamuno," in *El Español* (Madrid), April 10, 1950.
—. "Datos para una biografía," in *El Español* (Madrid), April 4, 1950.
Altolaguirre, Manuel. "Don Miguel de Unamuno," in *Revista hispánica moderna* (New York), (January 1940), pp. 17–24.
Alvarez de Miranda, Angel. "El pensamiento de Unamuno sobre Hispanoamérica," in *Cuadernos hispanoamericanos* (Madrid), Vol. 13 (January–February 1950), pp. 51–74.
Aragón Gómez, Bartolomé. *Síntesis de economía corporativa* with Prologue by José María Ramos Loscertales (Salamanca: Librería "La Facultad," 1937).
Araquistáin, Luis. "Una entrevista con Unamuno." A typewritten article seen by the author in the files of Don Federico de Onís at the University of Puerto Rico, in December, 1960.
Azaña, Manuel. *Tres generaciones del Ateneo* (Madrid: [Editorial del Ateneo ?], 1930).
Basave, Dr. Agustín Jr. *Miguel de Unamuno y José Ortega y Gasset: un bosquejo valorativo* (México: Editorial Jus, 1950).
Benítez, Hernán. "La crisis religiosa de Unamuno" in *Revista de la universidad de Buenos Aires*, Vol. III, No. 9 (January–March 1949), pp. 11–88.
—. "Unamuno y la existencia auténtica" in *Revista de la universidad de Buenos Aires*, Vol. II, No. 7 (July–September 1948), pp. 11–45; Vol. II, No. 8 (October–December 1948), pp. 263–293.
— (ed.). "Cartas inéditas de Miguel de Unamuno y Pedro Jiménez Ilundain" in *Revista de la universidad de Buenos Aires*, Vol. II, No. 7 (July–September 1948), pp. 47–87; Vol. II, No. 8 (October–December 1948), pp. 295–357; Vol. III, No. 9 (January–March 1949), pp. 89–179; Vol. III, No. 10 (April–June 1949), pp. 473–533.
Blanco Aguinaga, Carlos. *El Unamuno contemplativo* (México: Publicaciones de la Nueva Revista de Filología Hispánica, 1959).

Bromberger, Merry. "El caso de don Miguel de Unamuno y la militarada española" in *Repertorio americano* (San José, Costa Rica), Vol. XXXIII, No. 2 (January 16, 1937), pp. 37–38.

Brouwer, J. "Entrevista del hispanista holandés Dr. J. Brouwer con don Miguel de Unamuno, en el mes de setiembre de 1936," in *Repertorio americano* (San José, Costa Rica), Vol. XXXIII, No. 14 (April 10, 1937), pp. 217–218.

——. Typewritten article dated January 1937, in the possession of Federico de Onís, University of Puerto Rico.

Carlyle, Thomas. *Sartor Resartus* (University Edition; Chicago: Hooper, Clarke & Co., 1868).

Chambers, Whittaker. *Witness* (New York: Random House, Inc., 1952).

Clavería, Carlos. "Unamuno y Carlyle," in *Cuadernos hispanoamericanos* (Madrid), Vol. 10 (July–August 1949), pp. 51–87.

Corominas, Pedro. "El trágico fin de Miguel de Unamuno," in *Ateneo* (1938), No. 157.

*Cuadernos de la cátedra Miguel de Unamuno.* 9 vols. (Salamanca: Editorial Universitaria, 1948–1959).

Ferrater Mora, José. *Unamuno: bosquejo de una filosofía* (Buenos Aires: Losada, 1944).

García Bacca, Juan David. *Nueve grandes filósofos contemporáneos y sus temas.* 2 vols. (Caracas, Venezuela: Imprentas Nacionales, 1947).

García Blanco, Manuel. "Don Miguel de Unamuno y sus poesías," in *Acta salmanticense* (Universidad de Salamanca), Vol. VIII (1954).

García Martí, Victoriano. *El Ateneo de Madrid (1835–1935),* (Madrid: Biosca, 1948).

González Caminero, Nemesio. *Unamuno* (Santander: Universidad Pontificia Comillas, 1948).

González-Ruano, César. *Miguel de Unamuno* (Second Edition; Barcelona: Ediciones G. P., 1959).

Granjel, Luis S. *Retrato de Unamuno* (Madrid: Ediciones Guadarrama, 1957).

Grillo, Max. "Conversando con Unamuno," in *Revista de América* (Bogotá, Colombia), Vol. IV, No. 10 (October 1945), pp. 52–56.

"Homenaje a Miguel de Unamuno," in *La Torre: revista general de la universidad de Puerto Rico,* Vol. IX, Nos. 35–36 (July–December 1961).

Ichaso, Francisco. *Defensa del hombre* (Habana: Ensayo Cubano, Editorial Trópico, 1937).

Laín Entralgo, Pedro. *La generación del noventa y ocho* (Buenos Aires: Espasa-Calpe, 1947).

*Libro homenaje al profesor don Agustín del Cañizo con motivo de su jubilación* (Madrid: Editorial Universitaria, 1946).

*Life* (Chicago), December 21, 1953, pp. 31–32.

Menéndez Pidal, Ramón. "Recuerdos referentes a Unamuno," in *Cuadernos de la cátedra Miguel de Unamuno,* Vol. II (Salamanca: Editorial Universitaria, 1951).

Onís, Federico de. "Bibliografía de Miguel de Unamuno" in "Homenaje a Miguel de Unamuno," in *La Torre: revista general de la Universidad de Puerto Rico,* Vol. IX, Nos. 35–36 (July–December 1961), pp. 601–636.

——. "Mi primer recuerdo de Unamuno," in *Strenae: estudios de filología e historia dedicados al profesor Manuel García Blanco,* Vol. XVI (Salamanca: Editorial Universitaria, 1962), pp. 375–378.

——. "Unamuno íntimo," in "Cursos y conferencias," *Revista del colegio libre de estudios superiores* (Buenos Aires), (July–September 1949), pp. 241–260.

——. "Unamuno profesor" in *Revista hispánica moderna* (New York), (October 1934), p. 78.

Oromí, Miguel. *El pensamiento filosófico de Miguel de Unamuno: filosofía existencial de la inmortalidad* (Madrid: Espasa-Calpe, 1943).

Portillo, Luis. Typewritten article in the possession of Federico de Onís, University of Puerto Rico.

Prieto, Indalecio. "La repatriación de Unamuno," in *Acción* (Montevideo), (January 7, 1950).

Pritchett, V. S. *The Spanish Temper* (New York: Alfred A. Knopf, Inc., 1954).

Puccini, Mario. "Unamuno y D. Pedro Eguillor," in *La Gaceta Regional* (Salamanca), December 31, 1937.

Reyes, Alfonso. "Unamuno dibujante," in *Simpatías y diferencias* from *Colección de escritores mexicanos*, Vol. II (Mexico: Editorial Porrúa, 1945), pp. 223–225.

Río, Angel del. "Miguel de Unamuno vida y obra," in *Revista hispánica moderna* (New York), (October 1934).

Romera-Navarro, Miguel. *Miguel de Unamuno* (Madrid: Sociedad general española de librería, 1928).

Sánchez Barbudo, Antonio. *Estudios sobre Unamuno y Machado* (Madrid: Ediciones Guadarrama, 1959).

Santos Torroella, Rafael. "Los poetas en su dolor," in *La estafeta literaria,* (Madrid), (November 30, 1945).

Villarrazo, Bernardo. *Miguel de Unamuno: glosa de una vida* (Barcelona: Editorial Aedos, 1958).

Wills, Arthur. *España y Unamuno: un ensayo de apreciación* (New York: Instituto de las Españas, 1938).

Zuazagoitia, Joaquín. *Algunos escritores vascongados desde 1874* (Bilbao: [n. p.], 1920).

Zubizarreta, Armando. "Diario," in *Mercurio Peruano* (Lima), (April 1957).

——. *La inserción de Unamuno en el cristianismo: 1897.* Pamphlet (Salamanca: [n. p., n. d.]).

——. *Unamuno en su "nivola"* (Madrid: Taurus, 1960).

# Selected Works by Miguel de Unamuno

For a complete bibliography on Unamuno the reader is referred to "Bibliografía de Miguel de Unamuno," by Federico de Onís, in *La Torre: revista general de la universidad de Puerto Rico*, Vol. IX, No. 35–36 (July–December 1961), pp. 601–636.

*agonía del cristianismo, La* (Madrid: Renacimiento, 1931).

*Amor y pedagogía* (Second Edition; Madrid: Espasa-Calpe, 1934).

*Andanzas y visiones españolas* (Second Edition; Buenos Aires: Espasa-Calpe, 1941).

*Cancionero* (Buenos Aires: Editorial Losada, 1953).

*Cincuenta poesías inéditas* (Madrid: Ediciones Papeles de Son Armadans, 1958).

*ciudad de Henoc: comentario 1933, La* (México: Séneca, 1941).

*Cómo se hace una novela.* With "Retrato" by Jean Cassou. (Buenos Aires: Editorial Alba, Araujo Hnos., 1927).

*Contra esto y aquello* (Fourth Edition; Buenos Aires: Espasa-Calpe, 1941).

"De Fuerteventura a París" in *Nuevo Mundo* (Madrid), (September 1924).

*De Fuerteventura a París* (Paris: Editorial Excelsior, 1925).

*Dos discursos y dos artículos* (Madrid: Sección Editorial de Historia Nueva, 1930).

*Ensayos.* 8 vols. (Madrid: Residencia de Estudiantes, 1916–1918).

*Epistolario a Clarín* (Madrid: Ediciones Escorial, 1938).

*espejo de la muerte, El* (Madrid: Compañía Ibero-Americana de Publicaciones, 1930).

*Niebla* (Madrid: Renacimiento, 1914).

*Obras completas.* 7 vols. With Prologue by Manuel García Blanco. (Madrid: Afrodisio Aguado, 1950–1959).

*Obras selectas.* With Prologue by Julián Marías, and "Retrato" by Gómez de la Serna. (Madrid: Editorial Pleyade, 1946).

*Paz en la guerra* (Third Edition; Madrid: Compañía Ibero-Americana de Publicaciones, 1931).

*Poems.* Translated by Eleanor Turnbull (Baltimore: Johns Hopkins Press, 1952).

*Poesías* (Bilbao: Rojas, 1907).

*Por tierras de España y Portugal* (Madrid: Renacimiento, 1911).

*Rosario de sonetos líricos* (Madrid: Afrodisio Aguado, 1950).

*Teatro* (Barcelona: Editorial Juventud, 1954).

*Teresa: rimas de un poeta desconocido.* With Prologue by Rubén Darío. (Madrid: Renacimiento, 1923).

*Tragic Sense of Life in Men and in Peoples, The.* Translated by J. E. Crawford Flitch, with an Introduction by Salvador de Madariaga. (London: Macmillan and Company, Ltd., 1926).

with Angel Ganivet. *El porvenir de España* (Madrid: Renacimiento, 1912).

with Pedro Jiménez Ilundain. "Cartas inéditas de Miguel de Unamuno y Pedro Jiménez Ilundain," edited by Hernán Benítez, in *Revista de la universidad de Buenos Aires.* Vol. II, No. 7 (July–September 1948), pp. 47–87; Vol. II, No. 8 (October–December 1948), pp. 295–357; Vol. III, No. 9 (January–March 1949), pp. 89–179; Vol. III, No. 10 (April–June 1949), pp. 473–533.

# INDEX